Fundamentals of Computers and Information System

Niranjan Shrivastava

&

Kogent Learning Solutions Inc.

Published by:

ISBN : 978-93-5119-191- 9

Reprint : 2014

Printed at : Durga Enterprises Bawana Ind. Area Delhi

Preface

The Dreamtech Management Textbook Philosophy

"You can be appointed a manager, but you are not a leader until your appointment is ratified in the hearts and minds of those who work with you."

John Adair – Author on Leadership and Management

With a strong student orientation, our Management series aims at continuous improvement of readers to help them turn out to be leaders, not just appointed managers. The series offers an absolute package of theoretical concepts and practice exercises to the readers ranging from students of prominent B-schools to the professionals at the pinnacle of their careers. The pedagogical style of the books keeps pace with the needs and aspirations of the students and teachers, prudently adopting the current trends in management education and profession. Easy to use, comprehensive, lucid, and enriched text developed to encourage critical thinking and application by means of activities, tips, and case studies are the hallmark of our books in the series. In addition, you would also find the intricacies of various topics and concepts of management in a simplified manner. The cognitive deliberation of our books is endorsed by our continuous approach for the development of content with re-modeled thinking, innovative planning, and emerging needs of change management. In addition, a continuous interaction of our authors with the teaching community provides us an edge to prevent the constraints in teaching-learning context.

Table of Contents

Introduction

Dreamtech Press team congratulates you on purchasing **Fundamentals of Computers and Information System** book and making a right decision to that end! Your decision to purchase the book spells your requirement of developing the right attitude and the requisite skills for learning the basics of computers that every manager should know. This book promises to offer all this along with the knowledge required to help you in understanding the need and role of computers in management. This book keeps you abreast with the basic and new technologies of computers so that they can be implemented in the business environment.

Computers have re-defined the way of performing business operations with the introduction of various software applications, such as Microsoft Word and Excel. To reap the utmost benefits of these applications, you should be able to leverage the full potential of these software techniques. This helps you to have a better hold over business operations, channelize productivity of employees, and achieve strategic goals.

In modern times, the business owners and enterprise decision makers need to communicate and share files, information, or other relevant documents with each other to perform various tasks. The concept of networking allows you to connect the computers of an organization over an Intranet-based system or Web-based environment so that the computers can communicate with each other and facilitate the sharing of resources over the network.

This book provides an insight into the fundamental concepts and structure of a computer, explores the applications of Microsoft office, describes the importance and role of database management system in maintaining records, and explores the need of Internet and networking in the business world. Finally, the book introduces the concept of management information system, knowledge management, artificial intelligence, and information system security and control.

Wish you a happy reading!!

Unique Features of the Book

The following are some of the unique features of this book:

- Provides ample content coverage to suit your specific learning and skill building requirements
- Includes a number of illustrations and applications to ensure better understanding as well as retention of concepts
- Includes specific instructions for teachers at relevant places to ensure that the students are able to build the requisite skills under their guidance
- Includes case studies that help the students to understand the concepts in the practical perspective and develop the analytical skills to manage diverse situations
- Provides a comprehensive learning structure by using various teaching elements, such as objectives, summary, case studies, and key terms to ensure effective learning

Cognitive Elements

All the chapters offer you with a comprehensive learning structure that begins with the objectives of each chapter. The introduction of the chapter familiarizes you with the subject matter and orients you towards the professional perspective of what you will learn in the respective chapter. The chapters are adequately supplemented with figures and illustrations wherever required. At the end of each chapter, an exhaustive summary and a list of key terms are given to help you to easily recap what you have learned and enhance your retention.

To facilitate the process of learning as well as better retention of concepts, we have provided some opulent cognitive elements. The cognitive elements used in this book include:

Chapter Objectives: Help you to align your learning path to achieve the specified objectives of each chapter

Introduction

Introduction: Orients you to the appropriate perspective of learning by providing an advanced view of the contents in the chapter

Related Questions: Showcases the questions about the concepts being taught in the chapter

Talk to teacher: Provides the questions that need to be discussed with the teacher

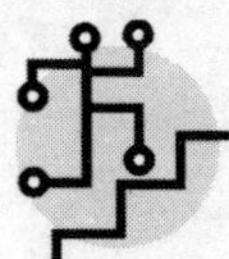

Activity: Enlist action-based questions related to concepts

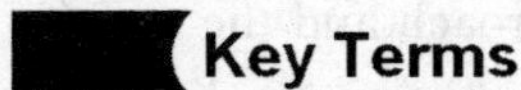

Key Terms: Enlist the major important terms used in the chapter with their meanings and definitions

Case Study: Describes interesting cases and real-world demonstrations of the concepts being taught in the chapters

Exercise: Includes numerical questions to help the students in practicing and reinforcing the important concepts learned in the chapter

The Book at a Glance

Chapter 1: Introduction to Computer Systems, introduces you to the fundamental concepts of computer, such as its history, basic parts, and structure. The chapter also explores different types of computers along with the discussion of its hardware and software components.

Chapter 2: Getting Started with Word 2010, explains the theoretical perspectives and various implementation aspects of Microsoft Word 2010. The chapter also makes you familiar with editing and formatting tasks that are performed in Microsoft Word 2010.

Chapter 3: Getting Started with Excel 2010, introduces the fundamental concepts of Microsoft Excel 2010, such as workbook, worksheet, and data ranges.

Chapter 4: Getting Started with PowerPoint 2010, explains the fundamental concepts of PowerPoint 2010, such as its history and features. You also learn how to perform various operations in PowerPoint, such as creating a presentation, opening an existing presentation and saving a presentation.

Chapter 5: Microsoft Access 2010, explains the fundamental concepts of Access 2010, such as database, tables, and fields. You also learn how to perform various operations in Access2010, such as creating a database, opening an existing database and creating a table in a database.

Chapter 6: Introduction to Networking, explores the basic concepts of networking and discusses various hardware devices used in networking. Various other concepts, such as transmission media, security, virus, antivirus, and firewall have been explained in the chapter.

Chapter 7: Introduction to Management Information System, introduces you to the definition, components, trends, types and framework of information systems. The chapter also elaborates on different aspects of management information system with its need and role in an organization.

Chapter 8: System Development and Design, helps in understanding the system approach and the concept of system. The chapter provides an overview of system analysis and elaborates the traditional system development lifecycle. The chapter also explains the aspects of system design and the system development methodologies.

Chapter 9: Knowledge Management and Artificial Intelligence in Business, brings an insight of knowledge management with information systems by discussing about the scope of knowledge in business and explores the concept of knowledge management in organizations. Later the chapter explains the concept of artificial intelligence along with its application, evolution, components and the concept of expert systems.

Chapter 10: Information System Security and Control, explores the ethical aspects of information technology by examining the importance of ethics in information technology and finding out the ways that help in achieving ethics in the use of information technology. The chapter discusses about the ethical challenges in information technology and explains its security management and control. Along with discussing about various security issues it explains the management of risk involved in application of information technology in business.

CHAPTER 1

Introduction to Computer Systems

CHAPTER STRUCTURE

CHAPTER OBJECTIVES

- Learn about computer and its features
- Know about the basic parts of a computer
- Learn about the different types of computers
- Explore about computer hardware and software
- Explore about operating system
- Understand the types and functions of operating system
- Learn about Windows operating system

1.1 Introduction

The term computer is derived from the word compute, which means to calculate. In simple words, a computer is an electronic device, which takes input from the user in the form of data, processes that data according to the instructions given by the user, and displays the output on the screen. Initially, invented to just calculate basic mathematical and astronomical problems, computers are now used in almost all the domains including business, academics, defense, budgeting, research, engineering, medicine, and space exploration. In today's world, computer has almost become a necessity of man, as it greatly simplifies and quickens the process of performing various tasks.

Consider a scenario of an organization where all the details of employees, customers, and products need to be maintained on a daily basis. Earlier, all these records were generated and maintained manually, which was a tedious, time consuming, and error-prone process and required a lot of manual labor. However, nowadays, with the help of computers, all this work can be performed easily and much more accurately by a single person.

Apart from maintaining the day-to-day records of an organization, computer also helps to perform various other tasks, such as generating the revenue and comparing the annual sales records of the organization. To generate revenue, an executive just needs to provide the expenses incurred, sales, purchases, and other details of the business as input to the computer. After receiving the required information, the computer processes the data to generate the revenue of the organization. Finally, the generated output, in our case the revenue of the organization, is displayed on the monitor of the computer. This entire process is done very quickly as compared to manual processing. Earlier, computers were very large in size and consumed a lot of power. However, with the passage of time, more enhanced technologies were used to reduce the size and power consumption of computers.

The soul of computer is operating system (OS). OS is a set of programs that controls the hardware of a computer and enables it to communicate and operate with the computer software. As a computer understands and receives instructions only in machine language, the OS converts the input and instructions given by a user into the machine language that can be understood by the computer, which then processes the data according to the given instructions to produce the output. The OS again converts the generated output from machine language to the high-level language, understandable by the user, before displaying it on the computer screen.

This chapter familiarizes you with computers and operating system. The chapter discusses basic parts of a computer and different hardware, software and storage devices of computers. Next, it covers the functions, type ad classification of the operating system. Towards the end, the chapter explains about the elements of the GUI based operating system.

1.2 Defining Computer

As already discussed, a computer is a machine that accepts the input in the form of data or information, and processes it according to the instructions provided by the user to produce the desired output. Consider an example where you need to obtain the sum of all the digits from 1 to 10. In this case, the digits are the data or the input and the command to add all these digits is referred as the instruction given to process the data. The final result, in this case 55, is displayed as the output on the computer screen. The following are some of the features of a computer:

- **Speed:** Refers to the rate at which a computer performs all its operations. A computer processes all the computations in fractions of seconds.
- **Storage and reliability:** Refers to the storage capacity of a computer, that is, how much information can be stored in a computer. The reliability feature helps the computer to generate the output at the location specified by a user.
- **Accuracy:** Refers to the degree of accurate results generated by the computer. As you know that computer is an electronic machine, which processes on the basis of the input provided by a user. It generally produces 100% accurate results provided the data and instructions given by the user are correct.
- **Versatility:** Allows you to use computers in almost every field or domain, such as teaching, training, entertainment, accounting, and hospitality, to perform the desired task.

A computer consists of software and hardware devices that interact with each other to produce the desired output. Different hardware devices are used to perform different functions, such as keyboard and mouse are used to provide input to the computer; whereas, printer or monitor are used to display the output generated by the computer. The applications and programs that are used to provide processing instructions to a computer come under the category of software.

Figure-1 shows the software programs and hardware devices involved in processing data:

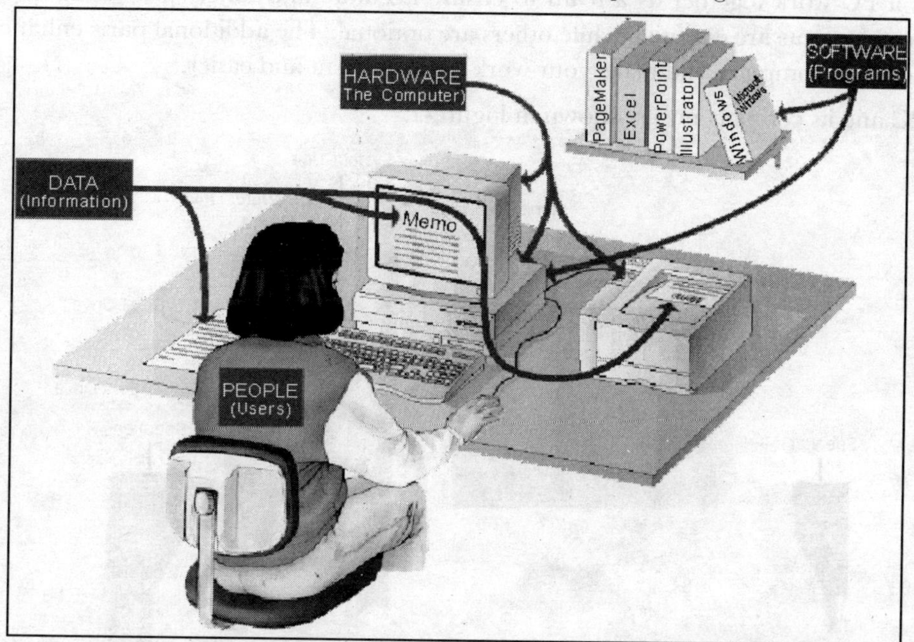

Figure-1: Displaying the Hardware Devices and Software for Data Processing

As you can see from Figure-1, a computer can contain various software applications, such as PageMaker, Excel, PowerPoint that are used to process data according to the instructions given by the user. The data processed by a computer is referred as output or information.

A computer performs the following tasks:

- Accepts the data and processing instructions from the users in the form of input
- Processes data or executes the commands provided by the user with the help of its hardware and software components.
- Displays or stores the result obtained after processing the data or executing the command.

Let us now explore the basic parts of a computer..

1.3 Exploring the Basic Parts of a Computer

A computer consists of various components, such as CPU, monitor, mouse, and keyboard. Depending upon your requirements, you can also attach some additional accessories, such as speakers, microphone, and headphone, to your computer. The main components of computers are as follows:

- **CPU:** Processes data according to the instructions given to it, by a user. It consists of two parts, namely Control Unit (CU) and Arithmetic Logic Unit (ALU). The CPU processes the instructions given to it by successful coordination between the unit and its two parts.
- **Monitor:** Displays the output of a program. It is a television-like equipment, which can be monochrome (black and white), Liquid Crystal Display (LCD), Video Graphics Array (VGA), or Super Video Graphic Array (SVGA).

- **Mouse:** Refers to a component that fits inside a palm and contains buttons (two or three) to handle the motion of a cursor and control the graphical user interface (GUI) of the computer.
- **Keyboard:** Refers to a device that contains keys to feed information into the computer. Generally, a keyboard is available in two models: the standard model with 83-84 keys and the enhanced model that contains 104 keys or more.

The components in a PC work together as a team to ensure accurate and timely processing of tasks. As mentioned earlier, some of the components are essential, while others are optional. The additional parts enhance the range of tasks that can be performed on a computer and make your work more efficient and easier.

The structure of a PC and its components are shown in Figure-2:

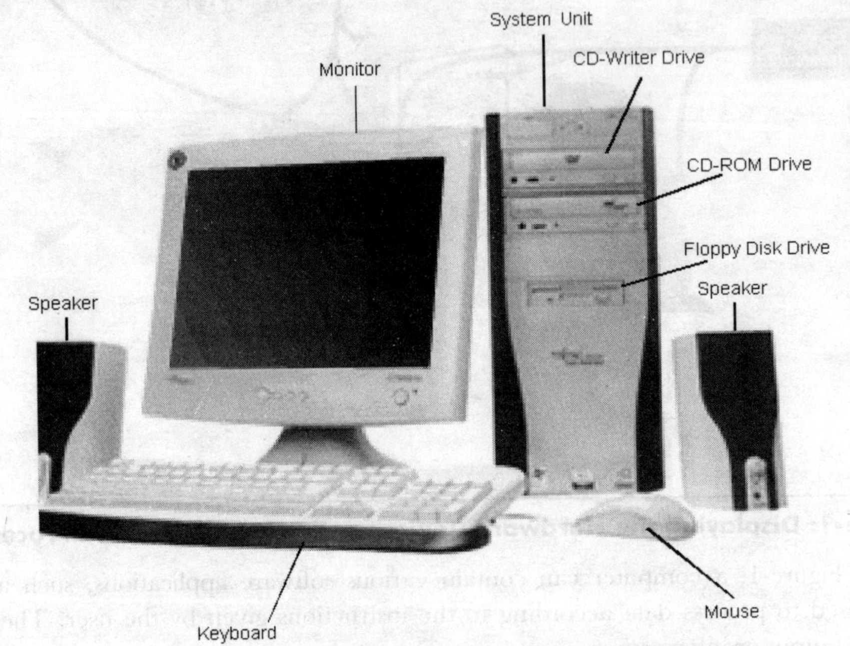

Figure-2: Showing PC and its Components

In Figure-1, various components of a PC, such as mouse, speaker, monitor, system unit, and keyboard, can be seen. The essential and the optional components of a computer are listed in Table-1:

Table-1: Basic and Optional Components of a Computer

Basic Components	Optional Components
Processor	Printer
Hard disk	Scanner
RAM	Modem
Display/Video card	Digital Versatile Disc (DVD) drive
Keyboard	Speakers
Drives: Hard Disk, Floppy	Zip Disk and Compact Disc Read-Only-Memory (CD-ROM Drive)
Mouse	
Monitor	

Now that you are familiar of the basic parts of a computer, let us move on to learn about the basic structure of a computer.

Activity-1

1. What is computer?

2. With the help of a neat schematic diagram, explain the basic parts of a computer.

1.4 Describing Computer Hardware

We have mentioned earlier that computer component or device that you can see and feel is known as hardware. In other words, the physical components of a computer are known as computer hardware. Some hardware components are already attached to a computer, such as monitor and keyboard; however, depending upon your requirements, you can also install additional hardware components, such as a scanner or printer. In computer terminology, there are three broad categories of hardware devices:

- Input devices
- Output devices
- Storage devices

Let us learn about each of these devices in detail.

1.4.1 Input Devices

A device that lets you enter data or instructions in a computer is known as an input device. For example, you enter text in a document using a keyboard. In this example, keyboard is an input device that is used to provide data to the computer.

In this section, you learn about the following input devices:

- Keyboard
- Voice speech devices
- Mouse
- Scanner
- MICR
- OMR
- Bar code reader
- Digital camera

Keyboard

A keyboard looks similar to a typewriter, which contains various alphabetic, numeric, and function keys. A numeric keypad is located on the right-hand side of the keyboard. Numeric keys have the same placement as a 10-key calculator, which allows the operator to enter numbers rapidly. You can find various function keys, such as Caps Lock, Enter, Shift, Alt, and Ctrl keys that are used to perform various tasks. For example, when the Caps Lock key is on, the alphabets that you type with the keyboard are displayed in upper case. The keyboard that we use is known as QWERTY keyboard, which is also called the Universal keyboard. Christopher Sholes, the inventor of the typewriter, designed the arrangement of characters on a QWERTY keyboard in 1868. Generally, keyboards are available in two models: standard model with 83-84 keys and enhanced model with 104 keys or more. Figure-3 shows a standard QWERTY keyboard.

Figure-3: Standard QWERTY Keyboard

A brief description of the various keys present on the QWERTY keyboard is given as follows:

- **Typewriter keys:** Include letters, numbers, and punctuation symbols. The typewriter keys are used to type data.
- **Function keys:** Include keys labeled from F1 to F12 located at the top end of the keyboard. The functions that they perform depend on the software you use.
- **Cursor control keys:** Appear as Left, Right, Up, and Down arrow keys. These keys enable you to move the cursor to the left, right, up, or down the screen.
- **Numeric keys:** Appear just below the function keys along with some special characters printed on the topside. In addition, the right-hand side of the keyboard contains the numeric key pad comprising calculator-like keys. Some of these keys have double functions. The switch over between the two functions of a numeric key pad is controlled by the key marked Num Lock. For example, the key marked 7 works as a Home key only when the Num Lock key is OFF. When the NUM LOCK key is ON (indicated by the green light on top of the keyboard), the keys marked 1, 2, 3, 4, 5, 6, 7, 8, 9, and 0 function as numeric keys, and on pressing any one of them, a number is displayed on the screen.
- **Page Up and Page Down keys:** Allow you to move to the preceding and next pages of the document, respectively.
- **Home and End keys:** Allow you to move the cursor to the top and bottom of the document, line, or window, respectively.
- **Caps Lock key:** Allows you to type text in upper case. Generally, an alphabet is typed in lower case. If you press the Caps Lock key once (when the Light-Emitting Diode (LED) status indicator of Caps Lock is lit), any letter you type appears in upper case (capital). This effect can be reversed by simply pressing the Caps Lock key once again.
- **Shift key:** Allows you to type text in upper case. An alphabet appears in upper case if you press the Shift key along with the letter key. However, if the Caps Lock is ON, this effect is reversed. Where there are two symbols or characters on a key, pressing the key along with the Shift key displays the upper symbol, such as ~, ! , @, #, $, %, ^, &, *, ( ), _, +, |, :, {, }, ", :, <, >, and ?.

- **Ctrl and Alt keys:** Allow you to carry out special actions. For example, pressing the Ctrl and C keys together allows you to copy the selected item or text. By pressing the Ctrl, Alt, and Del (Delete) keys together, the Windows Task Manager window opens, which allows you to end the process that is not responding.
- **Enter key:** Allows you to start processing the data. In case of software, such as MS Word, pressing the Enter key moves the cursor to the next line. The Enter key is also referred to as the Return key.
- **Tab key:** Moves the cursor along a line to a preset point. It lets you indent paragraphs and line-up columns, text, or numbers in a document. In some software, the Tab key helps you to move from one option to another in a menu.
- **Esc (Escape) key:** Allows you to cancel or ignore the entry or command that you have just entered in an application.
- **Delete and Backspace keys:** Erase a space or a character (one space/character at a time) in a document. The Delete key erases the character that is placed on the right-hand side of the blinking cursor. On the other hand, the Backspace key erases the character on the left-hand side of the blinking cursor.

Mouse

Mouse is a handheld device that allows you to control your computer without typing instructions from the keyboard. The user places the palm of the hand over the mouse and moves it across a mouse pad; thereby, moving the mouse pointer on the screen. You can select icons, open programs, and select commands present in a program by moving the mouse pointer.

A mouse has one primary button (left button) and one secondary button (right button). The primary button is used to carry out most of the tasks; whereas, the secondary button is used in special cases, such as opening shortcut menus. You can select icons and commands by positioning the tip of the mouse pointer over the desired choice and clicking the mouse button. A small wheel between the mouse buttons lets you scroll through the documents and Web pages. To scroll down, roll the wheel backward (toward you), and to scroll up, roll the wheel forward (away from you).

Some computers have a wireless mouse, which means that the mouse is not physically connected to the computer. Instead, it relies on infrared or radio waves to communicate with the computer. These wireless mice are more costly when compared to serial and bus mouse because these mice do not contain a cord that might interfere a user working with it.

Figure-4 shows wireless mice:

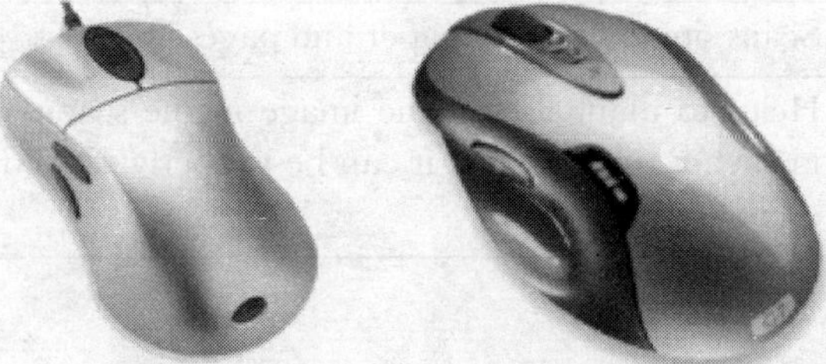

Figure-4: Showing wireless mice

Voice Speech Devices

Nowadays, headphones are accompanied with built-in mike. At home, you can use a headphone and a mike for voice-based chatting and making phone calls over the Internet. You can hear the voice and speak to your friends simultaneously by using a headphone.

Figure-5 shows a headphone and a mike:

Figure-5: Headphone and Mike

Scanner

The scanner is a device that can transfer typed or handwritten texts, graphs, diagrams, and photographs to the computer. Instead of making a duplicate copy on a paper of the required data or photograph, the scanner stores them in the memory of the computer. Scanners can be used for storing photographs and important documents in their original form. Figure-6 shows desktop and handheld scanners.

Figure-6: Desktop and Handheld Scanners

Let us now discuss the features of these two types of scanners.

Table-2 lists the working and features of desktop and handheld scanners:

Table-2: Working and Features of Desktop and Handheld Scanners

Scanner Name	How it Works	Features
Desktop Scanner	Scans single sheets of paper and pages of a book	Expensive and less compact
Handheld Scanner	Helps to manually set the image in the scanner in such a manner that it can be properly viewed on the monitor	Inexpensive

MICR

MICR stands for Magnetic Ink Character Reader. MICR is the character recognition system that uses a special ink referred as *magnetic ink* and characters to facilitate a secure way of information processing. When the document that uses this special ink needs to be read, it has to be passed through the machine which reads and translates it into characters. It is mainly used in banks where the information (cheques number and sort number) that is printed on cheques is written by the magnetic ink. Figure-7 shows a cheque having magnetic ink:

Figure-7: Cheque having Magnetic Ink

MICR are advantageous as it is highly secured and forging is difficult. Additionally, the documents can also be read even after they are being folded or split. The drawbacks associated with MICR is that the MICR encoders and readers are expensive. Also, MICR system could accept only a few characters.

OMR

OMR stands for Optical Mark Recognition. OMR is the process of extracting the human marked data from the forms that are usually related to the surveys and various types of tests. In OMR, special pre-printed forms are designed with boxes that are filled or marked by the user using a dark pencil or ink as shown in Figure-8. OMR reads these kinds of forms and translates the marks to electrical pulses. Then, these pulses are passed to a computer for further processing.

OMR is commonly used in areas where you need to select an option out of a given set of responses. Generally, OMR is used in cases where the volume of data to be processed is very large.

OMR becomes a best choice when:

- The question paper includes answers in the form of a set of alternatives
- Several types of surveys where responses are restricted to either one or more out of a given set of alternatives
- Order forms that contains a small choice of items
- Timesheets of employees for marking the start and stop time

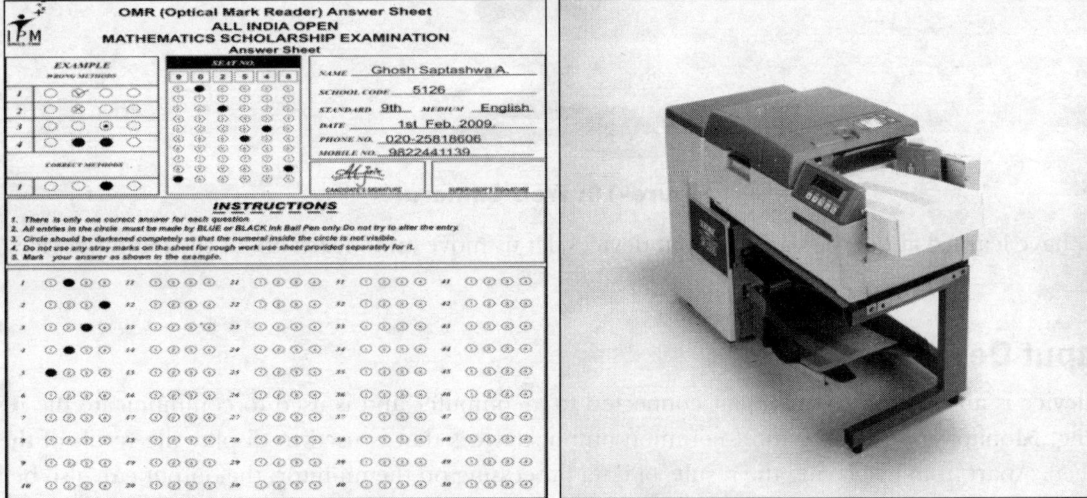

Figure-8: OMR Sheet and OMR Machine

OMR is useful to input large volumes of data with reliability and speed. Additionally, the information is entered directly from the source and this minimizes the probability of unreliable data. On the other hand, regarding the limitations, accurate printing on forms is required.

Bar Code Reader

Bar code is a combination of black color parallel lines of varying widths. The white space between these lines carries the code. This machine-readable code is sensed and read by a special input device called a bar code reader, shown in Figure-9. This reader uses reflective light to capture the code, then fed the read code to the computer. The computer interprets the information from the spacing and thickness of the bars.

Figure-9: Bar code reader

The bar code reader is also known as point of sale (POS) scanner as in supermarkets for capturing the information of the product. It also finds application in libraries for maintaining the database.

Digital Camera

A digital camera or a web camera is a video camera attached directly to a computer. You can easily connect cameras to your computer through a USB port (earlier cameras were connected through a card or parallel port). A software is connected to the camera to hold an image from the camera periodically. For example, the software might hold a still image from the camera once every 30 seconds. The software then turns that image into a normal Joint Photographic Experts Group (JPEG) file and uploads it to your Web server. Now, this JPEG image can be placed on any Web page and can be accessed anywhere and anytime provided you have an Internet connection. You can also upload your images on the Internet by using the free Web space provided by several organizations. Figure-10 shows a Web camera.

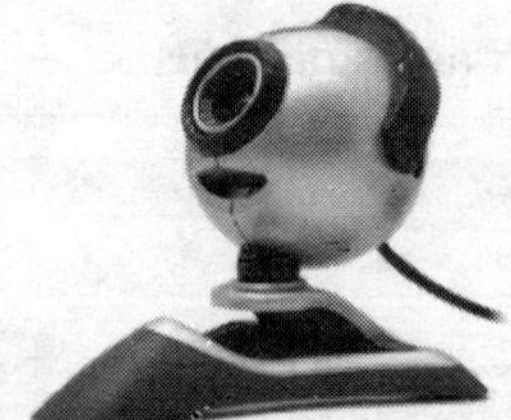

Figure-10: Web Camera

Now that you have learned about the various input devices, let us move on to learn about the output devices in the next section.

1.4.2 Output Devices

The output device is an electronic equipment connected to a computer and is used to communicate the results of the data processing. Monitor is one of the most-common output devices that is used to display the result of the processed data on a screen. Apart from displaying the results of data processing on the monitor, the output can also be transferred from a computer to various output devices, such as printer and speaker. These output devices need to be additionally attached to the computer and provide the output received from the computer in various forms, such as text, image, sound, or any other media.

Let us now learn about the output devices in detail.

Visual Display Unit

A monitor of a PC works similar to a television screen and displays text characters and graphics in colors or shades of grey. A monitor is also known as a screen, display, or Cathode Ray Tube (CRT). Anything that you have typed from the keyboard is displayed on the monitor. When a program is executed, the information or the output is displayed on the monitor. However, the results shown on the screen are only temporary and not permanent unless they are saved in the hard disk. At present, various types of monitors are available in the market, such as the monochrome (single color) monitor and color monitor. The monochrome monitor and the color monitor differ in terms of their resolution (which means the sharpness of the image on the screen). The cost of the monitor varies according to its resolution. Generally, color monitors have higher resolution as they are used for specialized jobs, such as creating graphics and images.

Figure-11 shows CRT and LCD monitors:

Figure-11: Displaying the CRT and LCD Monitors

Printer

A device that prints images, numbers, alphabets, and graphs on a sheet of paper is known as a printer. After creating a document on a computer, you can print the content of the document if you want a hard copy of the document, which is generally called a printout. The speed of a printer is rated either by pages per minute (ppm) or characters per second (cps). You can use colored printers to get the colored print outs of the documents. The colored printers are more expensive than the normal printers.

The following are the three popular types of printers available in the market:

- Dot matrix printer
- Inkjet printer
- Laser printer

Let us discuss each of them in detail.

Dot Matrix Printer

The dot matrix printer uses metal pins in the print head to create text and graphics in the form of dots on the paper, as shown in Figure-12. In a dot matrix printer, an ink-soaked ribbon is placed between the paper and the print head. The print head refers to that part of the printer, which transfers a character or image on the paper. The print head strikes against the ribbon with considerable force and the impact causes an impression of the text on the paper. The number of metal pins in the print head of the dot matrix printer determines the quality of the printout. The number of metal pins varies from 9 to 24. The more the number of pins in the print head, the better the quality of printout. A dot matrix printer that contains 24 metal pins produces the best quality.

Dot matrix printers are ideal for printing multi-part documents, such as invoices and receipts. They are also used in carbon copy printing, where you can create multiple copies of the document when it is printed for the first time.

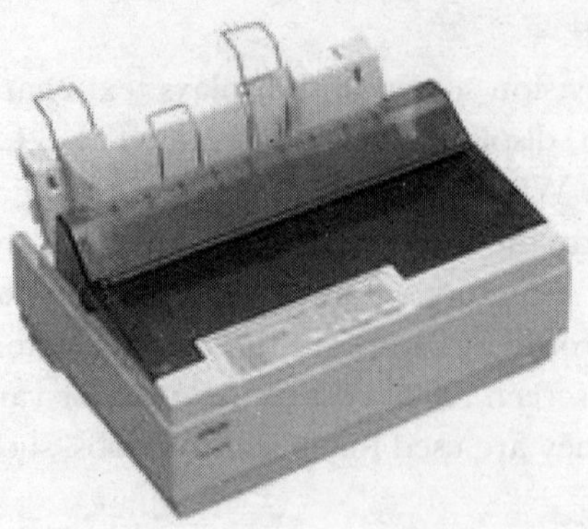

Figure-12: Dot matrix printer

Inkjet Printer

The inkjet printer is more efficient than the dot matrix printer. Similar to a dot matrix printer, the inkjet printer also has a print head; however, the inkjet's print head does not have metal pins that come out from the print head. Instead, it has several tiny nozzles that spray ink on the paper. Each nozzle is thinner than a hair.

The print head of the inkjet printer is known as a print cartridge, which contains nozzles and ink. Therefore, when no more ink is left in the print cartridge, the entire print cartridge is replaced by another print cartridge. An inkjet cartridge has 50 or more nozzles instead of 9, 18, or 24 metal pins that a dot matrix printer has. Due to this, the printing quality of an inkjet printer is better than that of the dot matrix printer. Moreover, every time the printer cartridge is replaced, the printer gets a new print head. Figure-13 shows a inkjet printer.

Figure-13: Inkjet printer

Color inkjet printers usually have a black cartridge for normal printing and a separate color cartridge for colored ink or even separate cartridges for each color. Buying an inkjet printer that uses a single cartridge for colors is cheaper when used for a short period, but proves to be more expensive in the long run. This is because black ink is consumed by the printer more quickly than the colored ink. Therefore, even if you have colored ink left in the print cartridge, the printer is unable to produce a printout with exact color scheme due to the non-availability of the black ink. Therefore, it is always advisable to buy an inkjet printer model with separate cartridges for black ink and colored inks.

A drawback of the inkjet printer is that it sometimes spreads ink on the paper. If the paper gets too wet with ink, the printout becomes useless. The ink also spreads on the paper if someone touches the printed page before the ink dries. The ink can also soak or bleed down the paper. Different ink manufacturers have responded to this problem in different ways. However, the easiest way to avoid this problem is to use good quality paper for printing, such as glossy sheets.

Laser Printer

The laser printer uses a beam of laser for printing. Laser printers work on the principle of electro-photography used in the photocopy machine. The primary principle at work in a laser printer is static electricity, which is simply an electric charge induced or generated on an insulated object, such as a human body. Figure-14 shows a laser printer:

Figure-14: Laser Printer

In contrast to dot matrix and inkjet printers, which produce printouts by printing characters and line by line printing, respectively, a laser printer is a page printer that finishes the printout in a single rotation of the print head assembly. During the printing process, a laser printer converts the entire text or image into a raster image, which is then processed by a Raster Image Processor. This processor scans the entire page, line by line, and stores a bitmap of the page in the memory of the printer. Laser printers cannot handle different paper sizes.

Plotters

A plotter, similar to a printer, produces hard-copy output. Plotters, which produce high-quality color graphics, are usually categorized based on whether they use pens or electrostatic charges to create images. A continuous-curve plotter is used to draw maps from stored data. Computer-generated maps can be retrieved and plotted or used to show changes over time. Plotters are generally more expensive than printers, ranging from about $1,000 to $75,000 or more. Plotters are ideal for engineering, drafting, and many other applications that require intricate graphics. Figure-15 shows a plotter.

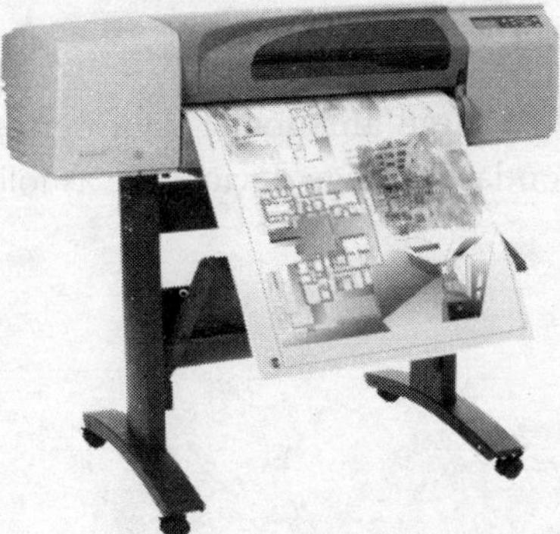

Figure-15: Plotter

Speakers

Speaker is an output device that converts the electric signals received from the computer into sound waves. While buying a speaker, you should ensure that it has a built-in amplifier, and is magnetically shielded so that it does not interfere with the picture quality of the monitor.

Figure-16 shows the speakers of a computer:

Figure-16: Speakers

Nowadays, a wide range of speakers, with varying quality and size, are available in the market. In desktop computers, speakers need to be attached as additional devices; whereas, they are built-in, by default, in laptops and notebook computers.

1.4.3 Storage Devices

Storage devices are used to store data. This data can be used either by the system or by the user for accomplishing a desired task. Memory devices are categorized as:

- Primary storage devices
- Secondary storage devices

Let's discuss each of these devices in detail.

Primary Storage Devices

Primary storage devices are also referred as internal/ main memory, main memory, or primary storage. It is a storage location that holds memory for short periods of time while the computer is on and is called as *volatile memory*. The primary memory is also known as the **Immediate Access Store (IAS)**.

The CPU reads the data and programs that are stored on the secondary devices by moving them to the main memory (temporarily) as long as the programs are being processed. This happens because the secondary storage is much slower than the main memory. Thus, when data and programs are available in the main memory, they can be easily retrieved by CPU in much lesser time. Computer **RAM** and **cache** are both examples of primary storage devices.

Secondary Storage Devices

Secondary storage devices are used to store a large amount of data permanently, which is not possible by using the primary memory. Some of the common secondary storage devices are as follows:

- Hard disks } Magnetic Media
- Floppy disks
- CD ROMs } Optical Media
- DVDs
- Pen drive } Flash Drive
- SD card

Magnetic Storage Devices

Hard disk, floppy disk and tape drives are the examples of magnetic storage devices. A magnetic storage device uses a magnetic head to read and write data. The surfaces of these devices coat with a magnetisable medium such as iron oxide. For storing data, the principle of polarisation is used. Accordingly, all the ions of the magnetisable material are aligned in one direction. The orientation of the magnetic field is used to represent data.

Figure-17 shows the floppy disk.

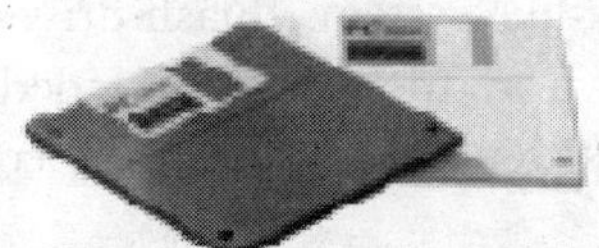

Figure-17: Floppy disk

Magnetic medium performs the following operations:

a. **Writing a magnetic medium:**

- ⇨ *Read/Write head* (electromagnet) records information by transforming the electrical pulses into the magnetic field of varying behavior.
- ⇨ When the magnetic particles pass under the read/write head, the magnetic field enforces the rearrangement of particles into some meaningful pattern.

b. **Reading a magnetic medium:** Sensing the specified pattern and then transforming it into electronic impulses.

Optical Storage Devices

CDs (compact disc) and DVDs (digital versatile disc) are the examples of optical storage devices. These discs are a special medium that store ad retrieves the data using a laser light. It works on the principle of electro-mechanics. Figure-18 shows a compact disc (CD).

Figure-18: Compact Disc

Optical storage media differs from the magnetic media as how it is read and written:

a. Reading an optical storage medium:

- ⇨ It uses the focused laser beams to read the specified pattern (which are microscopic) on the optical disks.
- ⇨ Pits (indentation) absorb the laser light.
- ⇨ The optical storage device is a light sensor and since no light is emitted, 0 pit is recorded.
- ⇨ *Lands* are the flat reflective areas, which help in bouncing the light back. Lands are read as 1.

b. Writing an optical storage medium:

- ⇨ It varies as per the type of optical media.
- ⇨ Each CD type is written in a different manner.

Flash Memory

Pen drive and SD cards are the examples of flash memory. Pen drive gets integrated with a universal serial bus (USB) connector. The flash memories are also known as a USB flash drive, which is typically a small, lightweight, removable, and rewritable device.

USB flash drives offer potential advantages over other portable storage devices, particularly the floppy disk. They are more compact and faster than any other external storage medium. They store more data, are more reliable due to their lack of moving parts, and have a more durable design. Additionally, it has become increasingly common for computers to ship without floppy disk drives. USB ports, on the other hand, appear on almost every current mainstream PC and laptop.

These types of drives use the USB mass storage standard, supported natively by modern operating systems, such as Windows, Mac OS X, Linux, and other Unix-like systems. Flash drives are active only when they are plugged into a USB connection and draw all necessary power from the supply provided by that connection. These drives will not work unless plugged directly into a host controller (the ports found on the computer itself) or a self-powered hub. This is a removable device.

Figure-19 : USB flash drive

1.5 Describing Computer Software

Software is a set of computer programs and related data that are used to provide instructions to a computer to perform a specific task. Computer programs are step-by-step instructions that instruct a computer on how to carry out operations and proceed with a particular task. In contrast to hardware, software is intangible, which implies that it cannot be touched or seen. Depending upon the functions that it performs, software are of two types:

- System software
- Application software.

Let us discuss each of these types in detail.

1.5.1 System Software

The system software consists of programs, languages, and documentation supplied to the end user by the manufacturer of the computer. This type of software is required to use the computer efficiently and conveniently. It allows the application developers to write and develop their own programs. Some common examples of the system software are operating systems (Windows 2000, Windows XP, Windows Vista, and Windows 7) and drivers (sound card driver, display driver).

Figure-20 shows the desktop of Windows 7, which is a type of system software.

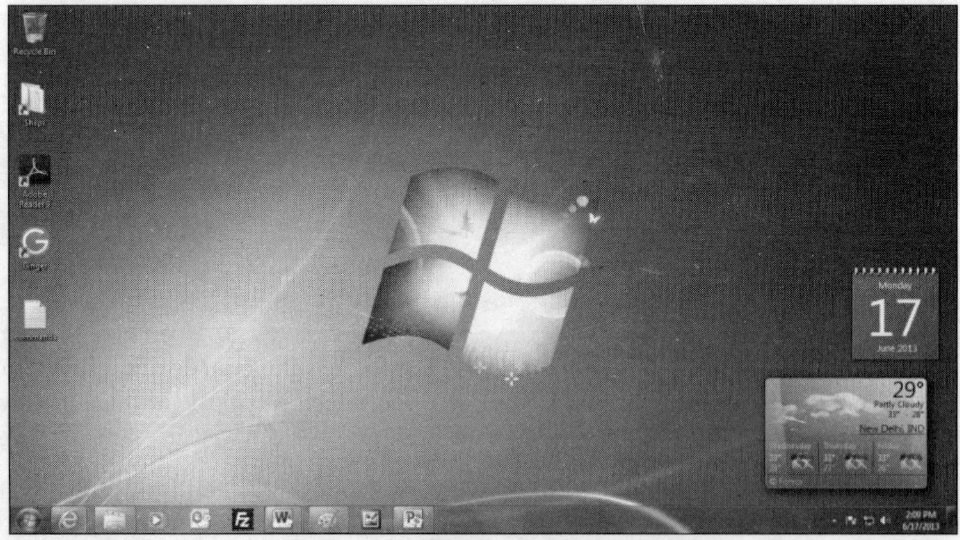

Figure-20: Desktop of Windows 7

Language Processor

A language processor is a type of system software that helps to translate the source code (the program written in a code editor, such as Notepad) developed by using a High Level Language (HLL), such as C++ or Java, into the machine code. Programmers prefer to write their programs using HLL because it is much easier to write the code in such languages. However, the code written in HLL has to be converted to the machine language so that it can be processed by the computer. The software that interprets and executes the machine language is called language processor.

Types of System Software

Three types of language processors are commonly used to convert HLLs into the machine language.

- **Compiler:** Refers to the language processor that is used to convert or translate the HLL program code into the machine code (object code). The object code thus produced can be understood and executed by your computer. A compiler is different from an interpreter as the former converts the entire HLL program in one go and displays all the errors of the program along with the line numbers. After the errors have been removed, the program is recompiled and the compiler is no longer required in the main memory since the object program is available for execution.
- **Interpreter:** Refers to a language processor that converts a program written in HLL into the machine language. In this case, the interpreter converts and executes the program line by line. If the interpreter finds an error in any line, it reports that error at the same time and the conversion process does not resume until that error is removed or rectified. The interpreter must always be present in the main memory every time the program is executed. This is because every time the program is run, it is first interpreted and then executed.

  Compilers and interpreters are important tools for any programming language to translate HLLs into object or machine code.

  Compilers are good for long programs; whereas, interpreters are good for short ones. However, combining interpreters and compilers to process a single program is the best way of translating an HLL program into a machine program (or object code).
- **Assembler:** Refers to the language processor that converts a program written in an assembly language (code) into the machine language (code). An assembly language is a low level programming language that uses simple instructions written in English letters (known as mnemonics) for programming. Figure-21 illustrates the conversion of code (to add two numbers) written in an assembly language (mnemonics form) into the machine language using an assembler:

Assembly Code	Assembler	Machine Code

_asm{
MOV AX 4
MOV BX 6
ADD AX,BX
}
	⇨	010101011
		011101110
		011010110
		011011101

Figure-21: Converting Assembly Code into Machine Code Using an Assembler

1.5.2 Application Software

As compared to system software, which controls the working of the hardware components of a computer, an application software mainly focuses on executing a particular set of functions or instructions provided by the user. Consider a scenario where you need to maintain the records of employees of an organization. Now depending upon your requirements and the format in which you want to present your data, you can prepare this record by using various application programs, such as Word processing or a spreadsheet program.

Some of the most-commonly used application software are as follows:

Word Processing Program

Enables the PC to function similar to a sophisticated typewriter. This software allows you to type words in a document or copy and paste the selected text in the document. Further, word processing programs also count your words and even check spellings. Some popular word processing programs are Microsoft Word and WordPad. The Microsoft word 2010 window is shown in Figure-22:

Figure-22: Word Processing Program (Microsoft Word 2010)

Spreadsheet Program

Allows you to perform a lot of calculation in a computer. A spreadsheet is made up of cells arranged in a grid. Each cell can contain a numeral value, text, or formula. A spreadsheet can include charting tools that allow you to plot the values stored in the rows and columns of a sheet as a graph or a chart. The Microsoft Excel 2010 window is shown in Figure-23:

Figure-23: Microsoft Excel 2010 Spreadsheet

Database Program

Allows you to store, sort, and retrieve large amount of data. Invoices or orders, which may be in large numbers, can be managed better by using a database program. Database software allows you to add new information as a record in a database, search information through previously stored data in a database, and print records from the database. For example, an organization might require a database to store information about its products, suppliers, employees, and customers. Nowadays, the most widely used database program is MS Access 2010, which is shown in Figure-24:

Kogent

EmployeeID	Employee N	Address	Salary detail	Click to Add
012	meenakshi	New delhi	10000	
013	Kinshuk	chandni chowk	10500	
014	Heena	Laxmi nagar	11000	
015	Priya	Dhaula kuan	11500	
016	pooja	Gurgaon	12000	

Figure-24: Microsoft Access 2010 Spreadsheet

Presentation Program

Enables you to represent information in a number of attractive formats. These programs help you to prepare reports and presentations for personal as well as commercial purposes. Figure-25 shows the most-commonly used presentation program, that is, MS PowerPoint 2010.

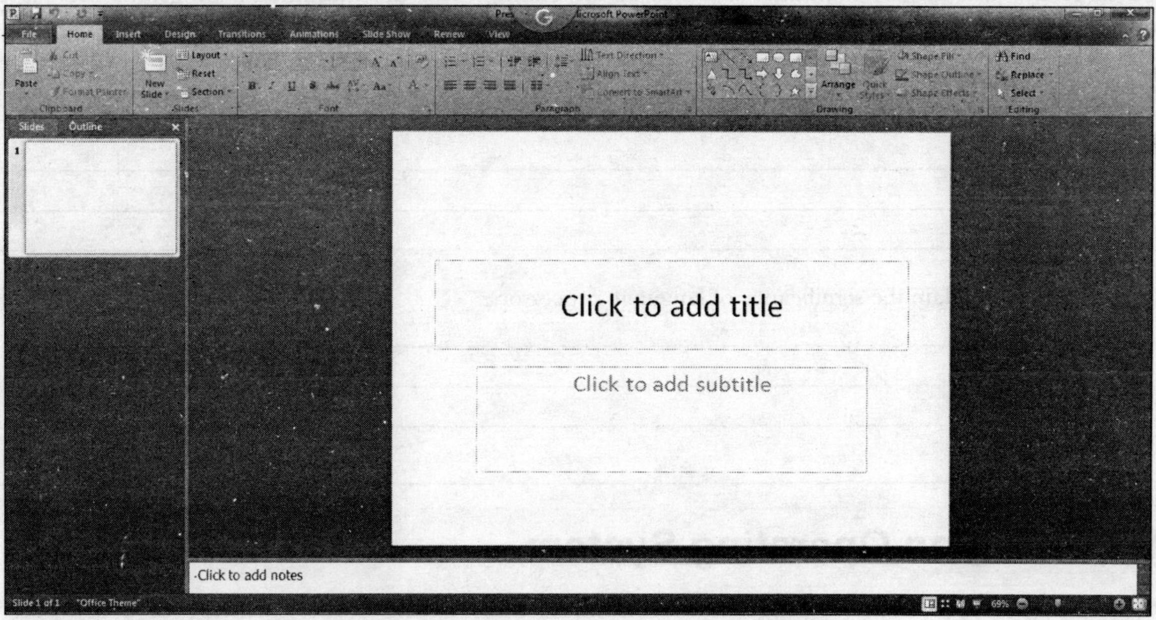

Figure-25: Microsoft PowerPoint 2010

Browser

Allows you to view Web pages. The two most popular browsers are Netscape Navigator and MS Internet Explorer. Both are graphical browsers, which mean that they can display graphics as well as text. In addition, most modern browsers can present multimedia information, such as sound and video, though they require plug-ins for some formats. Figure-26 shows a window of the Internet Explorer.

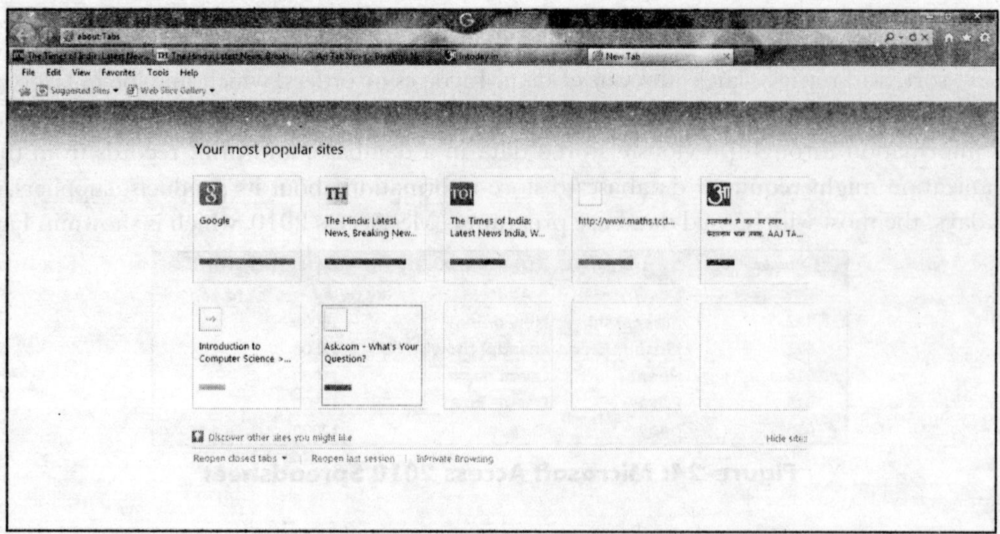

Figure-26: Internet Explorer

Multimedia Software

Allows you to create and modify animations. Some of the examples of the multimedia programs are Flash, Maya, Macromedia Director, and Sound Forge.

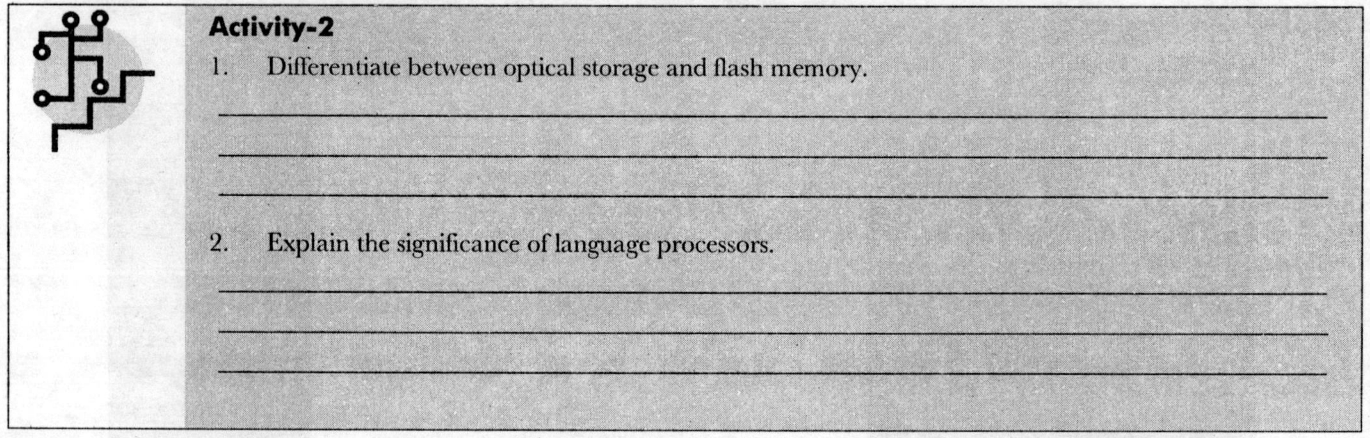

Activity-2

1. Differentiate between optical storage and flash memory.

____

____

____

2. Explain the significance of language processors.

____

____

____

1.6 Exploring an Operating System

As already discussed, OS is a set of programs that controls and supervises the hardware of a computer system. Depending upon the specific tasks and operations that they perform, OS programs are generally divided into two categories—control and service.

A control program is the main program in most of the OSs and is also known as monitor, executor, executive, or kernel. Control programs manage application programs and activities of all the hardware components of a computer system. They help in allocating resources to different devices of a computer. For example, during the processing of an input or output device, the CPU time is allocated to the device by the control programs. These programs also manage the scheduling and execution of multiple jobs.

Service programs provide various services to the users of a computer system to perform the required tasks. Some examples of a service program are language translator and utility programs. The language translator, such as compiler or interpreter, helps to convert programs into machine language instructions so that these instructions can be executed by the computer. The utility programs perform routine functions, such as loading/saving a program and keeping track of files stored on a disk.

1.6.1 Types of Operating System

Depending upon the size, efficiency, and the purpose for which a computer is designed, different types of OSs are used in different computers. For example, personal computers mainly use OSs, such as Microsoft Windows, Linux, and Mac; whereas, more complex configurations, such as UNiplexed Information Computing System (UNIX) and XENIX are used in supercomputers and multiuser systems. Some of the major categories of an OS are as follows:

- **Single-program OS:** Allows only a single program to execute at a single point of time. The program must be executed completely before the execution of the next program.
- **Concurrent OS:** Allows the CPU to execute more than one program concurrently. CPU switches its attention between programs according to the requests received for processing and executing statements. This processing happens so fast that it appears that the programs are being executed simultaneously.
- **Time-sharing OS:** Allows multiple users to access a single computer system. The attention of the CPU is switched among users. When multiple users are accessing an OS at the same point of time, each user gets uninterrupted access to the CPU. In case the number of users increases beyond the maximum user handling capacity of the OS, the processing capability of the OS would get slow.
- **Multiprocessing OS:** Allows you to execute multiple programs simultaneously on a computer that has several CPUs. Many computer systems, such as mainframes and supercomputers have more than one CPU.
- **Virtual-storage OS:** Allows you to use a secondary storage device as an extension of primary storage. A virtual-storage OS swaps the portions of program between the secondary storage device and primary storage according to the processing needs of a user, creating an illusion that there is enough memory in the primary storage of the computer.
- **Real-time OS:** Allows a computer to control or monitor tasks performed by other machines and users by responding to the input data in the required amount of time. Generally, an immediate response by the OS is necessary to control the processes and a periodic response is necessary to monitor the processes.

1.6.2 Functions of Operating System

After discussing various types of OSs and their programs, let us discuss the functions that an OS performs. In this section, you learn about the following functions of an OS:

- Processor management
- Job scheduling
- Memory management
- Virtual storage
- Device management
- Information management

Let us explore each of these functions in detail.

Processor Management

Processor management refers to task of managing processes (tasks or jobs) allocated to a processor. A processor is a hardware device that executes instructions sent by either a user or computer. Nowadays, most of the computers are equipped with multiple processing feature, also known as multiprogramming, that allows them to execute multiple tasks simultaneously. In multiprogramming, to execute multiple processes at a single point of time, the CPU time needs to be shared among all the processes. This means that all the programs are stored in the computer's memory and each user is allocated only a fraction of CPU time for the execution of programs.

When a program is submitted to CPU, it may be in any one of the following three states:

- **Running:** Refers to a stage in which the instruction sequence of a program is being executed by a processor
- **Ready**: Refers to a stage in which a process is ready to be executed and is waiting for the allocation of a processor
- **Blocked:** Refers to a stage in which a process is blocked when it is waiting for an event to occur before continuing execution. For example, when you paste the copied content in a document, the processing of the document is blocked until the process of pasting the content is completed.

Figure-27 displays all the three states of a program:

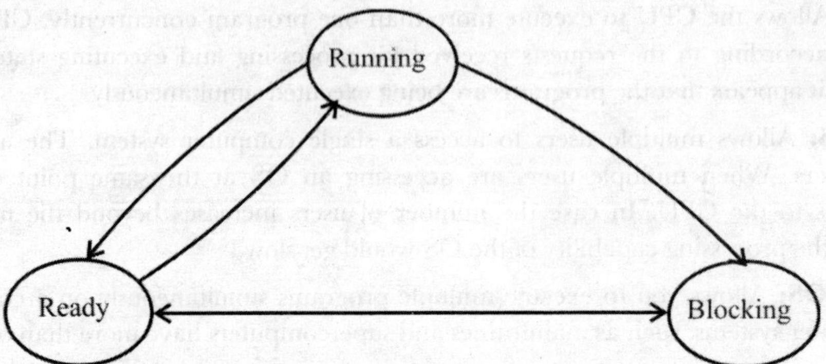

Figure-27: Displaying the Process State

Job Scheduling

Job scheduling, often called process scheduling, is a process of assigning tasks to CPU according to their priority levels and available resources. In a multiprogramming environment, scheduling of multiple jobs ensures smooth execution, as it minimizes the chances of deadlocks and clashes among the jobs for the CPU time. When a user submits a job for execution, the system considers various factors, such as the time of arrival of the job, processing requirement of the job, and type of the job that is whether the job is compute-bound or I/O-bound. These factors are essential to select the appropriate scheduling technique for the job. There are two types of scheduling, which are as follows:

- **Non-preemptive scheduling:** Here a scheduled job is always completed before another scheduling decision is made. In other words, the jobs are completed in the order in which they are scheduled.
- **Preemptive scheduling:** Here a decision regarding the scheduling of a job can be made during the execution of the job. On the other hand, in non-preemptive scheduling, the decision can only be made after the execution of the job. In the preemptive scheduling, the job, which is in the state of execution, may be forced to release the processing time of the processor so that the execution of some other job can take place.

Memory Management

An OS plays an important role in managing the memory of a computer by allocating the portions of memory to the programs and releasing the unused memory for reusability. Some of the important memory management techniques are:

- **Single contiguous allocation:** Here, the physical memory is allocated to the OS and is also used by the computer users. In this type of allocation, a job is assigned to the core memory, but the job generally uses only a small amount of the memory. The CPU is occupied by the job until its execution is completed, which results in waste of time and resources. Therefore, multiple tasks cannot be performed in a system simultaneously.
- **Partitioned allocation:** Here, the approach is based upon the partitioning of memory to accommodate more programs in the main memory. This technique is introduced to solve various problems faced in single contiguous allocation system, such as wastage of time, memory, and resources.

Virtual Storage

Virtual storage is a primary storage that does not actually exist; however, it gives an illusion of the primary storage to the programmers. The computer system itself maintains this illusion through a combination of hardware and software techniques. Virtual storage is shown in Figure-28:

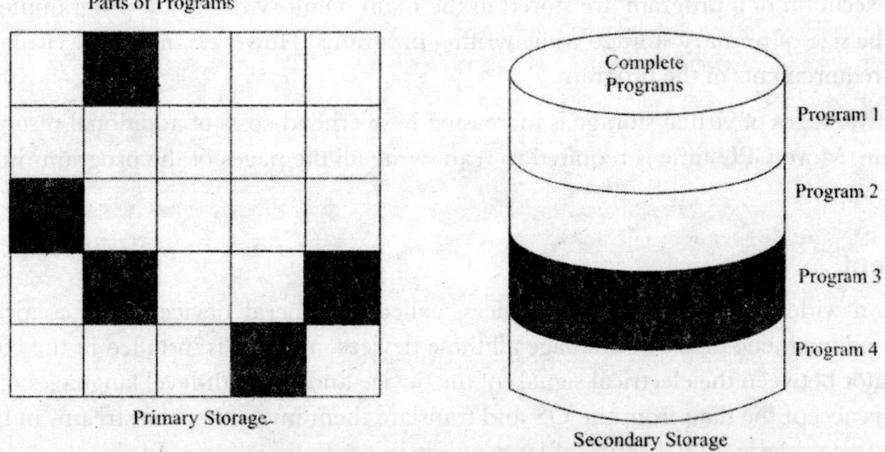

Figure-28: Displaying an Overview of Virtual Storage

To execute a program, each of its instructions must be stored in the real primary storage. However, it is not essential that all the instructions of the program should be available at the same time and at the same place. A virtual storage involves storing only those instructions, which are required for the current execution of the program in primary storage. The remaining instructions can be stored on a secondary storage device, such as disks.

Virtual storage allows a computer to execute a program even though only a part of the program is in primary storage. The parts of a program are called pages, which can be swapped in and out of primary storage on the basis of their requirement during the execution of the program. The process of swapping of pages in and out of the primary storage is known as paging.

Figure-29 shows the working of the process of paging:

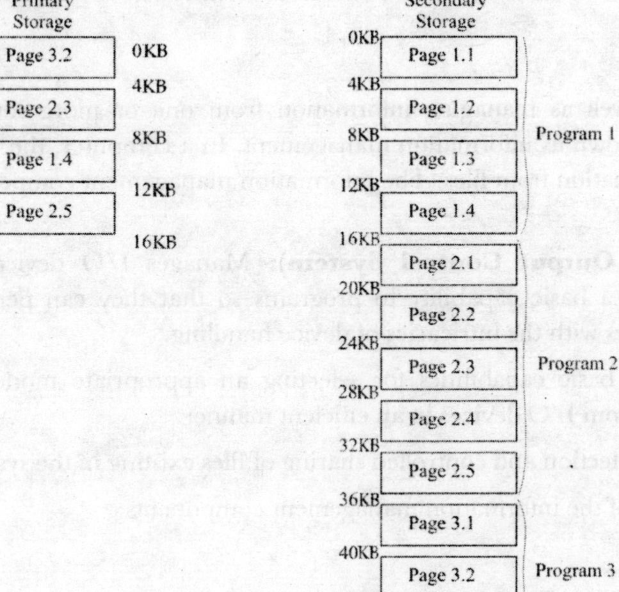

Figure-29: Paging in a Virtual Storage System

Figure-10 depicts the primary storage of 16 KB and the three programs, Program 1, Program 2, and Program 3, which would require 48 KB for their execution. However, because of the virtual-storage capability, the CPU can execute all the three programs concurrently even though there is only 16 KB of primary storage available.

Virtual storage has two major advantages. First, it helps in full utilization of the CPU resources as only the pages that are required for the execution of a program are stored in the main memory. Second, programmers no longer need to be concerned about the size of primary storage while writing programs. However, in case of virtual storage, there is no limit for the memory requirements of the program.

One of the main disadvantages of virtual storage is increasing in overhead costs of additional resources required for the execution of a program. More CPU time is required to read/write all the pages of the programs in and out of the main storage.

Device Management

A computer includes a wide assortment of I/O devices, called peripheral devices, such as printers, card readers, magnetic tape units, and magnetic disks. To manage all these devices, a driver is installed in the computer system. The driver acts as a translator between the electrical signals of the device and the high-level languages of OS and application programs. The drivers accept the data from the OS and translate them into either the streams of bits that are stored at specific locations on storage devices or a series of laser pulses in case of a printer. In this way, an OS can manage a device, which is attached to the computer, with the help of an appropriate driver.

The various characteristics of a device are as follows:

- **Speed:** Refers to the rate at which a task is performed by a device. The speed of one I/O device may differ from another. For instance, cartridge tape works slower than a floppy disk in terms of retrieving data.
- **Data Representation:** Allows devices to display data in different forms, such as American Standard Code for Information Interchange (ASCII) code and Binary-Coded Decimal (BCD).
- **Shareability:** Refers to the shareable or non-shareable characteristic of a device. For example, floppies and hard disks are shareable because they can handle successive requests from different programs; whereas, keyboards are non-shareable devices.
- **Data Transfer:** Allows devices to transfer data in various forms, such as characters, words, bytes, and records.

Information Management

The process of collecting as well as managing information from one or more sources and then distributing that information to the devices is known as information management. In a computer, the OS provides convenient ways for storing and accessing the information from files. The information management components of the OS are structured as follows:

- **Physical IOCS (Input Output Control System):** Manages I/O devices and ensures that they work independently. It provides a basic capability to programs so that they can perform their own I/O operations without involving themselves with the intricacies of device handling.
- **Logical IOCS:** Provides basic capabilities for selecting an appropriate mode for organizing data. It is also responsible to access data from I/O devices in an efficient manner.
- **File System:** Provides protection and controlled sharing of files existing in the system.

Figure-30 shows the hierarchy of the information management components:

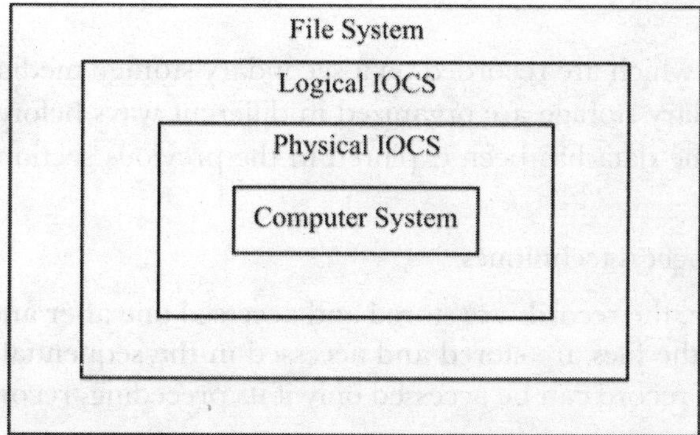

Figure-30: Displaying the Hierarchy of Information Management Components

As the information is stored in the form of files, let us discuss how these files are structured in a computer.

File Organization

The data supplied to a computer must generally be organized in a predetermined way to satisfy the numeric, alphabetic or alphanumeric (numeric and alphabetic) forms demanded by a particular program in use. The basic hierarchy of data organization, going from the general to the specific, is database, file, record, and field.

A database is a collection of related records stored together in a logical way. On the other hand, a file is a collection of similar type of data appearing under a single name. A file may be further divided into more descriptive subdivisions called records. A record is a collection of related data items treated as a single unit. For example, in the payroll database of an organization, the salary details of all the employees are maintained. Therefore, for each employee a particular record containing various details, such as Basic Pay, D.A., and H.R.A., would be defined. In this example, the payroll is a database that maintains similar type of records, that is, the salary details of the employees. These salary details are subdivided in the form of records containing Basic Pay, D.A., and H.R.A. for each employee. Each individual item of data stored in a record is known as a field. Each record may contain one or more fields. In this payroll example, there can be many fields, such as employee name, Basic pay, D.A, and H.R.A.

A field may be of fixed-length or variable-length. A fixed-length field is one where a specific number of characters can be provided. For instance, if the length of a field is fixed up to 30 characters and only 25 characters are used, then five empty spaces are stored with the data.

In a variable length field, the length of the field varies according to the data to be entered. The hierarchy of data for processing is shown in Figure-31:

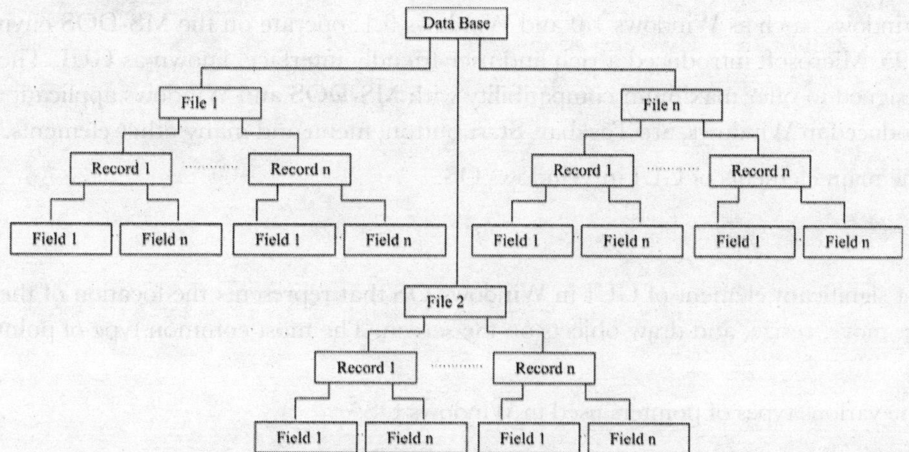

Figure-31: Displaying the Hierarchy of Data for Computer Processing

After learning about the hierarchy in which the data is stored, let us discuss various ways in which a file containing the data can be accessed.

File-Access Methods

Data items are organized into files, which are recorded on a secondary storage medium, such as disk or tape. The data items or locations of files on secondary storage are organized in different ways before they can be stored and retrieved. The ways or hierarchy of storing the data has been explored in the previous section. Let us now discuss how the files can be accessed.

The following are the different file-access techniques:

- **Sequential access file:** Here, the records are stored and accessed one after another. For example, magnetic tape is a storage medium in which the files are stored and accessed in the sequential manner. You should note that in sequential access, an individual record can be accessed only if its preceding records have been read.
- **Direct access file:** Here, a record is read directly from a disk without reading all the preceding records. In the direct access method, the order of the storage of records is immaterial; therefore, it is the fastest file accessing method.
- **Indexed-sequential access file:** The approach of accessing disk records directly with the help of an index is known as indexed-sequential access file. In this method, the computer uses file handling programmed routines during the creation of records to establish an index on the disk itself. The index indicates where each record is located. The concept is similar to the index found at the end of a book, which specifies the page where each item of information can be located. The disk index indicates the locations (track and sector) of each record, where a particular record can be found. A key data field in each record, indicated by the programmer, is used by the computer as the basis for establishing address information in the index.

1.7 Exploring Features of Windows OS

Windows OS is a set of programs that acts as a link or interface between the user and computer hardware. The latest Windows OS is Windows 8. In this book, you learn how to work with various applications, such as Microsoft Office, Internet Explorer, and Outlook Express, in Windows 8. In this section, you get acquainted with the interface of the Windows 8 edition.

Let us explore the new features of Windows OS.

1.7.1 Graphical User Interface

GUI is a type of user interface that allows the users to interact with the applications and programs easily. In other words, GUI is an interface that uses the advantages of the graphical capabilities of a computer to allow the users to work with the programs easily. GUI was firstly designed by Xerox Corporation's Palo Alto Research Center in 1970s. This type of interface provides graphical icons to perform various tasks, such as clicking a folder icon by the user. The earlier versions of Windows, such as Windows 1.0 and Windows 3.1, operate on the MS-DOS environment. With the release of Windows 95, Microsoft introduced a rich and user-friendly interface, known as GUI. The improved versions of Windows were designed to offer maximum compatibility with MS-DOS and Windows applications. The elements of GUI, which are introduced in Windows, are Taskbar, Start button, menu and many other elements.

Let us learn about the main elements of GUI in Windows OS.

Pointers

A pointer is the most significant element of GUI in Windows OS that represents the location of the pointing device. It can be used to select, move, resize, and draw objects on the screen. The most common type of pointer in Windows OS is of an arrow shape.

Figure-32 displays the various types of pointers used in Windows OS:

Figure-32: Displaying Different Types of Pointers

Menus

Menus in Windows help a user to execute commands by selecting a particular option from a list of options. Each option in a menu can be used to perform a specific function. Menus in Windows are commonly grouped into two categories:

- **File menu:** The File menu contains a list of options for file-related tasks. Figure-33 displays the File menu in Windows 7.

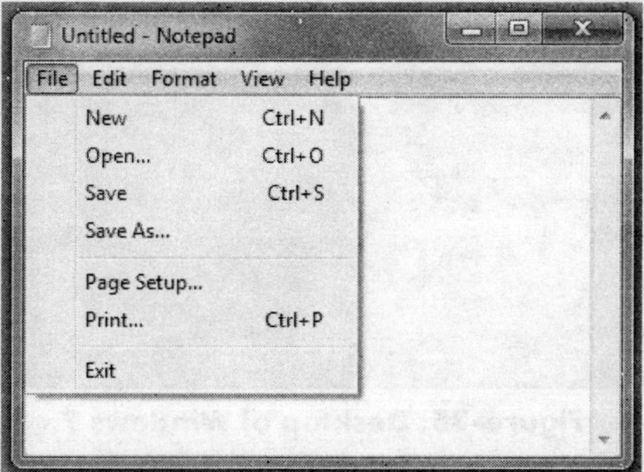

Figure-33: File Menu of the Notepad application of Windows 7

- **Context menu:** The context menu is visible only when the user clicks the right mouse button. It displays the options related to the selected object. Figure-34 displays the context menu in Windows 7:

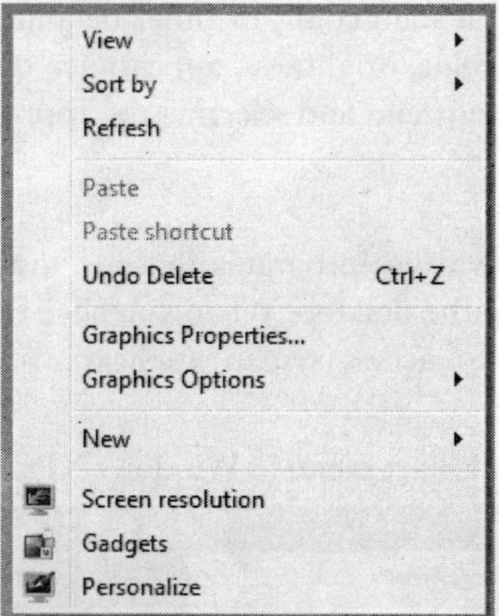

Figure-34: Context Menu in Windows 7

Desktop

Desktop is the primary screen area that appears after you log on to a computer. In Windows, desktop comprises the Start Menu button, Taskbar, icons, and background. The Start menu button contains a list of applications or programs. The Taskbar is located at the bottom of the desktop. It displays the list of currently-running programs. You can switch from one program to another by clicking the corresponding icons from the Taskbar. Figure-35 displays the desktop of Windows 7.

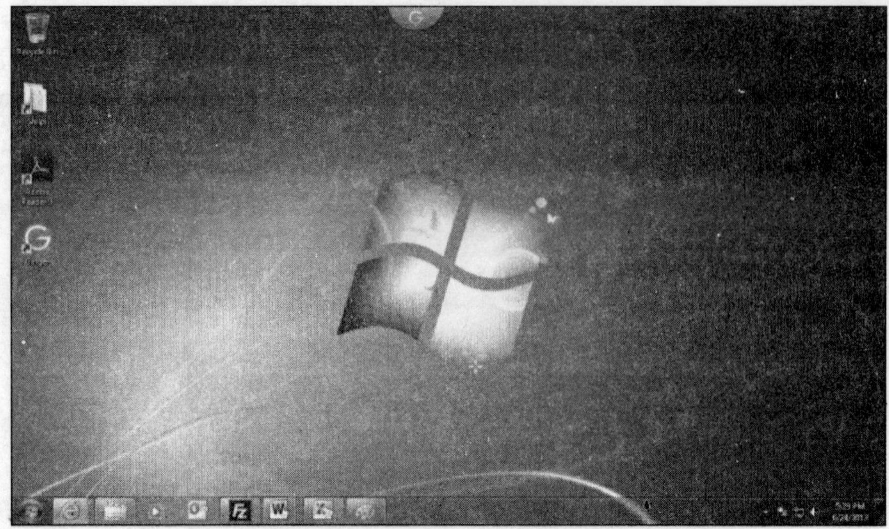

Figure-35: Desktop of Windows 7

Now, let us discuss about each of these components of desktop in some detail.

Background

Background is a picture or pattern displayed on the desktop of a computer. The desktop background, also known as wallpaper, can be a picture of your choice, a solid color, or other default wallpapers available in Windows. You can change the settings of the desktop, such as color, brightness, appearance of wallpaper, and size and color of icons and folders by right clicking anywhere on its background and selecting the appropriate options from the context menu.

Start Menu Button

The Start menu button helps you to start various programs that are available in your computer. In Windows, this button is located at the bottom left corner of the desktop. When you click the Start menu button, the Start menu opens displaying various options that help you to access system applications, system settings, printer, and Start menu properties.

Figure-36 displays the Start menu button and Start menu in Windows XP:

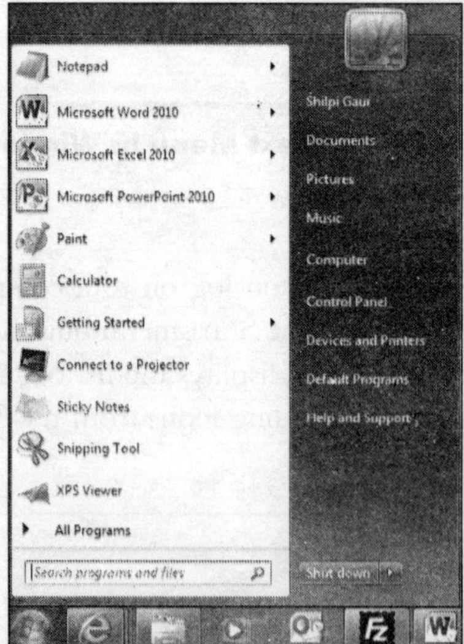

Figure-36: Displaying the Start Menu

The Start menu also allows you to perform various crucial tasks, such as restart or shutdown the system and install and uninstall new programs.

Taskbar

Taskbar is displayed at the bottom of the desktop and is used to launch applications. It includes the Start menu button, Quick Launch bar, Taskbar buttons, and notification area. The Quick Launch bar contains the shortcuts of various useful programs, such as Internet Explorer, Command Prompt, and Windows Media Player. The notification area in the Taskbar displays the system and application features (that may or may not be currently present on the desktop), time, and volume icon. Notifications are small shortcut windows displayed in the notification area of the Taskbar. These notifications display the status of currently running programs, new programs, and the detection of new devices.

Figure-37 displays the Taskbar of Windows 7 with single running task:

Figure-37: Displaying the Taskbar of Windows 7

Icons

In Windows, an icon is a small graphic or symbol that represents a program, file, folder, or device. The icons for some of the commonly-used features, such as Network, My Computer, and Recycle Bin are displayed on the desktop, by default. Apart from these icons, there is an icon for each application, which is displayed on the Taskbar, if the application is running. The documents with same extensions are represented by a common icon or symbol.

Figure-38 displays various desktop icons:

Figure-38: Displaying Various Desktop Icons

On the basis of your requirements, you can add or remove icons from your desktop. You should note that when you start Windows for the first time (after installing Windows on your computer), only the Recycle bin icon is displayed on the desktop. In Windows-based OS, the Recycle Bin represents a location where deleted files and folders are temporarily stored.

1.8 Tools of Windows Operating System

Computers are advancing day by day. They are becoming more complex day by day in terms of technology. On the other hand, the computers are becoming easier to use and coming with a variety of applications. Every application is for specific purposes and take its own space in the computer memory. Managing a collection of applications and system performance is not an easy task. Some special applications called tools are designed to provide trouble-free access and improved performance. These tools are an important part of any operating system. Tools helps in executing particular task. Let's learn about few tools available in windows 7.

1.8.1 Desktop Gadget Gallery

The Windows Sidebar feature introduced with Windows Vista has been replaced by Desktop Gadget Gallery in Windows 7. While working on the computer, there may be certain information or tools that you need to use very often. For instance, you may be frequently using the calendar, going through the contacts, and keeping track of the current news. Windows 7 eases the access to such information and tools by presenting the desktop gadget gallery in which you can display gadgets on the right side of the Desktop, as shown in Figure-39.

Figure-39: Desktop gadget gallery

The desktop gadget gallery provides the frequently used information and tools in the form of small programs known as gadgets. Windows 7 provides few gadgets such as clock and calendar that you can add, remove, and organize on the desktop gadget gallery.

1.8.2 Performance Improvements

Performance is one of the key aspects that concern all computer users. The performance features of Windows 7, such as starting up, shutting down, and resuming from sleep mode, has been improved. Following are the various tools included in Windows 7 that helps you to improve the performance of your computer:

- **Performance Information and Tools:** Indicates the performance and overall capability of the computer hardware
- **Windows Experience index:** Measures the capability of software and hardware of your computer and expresses the measurement as a number called base score
- **ReadyBoost:** Speeds up the computer by using an external storage device

Open Performance Information and Tools by clicking the **Start → Control Panel → System and Maintenance → Performance Information and Tools**. You can view the performance of your computer in the **Performance Information Tools** window, as shown in Figure-40.

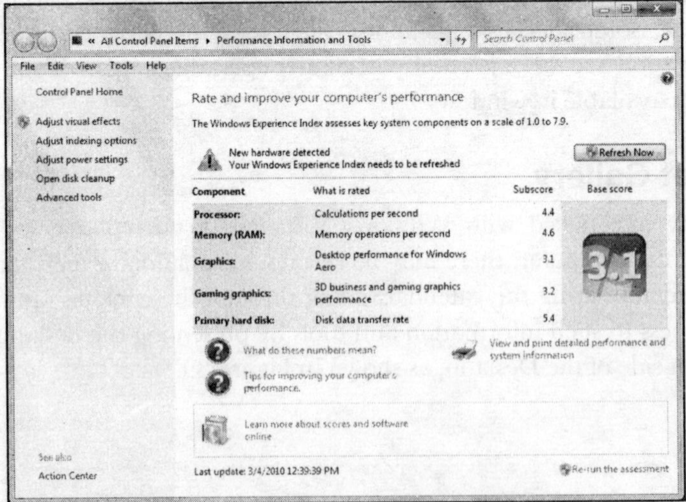

Figure-40: Performance Information Tools

In the Performance Information Tools window, you can perform the following tasks:

- Adjust visual effects by changing how menus and windows appear on screen.
- Adjust the searching option by queuing up the location of files and folders present on your computer and saving it as an index. This process is known as indexing files and folders. In Windows 7, you can specify indexing options such as specifying or adding commonly used files. Once you have indexed these files, the search for the indexed files or folders would be much faster than non-indexed files and folders.
- Adjust power settings so that the computer efficiently resumes from power saving settings.
- Open disk cleanup to delete unnecessary and temporary files saved on the hard disk.
- Access advanced tools such as Event Viewer (helps in viewing and scheduling events on your computer), Disk Defragmenter (helps you to defrag the hard disk), and System Information (helps you to acquire hardware related information), so that the problems of the system can be solved efficiently.

Activity-3

1. Discuss memory management function of the operating system in detail.

____

____

____

2. Explain how to monitor the performance of a computer system.

____

____

____

1.9 Commands of Windows Operating System

Command is an alternate solution for GUI. Windows 7 offers run command, that starts an application. Run command is helpful in situations when windows is not working properly. Run conmand offers an alternative solution to access the computer system through command line interface.

Press windows button and key R from the keyboard to give the command. Type any of the commands, as per the requirement, from the list of commands given in the Table-3.

Table-3: List of run commands for windows7

Program name	Run command
About Windows version details	winver
Calculator	calc
Control Panel	control
Disk cleanup	cleanmgr
Disk defragmenter	dfrgui
Internet Explorer	iexplore
Magnifier	magnify
Microsoft word	winword
Microsoft Excel	excel
Microsoft Powerpoint	powerpnt

Table-3: List of run commands for windows7

Program name	Run command
Notepad	notepad
Sticky note	stikynot
Windows explorer	explorer
Windows media player	wmplayer
WordPad	write

Case Study: Create a Report about various I/O Devices

Krish has to submit a report in college that provides a good coverage about various input and output devices till date. Use the information provided in the chapter on the input and output devices and also search for more information regarding the devices from various sources, such as books and Web.

Question:

Q1. Assuming you are Krish, create a report with the gathered information covering as much information as possible for clearly explaining the idea and concept of the report.

*(*Case study presented is the proprietary information of the respective organization, and is used here specifically and only for educational purpose.)*

With this, we come to the end of the chapter.

Let us now summarize the main topics learned in this chapter.

1.10 Summary

In this chapter, you have learned about the working of a computer and its four basic operations, namely, input, processing, output, and storage. You have also learned about input, output and storage devices. The concepts of the software, covering system software, language processors and application software are also discussed in the chapter. Finally, the chapter has helped you to learn about the operating system.

1.11 Key Terms

- **Computer:** Refers to an electronic device, which takes input from the user in the form of data and instructions. On receiving the instructions from the user, the computer processes the data and generates some output and displays it to the user.
- **CPU:** Refers to the brain of a computer and consists of CU and ALU as its integral parts. Actual processing of instructions takes place in the CPU. A CPU is usually located in a tower-shaped cabinet.
- **Monitor:** Displays the output of a computer. It is television-like equipment, which can be monochrome (black and white), LCD, VGA, or SVGA.
- **Mouse:** Refers to a component that fits inside a palm and contains buttons (two or three) that help you to work on a computer conveniently.
- **Keyboard:** Refers to a device that contains keys to feed information into the computer.
- **Desktop computer:** Refers to the computers that are small in size and primarily used in an office or home without the need to be connected to a larger computer. These computers are also called PC.

- **Operating System:** Refers to system software that works as a middle layer between a user and computer. OS is used to translate the user input in the language that a computer can understand and process the converted language to generate output.
- **Sequential Access File:** Refers to a mode in which records are stored and accessed one after another.
- **Direct Access File:** Refers to a mode in which a record is read directly from a disk without reading the preceding records.
- **GUI:** Refers to an interface that helps the user to use the programs on a computer system.

1.12 Exercise

Multiple Choice Questions

Q1. Which storage device has the lowest capacity?

a. Magnetic tape
b. Floppy disk
c. Pen drive
d. Hard disk

Ans. b

Q2. Which of the following mnemonics is used in machine level language?

a. Hexadecimal code
b. Binary code
c. Octal code
d. Decimal code

Ans. b

Q3. Which one of the following is not an example of control programs?

a. Resource Allocation
b. Job Management
c. Data Management
d. Language Translator

Ans. d

Q4. Which one of the following is not a function of an operating system?

a. Data Transfer
b. Processor Management
c. Job Scheduling
d. Virtual Storage Management

Ans. a

Q5. Which one of the following is not a state of a program that is submitted to Central Processing Unit for its processing?

a. Running
b. Start
c. Ready
d. Blocked

Ans. b

Q6. The operating system is:

a. Application Software
b. System Software
c. Language Processor
d. None of the above

Ans. b

Q7. Which of the following is a high level language?

a. FORTRAN
b. COBOL
c. PL/I
d. All of the above

Ans. d

Q8. DVD stands for ________.

a. Digital Versatile Disc
b. Digital Vary Disc
c. Demo Versatile Disc
d. Dynamic Video Disc

Ans. a

Q9. Run command for Microsoft Word is ________.

a. Word
b. mw
c. Winword
d. msword

Ans. c

Q10. Bar code reader is a/an ________ device.

a. Input
b. output
b. Storage
d. processing

Ans. a

Short Answers Type Questions

Q1. What are the main characteristics of a computer?
Q2. Explain in detail the basic parts of a computer.
Q3. What is the role of an operating system in a computer?
Q4. List the major functions of control programs.
Q5. What are the advantages of virtual storage?
Q6. Explain the disadvantages of virtual storage.
Q7. Differentiate between MICR and OMR?
Q8. Explain the possible states of a program when it is submitted for execution to the CPU.
Q9. Compare system software and application software?
Q10. What do you understand by Graphical User Interface?

Microsoft®
Word 2010
Starting

CHAPTER 2

Getting Started with Word 2010

Office

CHAPTER STRUCTURE

CHAPTER OBJECTIVES

- Explore the history of Microsoft Word
- Start and quit Word 2010
- Explore the interface features of Word 2010
- Create, open, and save documents in Word 2010

2.1 Introduction

In today's technology-driven world, activities such as creating and managing documents have become an integral part of every organization. These documents serve as a resource of information, which, in turn, helps in business activities, such as information analysis, knowledge sharing, decision making, and planning. For example, in an organization, there are various departments, such as inventory, sales, and Human Resource (HR). Each of the departments needs to maintain some data and information related to employees, daily transactions carried out in each department, and records that need to be maintained for future references. Managing and maintaining the information, data, and records manually on paper files can be a cumbersome job. Instead, a word processor can be used to cater to these needs. A word processor is a software application or program that allows you to create, edit, and save documents electronically. When you create a document in any word processor, some text in the document can be edited by adding, moving, or deleting text. You can also change and save the structuring of paragraphs and sentences in the document; and if required, you can print the document to keep a hard copy of it.

Some of the popular word processors include WordPerfect, WordPad, AbiWord, and Microsoft Word. The most popular word processor in use today is Microsoft Word. One of the widely used versions of Microsoft Word is Word 2010, which is included in Microsoft Office 2010. Word 2010 offers a host of modern, enhanced, innovative, and extensive features and tools. It provides a new and improved user interface that is convenient to use.

Word 2010 allows you to create professional-looking documents easily and quickly by using the predefined templates. The documents can have different formatting styles, themes, pictures, shapes, and tables. Word 2010 also allows you to save your documents as a Portable Document Format (PDF) or XML Paper Specification (XPS) file. In addition, you can take a print of the documents created in Word 2010.

Note: *XML stands for eXtensible Markup Language.*

In this chapter, you learn about the history of Microsoft Word. Then the chapter explains how to start and quit Word 2010. Further, you learn about the essential user interface features of Word 2010. The chapter also explains how to create a document in Word 2010, save it, open an existing document, and close an open document.

Now, let us start the chapter by briefly exploring the history of Microsoft Word.

2.2 History of Microsoft Word

The inception of Word can be traced back to one of the earliest word processors, named Bravo. Word was first released in 1983 with the name Multi-Tool Word, which was later renamed as Microsoft Word and released again in the same year for the International Business Machines Personal Computer (IBM PC). Although Microsoft Word provided features, such as line breaks and bold and italicized text in a document, it failed to make an impact in the market. In 1985, Word was released for Macintosh systems. Due to the popularity of Word for Macintosh, subsequent versions of Word, namely, Word 3.0, Word 3.01, and Word 4.0, were released.

The first version of Word for Windows operating system was released in 1989. With the next release—Word for Windows 2.0—Microsoft had captured a huge portion of the market. In 1995, Microsoft released Word for Windows 95 as a part of Microsoft Office 95, which introduced some new features, such as spell checking and repairing of documents. The next release of Word—Microsoft Word 97—provided customizable user interface, numerous toolbars, and hierarchical menus. Word 97 was also the first version of Word to have an Office Assistant. As the user interface of Word 97 was exhaustive, people found it difficult to work with it. Later versions of Word—Word 2000 and Word 2003—were released with Office 2000 and Office 2003, respectively.

With the release of Word 2003, Word was officially named as Microsoft Office Word. The next version of Word—Word 2007—was released to be used in businesses in November 2006. Later, in January 2007, Word 2007 was released all over the world to be used by the common people. It has been stated earlier that various enhanced and contemporary features were included in Word 2007, which can assist you in creating good-quality documents. Note that the latest version of Word is Microsoft Word 2010; and, this book focuses on MS Word 2010, as it is commonly used by the people.

Now that you have learned about the history of Word, let us proceed to learn to work with Word 2010.

Activity-1

Using the Internet, explore and find out the new features introduced in Word 2010 and compare them with the previous versions of Microsoft Word.

____

____

____

2.2.1 Exploring New Features of Microsoft Word 2010

MS Word 2010 introduces several new and improves features, such as improved WordArt, Screenshot, Remove Background, Artistic Effects, Protected View, and enhanced Themes. These new features provide a professional looks to your document. Also, the new user interface of MS Word 2010 makes it more attractive and eye-catching as the user gets all the commands and options in front of the eye. These new and improved features of MS Word 2010 are defined as follows:

- **Screenshot:** Provides the facility to capture a picture of any document or screen and use it in the document. You can use this tool by simply clicking the Insert tab and selecting the Screenshot command under the Illustrations group.
- **Improved WordArt:** Provides improved WordArt with great color combinations to create stylized text, which cannot be created using normal formatting. You can use WordArt by clicking the Insert tab on the Ribbon and selecting the WordArt command under the Text group.
- **Enhanced Themes:** Provide consistent style, look, and feel to the entire document; thereby helping the users to change the fonts and colors in the document. You can view the themes by clicking the Page Layout tab and selecting the Themes command under the Themes group.
- **Customize Quick Access Toolbar:** Helps in showing the options, which are used more commonly and frequently in the document while creating it. The Quick Access Toolbar is located at the top left-hand side corner of the MS Word window. By default, the Quick Access Toolbar shows the three options, namely, Save, Undo, and Redo options. The Customize Quick Access Toolbar is used to add or remove commands in the Quick Access Toolbar. You can also add more commands in the Quick Access Toolbar by selecting the More Commands option from the Customized Quick Access Toolbar.
- **Improved Ribbon:** Provides an easier and faster access to all the commands available in MS Word 2010. You can also customize the Ribbon by creating custom tabs and groups, which contain regularly used commands. The Ribbon can be defined as an interface that contains an arrangement of command buttons and icons, and manages commands as a set of tabs.
- **Artistic Effects:** Helps in applying special types of effects to the images inserted in a document. When the picture is selected in a document, the Format tab appears on the Ribbon.
- **Remove Background:** Refers to as an important feature, which helps in removing the background of a picture. With the help of this feature, you need not required any picture editing software, such as Adobe Photoshop to remove the background of a picture. You can remove the background of the picture by selecting the picture, the Picture Tools contextual tab, which consists the Format tab, is appeared. After this, select the Removal Background command under the Adjust group to remove the background of the picture
- **Protected View:** Helps in providing security to the computer against viruses and also to the document against unauthorized modification. When you download a document from the Internet and try to open it, the protected mode disables the editing feature. In such a case, the user is only able to view the contents of the document.

Therefore, if the user confirms that the document is valid or is from a trusted source, he/she can enable editing by clicking the Enable Editing button on the Ribbon.

- **Improved Navigation pane:** Provides the improved search facility, which helps in finding information in the document very easily and quickly. In the earlier versions of MS Word, you had to press the CTRL + F keys from the keyboard to find information in a document. In MS Word 2010, press the CTRL + F keys to open the Navigation pane, which displays the results of the search in a single pane. The Navigation pane also allows you to view the document and browse the pages and headings in the document. Further, it helps you to find a particular text or object in the document.
- **Access and share your documents:** Provides access to the documents from anywhere on the Web. When you publish documents online, you are able to see or edit the documents from any computer connected to the Internet.

Let us now learn how to start and quit Word 2010.

2.3 Starting and Quitting Word 2010

Before you actually start working with Word 2010, you must first know how to start and close it once you are through with your work. Therefore, let us first learn how to start Microsoft Word 2010 in the following subsection.

2.3.1 Starting Word 2010

As you know about the MS Word, which is a word processing system, which helps in creating, managing, and maintaining the document more efficiently and effectively. A word processing application also helps in time saving as it allows to reuse the contents without retype it. There are two ways to start MS Word 2010. Let's perform the following steps to simple start MS Word 2010, which are defined as follows:

1. Click the **Start** button in the **Task** bar. The **Start** menu appears.
2. Click the **All Programs** option from the **Start** menu.
3. Click the **Microsoft Office** folder from the menu. A list of options related to the **Microsoft Office** suite appears.
4. Click the **Microsoft Word 2010** option from the list, as shown in Figure-1:

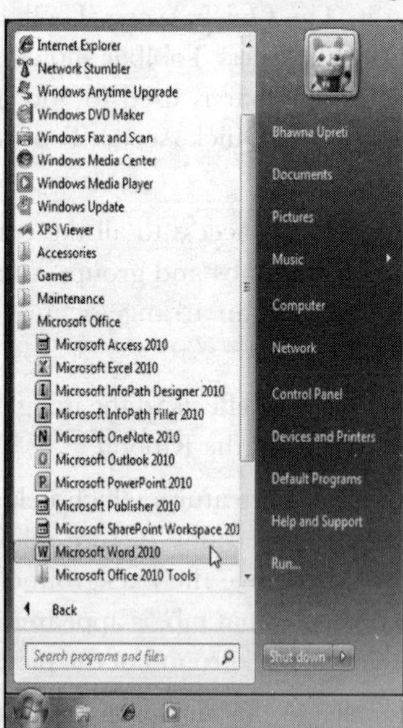

Figure-1: Displaying How to Start Word 2010 from the Start Menu

This opens the Word 2010 window, as displayed in Figure-2:

Figure-2: Displaying the Word 2010 Window

2.3.2 Quitting Word 2010

You can exit from the MS Word 2010 application after completing the work in the document. You can close the document in two ways, namely, closing a document by using the Close option under the File tab and quitting MS Word 2010 by using the Exit option under the File tab; however, there is a difference between them. When we are closing a document by using the Close command under the File tab, it means we are closing the currently working document. On the other hand, when we are quitting from the MS Word 2010 application by using the Exit command under the File tab, it means we are closing all the currently working documents of the MS Word 2010 application. Let's perform the following steps to quit from MS Word 2010 application:

1. Click the File tab on the Ribbon. The Backstage view appears.
2. Select the Exit button from the Backstage view, as shown in Figure-3:

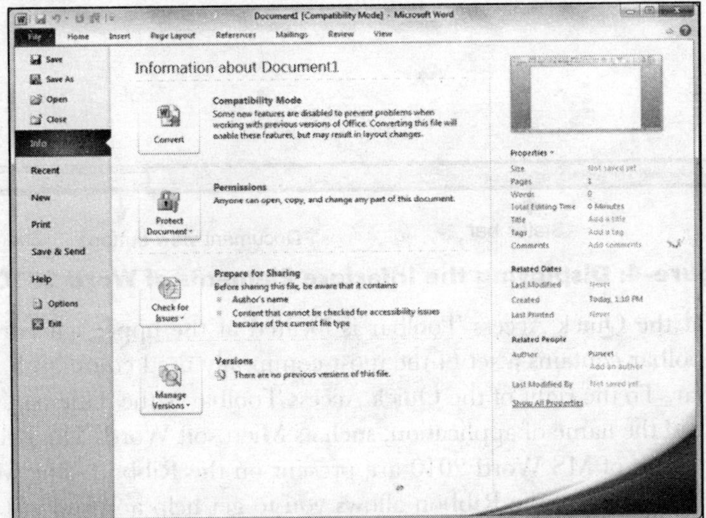

Figure-3: Showing the Context Menu for the Office Button

Let us proceed further to get familiar with the user interface of Word 2010.

2.4 Exploring Word 2010 Interface Features

In the previous versions of MS Word (such as MS Word 2003), the user interface primarily constituted of different menus, submenus, and toolbars. Each menu, submenu, or toolbar, in turn, offered numerous commands to the users. Users of the previous versions of MS Word had to traverse through the menus and submenus to find the right command for a particular task. This is very time consuming process. To deal with this problem, Microsoft has renewed the user interface and has introduced a more compact and user-friendly user interface in MS Word 2007 and MS Word 2010.

The user interfaces of MS Word 2007 and MS Word 2010 are almost same; the only difference being that MS Word 2010 has introduced several new features, such as improved WordArt, improved themes, background removal, and other image editing features. In the user interface of MS Word 2010, most of the menus, submenus, and toolbars of the previous versions of MS Word have been replaced by the File tab and Ribbon. The user Interface of MS Word 2010 is as shown in Figure-4.

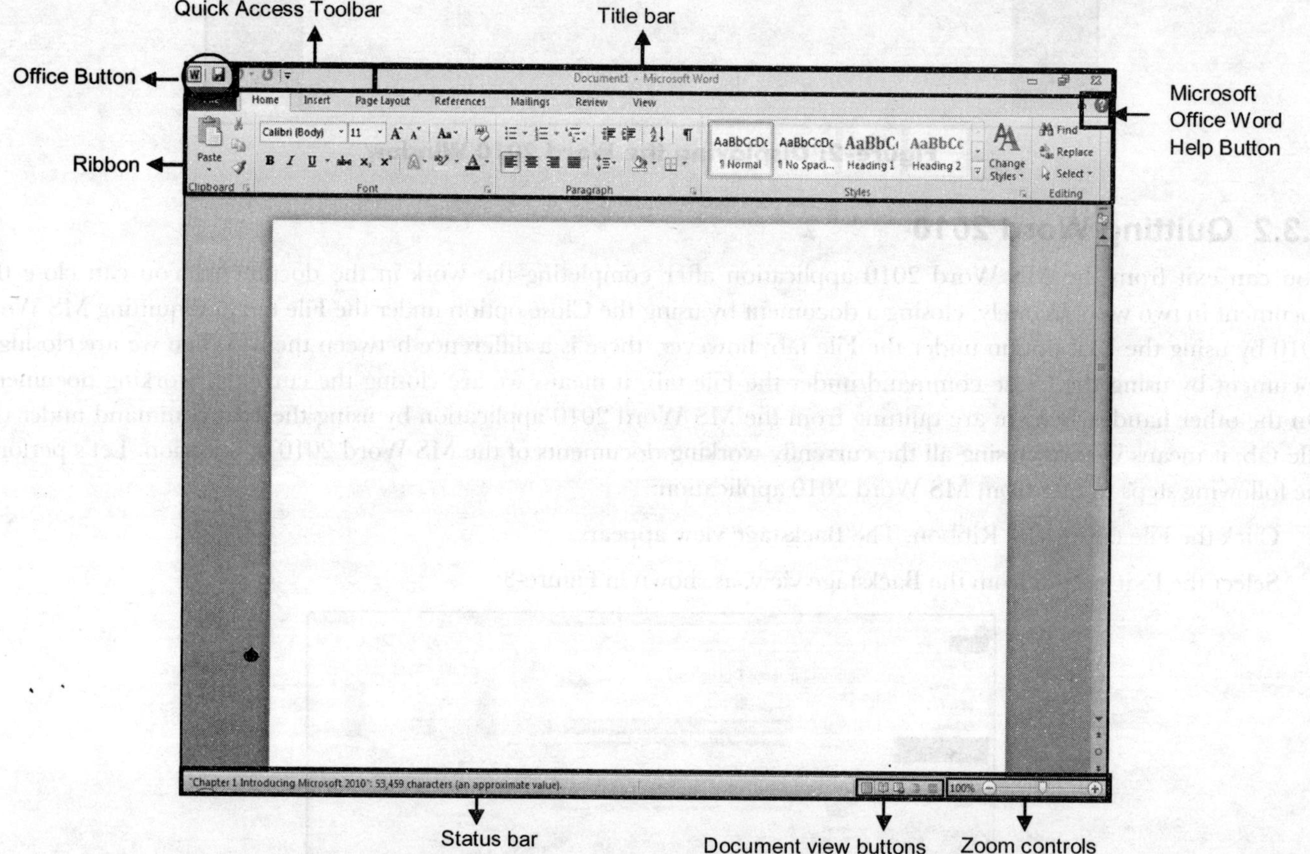

Figure-4: Displaying the Interface Elements of Word 2010

It can be seen in Figure-4 that the Quick Access Toolbar is located at the upper left corner of the MS Word 2010 window. The Quick Access Toolbar contains a set of the most commonly used commands. The File tab is located just below the Quick Access Toolbar. To the right of the Quick Access Toolbar is the Title bar, which displays the name of the currently open document and the name of application, such as Microsoft Word. The Ribbon appears just below the Title bar. Almost all the commands of MS Word 2010 are present on the Ribbon. The Microsoft Office Word Help button located at the upper right corner of the Ribbon allows you to get help and support for any problem regarding any aspect of MS Word 2010. The blank white area that you see below the Ribbon is where you can add and edit text.

The Status bar is located at the bottom of the MS Word 2010 window. It displays information related to the currently working document, such as the total number of pages in the document, the number of words in the document, and the track changes status. It also contains Zoom controls and buttons for different document views.

Now, the different components of the user interface of MS Word 2010 are defined as follows:

- **Quick Access Toolbar:** Contains commands, which are used more frequently in the document. The Quick Access Toolbar also provides one-click shortcuts to commands, such as Save, Undo, and Redo in a Word document. The Quick Access Toolbar is located at the top left corner of the MS Word window.
- **Tittle bar:** Helps in identifying the document. The Title bar contains the name of the document and also the name of the application, such as Microsoft Word.
- **Minimize, Maximize, and Close Buttons:** Help in controlling the MS Word window. The Minimize, Maximize, and Close buttons are located on the top right corner of the MS Word window. The Minimize button is used to minimize the MS Word window over the Task bar whereas the Maximize button is helps to restore or maximize the MS Word window. The Close button is used to close the document.
- **File tab:** Contains several options, such as Save, Save As, Open, Close, Info, Recent, New, Print, Share, Help, Options, and Exit, which is located just below the Quick Access Toolbar on the top left corner in the MS Word window. In MS Word 2010, the functionality of File tab is also known as the Backstage view. The Backstage view contains all the required options and sub options, such as Save, Print, Permissions, Versioning, Document Inspector, and Workflows, which help you to manage the documents or files easily. The Backstage view also helps you to hide recently used documents and provides access to file-related activities.
- **Ribbon:** Appears just below the Title bar in the MS Word 2010 window. It displays commands, features, and tools available in MS Word 2010. The commands are logically grouped under different tabs on the Ribbon. Each tab on the Ribbon corresponds to a particular task; for instance, the Insert tab contains the commands to insert pictures, shapes, and tables.
- **Dialog Box Launcher:** Refers to as a button that is presented in some groups on the Ribbon. This dialog box contains additional options that are not displayed as commands or options of the groups on the Ribbon. For example, when you click the dialog box launcher under the Font group of the Home tab, the Font dialog box appears. In the Font dialog box, you can select the Character spacing option, which is not displayed on the Ribbon, to set the spacing between the characters. The dialog box launcher icons are available on the right-hand side of the group name on the Ribbon.
- **Status bar:** Contains information related to the document. It displays the number of pages and words in the document and also the status of track changes (On or Off). The Status bar is located at the bottom left corner of the MS Word 2010 window.
- **Zoom Control:** Allows you to increase or decrease the size of the document according to the requirements. The Zoom command is present at the bottom right corner of the document window. You can set the zoom in or out of the document by moving the arrow that is located on the bottom right of the Zoom controls. The zoom option is also available under the Zoom group of the View tab.

Q1. Write a short note on the Ribbon element of Microsoft Word 2010.

Q2. Describe Quick Access Toolbar in brief.

2.4.1 Exploring the Common Features of MS Word Application

MS Word application provides several common features, such as Mini toolbar, which are also available in the earlier version of MS Word application. In MS Word 2010, these common features are improved and enhanced, which makes the MS Word application more user friendly, effective, and attractive. These common features are defined as follows:

- Mini toolbar
- Live preview

- Contextual tab
- Key tips
- Screen tips

Let's now learn each in detail. First start with the Mini toolbar, which is explained in the next section.

Mini Toolbar

The Mini toolbar can be defined as the context menu that appears when some text is selected in a document. The purpose of the Mini toolbar is to provide quick and easy access to frequently used formatting commands. You can directly select the common formatting commands from the Mini toolbar to format the selected text; thereby reducing the usage of the command tabs on the Ribbon. The Mini toolbar also appears above the context menu, which appears when a user right-clicks the selected text. The Mini toolbar is shown in Figure-5:

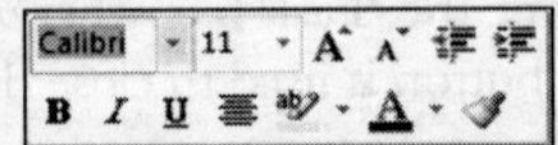

Figure-5: Mini Toolbar

Let's now learn about the live toolbar in the next section.

Live Preview

The live preview refers to as a very important feature of MS Word 2010 that enables the users to view the results or changes of the formatting or editing option by moving the mouse pointer over the options, before these changes are actually applied. With the live preview feature, you do not need to select each option to find the right option from the drop-down list of a particular command. You can simply place the mouse pointer over each of the options and see a preview of the effect that the selection of an option will cause to the selected text. When you place the mouse pointer away from the option, the live preview of that option disappears. The live preview is shown in Figure-6:

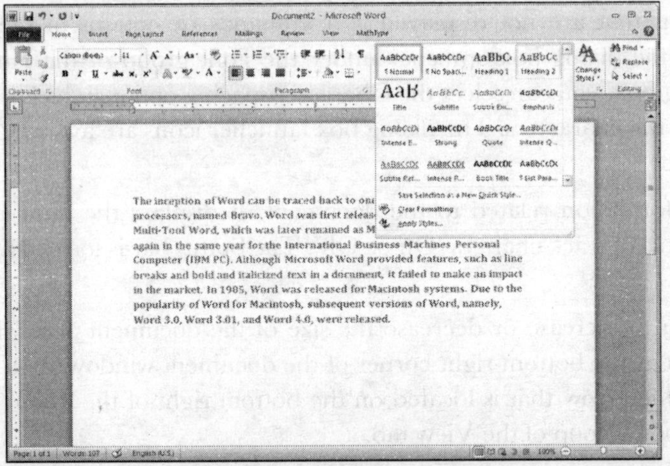

Figure-6: Live Preview

Let's now learn about the contextual tab in the next section.

Contextual Tab

In MS Word 2010, a contextual tab refers to a tab that appears when a particular object in a document, such as picture, Clip Art, shapes, and table, is selected. The contextual tab contains commands that are related to the selected object. For example, when you select a picture, the Format tab appears under the Picture Tools contextual tab, offering the options to modify or format the picture. Other examples of the contextual tab are the Design and Layout tabs under the Table Tools contextual tab, which provide commands to format a table. The contextual tab is shown in Figure-7:

Figure-7: Contextual Tab

Let's now learn about the Key Tips in the next section.

Key Tips

The Key Tips feature in MS Word 2010 allows you to access the commands on the Ribbon, File tab, and Quick Access Toolbar through the keyboard. A Key Tip can be a letter, number, or a combination of letters and numbers. To activate the Key Tips, simply press the Alt key from the keyboard. Next, press the key or the combination of keys that appear either above or below the name of the tabs or commands. The Key Tips appear on the top of the name of the tabs on the Ribbon and at the button of the Quick Access Toolbar, as shown in Figure-8:

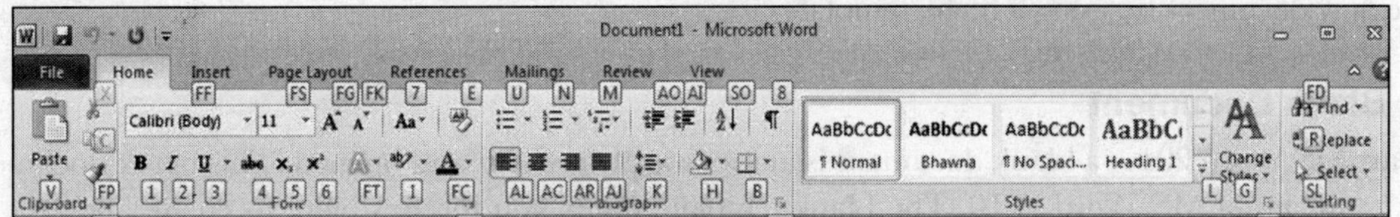

Figure-8: Key Tips

Let's now learn about the Screen Tips in the next section.

Screen Tips

Screen Tips are the small descriptions that appear when you move the mouse pointer over a command, button, or dialog box launcher. The Screen Tips show a brief description and, optionally, the keyboard shortcut of the buttons, commands, or dialog box launchers. MS Word 2010 also offers Enhanced Screen Tips that appear in slightly larger dialog boxes compared to the Screen Tips. Similar to Screen Tips, the Enhanced Screen Tips display a short description and keyboard shortcut of the commands, buttons, or dialog box launchers. They also display a small description of the action when you click a particular command, button, or dialog box launcher. For instance, when you place the mouse over a dialog box launcher, the Enhanced Screen Tip shows a picture of the corresponding dialog box, along with the description. In our case, we have moved the mouse pointer over the Paste option under the Clipboard group of the Home tab, as shown in Figure-9:

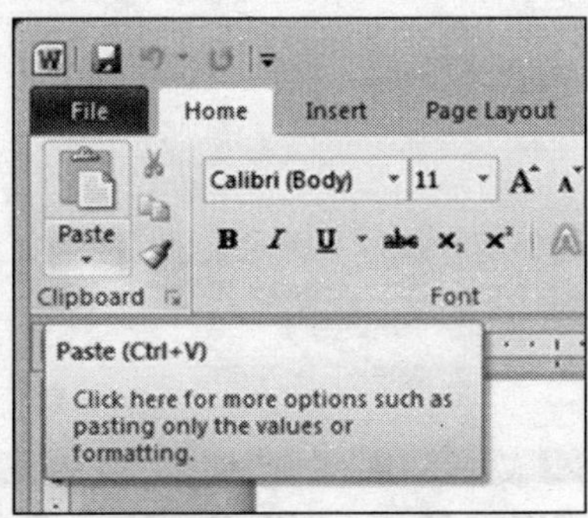

Figure-9: Screen Tips

Q1. Describe the Live Preview feature available in Word 2010.

Q2. What are Key Tips?

2.5 Creating, Saving, Opening, and Closing a Word Document

As learned earlier, you can use Microsoft Word 2010 for creating documents. You can also save these documents for future use and reopen them in Word whenever you want to rework on them. Therefore, let us now proceed further and learn how to create, save, and open documents in Word 2010.

2.5.1 Creating a New Document

Every document in MS Word 2010 is based on a template. A template is the basic model that provides the basic structure to create a document easily and quickly. Templates offer sets of different predefined visual elements that you can later customize according to your requirements. MS Word 2010 provides a wide range of templates with various layouts, fonts, styles, and colors. Some of the templates do not contain any elements, while others contain well-arranged and preformatted elements.

In MS Word 2010, you can create documents by using a blank template and installed template. Let's first understand how to create new document by using a blank template.

Creating a Blank Document

When you start MS Word 2010, a blank document is automatically created and opened. This blank document is based on the blank template of MS Word 2010. The blank template offers you the flexibility to create and edit documents according to your requirements and preferences. In case you want to create a blank document while you are working on another document, you do not need to start MS Word 2010 again. You can create a blank document from the already opened MS Word 2010 window.

Let's perform the following steps to create a blank document after you have started MS Word 2010:

1. Click the **File** tab on the Ribbon. A Backstage view appears (Figure-10).
2. Click the **New** tab in the Backstage view, as shown in Figure-10:

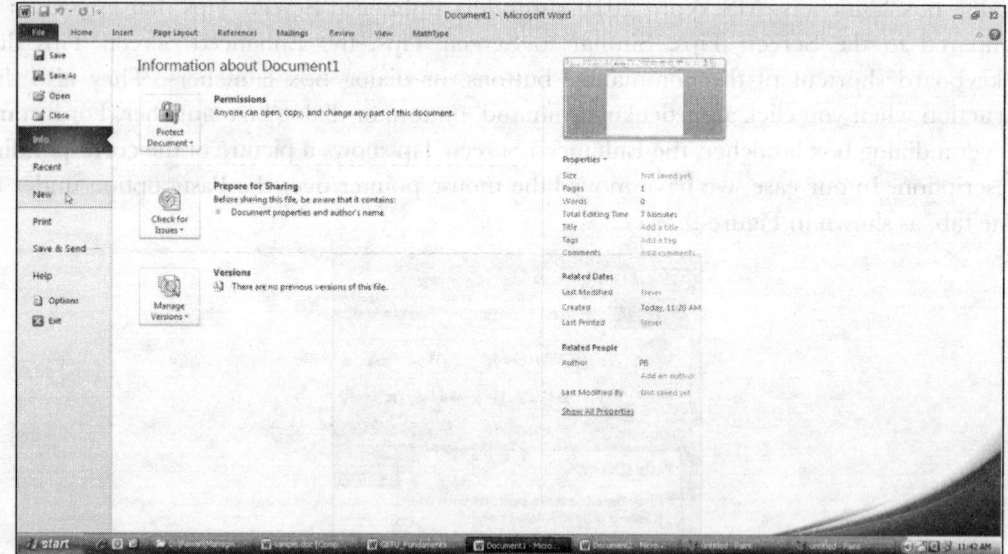

Figure-10: Displaying the Office Menu with the New Option Selected by Default

3. Select the **Blank document** option under **Available templates** category in the Backstage view (Figure-11).
4. Click the **Create** button in the Backstage view (Figure-11).

Figure-11: Showing the New Document Dialog Box

Now, the new blank document is created, as shown Figure-12:

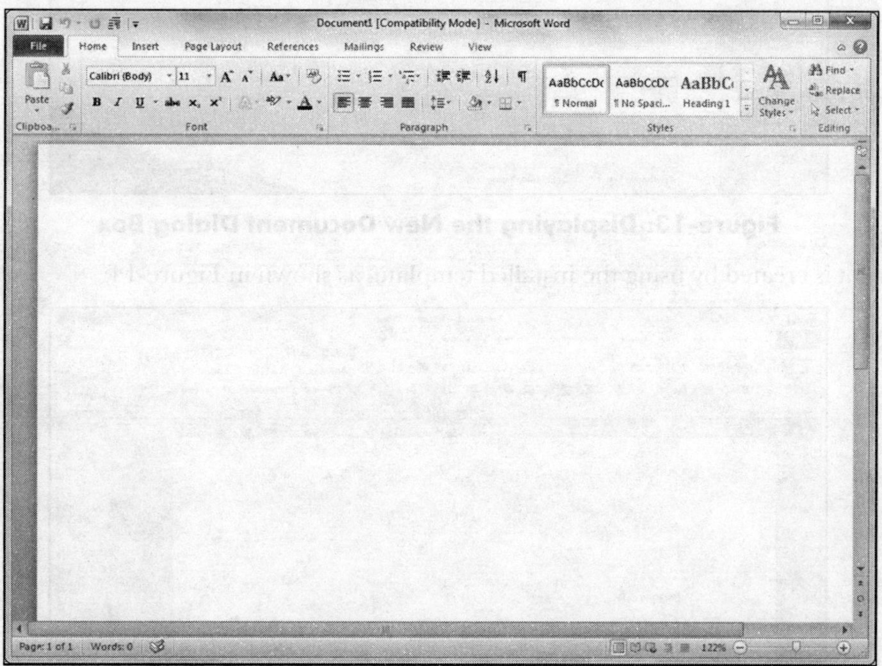

Figure-12: Showing the Blank Word Document

Let's now learn about the process of creating new document by using the installed template in the next section.

Creating a Document based on a Template

You can use templates, which are already installed in the computer or available as sample templates in MS Word 2010, to work quickly and effectively. With the help of the sample templates, you can save a lot of time and efforts while creating professional-looking documents.

Let's perform the following steps to create new document using the available installed or online template:

1. Click the **File** tab on the Ribbon. The Backstage view appears (Figure-13).
2. Click the **New** tab in the Backstage view (Figure-13).
3. Select the **Sample templates** option under the **Available Templates** category (Figure-13). The list of available templates appears (Figure-13)
4. Select the templates from the list. In our case, we have selected the **Adjacency Letter** template (Figure-13).
5. Select the **Template** radio button to create the template (Figure-13).
6. Click the **Create** button, as shown in Figure-13:

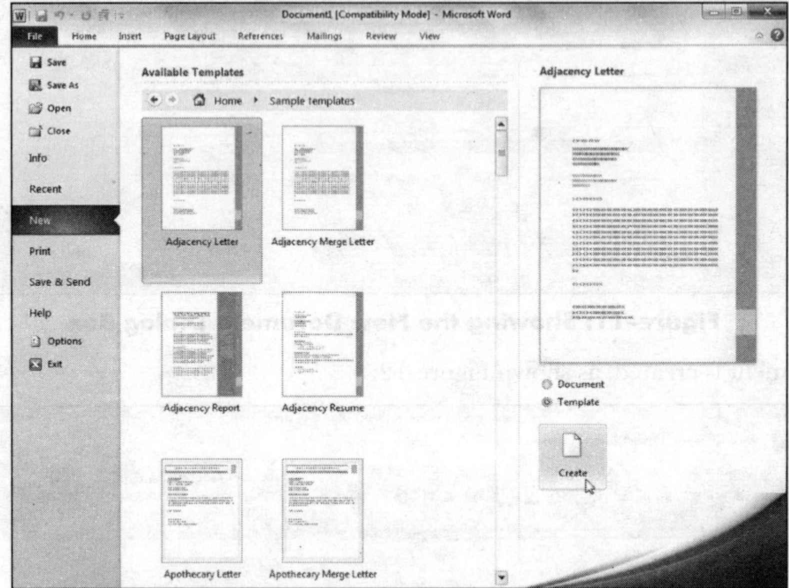

Figure-13: Displaying the New Document Dialog Box

Now, the new document is created by using the installed template, as shown in Figure-14:

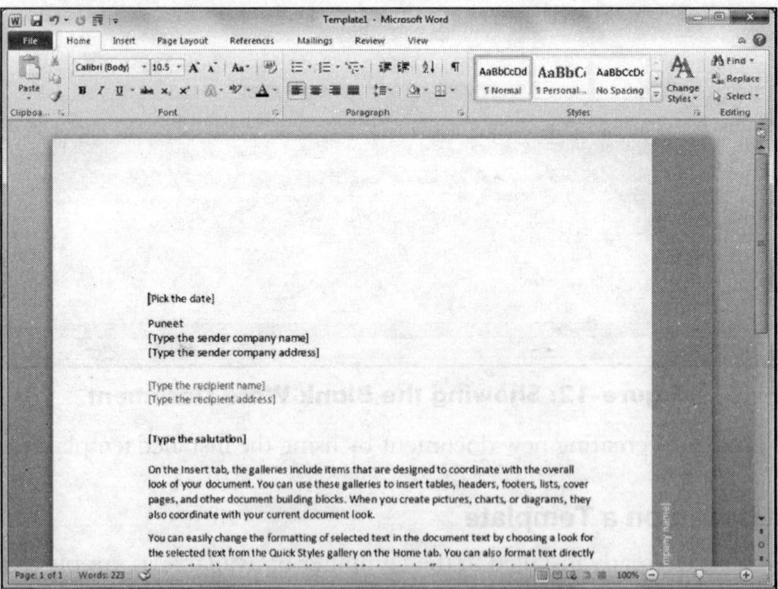

Figure-14: Displaying the New Document Based on the Selected Template

Let's now learn about how to save an existing document in MS Word 2010 in the next section.

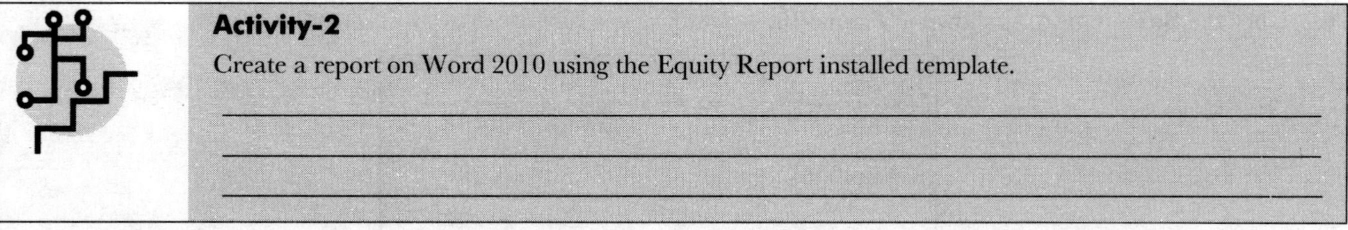

Activity-2

Create a report on Word 2010 using the Equity Report installed template.

2.5.2 Saving the Document

After you have created a new document, it is advisable to you that immediately save it. You need to save the document as frequently as possible to prevent any data loss due to any unexpected events, such as a power cut or system failure. By default, an MS Word 2010 document is saved as a file with the .docx extension. This extension indicates that the file is based on the new eXtensible Markup Language (XML) format. You can also save an MS Word 2010 document as a PDF file or as a document in the previous versions of MS Word such as Word 97-2003 document format.

In addition to this, protecting a document is also an important feature which helps to prevent unauthorized access of data and other useful information. In Microsoft Word, you can protect the document by protecting the document structure by assigning a password to open and edit the document.

Let's, perform the following steps to save your document:

1. Click the **File** tab on the Ribbon. The Backstage view appears (Figure-15).
2. Select the **Save** option from the Backstage view, as shown in Figure-15:

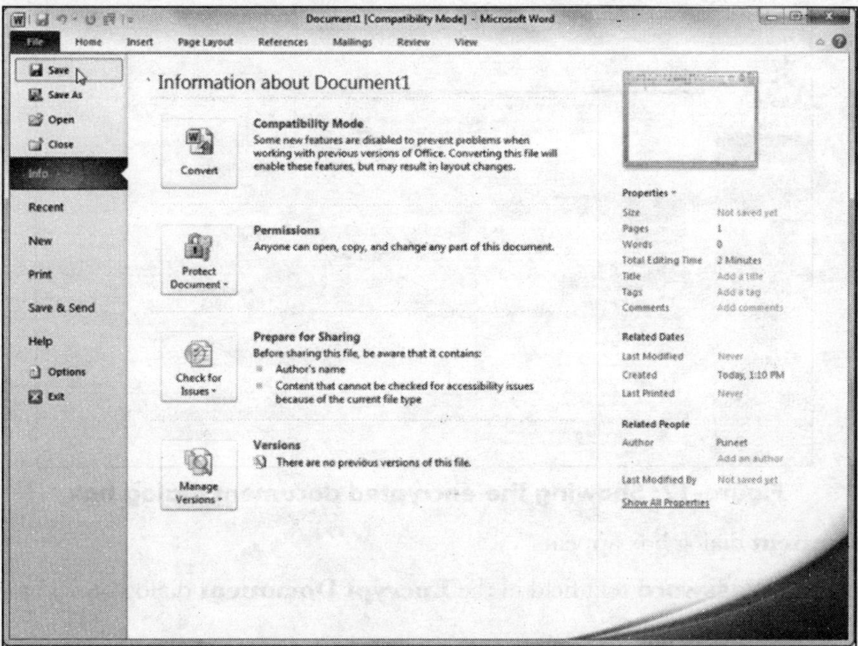

Figure-15: Displaying the Save As Dialog Box

The **Save As** dialog box appears (Figure-16).

3. Select the location where you want to save your document from the **Navigation** pane. In our case, we have selected **Desktop** (Figure-16).
4. Type the name of the document in the **File name** combo box. In our case, we have typed **Introduction to MS Word 2010** (Figure-16).
5. Select the format in which you want to save your document in the **Save as type** list box. In our case, we have selected **Word Document** option from the list (Figure-16).

6. Click the **Save** button, as shown in Figure-16:

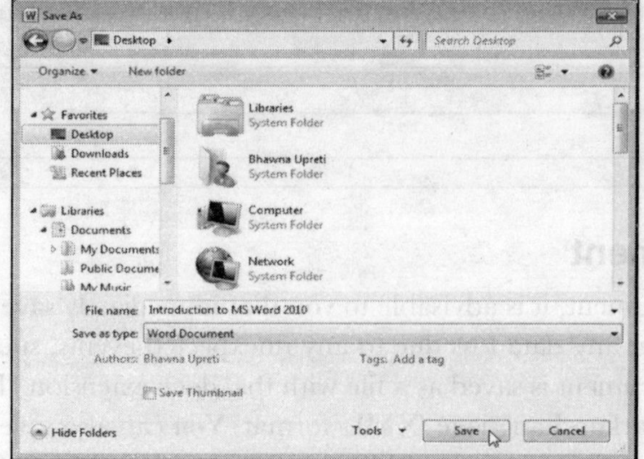

Figure-16: Displaying the Save As Dialog Box

Now the document is save with the name **Introduction to MS Word 2010**.

Let's now learn to assign a password to a word document.

1. Click the **File** tab on the Ribbon. The Backstage view appears (Figure-17).
2. Click the **Protect Document** button. A drop-down list appears (Figure-17).
3. Select the **Encrypt with Password** option from the drop-down list as shown in the Figure-17.

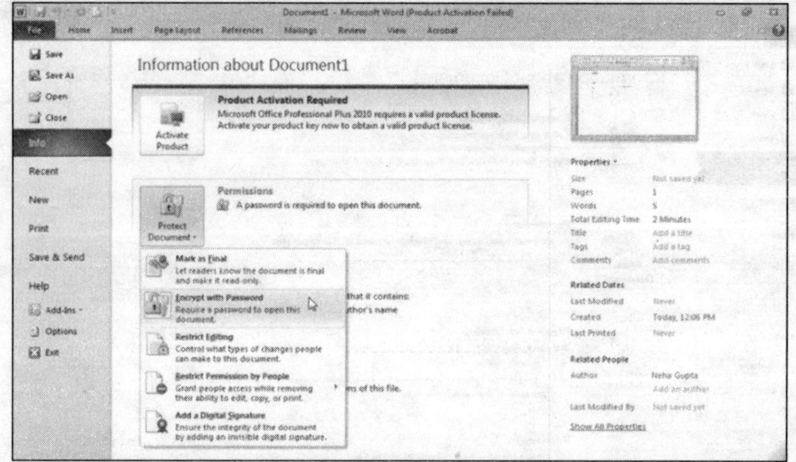

Figure-17: Showing the encrypted document dialog box

The **Encrypt Document** dialog box appears.

4. Type the password in the **Password** text field in the **Encrypt Document** dialog box (Figure-18).
5. Click the **OK** button (Figure-18).

   The **Confirm Password** dialog box appears (Figure-18).
6. Re-type the password in the **Password** text box (Figure-18).

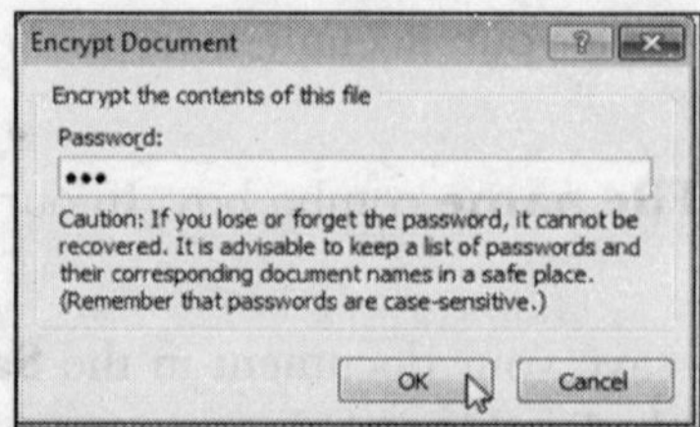

Figure-18: Displaying the Encrypt Document dialog box

Now, click the **OK** button as shown in Figure-19.

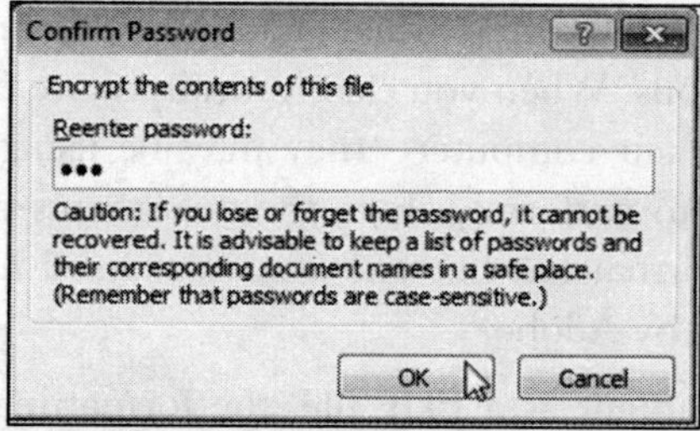

Figure-19: Displaying the Confirm Password dialog box

The document is now password protected. When you open the document, the **Password** dialog box appears where you type the password to open the document.

Saving a Document in Compatible Format

Suppose you are using the latest version of MS Word (that is, MS Word 2010) and other people in your office are using the previous versions of MS Word (say, MS Word 2003). In this situation, it may be possible that the other people are unable to open the document, which is created in MS Word 2010. This is because the extension of MS Word 2010 is .docx; which is not supported by the previous versions of MS Word.

To allow the people using the previous versions of MS Word to open and work with the MS Word 2010 document, you need to save the MS Word 2010 document in the previous versions format. In MS Word 2010, you can save the document in different versions, such as Word 97-2003 document or PDF.

Perform the following steps to save the document in the Word 97-2003 format:

1. Select the **File** tab on the Ribbon. The Backstage view appears.
2. Select the **Save** option. The **Save As** dialog box appears (Figure-20).
3. Select the location where you want to save the document from the **Navigation** pane. In our case, we selected the **Desktop** (Figure-20).
4. Type the name of the MS Word document in the **File name** combo box. In our case, we have typed **Introduction to MS Word 2010** (Figure-20).
5. Select the **Word 97-2003 document** option from the **Save as Type** combo box (Figure-20).
6. Click the **Save** button in the **Save As** dialog box, as shown in Figure-20:

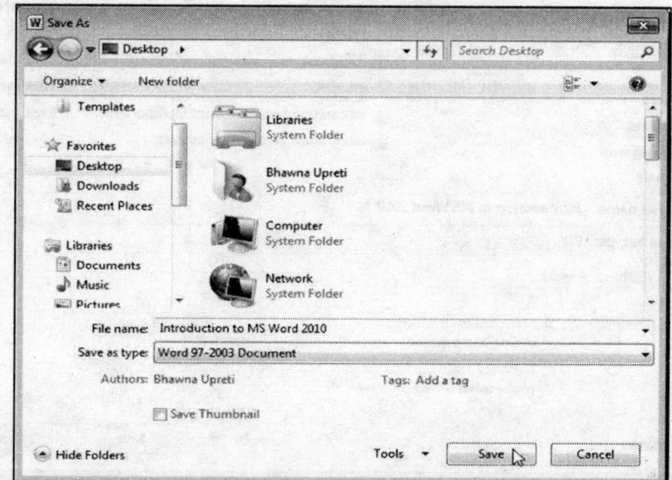

Figure-20: Displaying the Save As Dialog Box

Let's understand how to save a document as PDF, XPS, or Web Page in MS Word 2010.

Saving Document as a PDF File

In today's modern and technology-driven world, sharing of information in an easy and reliable way plays a very important role for making business decisions. When you electronically share documents with other people, some people might not have installed MS Word on their computer—they may be using other programs for creating and editing documents. To ensure that you are able to uniformly share the documents with others, MS Word 2010 allows you to save the documents as PDF files. This format has become a standardized mean of sharing information electronically due to free availability of Acrobat Reader by Adobe.

When you save an MS Word 2010 document as a PDF file, the formatting of the document remains unchanged. It means that the PDF file has the same formatting as that of the Word document, wherein you can read the contents in the file, but cannot modify them.

***Note:** Before you can save a Word 2010 document as a PDF file, you need to first install the Microsoft Save as PDF or XPS add-in. You can download this add-in from the following link:*

http://www.microsoft.com/downloads/

Perform the following steps to save a document as a PDF:

1. Select the **File** tab. The Backstage view appears.
2. Select the **Save** option. The **Save As** dialog box appears (Figure-21).
3. Select the location where you want to save the document from the **Navigation** pane. In our case, we selected the **Desktop** (Figure-21).
4. Type the name of the MS Word document in the **File name** combo box. In our case, we have typed **Introduction to MS Word 2010** (Figure-21).
5. Select the **PDF** option from the **Save as type** combo box (Figure-21).
6. Click the **Save** button in the **Save As** dialog box, as shown in Figure-21:

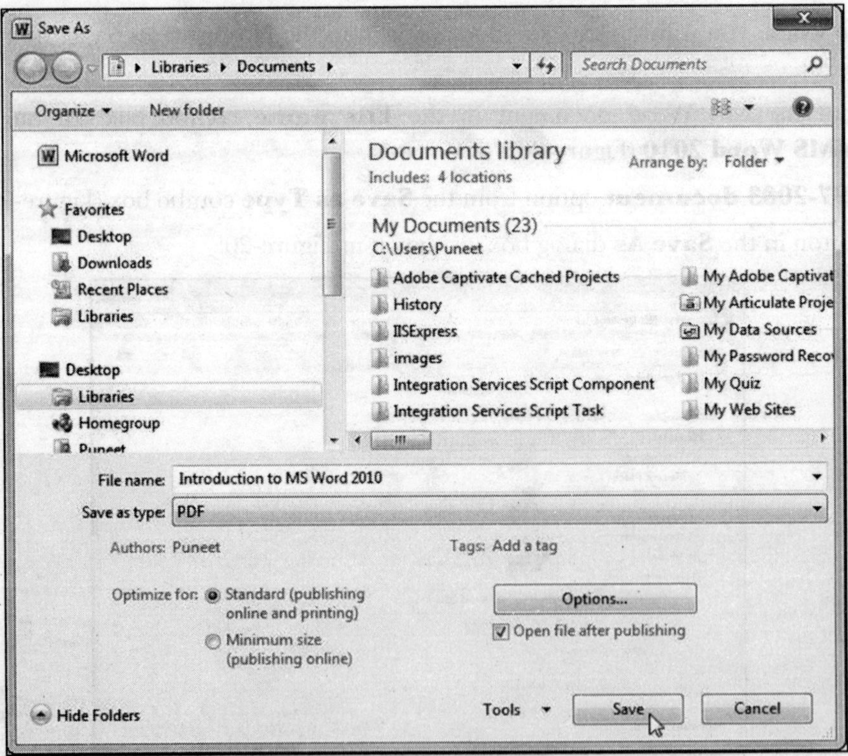

Figure-21: Displaying the Save As Dialog Box

Note: To view the PDF file, you need a PDF reader such as Adobe Acrobat Reader in your computer.

Let's now learn about the process of opening an existing document in the next section.

Tip: You can save further changes in your document by clicking the Save button ( ) on the Quick Access Toolbar. In this case, the Save As dialog box does not appear and the changes are saved automatically. If at any point, you want to change the location, type, or name of the saved document, click the Office button and then the Save As option.

2.5.3 Opening an Existing Document

In MS Word, you can open word documents that are saved at any location in the computer. After opening the saved document, you can make modifications to it or reuse its contents in some other document. Let's perform the following steps to open an existing document:

1. Click the **File tab** on the Ribbon (Figure-22). The Backstage view appears (Figure-22).
2. Click the **Open** button from the Backstage view, as shown in Figure-22:

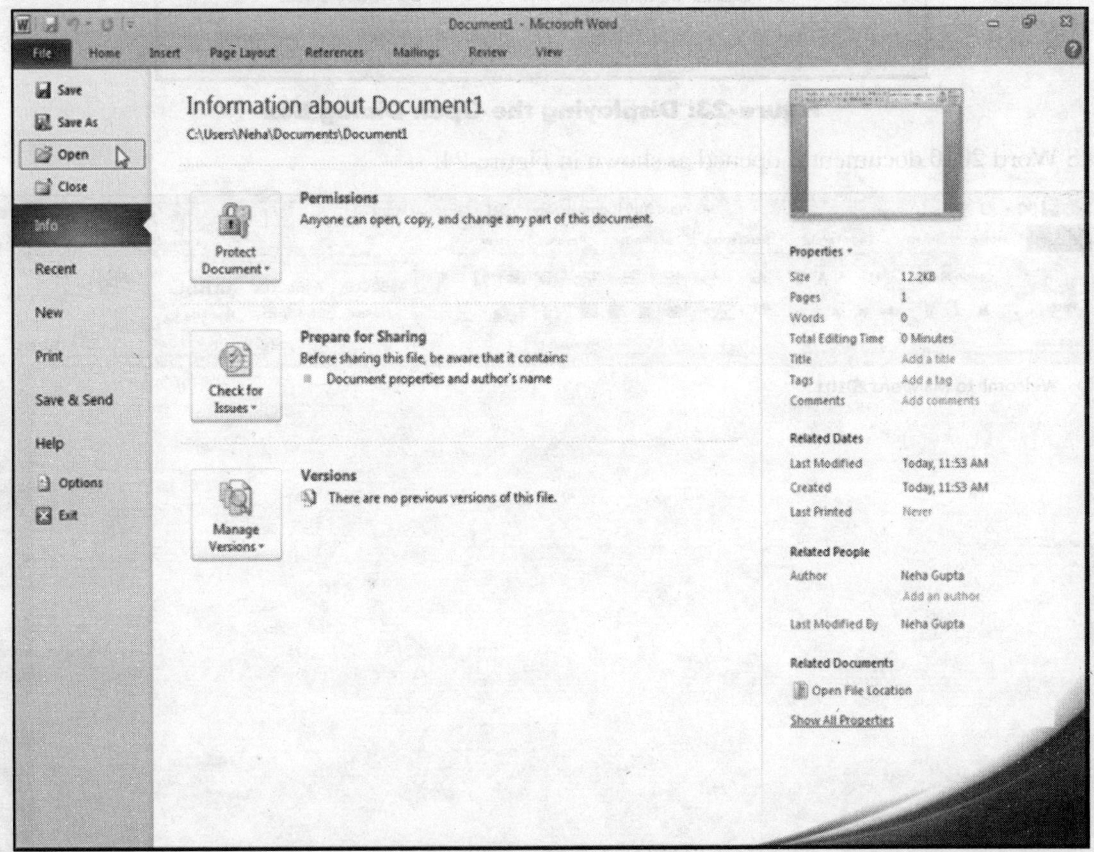

Figure-22: Showing Open as the Selected Option in the Office Menu

The **Open** dialog box appears (Figure-23).

3. Select the location in which the document is stored from the Navigation pane in the **Open** dialog box. In our case, we have selected **Desktop**. The list of document, which is stored in **Desktop** is appeared (Figure-23).
4. Select the document from the list. In our case, we have selected **MS Word 2010** (Figure-23).
5. Click the **Open** button in the **Open** dialog box (Figure-23).

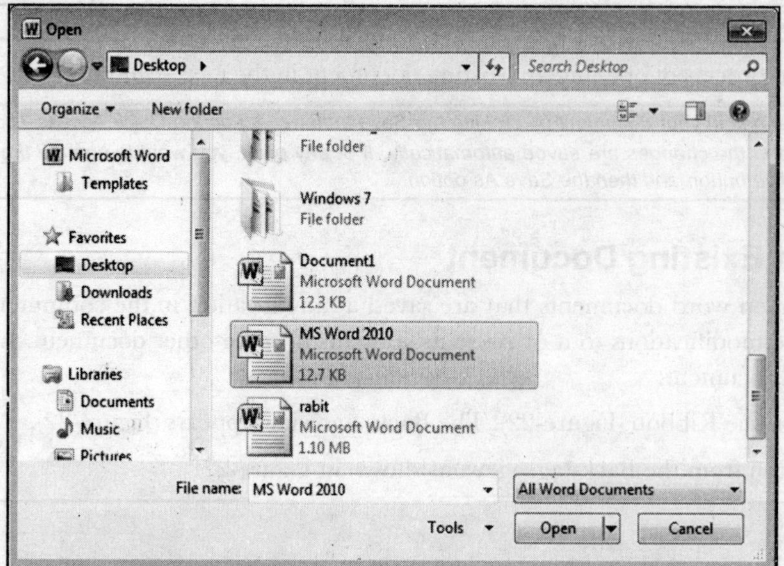

Figure-23: Displaying the Open Dialog Box

Now, the MS Word 2010 document is opened as shown in Figure-24:

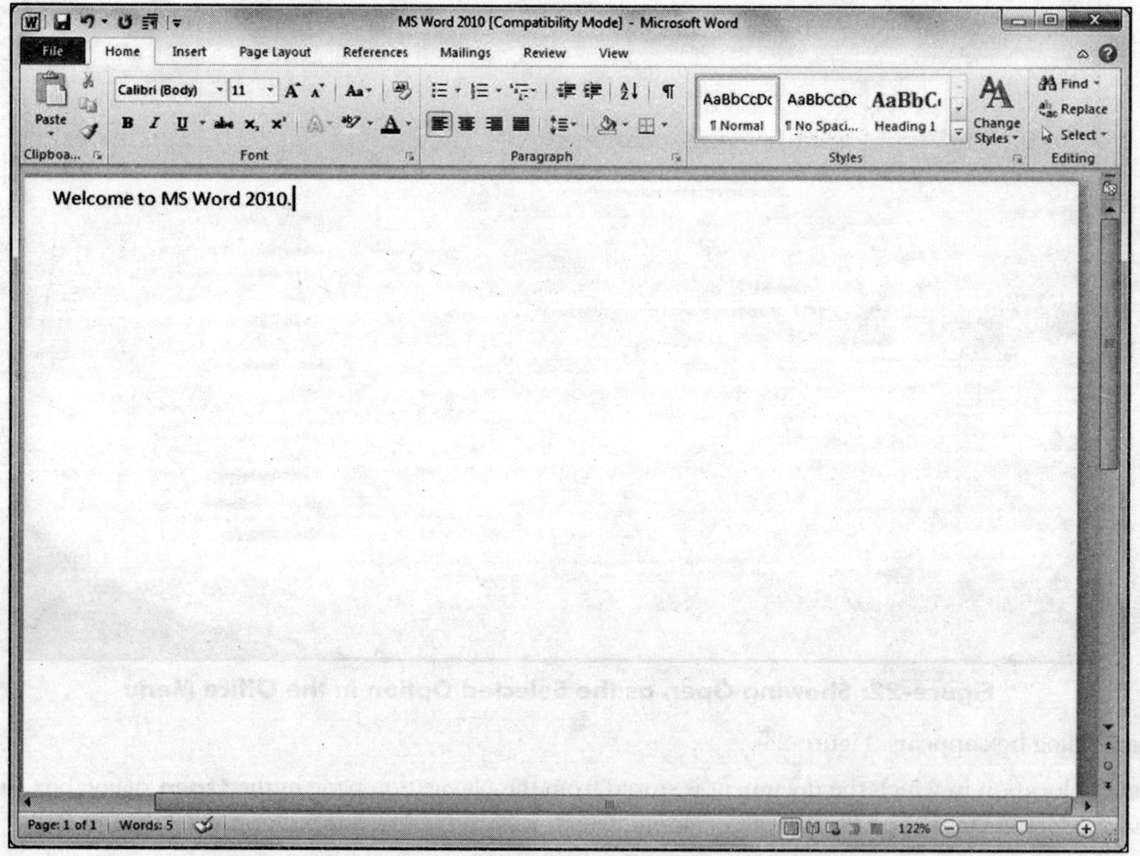

Figure-24: Showing the existing document

Let's now learn about the process of closing the currently opened document in the next section.

2.5.4 Closing the Document

After you have finished working with the MS Word 2010 document, you can close the document. There are two way to close the MS Word 2010 document. First, you can close a document by clicking the close button at the top right corner of the document window. Another, you can also close the currently open document by following these steps:

1. Click the **File tab** on the Ribbon. The Backstage view appears (Figure-25).
2. Select the **Close** option from the Backstage view, as shown in Figure-25:

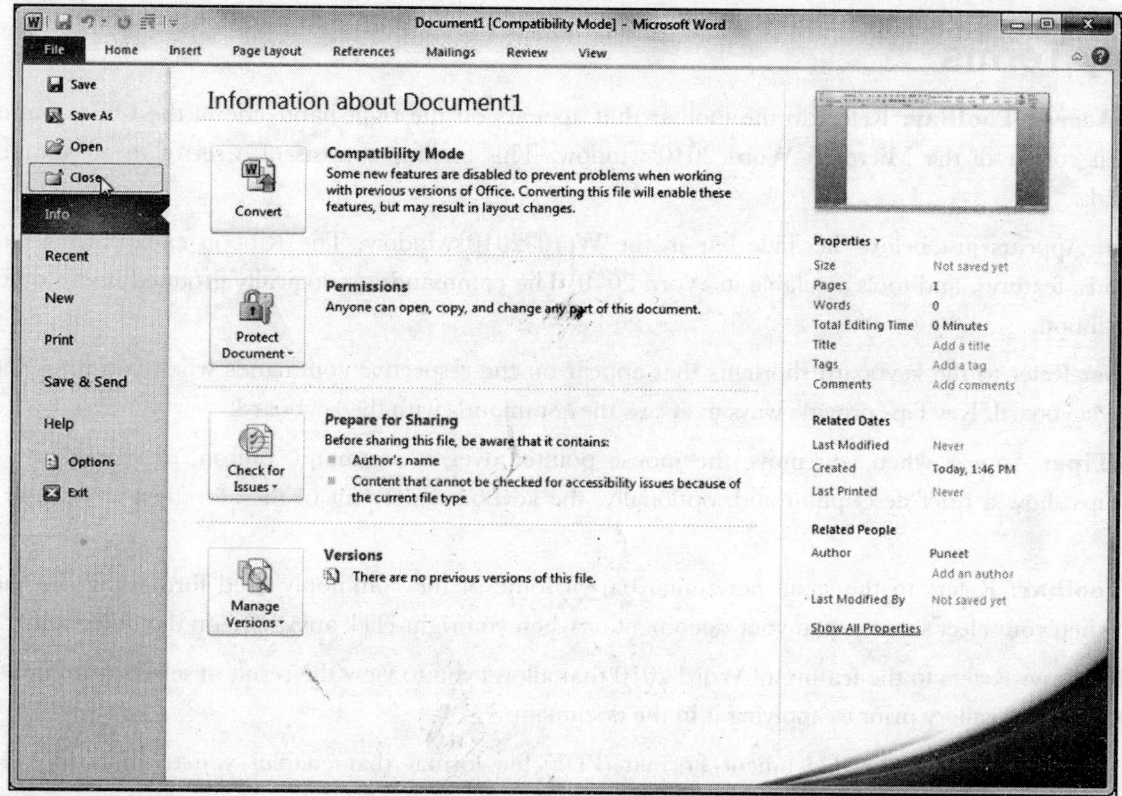

Figure-25: Showing the Office Menu with the Close Option Selected

After you have saved the contents of the document, the window is closed.

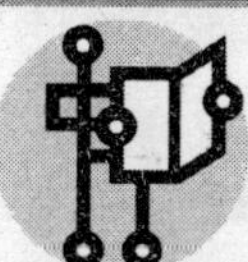

Case Study: Create a Report Using Word 2010

Neha needs to create a report using Word 2010. She needs to apply the following formatting details in her report:

- The first page of the report should have the report title
- The document should be password protected.
- After completion, the report should be saved as a pdf.

Questions:

Q1. Assuming you are Neha, write the steps that need to be used.

*(*Case study presented is the proprietary information of the respective organization, and is used here specifically and only for educational purpose.)*

2.6 Summary

In this chapter, you have learned about the history of Microsoft Word. You have learned how to start and quit Word 2010 using different options. You have also explored the interface features of Word 2010, wherein you have learned that menus, submenus, and toolbars of the previous versions of Word have been replaced by a button, that is, the Office button, and the Ribbon. Next, you have learned about the step-by-step procedures to create, save, open, and close a document in Microsoft Word.

2.7 Key Terms

- **Quick Access Toolbar:** Refers to the toolbar that appears on the right-hand side of the Office button on the upper left corner of the Microsoft Word 2010 window. This toolbar consists of a set of most commonly used commands.
- **Ribbon:** Appears just below the Title bar in the Word 2010 window. The Ribbon encapsulates most of the commands, features, and tools available in Word 2010. The commands are logically grouped under different tabs on the Ribbon.
- **KeyTips:** Refer to the keyboard shortcuts that appear on the respective commands when you press the **Alt** key from the keyboard. KeyTips provide ways to access the commands with the keyboard.
- **ScreenTips:** Appear when you move the mouse pointer over a command, button, or dialog box launcher. ScreenTips show a brief description and, optionally, the keyboard shortcut of the aforementioned user interface elements.
- **Mini Toolbar:** Refers to the small horizontal bar of some of the commonly used formatting commands that appear when you select some text in your document or when you right-click anywhere on the document.
- **Live Preview:** Refers to the feature of Word 2010 that allows you to view the result of selecting an option from a drop-down list or gallery prior to applying it in the document.
- **PDF:** Refers to the Portable Document Format (PDF) file format that enables you to uniformly share your documents with others.

2.8 Exercise

Multiple Choice Questions

Q1. With the release of which version was Word officially named as Microsoft Office Word?

a. Word 2003 b. Word 97

c. Word 2000 d. Word 2007

Ans. a

Q2. While starting Word 2010 using the Run command, the command you need to enter in the Run dialog box is:

a. Word 2010 b. winword

c. windows word d. Microsoft word

Ans. b

Q3. Which word feature allows you to see the keyboard shortcuts to access commands from the keyboard?

a. ToolTips
b. ScreenTips
c. Keyboard Shortcuts
d. KeyTips

Ans. d

Q4. Which interface element of Word 2010 provides a menu (Office menu) that has various menu items for some common and generic tasks such as creating, saving, opening, printing, and closing documents?

a. Microsoft Office Word Help button
b. Dialog Box Launchers
c. Command Tabs
d. Office Button

Ans. d

Q5. Which feature shows a brief description and optionally the keyboard shortcut of the button, command, or dialog box launcher?

a. ToolTips
b. ScreenTips
c. Keyboard Shortcuts
d. KeyTips

Ans. b

Q6. Which toolbar appears when you select some text in your document or when you right-click anywhere on the document?

a. Quick Access toolbar
b. Status bar
c. Mini toolbar
d. Ribbon

Ans. c

Q7. Which feature allows you to view the result of selecting an option from a drop-down list or gallery prior to applying it?

a. Live Preview
b. Quick Access toolbar
c. Ribbon
d. Mini toolbar

Ans. a

Q8. You can enlarge or shrink the document using which feature of Word interface?

a. Zoom Controls
b. Mini toolbar
c. Dialog Box Launchers
d. None of the above

Ans. a

Q9. You can uniformly share your document, even with users who do not have Word installed on their computer, by saving it as:

a. A WordPad File
b. A Notepad File
c. A PDF file
d. A Word 97-2003 file

Ans. c

Q10. Which interface command button is used to copy the formatting style of the selected text?

a. Change Case
b. Format Painter
c. Clear Formatting
d. Font Color

Ans. b

Short Answer Type Questions

Q1. How is the Quick Access Toolbar useful in Microsoft Word 2010?

Q2. What do you mean by command tabs and command sets?

Q3. Write a short note on the KeyTips feature of Word 2010?

Q4. Briefly explain ScreenTips and Enhanced ScreenTips?

Q5. How does the Live Preview feature works in Word 2010?

Q6. What are the various ways of creating a document in Word 2010?

Q7. How are installed templates useful in Word 2010?

Q8. What is the need for saving a Word 2010 document as a Word 97-2003 document?

Q9. Why is it sometimes required to save a Word 2010 document as a PDF file? What benefits does this provides?

Q10. What is a Mini toolbar?

Microsoft®
Excel 2010

Starting

Office

CHAPTER 3

Getting Started With Excel 2010

CHAPTER STRUCTURE

CHAPTER OBJECTIVES

- Understand the concept and usage of Microsoft Excel
- Comprehend the concept of Excel UI
- Explore the Excel options dialog box
- Comprehend the concept of Closing Microsoft Excel 2010

3.1 Introduction

In organizations, there is a need to save, organize, and manage the data proficiently. Nowadays, this data is maintained using spreadsheet applications that simplify the management of data. An application that allows you to arrange data in a grid of rows and columns is known as spreadsheet application.

Excel 2010, a part of Microsoft Office 2010, is a spreadsheet application that is used to manipulate and organize data. A file saved in Excel is called a workbook, which consists of various worksheets. A worksheet consists of various cells that together constitute a grid of rows and columns. A cell in a worksheet may contain numeric data, plain text, or a formula. Apart from the management of data, Excel 2010 also provides various formatting options to make your data attractive and presentable.

In this chapter, you learn the various features of Excel 2010 in detail. The chapter discusses how to perform basic operations in Excel 2010, such as creating a new workbook. In addition, you learn how to manage data in a worksheet. Towards the end, you learn how to close Microsoft Excel 2010.

3.2 Exploring New and Enhanced Features of Excel 2010

Excel 2010 is an application used to store, analyze, manipulate, and visualize data in an efficient manner. Excel helps to perform several numeric and non-numeric calculations. In organizations, Excel plays a vital role in preparing budgets, managing stock, and tracking the performance of the employees.

Excel 2010 is the latest version of Excel after Excel 2007. Various new and improved features in Excel 2010 help to analyze, manage, and share information in more ways than ever before. In addition, the latest version of Excel contains several new data analysis and visualization tools to help you track and highlight important data trends. Apart from this, Excel 2010 provides a user-friendly interface that uses a customizable pictorial system of tools and commands. Such an arrangement makes it easy for the user to both understand the tools and commands and access them from the Ribbon.

The new and enhanced features included in Excel 2010 are as follows:

- **Improved Ribbon:** Makes it easy to find commands and features in complex menus and toolbars. In Excel 2010, you can create custom tabs and groups and rename or change the order of the built-in tabs and groups. Apart from this, you can turn on or off various parts of the Ribbon and add your own custom shortcuts.
- **New Backstage View:** Refers to the view that appears when the File tab is selected. The File tab is a replacement of Office Button that was present in the previous version of Excel, that is, Microsoft Excel 2007. The Backstage view contains the options used while working with files, such as New, Open, Save, Info, and Print. When you select an option from the Backstage view, the various options related to that particular option appear on the right side of the Backstage view. For example, when you select the Recent option, the Recent Workbooks pane and Recent Places pane appears at the right side of the Backstage view.
- **New 64-bit version support:** Enables you to take the advantage of 64-bit machines to create larger workbooks with a size up to 4 GB. You need special hardware to run the 64-bit version of Excel 2010. The commonly used version of Microsoft Excel is 32-bit.
- **New sparklines feature:** Allows you to create tiny charts that can be inserted in cells a long side your data in a worksheet. Sparklines are very useful when you want to show a trend or know the status of a business at a glance.
- **New slicer feature:** Allows you to easily filter data from pivot tables.
- **Enhanced image editing feature:** Provides the facility to capture a screenshot and add it to a worksheet. Excel 2010 also provides additional SmartArt graphic layouts and artistic effects such as pencil sketch, line drawing, plastic wrap, and paint strokes. Apart from this, Excel 2010 allows you to have better control over the quality of an image by adjusting the color, brightness, contrast, or sharpness of the image.

- **New paste with live preview feature:** Enables you to save time when reusing content within Excel 2010 or across other programs. You can use this feature to preview various paste options such as Keep Source Column Width, No Borders, or Keep Source Formatting. The live preview feature enables you to visually determine how your pasted content will look before you actually paste it in the worksheet.
- **Enhanced Excel Services:** Provides four Microsoft Excel services, such as, improved user experience, better integration with SharePoint 2010 features, improved support for workbook features, and more support for developing applications.
- **Improved Protected View mode:** Provides protection from threats such as viruses that may be present in Excel files you download from the Internet or electronic mail. This facility allows you to read a file and check its content while reducing the risks that can occur. When you are sure that your file is safe, you can edit the file by clicking the Enable Editing button on the Message bar located just below the Ribbon.
- **Improved PivotTable:** Allows better control over the appearance of pivot table reports and provides an enhanced means for retrieving, sorting, and filtering data in a PivotTable.
- **Enhanced conditional formatting:** Provides new icon sets and formatting options in data bars, which you can use to illustrate your data and highlight important trends in it.
- **Enhanced functions:** Improves the accuracy of several Excel functions available in the Excel functions library. In addition, the names of some functions have been changed to more accurately reflect what they do.
- **New solver version:** Provides a new version of the Solver add-in, which you can use to perform What-if Analysis and find optimum solutions.
- **Enhanced Visual Basic for Applications (VBA):** Allows you to use VBA commands to create macros in Excel, instead of the old (Extended Learning Module) XLM format, which was used in the earlier versions of Excel to create macros.

Let us learn how to start Excel 2010.

3.2.1 Starting Microsoft Excel 2010

Before using the Microsoft Excel 2010, you need to start the application first. Perform the following steps to start Excel 2010 application:

1. Click the **Start** button present on the Taskbar. The Start menu appears (Figure-1).
2. Place the mouse pointer over **All Programs** option in the Start menu. A list of programs installed on your computer appears (Figure-1).
3. Click the **Microsoft Office** folder (Figure-1). A list of applications of the Microsoft Office suite appears (Figure-1).
4. Click the **Microsoft Excel 2010** option, as shown in Figure-1.

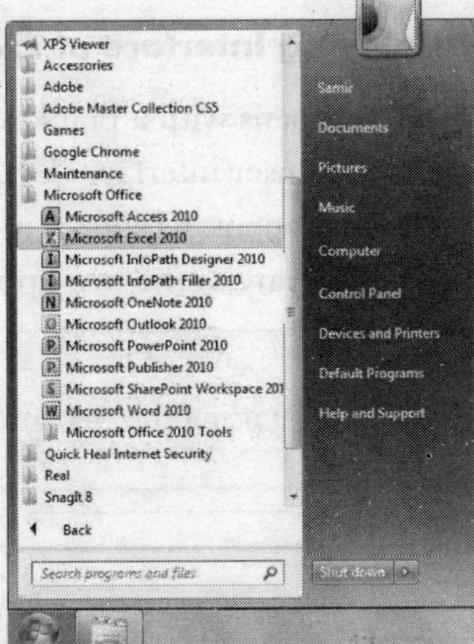

Figure-1: Selecting Microsoft Excel 2010

Perform the following steps to start Excel 2010 using the Run dialog box:

1. Click Start→Run.
   The Run dialog box appears (Figure-2).
2. Type excel besides the Open combo box in the Run dialog box (Figure-2).
3. Click the OK button, as shown in Figure-2:

The Excel 2010 application window appears, as shown in Figure-2:

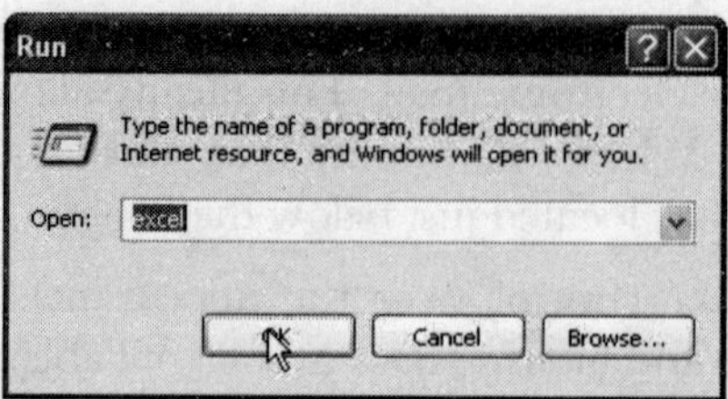

Figure-2: Starting Excel 2010 using the Run Dialog Box

A blank Excel 2010 workbook opens (Figure-3).

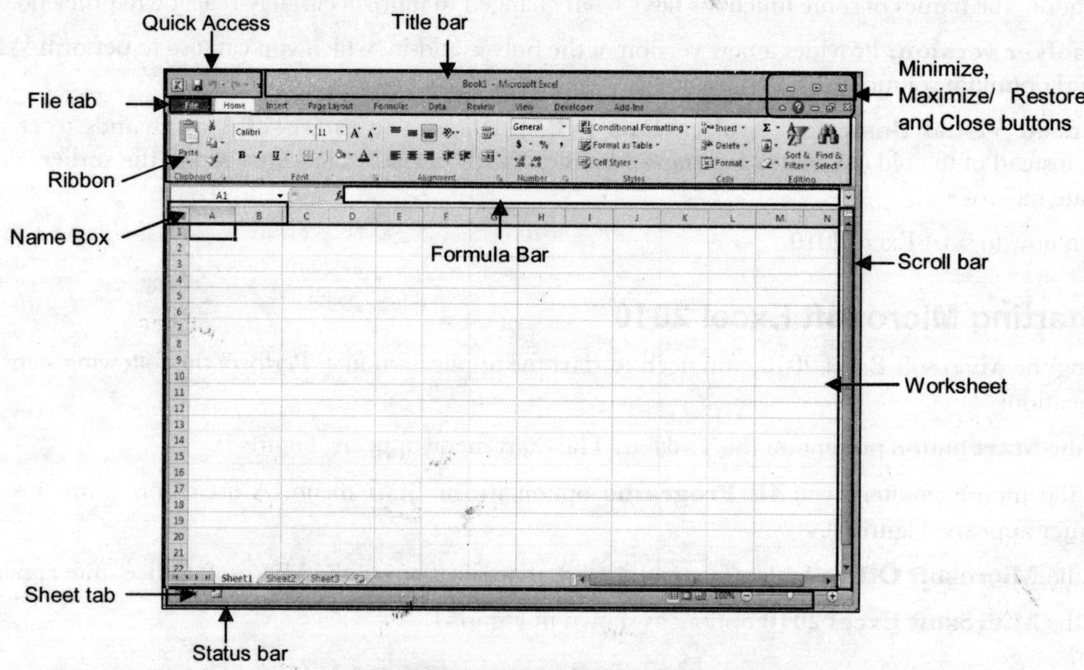

Figure-3: Displaying Interface of Excel 2010

As you can see in Figure-3, the Excel 2010 application opens with a blank worksheet on your computer. After starting the Excel 2010 application, let's explore its user interface (UI).

A blank Excel 2010 workbook, having three worksheets, opens, as shown in Figure-3:

Now, you know how Excel 2010 can be opened by using any of the two approaches.

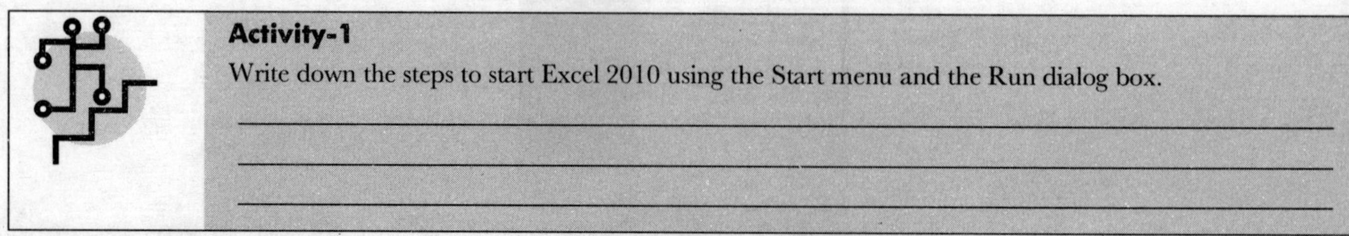

Activity-1

Write down the steps to start Excel 2010 using the Start menu and the Run dialog box.

Let us learn about the UI of Excel 2010 in the next section.

3.2.2 Introduction to Excel 2010 UI

The User Interface (UI) of Excel 2010 is similar to the Excel 2007 UI but has a lot of new features. The UI of Excel 2010 has a single strip at the top of the worksheet called the Ribbon, which contains the commands to perform common tasks. This arrangement ensures that the commands are placed at one convenient location and are visible at all times. By using this simple design, Excel 2010 is able to reduce its reliance on numerous toolbars and complicated menus and submenus. The Ribbon along with the File tab and Quick Access Toolbar in the UI provide you a bulk of Excel commands at your fingertips. As you know, when you start the Excel 2010 application, the application opens with a blank worksheet (named Sheet1) in a new workbook (named Book1) in the Excel application window (Figure-3). As you can see in Figure-3, the interface of Excel 2010 contains various components, which can be listed as follows:

- The File tab
- Quick Access Toolbar
- The Title bar
- The Minimize, Maximize/Restore, and Close buttons
- The Ribbon
- The Formula Bar
- The Name Box
- The Worksheet
- The Scroll bars
- The Sheet tab
- The Status bar

Let's discuss these components one by one in the following sections.

The File Tab

The File tab is present below the Quick Access Toolbar. When you select the File tab, the Backstage view appears that contains several options to help you work with an Excel file. Technically, the File tab is a replacement of Office Button that was available in Excel 2007, as the tab contains almost the same options that were available in Office Button, such as Save, Save As, Open, Close, Recent, New, Print, and Help. Figure-4 shows the File tab:

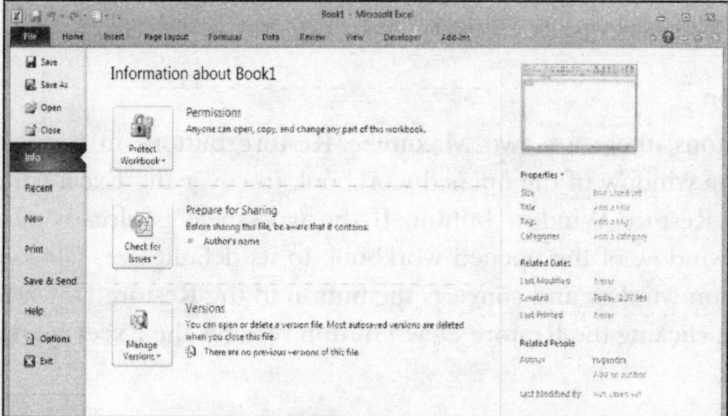

Figure-4: Displaying the File tab

After learning about the File tab, let's discuss Quick Access Toolbar.

Quick Access Toolbar

Quick Access Toolbar is located at the top left corner of the Excel application window and contains various buttons, such as New, Open, and Save, to perform common worksheet tasks. You can select the buttons that you want to display on Quick Access Toolbar by clicking the down arrow present in Quick Access Toolbar. A drop-down list containing various options appears. Simply select the option that you want to include in Quick Access Toolbar from the list. Th drop-down list also contains the More Commands option. Selecting this option displays the Excel Options dialog box You can use the Excel Options dialog box to add or remove buttons on Quick Access Toolbar. You can also customiz Quick Access Toolbar by right-clicking anywhere on the Ribbon and selecting the Customize Quick Access Toolba option from the context menu. Figure-5 shows Quick Access Toolbar of Excel 2010:

Figure-5: Displaying Quick Access Toolbar

After learning about Quick Access Toolbar, let's discuss the Title bar.

The Title Bar

The Title bar is present on the top of the Excel application window, adjacent to Quick Access Toolbar. The name c the application, that is, Microsoft Excel, and the currently opened workbook is displayed on the Title bar. All window based applications, such as Microsoft Word, Microsoft PowerPoint, and Notepad, have a Title bar. Figure-6 shows th Title bar of Excel 2010:

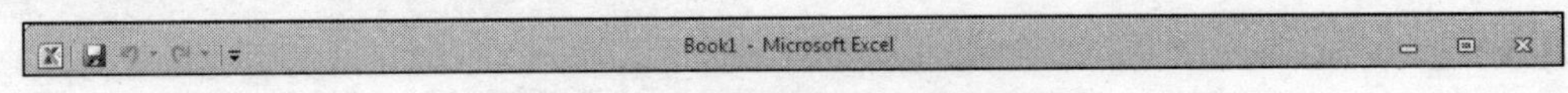

Figure-6: Displaying Title Bar

Now, let's discuss the Minimize, Maximize/Restore, and Close buttons

The Minimize, Maximize/Restore, and Close Buttons

The Minimize, Maximize/Restore, and Close buttons are located on the top right corner of the Excel applicatio window. Starting from the corner, if you move toward the left side, the buttons appear in the following order: Close Maximize/Restore, and Minimize. When you click the Maximize button, the button changes to the Restore button.

Let's discuss these buttons more detail in the following sections.

The Minimize Button

There are two Minimize buttons, present one below the other. Clicking the lower Minimize button minimizes th currently opened workbook and the minimize button changes to the Restore Up button, while clicking the uppe button minimizes the entire Excel application window.

The Maximize/Restore Button

Similar to the Minimize buttons, there are two Maximize/Restore buttons in Excel. Clicking the lower Maximiz button increases the size of the window of the opened workbook to cover the Excel window. This action also conver the Maximize button to the Restore Window button. If the worksheet is already maximized, clicking the Resto Window button restores the window of the opened workbook to its default size. Clicking the upper Maximize butto maximizes the Excel application window and converts the button to the Restore Down button. If the Excel applicatio window is already maximized, clicking the Restore Down button restores the Excel window to its default size.

The Close Button

Similar to the Minimize and Maximize/Restore buttons, there are two Close buttons in Excel. The lower Close butto is used to close the window of the opened workbook and the upper Close button is used to close the Excel applicatio window.

After learning about the Minimize, Maximize/Restore, and Close buttons, let's discuss the Ribbon.

The Ribbon

The Ribbon is located at the top of the Excel application window, just below the Title bar and Quick Access Toolbar. It is a strip that contains various commands. These commands are organized in logical groups, which are collected together under tabs. A group within each tab contains related commands. The Ribbon is designed to help you quickly find the commands that you need to complete a task. To reduce clutter, some tabs are shown only when they are needed. For example, the Picture Tools tab is shown only when a picture is selected.

Figure-7 shows the Ribbon of Excel 2010:

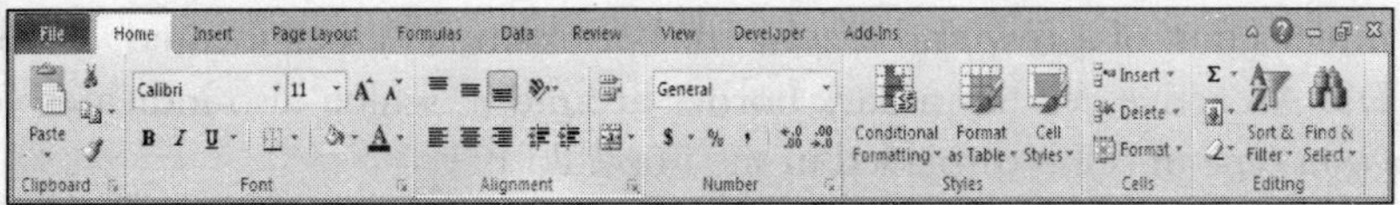

Figure-7: Displaying Ribbon

After learning about the Ribbon, let's discuss Formula Bar.

The Formula Bar

The Formula Bar is located between the Ribbon and the worksheet of a worksheet. This bar displays the data or formula stored in the selected or active cell. The Formula Bar can also be used to enter or edit a formula, function, or data present in a cell. Any data or formula that you enter in a cell appears in the Formula Bar. Next to the Formula Bar are the Cancel (☒) and Enter (☑) buttons. These buttons are only visible when Excel is in the edit mode, that is, when you begin typing an entry. To put Excel in the edit mode, simply click inside the Formula Bar. The Enter button enters the text you type into the cell and the Cancel button cancels your changes.

Figure-8 shows the Formula Bar of Excel 2010:

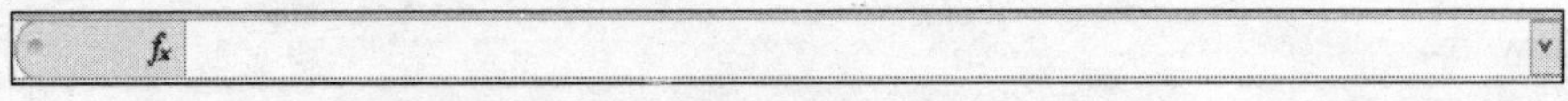

Figure-8: Displaying Formula Bar

After learning about Formula Bar, let's discuss the Name box.

The Name box

The Name box is displayed to the left of Formula Bar immediately below the Ribbon. It generally sows the address of the active cell and also displays the name of the selected cell, object, or range. You can see the address of the cell in the form of column–row, that is, when you select the first cell from the worksheet, the name A1 will be displayed within the Name box. Figure-9 shows Name Box of Excel 2010:

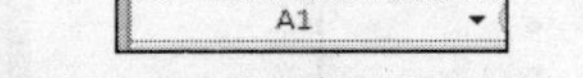

Figure-9: Displaying Name box

After learning about Name box, let's discuss the Worksheet in Excel.

The Worksheet

In Excel, the worksheet can be defined as the place where you enter data or records and perform various operations. The worksheet consists of rows, columns, and cells. Figure-10 shows worksheet of Excel 2010:

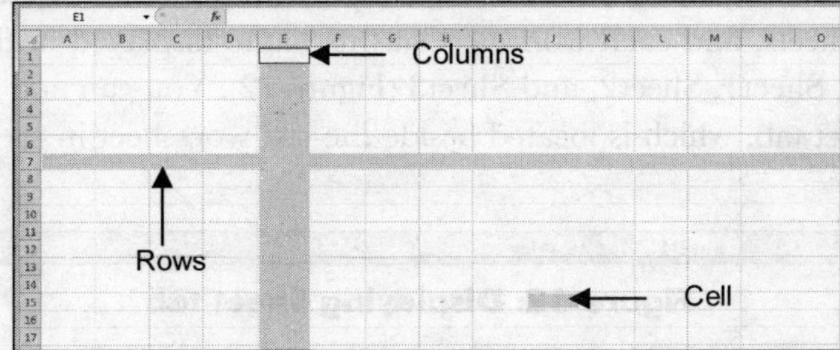

Figure-10: Displaying Components of Worksheet

As you can see in Figure-10, the worksheet consists of the following components:

- **Rows:** Refer to the horizontal areas in a worksheet where you can enter data. A worksheet in Excel can have rows numbering between 1 and 1,048,576. You can select all the cells of a particular row by simply selecting the number of the row.
- **Columns:** Refer to the vertical areas in a worksheet where you can enter data. A worksheet can have up to 16384 columns. These columns and are labeled as letters ranging from A to XFD. You can select all the cells of a particular column by simply selecting the heading of the column.
- **Cell:** Refers to the intersection of a row and a column. For example, a cell located at the interaction of column D and row 9 is called D9. An active cell has a dark border around it, which also indicates your current position on a worksheet. The data you type in cell is displayed in the Formula Bar.

After learning the worksheet, let's learn about scroll bars.

Scroll Bars

Scroll bars are the grey bars present at the right and bottom of a worksheet in the Excel window. The bars on the right of the Excel application window are known as vertical scroll bars and those at the bottom of the window are known as horizontal scroll bars. The scroll bars enable you to easily navigate through a worksheet. To use a scroll bar, you simply have to click the scroll bar and hold down the mouse button to drag the scroll bar in the desired direction. The following is a brief description of the two types of scroll bars:

- **The horizontal scroll bar:** Enables you to move a worksheet from the left to the right or vice versa in the Excel application window
- **The vertical scroll bar:** Enables you to move a worksheet from the top to the bottom or vice versa in the Excel application window

Figure-11 shows the scroll bars of Excel 2010:

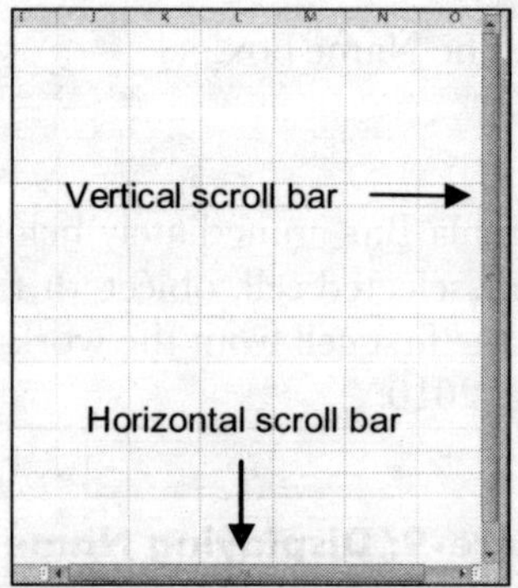

Figure-11: Displaying Scroll bars

After learning about scroll bars, let's discuss the Sheet tab.

The Sheet Tab

The Sheet tab is located beside the horizontal scroll bar and displays the various worksheets in a workbook. Workbooks can have any number of worksheets, and each worksheet has its name displayed in the Sheet tab. By default, a new workbook has three worksheets, Sheet1, Sheet2, and Sheet3 (Figure-12). You can add more worksheets to a workbook by selecting the Insert Worksheet tab, which is located beside the last worksheet in the Sheet tab. Figure-12 shows the Sheet tab of Excel 2010:

Figure-12: Displaying Sheet tab

Next, let's discuss the Status bar of the Excel 2010 UI.

The Status Bar

The status bar is located at the bottom in the Excel application window. This bar keeps you informed of Excel's current mode and any special keys that you may activate, such as Num Lock and Caps Lock. In addition, you can use the Status bar to select a new worksheet view and to zoom in and zoom out of the worksheet.

You can also customize the information displayed on the status bar by right-clicking anywhere on the bar and selecting the options from the context menu named Customize Status Bar according to your requirements. Figure-13 shows the status bar of Excel 2010:

Figure-13: Displaying Status Bar

Now that you are familiar with the various components of the Excel 2010 UI, let's take a detailed look at the various tabs and commands present on the Ribbon.

Q1. What is the use of the Quick Access Toolbar?

Q2. Define the Status Bars.

Q3. Explain the use of Zoom Controls and Formula Bar?

Q4. What is a Name Box?

3.3 Exploring the Ribbon

The Ribbon in Excel 2010 is a strip located above the worksheet and contains various commands that are organized in logical groups. These groups are collected together under tabs, such as Home, Insert, Page Layout, Formulas, Data, and Review. The commands displayed in the Ribbon depend on the currently selected tab. The Ribbon replaces the menus and toolbars found in earlier versions of Excel (prior to Excel 2007).The following is a brief description of the various tabs in Excel 2010:

- **Home:** Contains the commands that allow you to perform tasks such as formatting, aligning, inserting and deleting rows or columns; sorting and filtering numbers; applying style formatting effects; and finding and replacing data. Figure-14 shows the Home tab of Excel 2010:

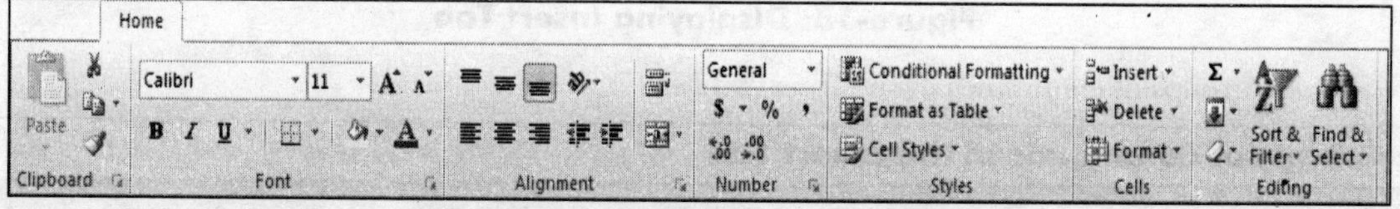

Figure-14: Displaying Home tab

Table-1 describes the groups of commands in the Home tab:

Table-1: Groups of Commands in the Home Tab

Group	Description
Clipboard	Contains the commands used to cut and copy data from one location in a worksheet and paste it within the same worksheet, to another worksheet of the same workbook, or to another workbook. The Format Painter command in this group allows you to copy and apply the formatting of one set of data to another set of data.
Fonts	Contains the commands used to change the name, size, style, and color of the fonts in a worksheet. In other words, the commands in this group allow you to change the appearance of a font.

Table-1: Groups of Commands in the Home Tab

Group	Description
Alignment	Allows you to align or control the position and layout of text in your worksheet. You can align text in two ways in Excel 2010, horizontally and vertically. This group contains the Top Align, Middle Align, Bottom Align, and Merge & Center commands.
Number	Contains the commands used to change the formatting of data in a cell.
Styles	Contains the commands to change the formatting style of a worksheet. The various formatting commands in Excel include Conditional Formatting, Format as Table, and Cell Styles.
Cells	Contains the commands to insert, delete, and format cells and worksheets. Using this group, you can insert, hide/unhide, and delete rows, columns, and worksheets.
Editing	Contains the commands to sort and filter data. The group also contains the commands to find and replace data in a worksheet.

- **Insert:** Allows you to insert a table, picture, slicer, chart, symbol, sparkline, header and footer, and different shapes in a worksheet. Figure-15 shows the Insert tab of Excel 2010:

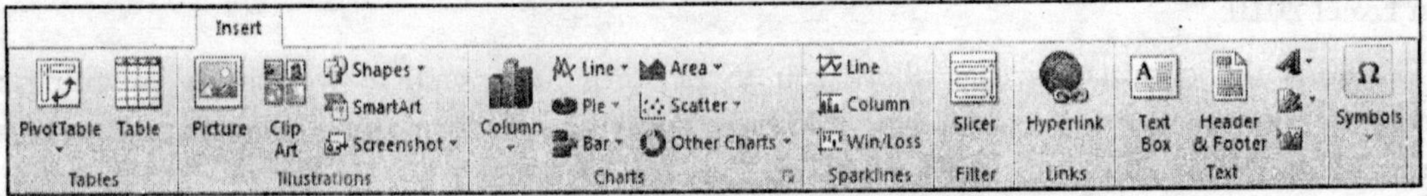

Figure-15: Displaying Insert Tab

Table-2 describes the groups of commands in the Insert tab:

Table-2: Groups of Commands in the Insert Tab

Group	Description
Tables	Contains the command to insert a simple table, a PivotTable, and PivotChart in a worksheet.
Illustrations	Contains the commands to insert pictures, cliparts, shapes, and SmartArts graphics in a worksheet. You can also use the commands in this group to take a picture of any part of a screen (a screenshot) and insert it in a worksheet.
Charts	Contains the commands to insert different types of charts in a worksheet.

Table-2: Groups of Commands in the Insert Tab

Group	Description
Sparklines	Contains the commands to insert different type of sparklines, including Line, Column, and Win/Loss in the cells of a worksheet.
Filter	Contains the command to filter pivot tables in a worksheet.
Links	Contains the command to insert hyperlinks in a worksheet.
Text	Contains the commands to insert text boxes, WordArt, objects, and headers and footers in a worksheet.
Symbols	Contains the commands to insert equations and symbols in a worksheet.

- **Page Layout:** Contains the commands that affect the overall appearance of a worksheet. These commands are arranged in various groups for easy access. Some of the commands present in this tab are Themes, Size, Background, Effects, and Gridlines. The commands related to printing, such as Print Area, Margins, and Print Titles are also present in this tab. Figure-16 shows the Page Layout tab of Excel 2010:

Figure-16: Displaying Page Layout Tab

Table-3 describes the groups of commands in the Page Layout tab:

Table-3: Groups of Commands in the Page Layout Tab

Group	Description
Themes	Contains the commands to apply themes to a worksheet. It also contains the commands to change the font, color, and effects of a theme.
Page Setup	Contains the commands to change the setting of a page. The various commands in the group include Margins, Orientation, Size, Print Area, Breaks, Background, and Print Titles.
Scale to Fit	Contains the commands to change the width, height and scale of the printing area in a worksheet.

Table-3: Groups of Commands in the Page Layout Tab

Group	Description
Sheet Options	Contains the commands to show and print gridlines and headings in a worksheet. Gridlines refer to the lines that appear in a worksheet to help you edit the worksheet as well as increase their adability of the worksheet.
Arrange	Contains the commands to change the arrangement of the objects placed in a worksheet. You can use this group to change the alignment of the objects, rotate the objects in a specific direction, and group different objects into a single object.

- **Formulas:** Allows you to insert a formula, name a range, and access the formula auditing tools. This tab controls how Excel performs calculations and displays results. The formulas are grouped according to their functionalities, such as Logical, Financial, Lookup & Reference, Text, and Math & Trig. Figure-17 shows the Formulas tab of Excel 2010:

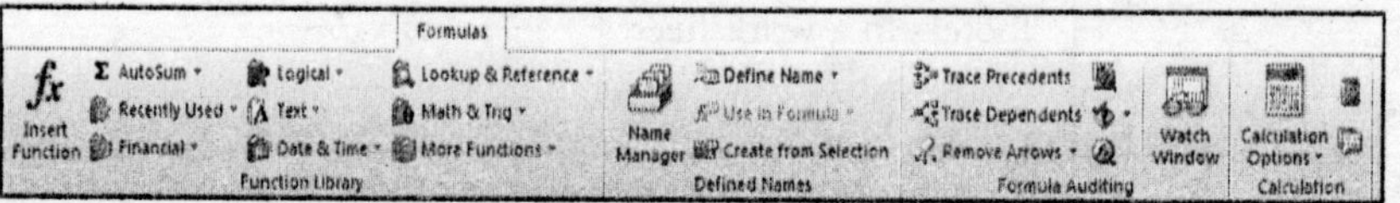

Figure-17: Displaying Formulas Tab

Table-4 describes the groups of commands in the Formulas tab:

Table-4: Groups of Commands in the Formulas Tab

Group	Description
Funtion Library	Contains the various categories of functions available in Excel. Each function category contains the functions related to the respective function category. For example, the Date & Time function category contains several function related to date and time, such as DATE, DAY, HOUR, and MINUTE. You can use these options to insert the date and time in different ways in your worksheet.
Defined Names	Allows you to create and organize the names of formulas, tables, and cell ranges used in a worksheet.
Formula Auditing	Contains the commands to audit a formula, such as Trace Precedents and Trace Dependents. Trace Precedents displays arrows to indicate what cells affect the value of the currently selected cell. Trace Dependents displays the arrows to indicate what cells are affected by the value of the currently selected cell.
Calculation	Contains the commands to specify the calculation mode for formulas. Besides the automatic calculation mode, you can set the manual calculation mode to perform a calculation.

- **Data:** Allows you to import data to a worksheet from external sources, such as Microsoft Access, Structured Query Language (SQL) Server, or the Internet. Various data-related commands and tools are also present in this tab, such as Sort, Filter, Data Validation, and Solver. You can use these commands to work on your worksheet data. For example, suppose you have employee information comprising employee ID, employee name, and employee salary, and you want to sort the information on the basis of employee name in ascending order, and also find the top 5 earning employees. In that case, you can use the Sort command to sort the employee information and the Filter command to find the top earning employees.

Figure-18 shows the Data tab of Excel 2010:

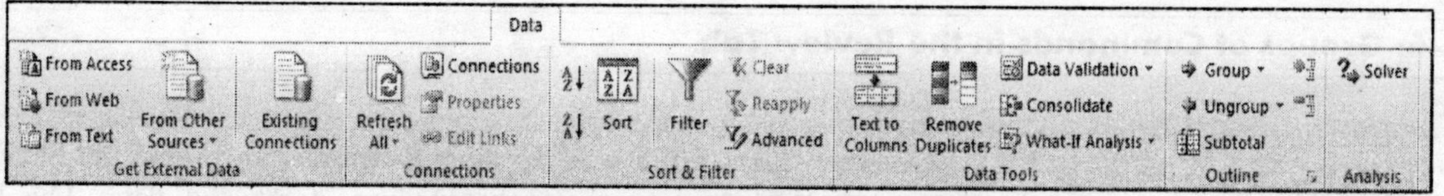

Figure-18: Displaying Data Tab

Table-5 describes the groups of commands in the Data tab:

Table-5: Groups of Commands in the Data Tab

Group	Description
Get External Data	Contains the commands that allow you to import data from external sources, such as Microsoft Access or the Internet, to a worksheet.
Connections	Contains the commands that allow you to establish a connection with the files or data located in the same computer or in a different computer, to import the files or data.
Sort & Filter	Contains the commands to sort data in ascending or descending order. The Filter command is used to display data based on certain criteria, such as the departments of an organization or regions of a country.
Data Tools	Contains the commands to remove duplicate values from a worksheet, validate the data entries made by a user, and combine data of different worksheets into single worksheet.
Outline	Contains the commands to group or ungroup rows and columns of a worksheet. This group also includes the commands to find the subtotal of cells in a worksheet.
Analysis	Contains the command to find the optimum solution of a formula by performing What-if Analysis.

- **Review**: Contains various tools to check spellings, translate words, add comments, and protect a workbook. You can protect workbook data from unauthorized access by using the Protect Sheet and Protect Workbook options available in the Review tab. Figure-19 shows the Review tab of Excel 2010:

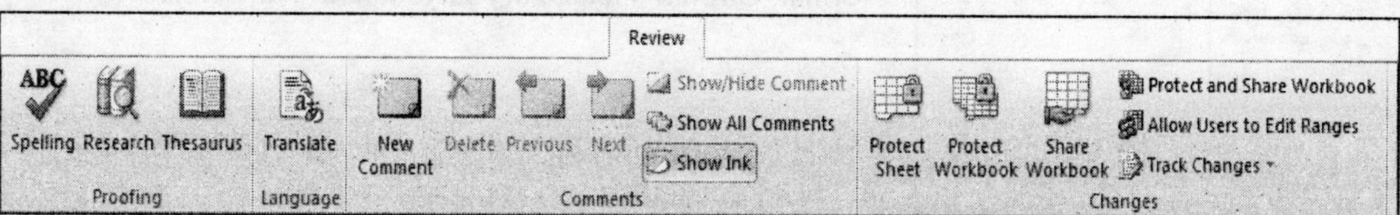

Figure-19: Displaying Review Tab

Table-6 describes the groups of commands in the Review tab:

Table-6: Groups of Commands in the Review Tab

Group	Description
Proofing	Contains three commands: Spelling, Research, and Thesaurus. The Spelling command is used to check the spelling of selected data. The Research command is used to search for additional information from reference books and research sites on the Internet. The Thesaurus command allows you to find the synonyms of words.
Language	Contains the command to translate the selected text into a different language.
Comments	Contains the commands to add, edit, and delete the comments in a cell. In addition, this group contains the commands that allow you to move to the next or previous comments.
Changes	Contains the commands to protect and share worksheets and workbooks, and track changes made in a worksheet.

- **View:** Contains the commands that allow you to view a worksheet in different ways. You can also show or hide gridlines or columns and row headings and zoom in or zoom out of your worksheet. In addition, you can create new windows and switch between the windows, freeze panes, or save multiple workbooks as a workspace. In addition, the commands in the View tab allow you to record, edit, or run macros.

  Figure-20 shows the View tab of Excel 2010:

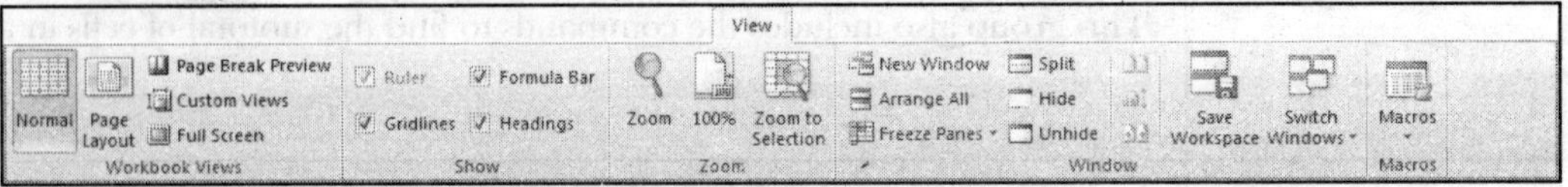

Figure-20: Displaying View Tab

Table-7 describes the groups of commands in the View tab:

Table-7: Groups of Commands in the View Tab

Group	Description
Workbook Views	Contains the commands to view a worksheet in different modes, such as Normal, Custom Views, Page Layout, and Full Screen.
Show	Contains the commands to show or hide the ruler, Formula Bar, gridlines, and headings in the Excel application window.
Zoom	Contains the commands that allow you to zoom in or out of a worksheet. For example, you can use the Zoom to Selection command to zoom a particular portion of a worksheet.

Table-7: Groups of Commands in the View Tab

Group	Description
Window	Contains the commands to view opened workbooks in different views. Apart from viewing workbooks, you can also split a workbook into two parts, switch to another workbook, or save and open multiple workbooks as a group by saving them as a workspace.
Macros	Contains the commands that allow you to view the macros present in a workbook as well as record a new macro. A macro is a set of instructions that you can use to automate repetitive tasks.

- **Developer:** Contains the commands needed to create, run, and edit macros. This tab also contains the command to import Extensible Markup Language (XML) files into a worksheet. Figure-21 shows the Developer tab of Excel 2010:

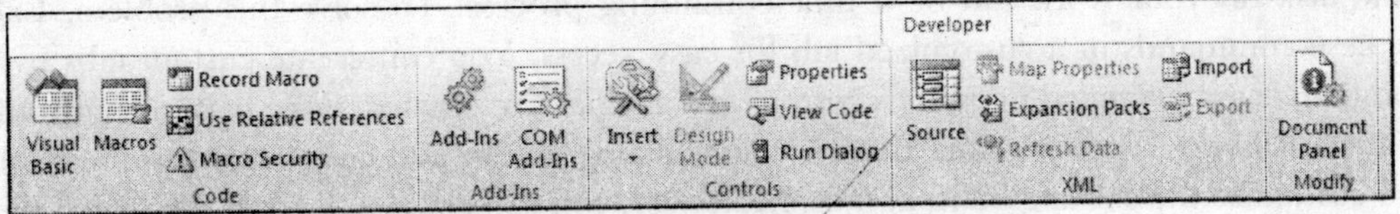

Figure-21: Displaying Developer Tab

Table-8 describes groups of commands in the Developer tab:

Table-8: Groups of Commands in the Developer Tab

Group	Description
Code	Contains the commands to create, run, and edit macros in a worksheet. For example, this group contains the Macro Security command, which is used to provide security to a macro at run time.
Add-Ins	Contains the commands to enable Excel's add-ins such as Solver, SnagIt, and Acrobat Reader. In addition, this group contains the Common Object Module (COM) Add-Ins command, which is useful for writing programs based on the COM architecture.
Controls	Contains the commands that allow you to add UI controls, such as buttons, textboxes, drop-down lists, and labels. This group is also useful for viewing the properties of the controls inserted in a worksheet.
XML	Contains the command for XML coding in Excel. It provides options to write XML source code, import and export XML files, and map and refresh XML data.
Modify	Contains the command that allows users to specify the important metadata (properties) of a Microsoft Office document of at any time, without having to leave a Microsoft Office application.

- **Add-Ins:** Provides commands of other applications that can be used with Excel. The Add-Ins tab does not necessarily display the same set of commands in different computers. The commands displayed in this tab depend on the applications installed on a computer. Figure-22 shows the Add-Ins tab:

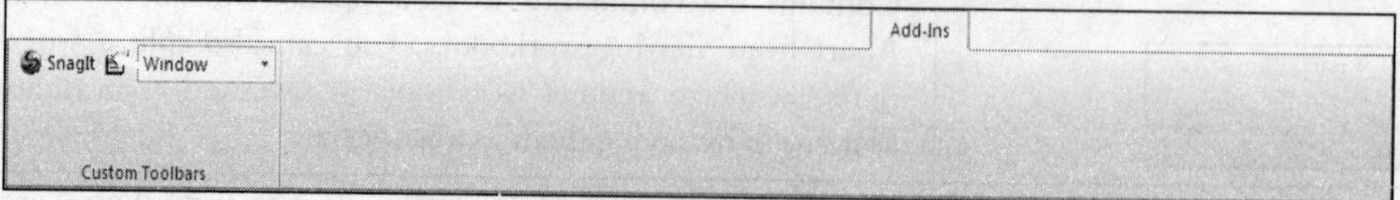

Figure-22: Displaying Add-Ins Tab

After learning the various commands available in the different tabs of the Ribbon in Excel 2010, let's move ahead and learn to customize the Ribbon.

3.3.1 Customizing the Ribbon

The commands that you use in your work are placed in different tabs and accessing these commands again and again to perform the same tasks in your work can be a time-consuming process. To solve this problem, Excel provides the facility to place these commands in a customized tab for easy access. You can create custom tabs by customizing the Ribbon. The commands are arranged in various custom groups that are created along with the custom tabs. You need to use the Customize Ribbon category of the Excel Options dialog box to add custom tabs to the Ribbon. Apart from this, you can also customize the existing build-in tabs. Moreover, you can change the order in which the tabs appear on the Ribbon and which groups of commands appear on each of these displayed tabs.

Perform the following steps to customize the Ribbon:

1. Select the **File** tab. The Backstage view appears, displaying various options (Figure-23).
2. Select the **Option** option from the Backstage view, as shown in Figure-23:

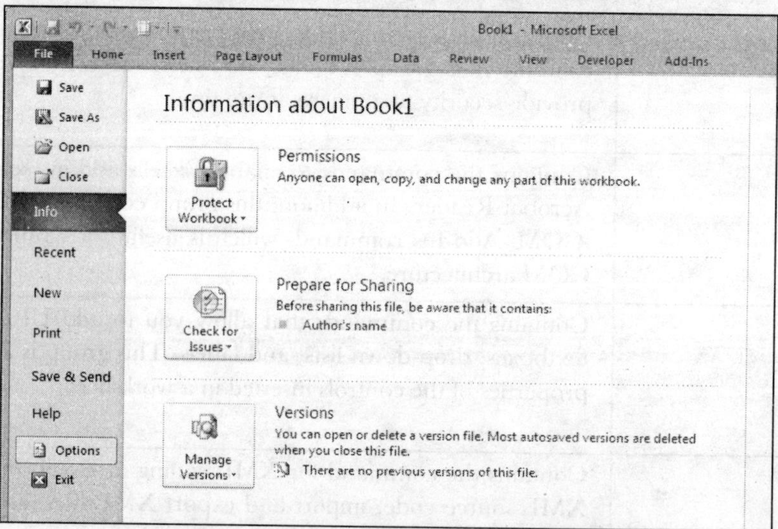

Figure-23: Displaying the Backstage view

The **Excel Options** dialog box appears (Figure-24).

3. Select the **Customize Ribbon** option in the **Excel Options** dialog box (Figure-24).

   The options related to the Customize Ribbon option appear on the right pane of the Excel Options dialog box.
4. Click the **New Tab** button to create a new tab (Figure-24).

The new tab appears under the Main Tabs list box, as shown in Figure-24:

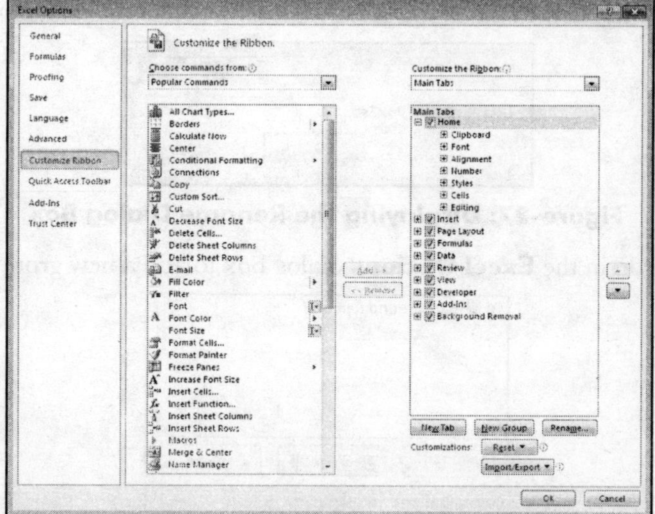

Figure-24: Displaying the Excel Options Dialog box

When you create a new custom tab, one custom group is created by default (Figure-25).You can add the commands for this group or create other custom groups. However, you first need to rename the tab.

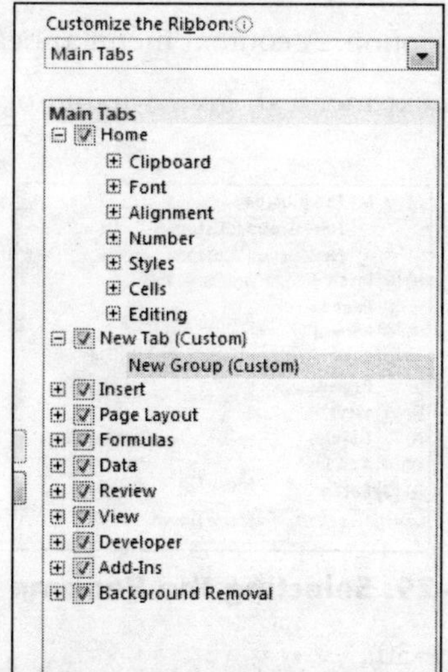

Figure-25: Creating New Custom Tab

5. Right-click the **New Tab (Custom)** option. A context menu appears (Figure-26).
6. Select the **Rename** option from the context menu to give a name of your choice to the new tab (Figure-26).

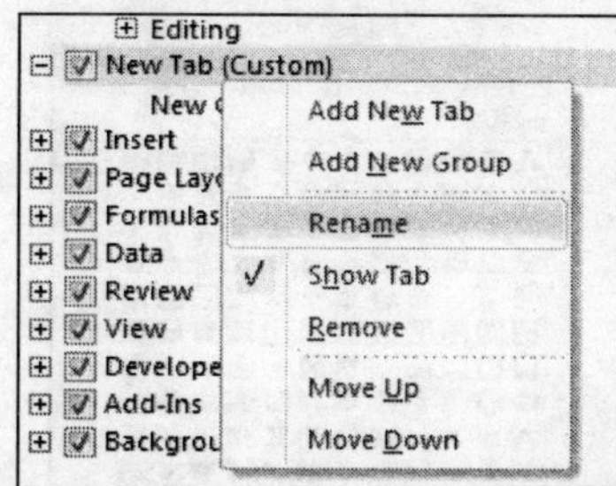

Figure-26: Selecting the Rename Option

The **Rename** dialog box appears (Figure-27).

7. Type a name for the tab in the **Display name** text box. In our case, we have typed **My Tab** (Figure-27).
8. Click the **OK** button to save the new name of the tab and close the Rename dialog box, as shown in Figure-27:

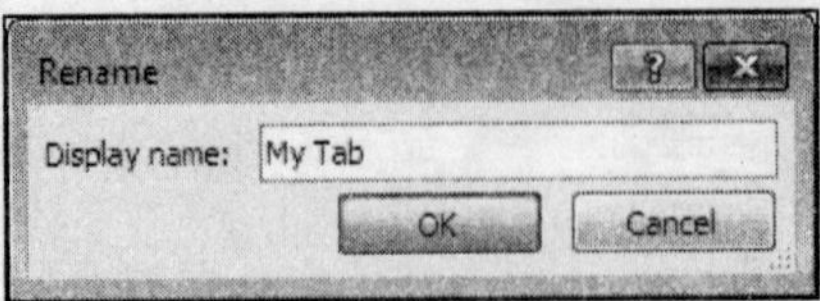

Figure-27: Displaying the Rename Dialog Box

9. Click the **New Group** button in the **Excel Options** dialog box to add a new group for the tab (Figure-28).

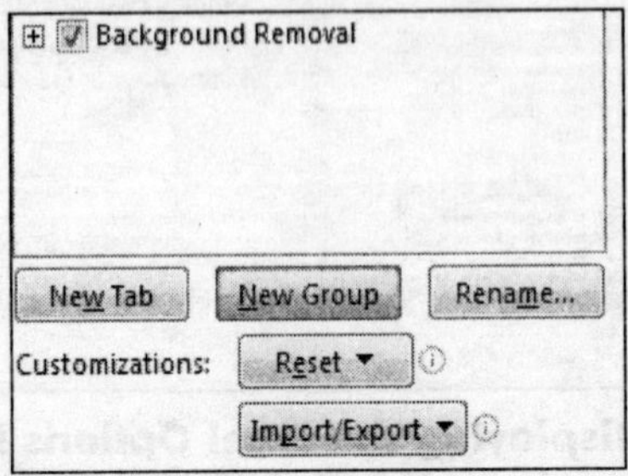

Figure-28: Using the New Group(Custom) Option

The **New Group** (Custom) appears under the **Main Tabs** list box (Figure-29).

10. Right-click the **New Group (Custom)** option. A context menu appears (Figure-29).
11. Select the Rename option from the context menu to give a name of your choice to the new group, as shown in Figure-29:

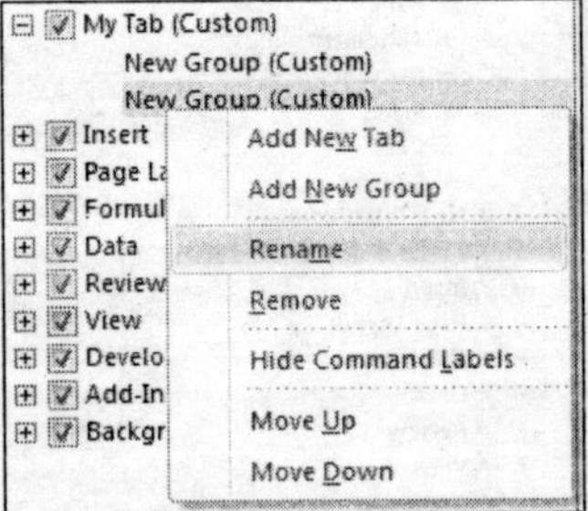

Figure-29: Selecting the Rename Option

The **Rename** dialog box appears (Figure-30).

12. Type a name for the new group in the **Display name** text box. In our case, we have typed **My Group** (Figure-30).
13. Click the **OK** button in the **Rename** dialog box to save the name of the group and close the dialog box (Figure-30).

Figure-30: Displaying the Rename Dialog box

Similarly, you can add the more new group and rename them in the **My Tab** tab. Now, let's add the commands for the **My Group** group in the **My Tab** tab.

14. Click the down arrow of the **Choose commands from** drop-down list in the **Excel Options** dialog box. A drop-down list appears (Figure-31).
15. Select an option from the drop-down list. In our case, we have selected the Commands Not in the Ribbon option, as shown in Figure-31:

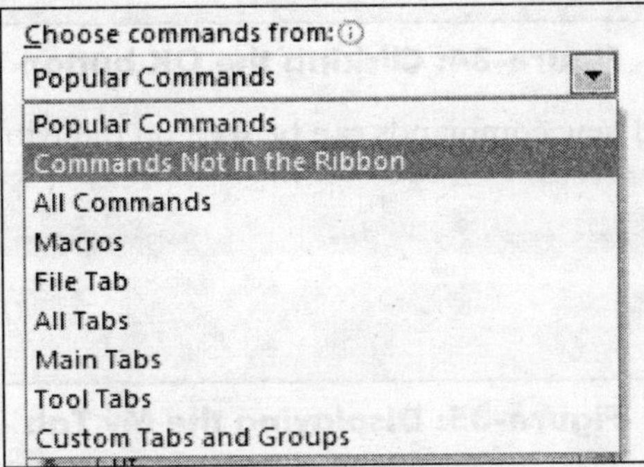

Figure-31: Selecting the Commands Not in the Ribbon

The various commands related to the selected option are displayed in the **Choose commands from** list box.

16. Select the commands that you want to add to the **My Group** group of the **My Tab** tab. In our case, we have selected the **Calculate Full** command (Figure-32).
17. Click the **Add** button to add the command (Figure-32).

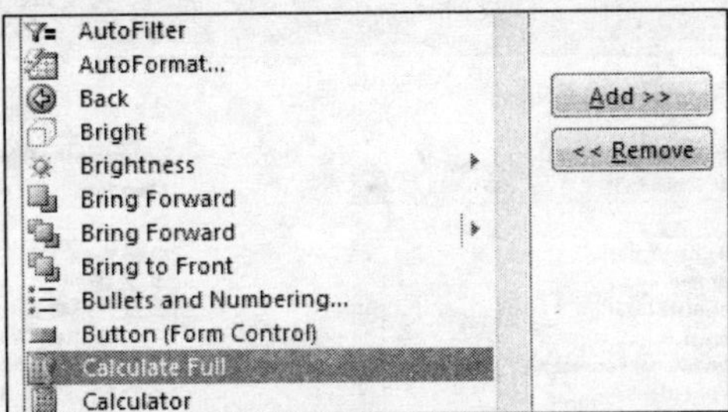

Figure-32: Selecting the Calculate Full Option

Similarly, you can add more commands to the **My Group** group. In our case, we have added the **Back**, **Shapes, Depth, Quick Print**, and **Dim** commands, as shown in Figure-33:

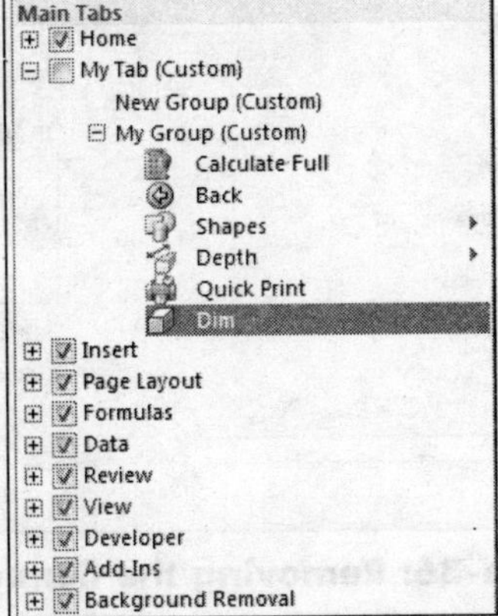

Figure-33: Selecting the Commands

18. Click the OK button in the Excel Options dialog box, as shown in Figure-34:

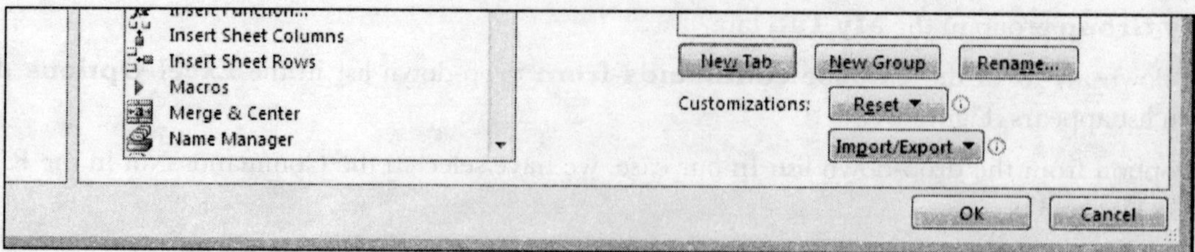

Figure-34: Clicking the OK button

The new tab with its custom groups and new commands can be seen on the Ribbon, as shown in Figure-35:

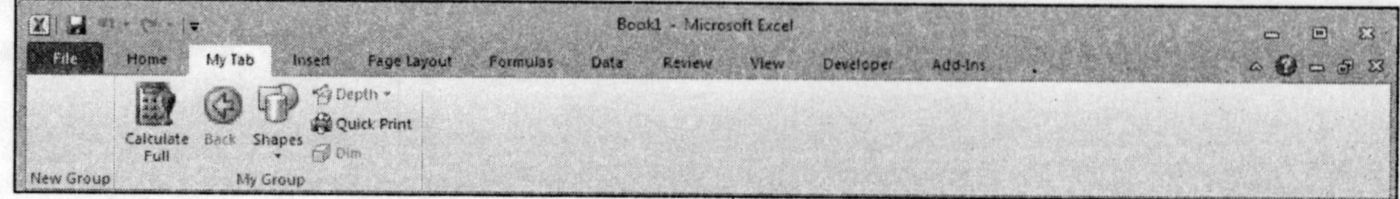

Figure-35: Displaying the My Tab

You can also delete commands that you no longer require from a custom group.

Perform the following steps to delete commands from a custom group:

1. Select the commands that you want to remove from the custom group (**My Group** in our case) under the **Main Tab** list box in the **Excel Options** dialog box. In our case, we have selected the **Dim** command (Figure-36).
2. Click the **Remove** button, as shown in Figure-36:

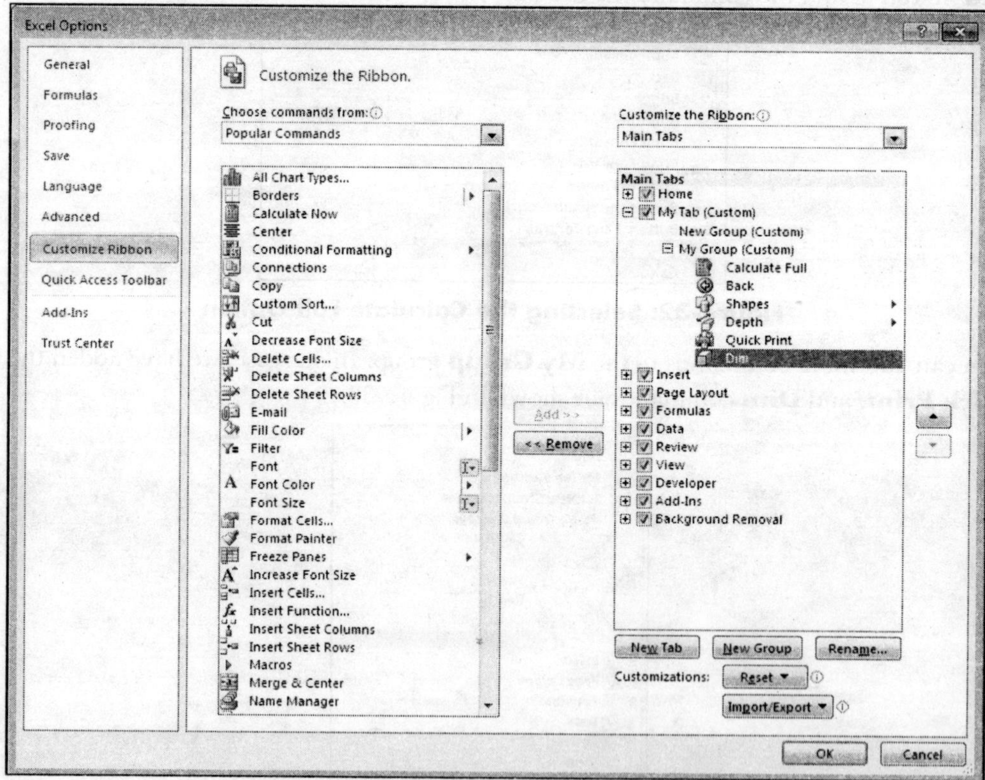

Figure-36: Removing the Commands

Similarly, you can select the other commands that you want to remove from the selected group.

3. Click the **OK** button to remove the selected command from the **My Group** group (Figure-34).

The command is removed from the Ribbon, as shown in Figure-37:

Figure-37: Displaying the My Tab Tab

After learning to customize the Ribbon, let's explore the Excel Options dialog box.

3.3.2 Exploring the Excel Options Dialog Box

The Excel Options dialog box performs the same function as the Control Panel, which is a part of the Microsoft Window graphical user interface (GUI).The difference between the two is that while the Control Panel provides options for a user to change the appearance or actions in an application, the Excel Options dialog box allows you to change the default settings of the Microsoft Excel application and enable/disable features. When you open the Excel Options dialog box (by clicking File→Options), you will find that the dialog box consists of two panes, the left pane and the right pane. The left pane displays a list of categories of Excel options while the right pane displays the options of the category that you click in the left pane. Figure-38 shows the Excel Options dialog box of Excel 2010:

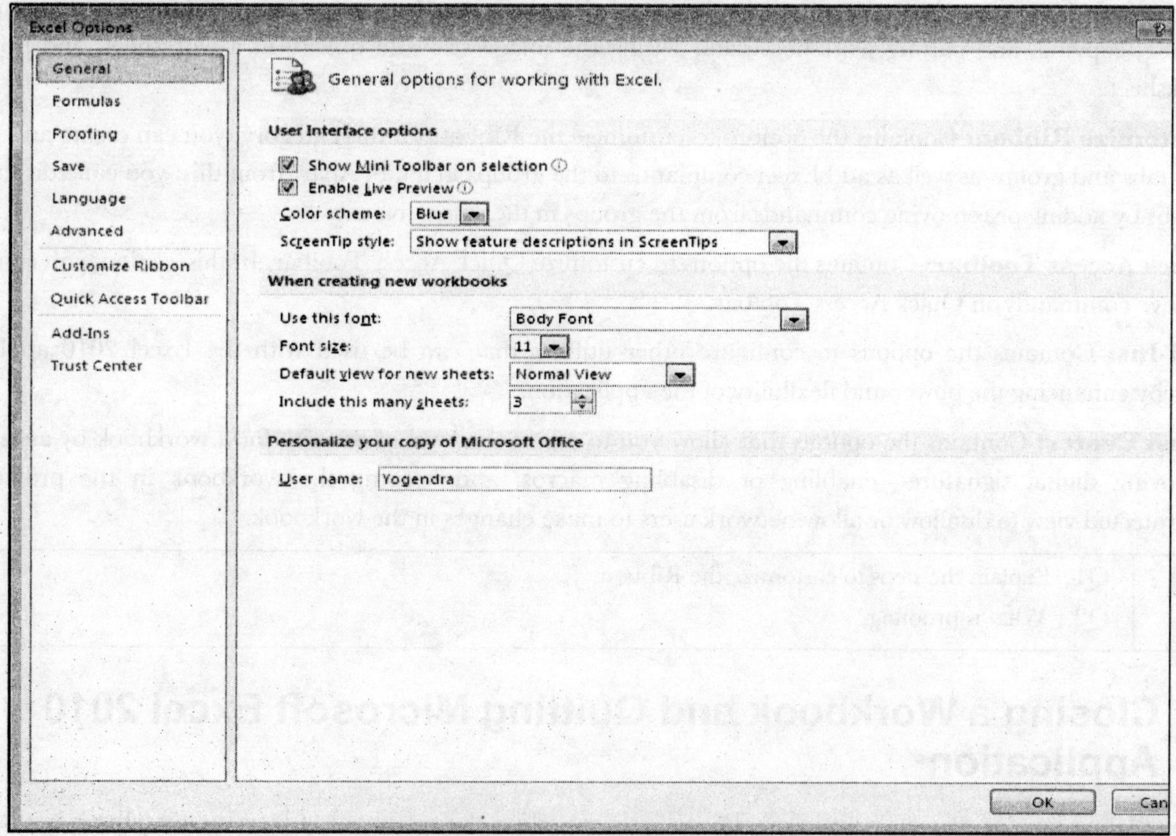

Figure-38: Displaying the Excel Options Dialog box

The following is a brief description of the list of categories that appear on the left pane of the Excel Options dialog box:

- **General:** Contains the options to customize the look and feel of the UI of Excel 2010, such as Show Live Preview, Color scheme, and ScreenTip style. This category also contains the options to specify the default font and font size for all new workbooks.
- **Formulas:** Contains the options that determine how Excel performs calculations by using formulas and checks for errors in them. This category also contains the Error checking rules section, which includes options that define the rules to check errors in formulas.
- **Proofing:** Contains the options that determine how Excel corrects and formats data, such as the AutoCorrect options button, which automatically correct misspelled words; the Ignore words in UPPERCASE option, which ignores the uppercase during a spell check; and the Custom Dictionaries option, which suggest alternate meanings of specified words.
- **Save:** Contains the options that determine how Excel saves a workbook. This category contains the options to set the time for auto saving your workbook, specify the default extension to save the workbook, and the default location to save recovered workbooks in case of power failure or shutdown of the computer without closing the workbook.
- **Language:** Contains the options to set language preferences for editing you data in a worksheet, where-in you can set the language specific features, such as dictionaries and grammar checking. This category also contains the option to select the language for the ScreenTip.
- **Advanced:** Contains advanced options to work with Excel. Some of these options include editing a worksheet, cutting, copying, and pasting worksheet data, setting the image size and quality in a worksheet, and printing a worksheet.
- **Customize Ribbon:** Contains the options to customize the Ribbon. In this category, you can create and remove new tabs and groups as well as add Excel commands to the groups in a tab. Apart from this, you can edit the built-in tabs by adding or removing commands from the groups in the respective tabs.
- **Quick Access Toolbar:** Contains the options to customize Quick Access Toolbar. In this section, you can add or remove commands on Quick Access Toolbar.
- **Add-Ins:** Contains the options to configure other utilities that can be used with the Excel 2010 application, thereby enhancing the power and flexibility of the application.
- **Trust Center:** Contains the options that allow you to adjust the level of security for a workbook by assigning or removing digital signatures, enabling or disabling macros, and keeping the workbook in the protected or unprotected view to disallow or allow network users to make changes in the workbook.

Q1. Explain the steps to customize the Ribbon.

Q2. What is proofing?

3.4 Closing a Workbook and Quitting Microsoft Excel 2010 Application

After completing your work on an Excel workbook, you can close the workbook. Once the workbook is closed, the Excel 2010 application window remains open on your computer screen. After you finish working on your workbook, you can quit or exit the Excel 2010 application. Excel 2010 prompts you to save the changes made in any opened worksheet before quitting the application.

Perform the following steps to close a workbook:

1. Click the **File** tab present on the Ribbon. The Backstage view appears.
2. Click the **Close option**, as shown in Figure-39:

Figure-39: Closing the Workbook

After closing the workbook, let's learn how to quit a Microsoft Excel 2010 application.

Perform the following step to quit the Microsoft Excel 2010 application:

1. Click the File tab present on the Ribbon (Figure-40). The Backstage view appears.
2. Click the **Exit** to exit from the Microsoft Excel 2010 application, as shown in Figure-40:

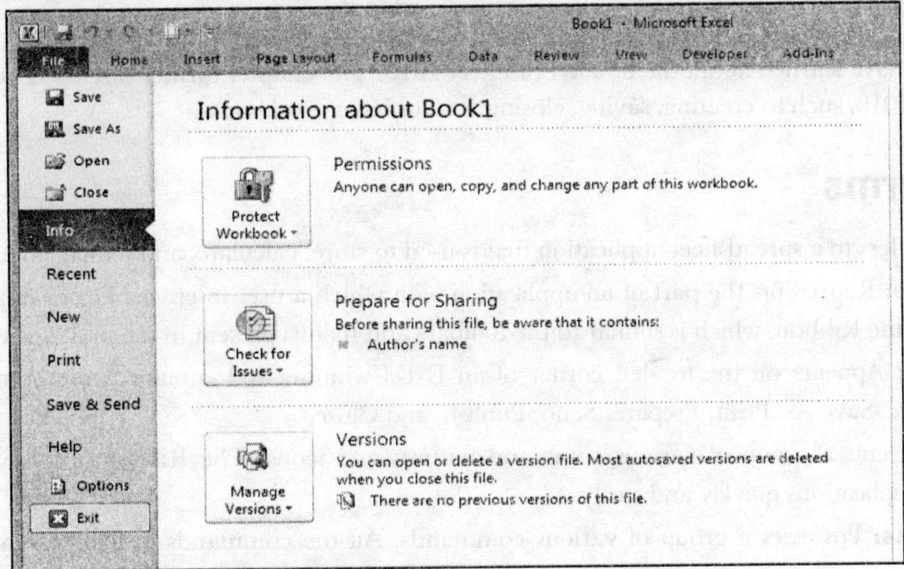

Figure-40: Clicking the Exit command

The Excel 2010 application closes.

Q1. Explain how to close Excel 2010 using the Office Button.

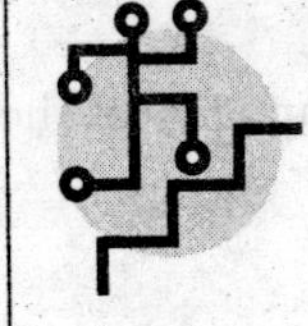

Activity-2

Explain the process of creating a workbook using a Blank Workbook template.

Case Study: Data Management in Krishna & Sons

Krishna & Sons is an organization that is engaged in transportation business and operates across India. The organization has a workforce of more than 3,000 employees. It also has approximately 800 trucks and 1200 lorries. As there is a large number of vehicles and employees, it has become extremely difficult for the organization to maintain the records of all the vehicles and employees manually. The organization wants to keep track of all the trucks and lorries engaged in the business. Therefore, it has decided to manage the data using Excel 2010.

Questions:

Q1. What would you do if you have given the responsibility to keep the record of resources of M/s Krishna & Sons?

*(*Case study presented is the proprietary information of the respective organization, and is used here specifically and only for educational purpose.)*

Now, let's recap the key points we have learned in this chapter.

3.5 Summary

In this chapter, you have learned about the new UI of Excel 2010. The chapter further discussed how to perform some basic tasks in Excel 2010, such as creating, saving, closing, and opening workbooks.

3.6 Key Terms

- **Excel 2010:** Refers to a spreadsheet application that is used to store, calculate, and manage data.
- **User Interface:** Represents the part of an application with which a user interacts. For example, the UI in Excel 2010 consists of the Ribbon, which is similar to the toolbars and menus present in the previous versions of Excel.
- **Office Button:** Appears on the top-left corner of an Excel window and contains various menu items, such as New, Open, Save, Save As, Print, Prepare, Send, Publish, and Close.
- **Ribbon:** Represents a group of various command buttons and icons. The Ribbon allows you to find out the features of the applications quickly and easily.
- **Command Sets:** Possesses a group of various commands. All the commands available in a command tab are organized in commands sets.
- **Live Preview:** Represents a unique feature that allows you to view formatting changes when the mouse pointer is kept over some formatting button.
- **Key Tips:** Allows you to use the commands displayed on the Ribbon with the use of keyboard.
- **Enhanced ScreenTips:** Represents pop-up boxes that provide information associated with the buttons and the menus. Enhanced ScreenTips is an upgraded version of the ToolTips, which exists in the previous versions of the Excel.
- **Formula Bar:** Displays the cell contents along with the formulas written for that particular cell. It appears at the right side of Name Box.

3.7 Exercise

Multiple Choice Questions

Q1. Which of the following commands is present in Excel 2010?

a. Mail Merge
b. Format Painter
c. Name Manager Insert
d. Cross-reference

Ans. b

Q2. Name Box in Excel 2010 is found:

a. Above the Ribbon
b. Right to the Quick Access Toolbar
c. Left to Formula Bar
d. Below the title bar

Ans. c

Q3. Which one of the following options helps to create a range?

a. Define Name
b. Name Manager
c. Create From Selection
d. Calculate Sheet

Ans. a

Q4. Spreadsheet Excel is a product of:

a. LINUX
b. Microsoft
c. Sun Solaris
d. None of the above

Ans. b

Q5. Which button is used to use a formula for a range:

a. Use in Formula button in the Defined Names
b. Unmerge Cells option from Merge & Center command
c. Insert Function button
d. Lookup & Reference button

Ans. a

Q6. Which one of the following is not a feature of Excel 2010?

a. Improved Ribbon
b. New Frontstage View
c. New sparklines feature
d. Improved PivotTable

Ans. b

Q7. VBA stands for

a. Visual Basic for Applications
b. Visual Business for Administration
c. Very Basic for Applications
d. Vary Beginners for Applications

Ans. a

Q8. How many types of scrollbars are available on Excel sheet?

a. One
b. Two
c. Three
d. Four

Ans. b

Q9. Status bar in the Excel 2010 is located at

a. Top
b. Bottom
c. Top left corner
d. Bottom left corner

Ans. b

Q10. Which one of the following is located at the top left corner of the Excel application window?

a. Scroll bars
b. Formula Bar
c. Title bar
d. Quick Access Toolbar

Ans. d

Short Answer Type Questions

Q1. Explain the use of the file tab.

Q2. Write the steps of starting Microsoft Excel 2010.

Q3. Make a list of various components of Excel 2010.

Q4. Explain the use of the Minimize, Maximize/Restore, and Close Buttons.

Q5. Explain the use of the Formula Bar.

Q6. Write the steps for closing and quitting Microsoft Excel 2010.

Q7. Explain the use of status Bar.

Q8. Give a brief description of two types of scroll bars.

Q9. Explain the components of the worksheet.

Q10. Write the use of title bar.

Microsoft®
PowerPoint® 2010

Starting

Office

CHAPTER 4

Working with Microsoft PowerPoint 2010

CHAPTER STRUCTURE

CHAPTER OBJECTIVES

- Describe the features of powerpoint
- Familiarise with the interface of powerpoint
- Discuss the basics of powerpoint
- Make the slides presentable
- Insert objects in a presentation
- Implement transition styles and animation to the presentation

4.1 Introduction

A presentation is a sequential collection of slides, where each slide displays some information in the form of text or graphics. Microsoft PowerPoint is the commonly used application to create presentations. It is presentation software that is available as a part of the Microsoft Office 2010 suite. A PowerPoint presentation can be used to explain some idea or concept to a group of people. For example, you can use it to create slide shows for presenting an idea to your clients, for explaining a concept to the employees of a company, or for teaching the students in a class. Microsoft PowerPoint provides some built-in features, such as special effects, animation, video trimming, compressing media, and drawing tools, used to enhance the clarity of your presentation. With the growth of technology, the improvised versions of PowerPoint are released from time to time, the latest version being the Microsoft PowerPoint 2010. This version of Microsoft is not much different from the earlier version, Microsoft PowerPoint 2007; however, it provides various new features, such as background removal and backstage view, in addition to those provided by PowerPoint 2007.

In this chapter, you learn about the new features of PowerPoint 2010. Next, you learn how to launch the PowerPoint application. Further, you learn about the PowerPoint interface. You also learn about different tabs available in PowerPoint 2010. The chapter explains how to create a presentation using different ways. Next, you will learn about how to apply date, time and slide number to the slides. Additionally, you will also learn about working with objects like clip art, shapes, images, video and audio clips. In the end, you learn how to to enhance your presentation.

Let's start by learning about the Microsoft PowerPoint 2010 features.

4.2 Exploring Microsoft PowerPoint 2010 Features

Microsoft PowerPoint 2010 is the latest entrant in the series of PowerPoint versions. This version is shipped with various enhanced features, such as artistic effects, transitions, animations, and the inclusion of the File tab. In addition, you can embed videos in PowerPoint 2010, which is one of the useful features to enhance the presentation and make it more alluring. Some of the new features of PowerPoint 2010 are as follows:

- **Backstage view:** Refers to the window that appears when the File tab is clicked. The Backstage view consists of some new options in addition to those present in the File menu of earlier versions, such as New, Open, Save, Info, and Print.
- **Built-in screen capture tool:** Allows you to take screen shots of the desired window directly from the PowerPoint application itself. In other words, you do not need to open an external screen capturing application, such as Snag It, to take screen shots.
- **Background removal:** Allows you to remove or modify background of an image, depending on the requirement. The background removal feature is useful when you want to emphasize on the desired part of an image.
- **Video insertion:** Allows you to add videos in a presentation. You can add videos in the presentation either from a file or from the Internet.
- **Video editing and cropping:** Enables you to edit and crop the videos in the similar way as you edit and crop the images in the earlier versions.
- **Collaboration and Sharing:** Allows you to collaborate and share the created presentation in an easier way. PowerPoint 2010 consists of compare and share features using which the presentation can be compared to other presentations as well as it can be shared by users present on the network.
- **Transition tab:** Consists of transition tools that you can apply on the presentation slides. The Transition tab is added in the PowerPoint 2010 interface; whereas, in the earlier versions of PowerPoint, some transition options were present in the Animation tab.
- **Microsoft Office Equation Editor:** Allows you to insert mathematical equations in a presentation.
- **Animation painter:** Allows you to copy the animation applied on an object to any other object contained in the presentation.

- **New animation options:** Consists of new animation options, such as Spin and Desaturate, along with the options available in earlier versions of Microsoft PowerPoint.
- **New photo editing tools:** Consists of additional editing tools for images, such as background removal.

4.3 Exploring Microsoft PowerPoint 2010 Interface

To create a presentation in PowerPoint 2010, you first need to launch PowerPoint 2010. Perform the following steps to start PowerPoint 2010 application:

1. Click the **Start** button present on the **Taskbar**. The **Start** menu appears (Figure-1).
2. Place the mouse pointer over **All Programs** option in the **Start** menu. A list of programs installed on your computer appears (Figure-1).
3. Click the **Microsoft Office folder** (Figure). A list of applications of the Microsoft Office suite appears (Figure-1).
4. Click the **Microsoft PowerPoint 2010** option, as shown in Figure-1:

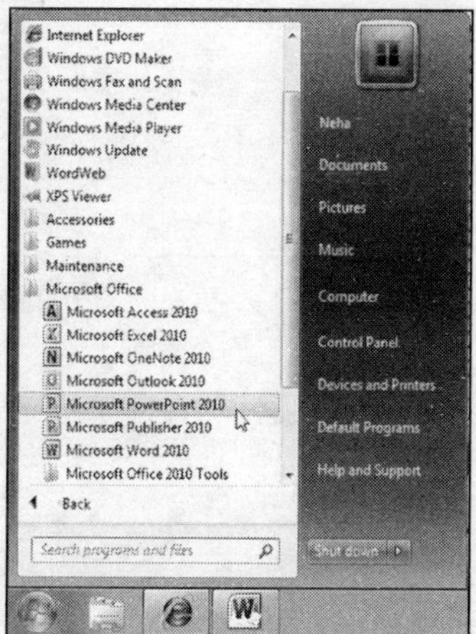

Figure-1: Displaying Start menu

The PowerPoint 2010 window opens and a new, blank presentation is displayed, as shown in Figure-2:

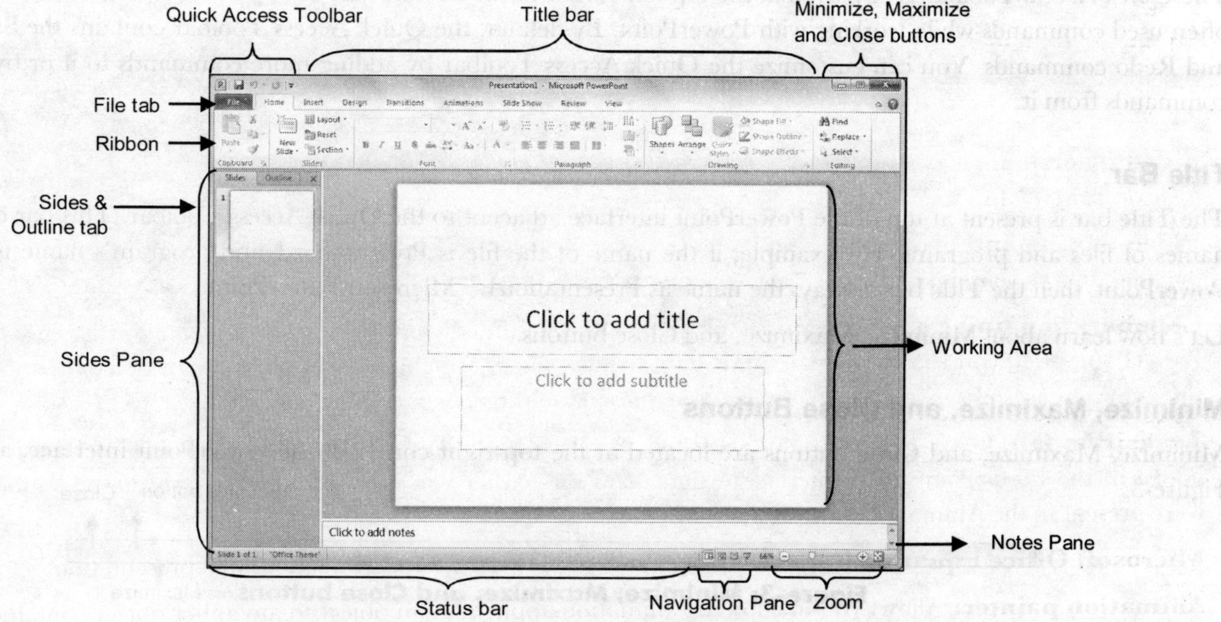

Figure-2: PowerPoint 2010 interface

The window that opens when you start PowerPoint is known as the interface of PowerPoint 2010. In the PowerPoint 2010 interface, you can create, design, and run presentations. Therefore, before performing these activities, let's first explore the interface in detail.

The major change introduced in PowerPoint 2010 as compared to earlier versions is that in the PowerPoint 2010 interface, the Office button has been replaced by the PowerPoint button and the File tab. The new interface groups the frequently used file commands, such as create, open, and save, inside the File tab and groups rest of the commands inside different tabs. The new interface is more intuitive, easier to navigate, and better suited for performing any task.

The PowerPoint 2010 interface consists of various components, which are as follows:

- Quick Access Toolbar
- Title bar
- Minimize, Maximize, and Close buttons
- File tab
- Ribbon
- Dialog box launcher
- Scroll bar
- Working area
- Slides and Outline tabs
- Slides pane
- Notes pane
- Status bar
- Navigation pane
- Zoom control

Let's discuss these components, one by one.

Quick Access Toolbar

The Quick Access Toolbar is displayed at the top-left corner of the PowerPoint 2010 interface. It contains a set of most often used commands while working with PowerPoint. By default, the Quick Access Toolbar contains the Save, Undo and Redo commands. You can customize the Quick Access Toolbar by adding more commands to it or by removing commands from it.

Title Bar

The Title bar is present at top of the PowerPoint interface adjacent to the Quick Access Toolbar. This bar displays the names of files and programs. For example, if the name of the file is Presentation1 and program's name is Microsoft PowerPoint, then the Title bar displays the name as Presentation1 – Microsoft PowerPoint.

Let's now learn about Minimize, Maximize, and Close buttons.

Minimize, Maximize, and Close Buttons

Minimize, Maximize, and Close buttons are located at the top-right corner of the PowerPoint interface, as shown in Figure-3:

Figure-3: Minimize, Maximize, and Close buttons

The role and purpose of each button is described as follows:

- **Minimize button:** Minimizes the current presentation window
- **Maximize button:** Maximizes the current presentation window
- **Close button:** Closes the current presentation window

File Tab

The File tab is located below the Quick Access Toolbar. This tab is also referred to as the Backstage view and consists of frequently used commands, such as Save, Save As, Open, Close, Info, Recent, New, Print, Share, Help, Options, and Exit. The Backstage view of the File tab is shown in Figure-4:

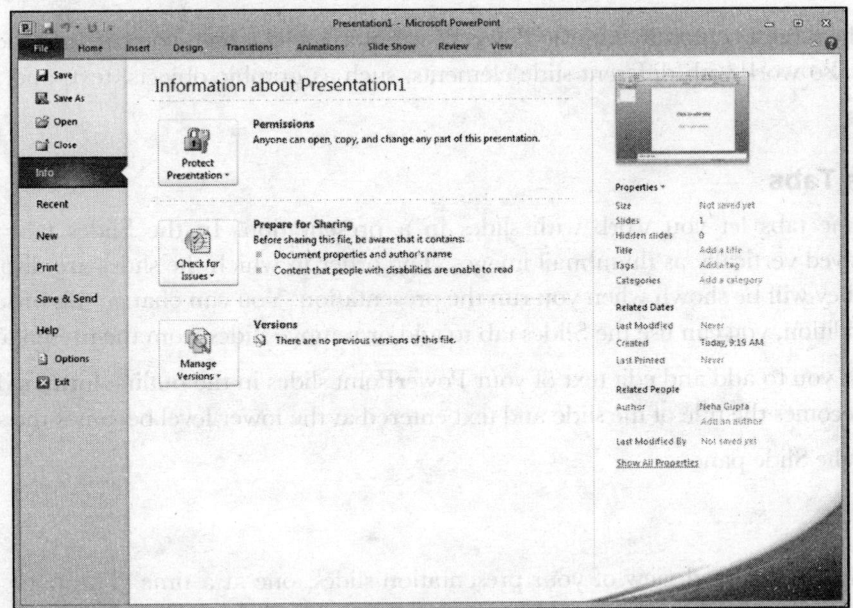

Figure-4: Backstage view of the File tab

Ribbon

Ribbon consists of almost all the commands and tools present in the menus and toolbars of the earlier versions of PowerPoint interface, in addition to new commands and tools. Depending on the specific category, all commands in Ribbon are grouped under some tabs, such as Home, Insert, Page Layout, References, Mailings, Review, and View. These are the basic tabs that are also referred to as Command tabs. The Ribbon is shown in Figure-5:

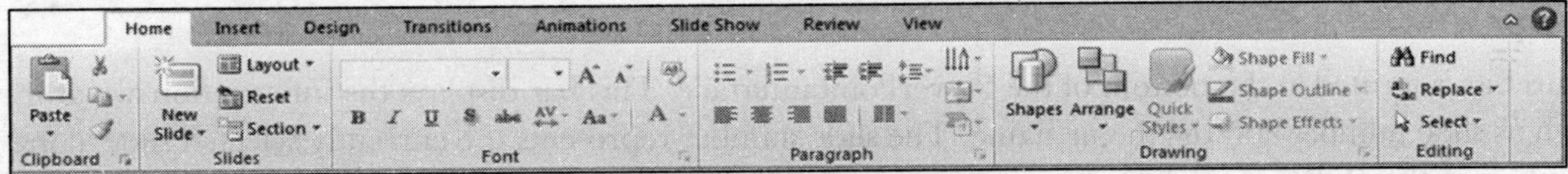

Figure-5: Ribbon

Following is the brief description of tabs present in the Ribbon by default:

- **Home:** Consists of commands to create and format slides.
- **Insert:** Consists of commands to insert objects in a presentation.
- **Design:** Allows you to work with themes, background, or page setup.
- **Transitions:** Consists of commands to apply, change, or remove the transition effects.
- **Animations:** Consists of commands to apply, change, or remove animations.
- **Slide Show:** Consists of commands to customize, setup, or monitor the slide show.

- **Review:** Consists of commands to proof check your presentation, set the language, work with comments, and compare the changes between different presentations.
- **View:** Allows you to view your presentation in different ways, such as normal and slide sorter.

Scroll Bar

The scroll bar appears at the right side of the PowerPoint interface. However, the scroll bar would only appear if there is more than one slide in a presentation. You can also scroll between different slides by using the up and down arrow buttons present in the scroll bar.

Working Area

The working area is the largest center area in the PowerPoint interface in which you can add the content of your slide. In this area, you can also work with different slide elements, such as graphic objects, text, and animations, which are inserted in the slides.

Slides and Outline Tabs

The Slides and Outline tabs let you work with slides in a presentation. In the Slides tab, all the slides of your presentation are displayed vertically as thumbnail images. The order in which the slides are displayed in the Slides tab is the order in which they will be shown when you run the presentation. You can change this order by moving the slides in the Slides tab. In addition, you can use the Slides tab to add or remove slides from the presentation.

The Outline tab allows you to add and edit text of your PowerPoint slides in the outline format. The text entered at the top-level in the slide becomes the title of the slide and text entered at the lower level becomes the subtitle of the slide.

Let's now learn about the Slide pane.

Slide Pane

The Slide pane displays an enlarged view of your presentation slides, one at a time. This pane allows you to edit the slides in your PowerPoint presentation. In the Slide pane, you can edit a slide by adding or removing text, pictures, and other content to or from it.

Notes Pane

The Notes pane is displayed below the Slide pane on the PowerPoint 2010 interface. In this pane, you can enter notes associated with the current slide. For example, you can specify note, such as this presentation is for kindergarten, if you are creating presentation for students.

Status Bar

The Status bar is located at the bottom of the PowerPoint interface. This bar displays the information about the current slide, such as slide number and the theme name. The slide number represents the currently selected slide along with the total number of the slides present in the presentation; whereas, the theme name represents the name of the theme applied to the presentation.

Navigation Pane

The Navigation pane provides four buttons, Normal, Slide Sorter, Reading View, and Slide Show. The Normal, Slide Sorter, and Reader buttons allow you to view slides in different views. The Normal button displays the slides in the normal view, the Slide Sorter button represents the slide sorter view in which all the slides are displayed on a single screen, and the Reading View button displays the slides in a reader view. The Slide Show button is used to display all the slides in the form of slide show.

4.4 Basics of the Presentation

In this section learn about the basics of the presentation that covers creation of a presentation, insertion of a slide, saving the presentation, closing the presentation and quitting the application. When you start PowerPoint 2010, it opens a new blank presentation by default. This blank presentation is based on the blank template of PowerPoint 2010. You can either work with the default blank presentation or create a new presentation based on a custom template. You can create a new presentation in PowerPoint 2010 by using the following templates:

- A blank template
- A template installed on your computer

Now, you learn how to create a new presentation using these ways, one by one.

4.4.1 Creating a Presentation using the Blank Template

In case you want to create a PowerPoint presentation completely on your own, then you can use the blank template in PowerPoint 2010. As the name suggests, the blank template opens a blank presentation. It offers only the basic visual elements of a presentation, such as a placeholder to add a title to a slide. The blank template gives a great deal of flexibility and liberty to create, edit, and design the PowerPoint presentation.

The following chain of steps should be followed to create a PowerPoint 2010 presentation by using a blank template:

File tab → New option → Blank presentation → Create (Figure-6).

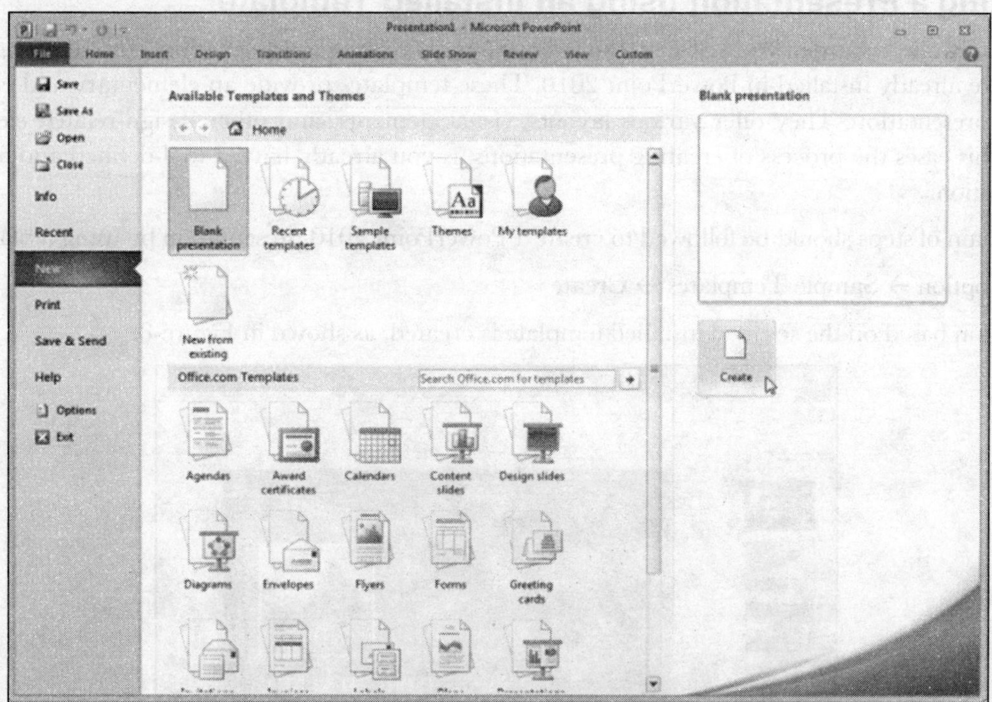

Figure-6: Creating a presentation

A new blank presentation is created with the name Presentation 2, as shown in Figure-7:

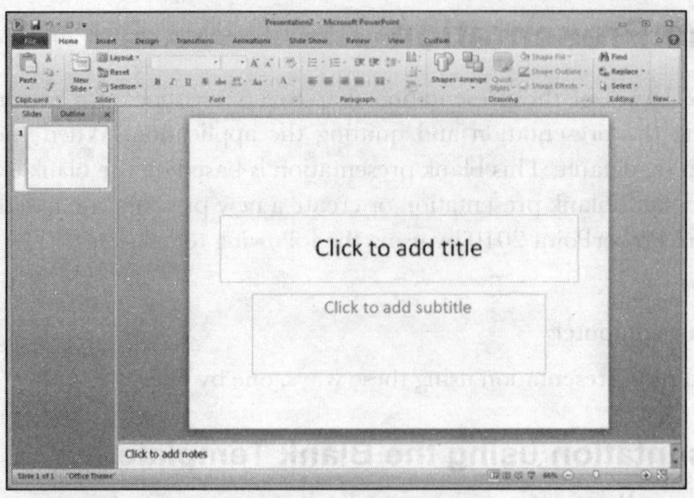

Figure-7: Displaying a new blank presentation

In Figure-7, you can see that a blank presentation contains a single slide with text boxes (placeholders) to enter a title and a subtitle. You can insert text, images, and add more slides to the blank presentation. You can also enhance your presentation by applying different styles and background to it.

4.4.2 Creating a Presentation using an Installed Template

In case you do not want to burden yourself with the tedious job of creating a presentation from scratch, you can use the templates that are already installed in PowerPoint 2010. These templates provide an elementary and easy-to-start-with layout for your presentation. They offer various layouts, visual elements, and other design-related elements to create presentations. This eases the process of creating presentations as you already have a well-defined and attractive outline for your presentation.

The following chain of steps should be followed to create a PowerPoint 2010 presentation by using a blank template:

File tab → New option → Sample Templates → Create

A new presentation based on the selected installed template is created, as shown in Figure-8:

Figure-8: New presentation based on the installed template

In Figure-8, you can see that the presentation has many slides. These slides have pre-written text and graphical content, which you can customize according to your requirements. In our case, we are not making any changes in the presentation.

Let's now learn how to insert a new slide in the presentation.

4.4.3 Inserting a New Slide

When you create a new presentation using a blank template, by default it has only one slide. However, a complete presentation usually contains many slides. Therefore, you frequently need to add new slides to your presentation. You can insert a slide in the presentation by clicking the **New Slide** icon present in the **Home** tab (Figure-9).

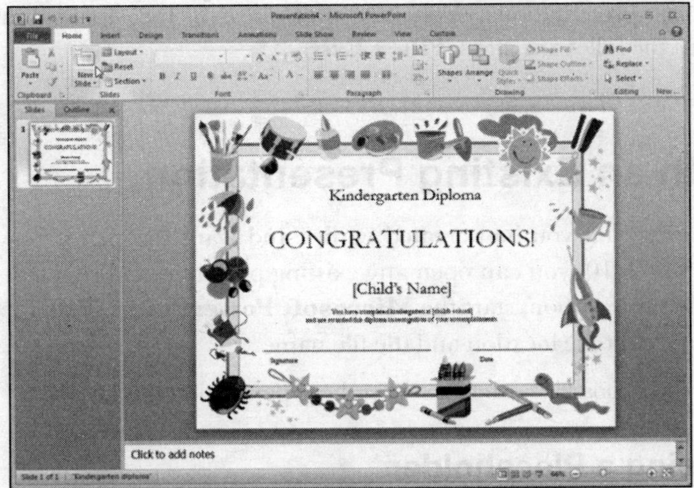

Figure-9: Presentation with one slide

The new slide is inserted in the presentation, as shown in Figure-10:

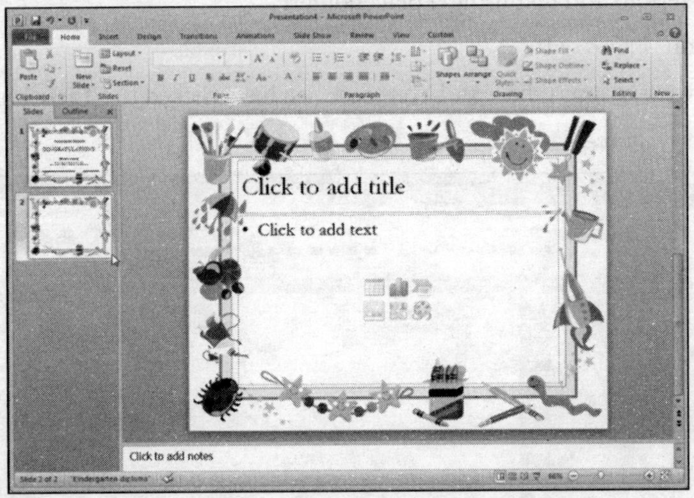

Figure-10: Insertion of new slide

4.4.4 Saving a Presentation

After creating a presentation based on a template, you can start designing and enhancing it. As you enhance your presentation, it becomes imperative for you to keep saving it as well. Saving your presentation makes your changes in the presentation permanent. You can save your presentation in many ways, some of which are as follows:

- For saving presentation in the default file format, do File→Save
- For saving presentation as a Portable Document Format (PDF), do File→Save As →Save As Type (select PDF)

After saving your presentation, further changes that you make in your presentation can be saved by simply pressing the CTRL+S key combination on the keyboar.

4.4.5 Closing the Presentation and Quitting PowerPoint

When you have finished working with a particular presentation, you can close that presentation. For this perform the following steps: **File→ Close.**

When you close a presentation, the PowerPoint 2010 window remains open on your desktop and you can create new presentations or open existing presentations. You can quit or exit the application after completing all your presentations. For this perform the following steps: **File→ Exit**.

The PowerPoint application gets close.

4.5 Working with an Existing Presentation

Suppose you have a presentation that you had created earlier and want to open it now for further modifications or enhancements. With PowerPoint 2010, you can open any existing presentation provided, you know the location where it has been saved. To open the presentation, start the **Microsoft PowerPoint 2010** application and proceed as given here: File → Open. From here select file location and the file name.

You can also use the CTRL+O keyboard shortcut to open the Open dialog box.

4.5.1 Adding Text using a Placeholder

In PowerPoint 2010, when you create a new presentation or add a new slide to an existing presentation, the slide appears with a placeholder to insert text; however, you can also add other objects, such as images, in the placeholder.

Let's perform the following steps to add text using a placeholder:

1. Create a new presentation (Figure-11).
2. Click the box where you want to insert the text. In our case, we have clicked the **Title** box (Figure-11).

   The placeholder appears (Figure-11).

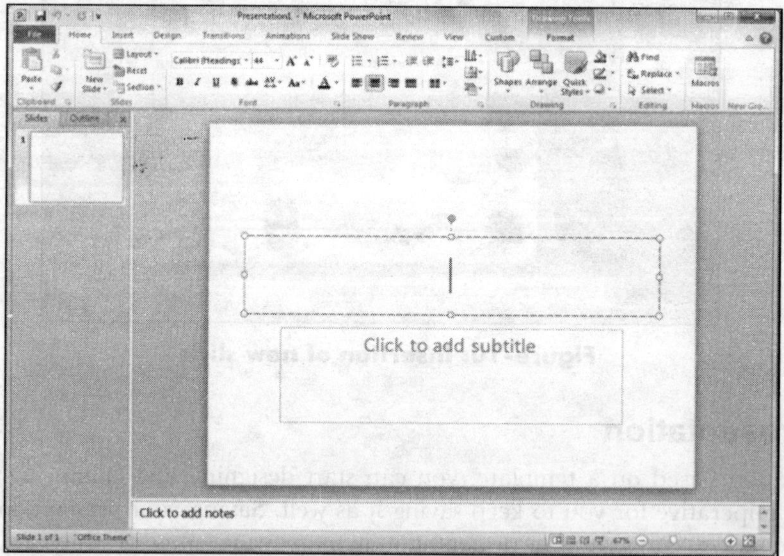

Figure-11: Displaying Title box

3. Type a title that you want to display on the slide. In our case, we have typed **Introducing PowerPoint 2010** (Figure-12).

   The inserted text appears, as shown in Figure-12:

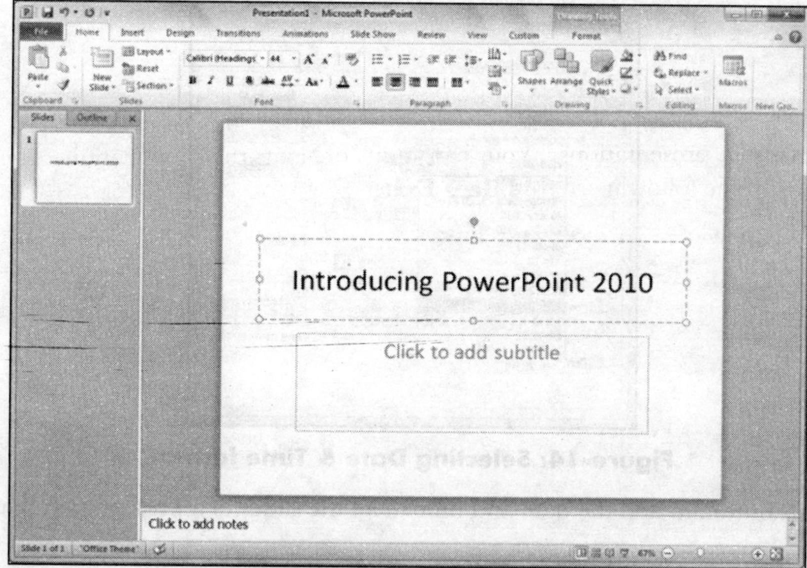

Figure-12: Inserting text in title box

Similarly, you can add more text in a slide depending on the requirement.

4.5.2 Adding Current Date and Time

You can add current date and time to one or all the slides of your PowerPoint presentation by using the Insert tab. By default, current date and time is displayed at the bottom left corner of a slide; however, you can display date and time at any other location in the slide.

Let's perform the following steps to add date and time in a slide:

1. Select the **Date & Time** option from the **Text** group of the **Insert** tab (Figure-13).

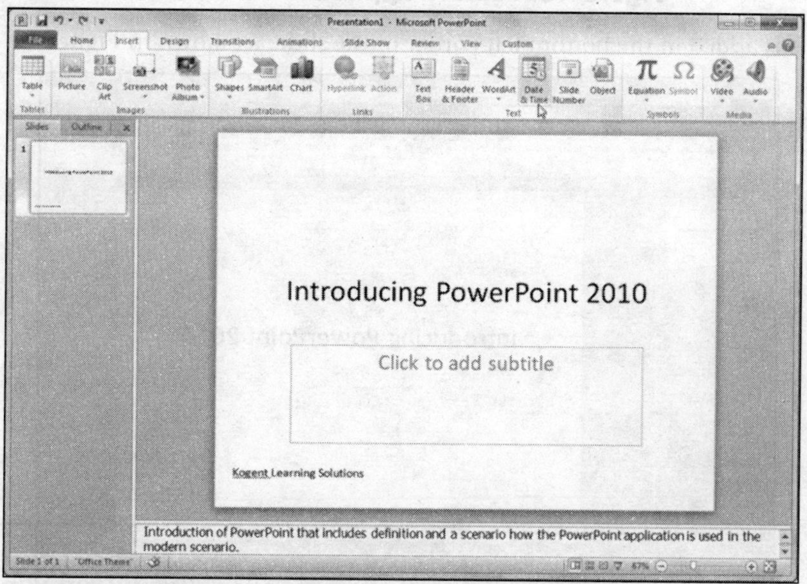

Figure-13: Selecting Date & Time option

The **Header and Footer** dialog box appears (Figure-14).

2. Select the **Date and Time** checkbox under the **Slide** tab (Figure-14).
3. Click the down arrow below the **Update Automatically** radio button (Figure-14). A drop-down list appears.
4. Select the desired date and time format from the drop-down list, as shown in Figure-14.

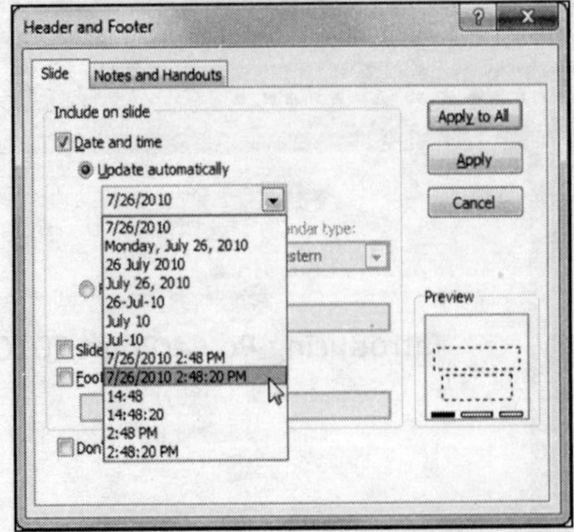

Figure-14: Selecting Date & Time format

5. Click the **Apply to All** button to add the date and time to all the slides of a presentation (Figure-15).

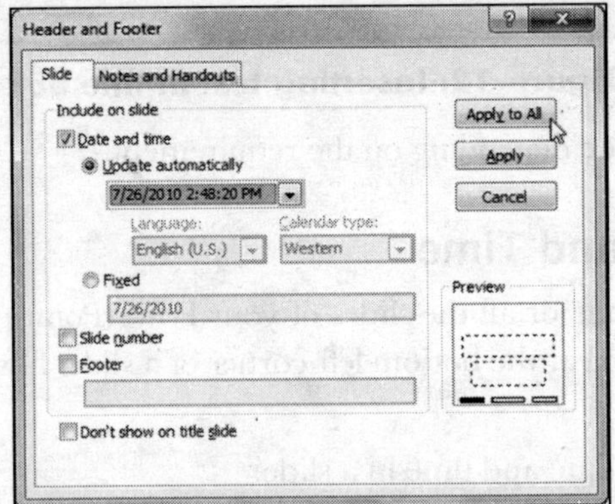

Figure-15: Feature applied to all slides

The current date and time is added in the bottom left corner of the slide, as shown in Figure-16:

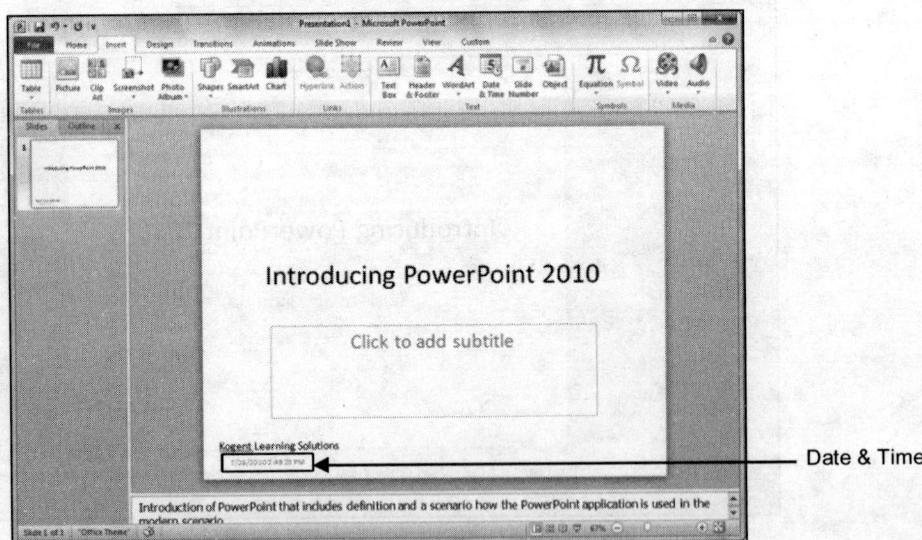

Figure-16: Showing Date & Time

Let's now learn how to add slide number.

4.5.3 Adding Slide Number

Adding slide numbers helps you to organize the sequence of the slides when needed. You can move slides up and down in the Slides pane as per the requirement. By default, the slide number appears at the bottom right of each slide; however, you can display it at any other location by dragging it.

Let's perform the following steps to add slide numbers in a presentation:

1. Select the **Slide Number** button in the **Text** group of the **Insert** tab (Figure-17).

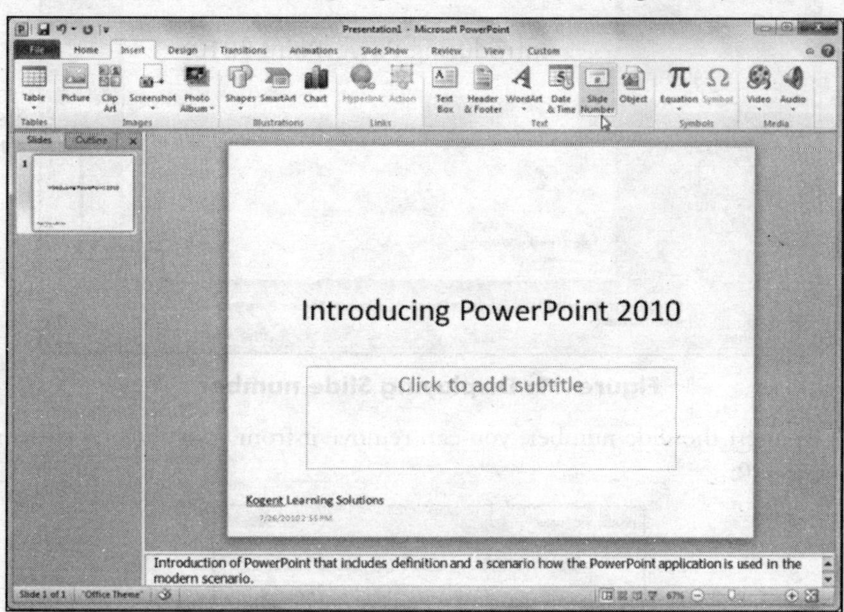

Figure-17: Slide without slide number

The **Header and Footer** dialog box appears (Figure-18).

2 Select the **Slide number** checkbox under the **Slide** tab (Figure-18).

3. Click the **Apply to All** button to add the slide number to all the slides of a presentation, as shown in Figure-18:

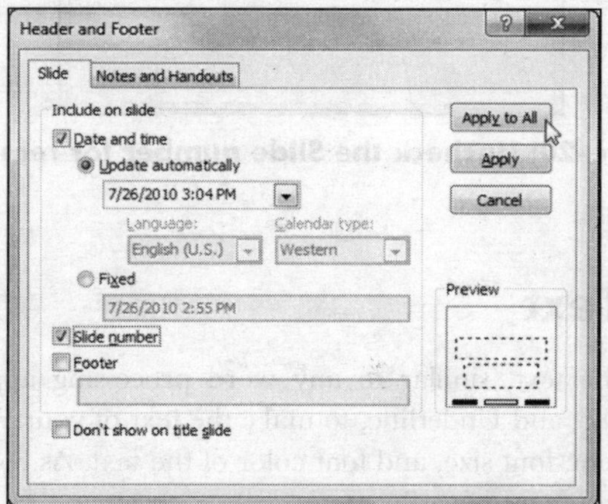

Figure-18: Applying slide number to all slides

The slide number is added in the bottom right of the slide (Figure-19).

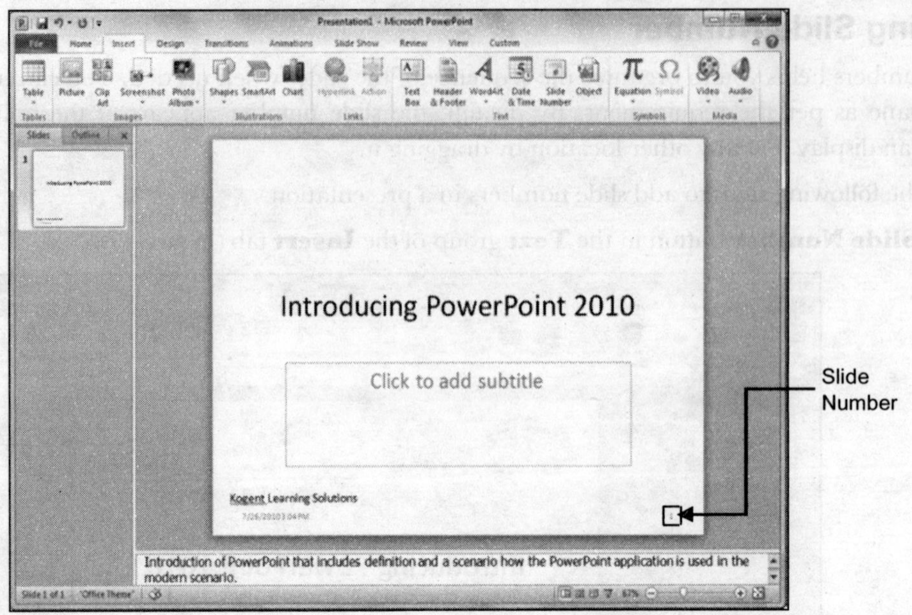

Figure-19: Displaying Slide number

In case you do not want to insert the slide number, you can remove it from your slide by clearing the **Slide number** checkbox, as shown in Figure-20:

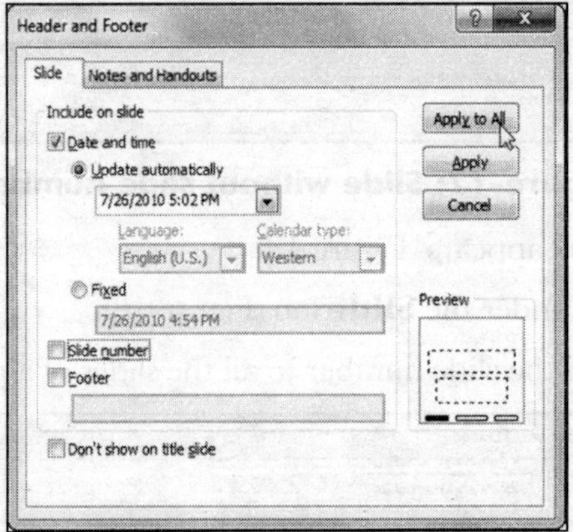

Figure-20: Uncheck the Slide number for removal

Let's now learn how to format the text.

4.6 Formatting the Text

PowerPoint allows you to format the text, similar to any word processing application. You can use some basic formatting features, such as Bold, Italic, and Underline, to make the text of your PowerPoint slides more readable and attractive. You can also change the font, font size, and font color of the text. As compared to the unformatted text, the formatted text grabs the viewer's attention more easily.

In the following sections, you learn how to apply formatting features to the text and work with font properties.

4.6.1 Applying Formatting Features

You can apply the basic formatting features, such as Bold, Italic, and Underline, to the text to emphasize it. These formatting features can be applied to the words or phrases that require special attention from the audience.

Let's perform the following steps to make the text bold:

1. Select the text that you want to make bold. In our case, we have selected **Introducing PowerPoint 2010** (Figure-21).

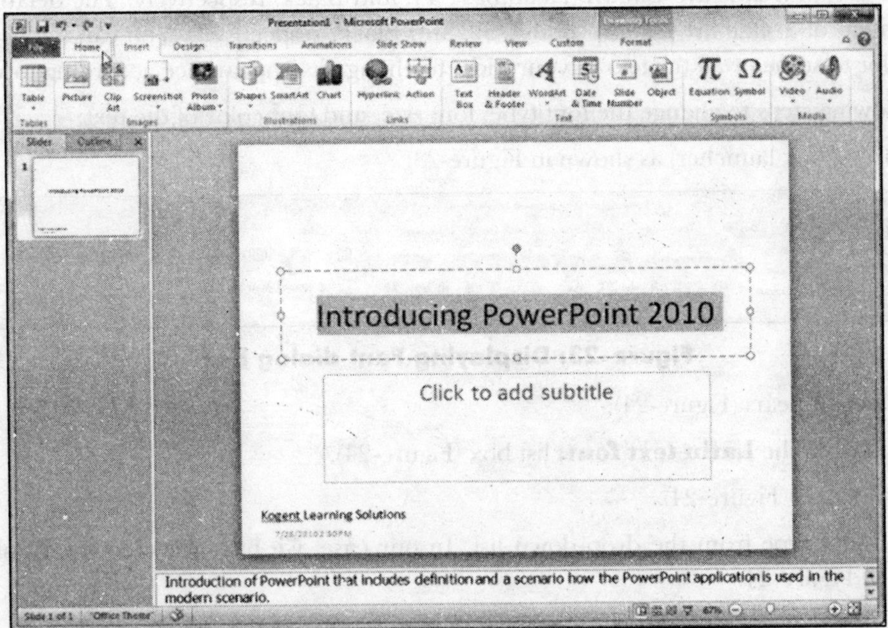

Figure-21: Selecting text

2. Select the **Home** tab (Figure-21). The **Home** tab opens (Figure-22).
3. Click the **Bold** button, as shown in Figure-22:

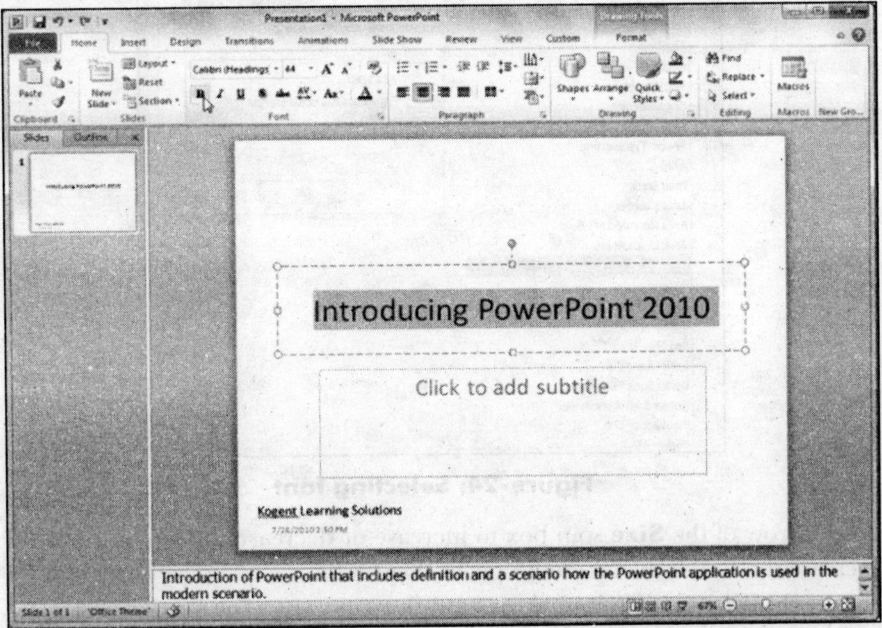

Figure-22: Applying formatting on selected text

You can also italicize the text by clicking the **Italic** button and similarly underline by clicking the **Underline** button.

4.6.2 Changing Font Type, Font Size, and Font Color of the Text

You can change the default font, font size, and font color of the text present on a slide. The default font, font size, and font color for the title text of a slide are Calibri (Headings), 44, and Black, respectively. The default font, font size, and font color for the content of a slide are Calibri (Body), 32, and Black, respectively. You can apply a different font type, font size, and font color to some or all the text of your slide, to change its appearance according to your requirements.

Let's perform the following steps to change the font type, font size, and font color of the text:

1. Click the **Font** dialog box launcher, as shown in Figure-23:

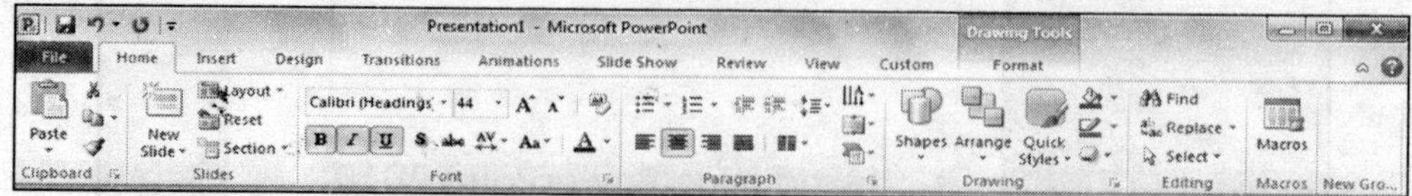

Figure-23: Displaying Font dialog box

   The **Font** dialog box appears (Figure-24).

2. Click the down arrow of the **Latin text font:** list box (Figure-24).

   A drop-down list appears (Figure-24).

3. Select the desired font type from the drop-down list. In our case, we have selected the **Baskerville Old Face** option, as shown in Figure-24:

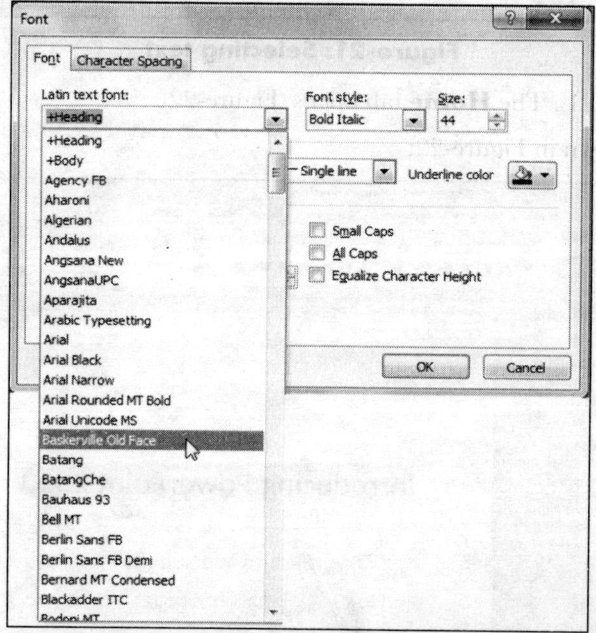

Figure-24: Selecting font

4. Click the up or down arrow of the **Size** spin box to increase or decrease the font size. In our case, we have clicked the up arrow to increase the size of the text to **45** pixels (Figure-25).

5. Click the drop-down arrow button beside the **Font color** option under the **Font** tab (Figure-25).

   The **Theme Colors** palette appears, displaying different types of colors (Figure-25).

6. Select the desired color from the **Theme Colors** palette. In our case, we have selected the **Red, Accent 2, Darker 25%** option (Figure-25).

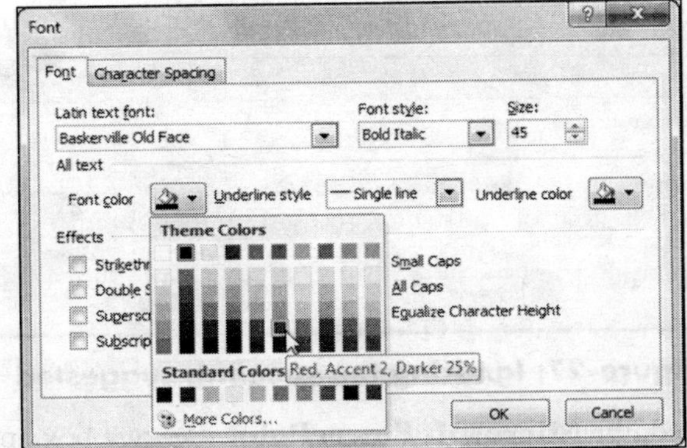

Figure-25: Selecting font color

7. Click the **OK** button.

The font of the selected text is modified, as shown in Figure-26:

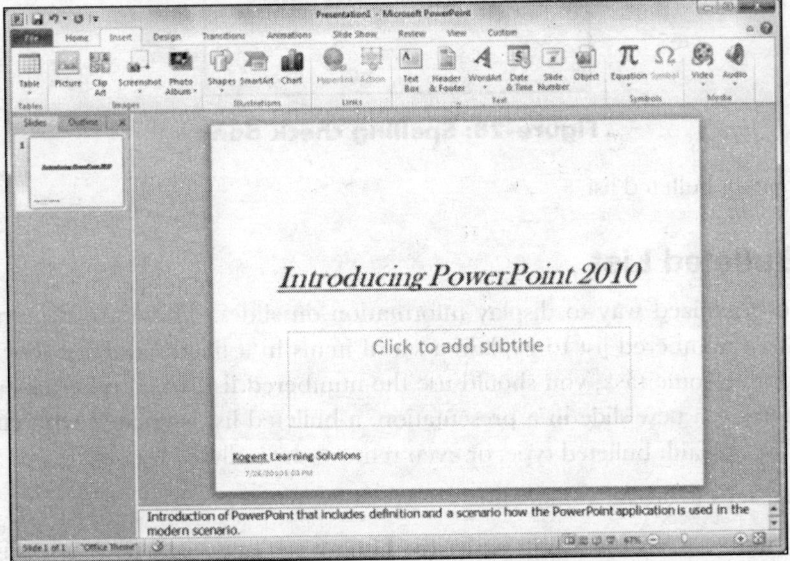

Figure-26: Text after formatting

Let's now learn how to check the spelling in presentation.

4.6.3 Performing Spell Check

PowerPoint provides you a spelling checker tool, which you can use to quickly determine spelling errors in your presentation. PowerPoint's spelling checker works in background and as you type a word, it immediately checks the word for spelling errors. It compares the word you have typed with the words present in PowerPoint's dictionary. If the spelling checker fails to find the word in the dictionary, it shows a spelling error by underlining the word with a red wavy line.

Let's perform the following steps to perform a spell check:

1. Open an existing presentation
2. Select the **Review** tab
3. Click the **Spelling** button.

   The Spelling dialog box appears (Figure-27). PowerPoint's spelling checker starts scanning the presentation for spelling errors when it finds the first misspelled word, it displays the word along with some suggested words in the Spelling dialog box.

4. Click the **Ignore** button in case if you do not want to change the word, as shown in Figure-27:

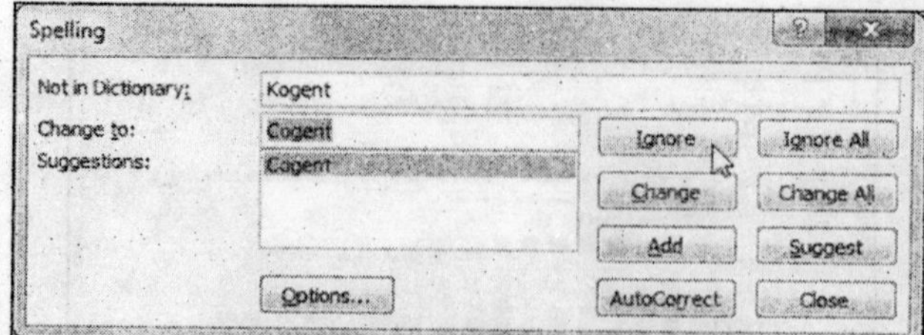

Figure-27: Ignoring the speeling suggested

When the spell check is completed, the **Microsoft PowerPoint** message box appears (Figure-28).

5. Click the **OK** button to close the message box, as shown in Figure-28:

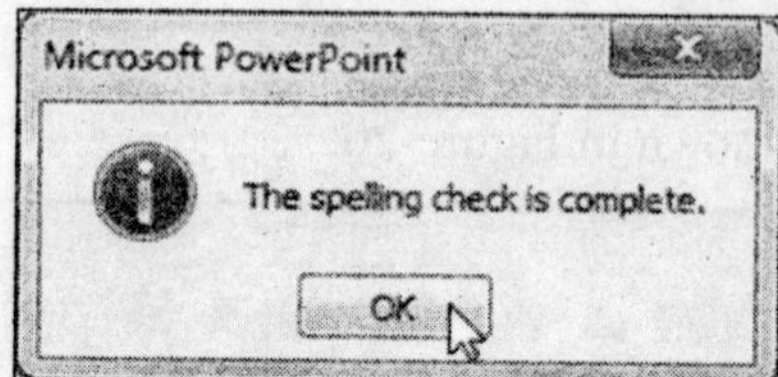

Figure-28: Spelling check done

Let's now learn how to create a bulleted list.

4.6.4 Creating a Bulleted List

Lists provide a better and organized way to display information on slides. There are two types of lists, bulleted and numbered. You should use a numbered list to explain a set of items in a fixed sequence. For example, if you need to explain the steps of performing some task, you should use the numbered list. In all other cases, you can use a bulleted list. By default, when you insert a new slide in a presentation, a bulleted list is created with circle as the bulleted type. However, you can modify the default bulleted type, or even remove the bulleted list.

Let's perform the following steps to create a bullet list:

1. Click the **New Slide** button of **Slides** group under the **Home** tab to insert a new slide (Figure-29).

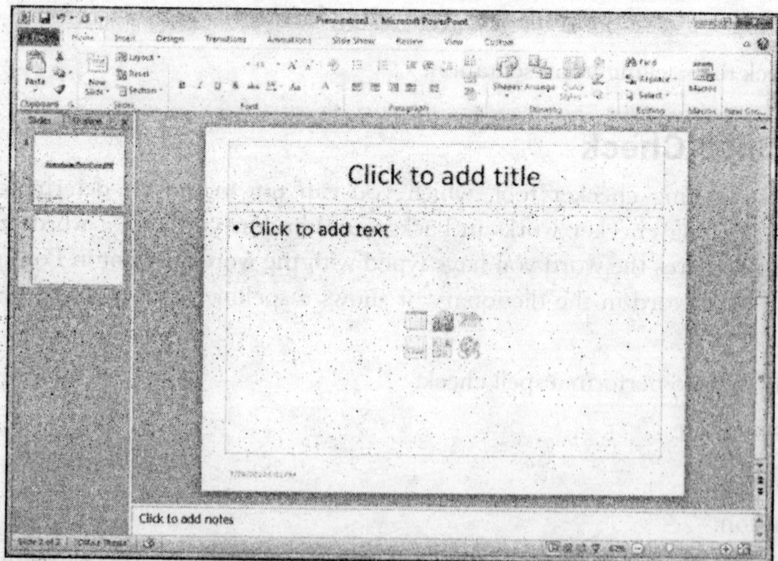

Figure-29: Displaying New slide

2. Insert the desired text in the slide (Figure-30). In our case, we have inserted the following text:

   ⇨ PowerPoint 2010 Features

   - ♦ Video conversion
   - ♦ Video cropping
   - ♦ Backstage view
   - ♦ Collaboration
   - ♦ Sharing

   The text is inserted in the slide, as shown in Figure-30:

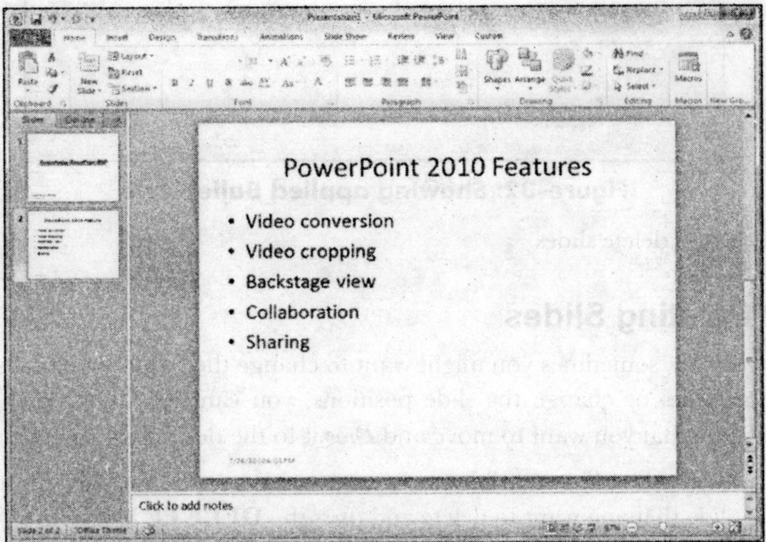

Figure-30: Showing Text added to the new slide

3. Select the bulleted list (Figure-31).
4. Click the down arrow of the **Bullets** button under the **Paragraph** group in the **Home** tab (Figure-31).

   A drop-down list appears with the default bullet type selected (Figure-31).

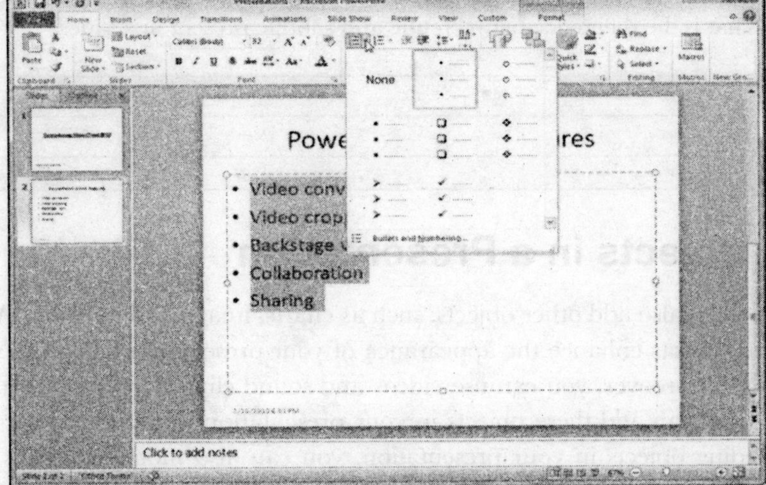

Figure-31: Selecting bullet style

5. Select the desired bullet type from the drop-down list. In our case, we have selected the **Star Bullets** type.

The desired bullet type is applied to the text, as shown in Figure-32:

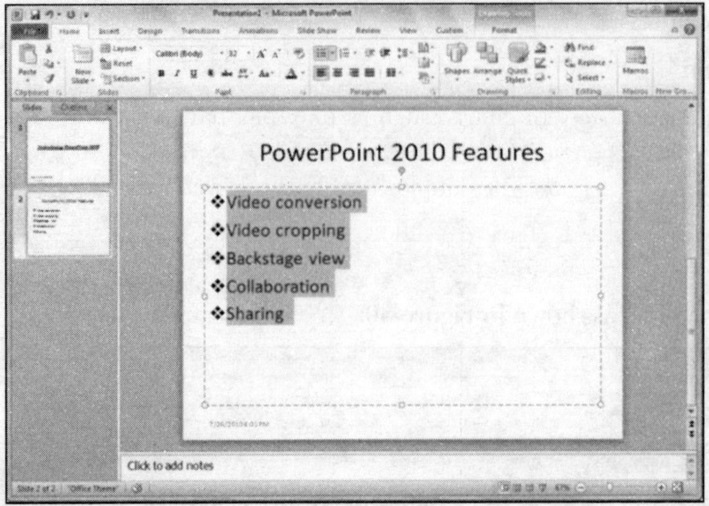

Figure-32: Showing applied Bullet style

Let's now learn how to move and delete slides.

4.6.5 Moving and Deleting Slides

After completing the presentation, sometimes you might want to change the sequence of the slides. In PowerPoint 2010, if you want to re-order the slides or change the slide positions, you can do so by moving the slides at the desired positions. Simply, *Select* the slide that you want to move and *Drag* it to the desired location.

At the time of creating a presentation, if some slides seem unnecessary and you wish to remove them, you can easily delete those slides. *Select* the slide that you want to delete and *press* the **DELETE** key.

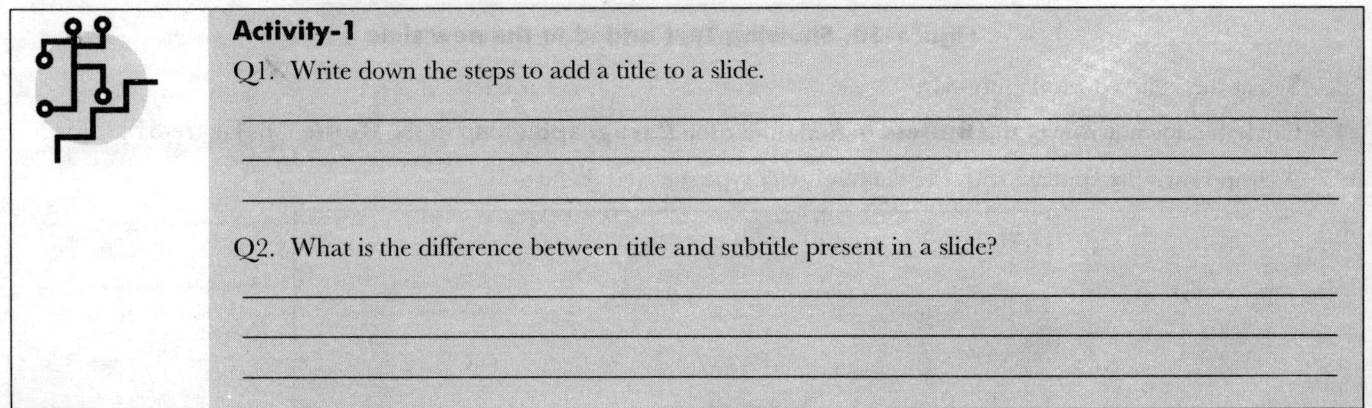

Activity-1

Q1. Write down the steps to add a title to a slide.

Q2. What is the difference between title and subtitle present in a slide?

4.7 Inserting Objects in a Presentation

Apart from adding text, you can also add other objects, such as charts, images, tables, WordArt, videos, and audio clips, in your presentation. These objects enhance the appearance of your presentation and grab viewer's attention easily as compared to the simple text. Moreover, you can use videos and sound clips in your presentation to make it lively and interesting to the viewers. You can add these objects in your presentation by using the options available in the Insert and Format tabs. After adding objects in your presentation, you can also modify them as per the requirement. For example, after adding an image in the presentation, you can change its color and background to match it with the background of the slides of your presentation. You can even crop some specific part of the image to emphasize more on that part.

4.7.1 Adding Charts to a Slide

A chart is a graphical representation of data or information. In simple words, you can say that a chart is a visual representation of a set of numbers. It can be used to communicate numeric information in a concise format. For example, you can use charts in your presentation to show sales revenue of your organization to the employees of your company. PowerPoint includes a variety of charts, such as line, pie, bar, area, and radar. Note that you can use the chart facilities in PowerPoint only when you have Microsoft Excel 2010 installed on your system. It is due to this reason that when you create a chart in PowerPoint, the data for the chart is stored in the Excel worksheet.

Let's perform the following steps to add a chart to a slide:

1. Create a new presentation.
2. Select the **Insert** tab (Figure-33).

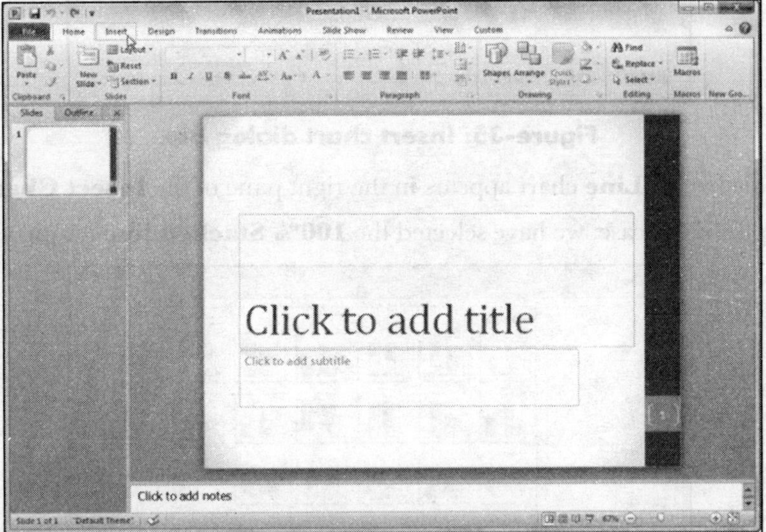

Figure-33: Displaying Insert tab

The groups present in the **Insert** tab are displayed (Figure-34).

3. Select the **Chart** button under the **Illustrations** group in the **Insert** tab, as shown in Figure-34:

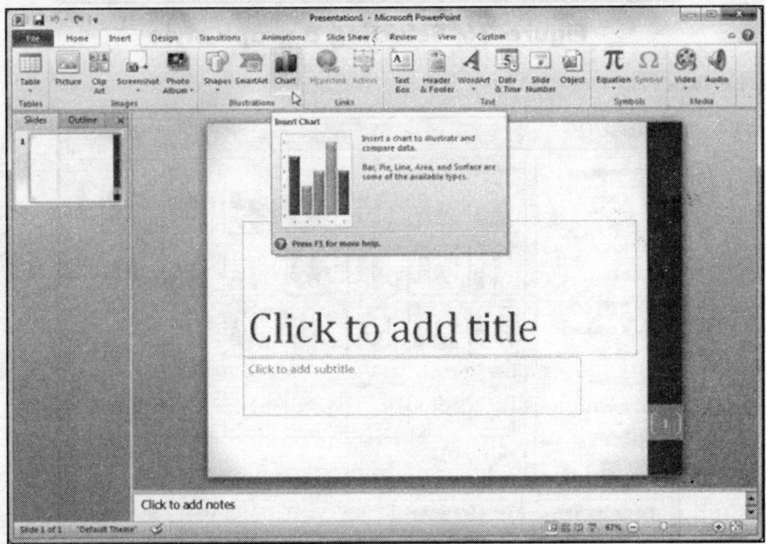

Figure-34: Displaying Chart button

The **Insert Chart** dialog box appears (Figure-35).

4. Select the desired chart type from the left pane of the **Insert Chart** dialog box. In our case, we have selected the **Line** chart (Figure-35).

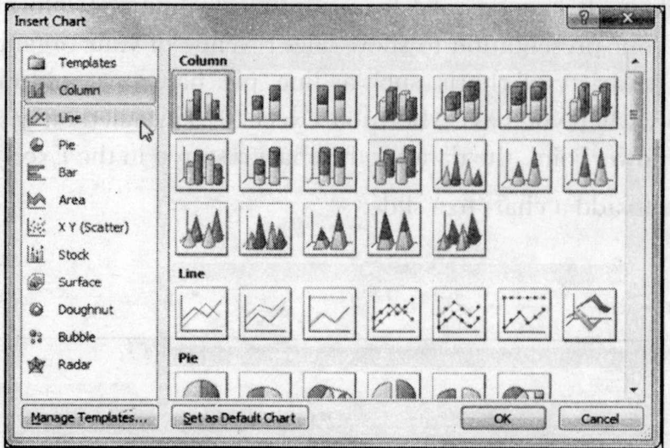

Figure-35: Insert chart dialog box

A list of graphs available for the **Line** chart appears in the right pane of the **Insert Chart** dialog box.

5. Select the desired graph. In our case, we have selected the **100% Stacked line** graph, as shown in Figure-36:

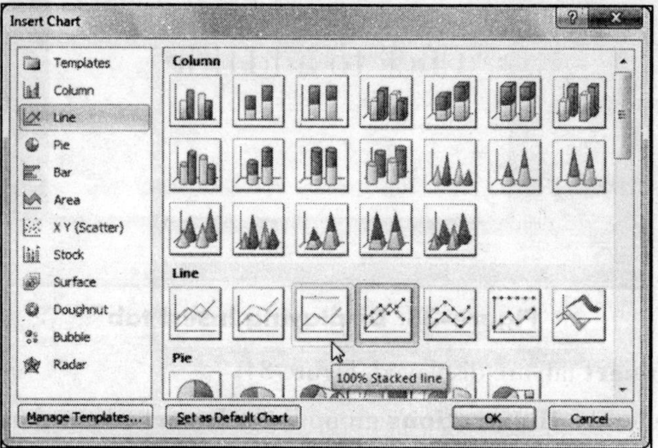

Figure-36: Selecting a graph style

6. Click the **OK** button (Figure-37).

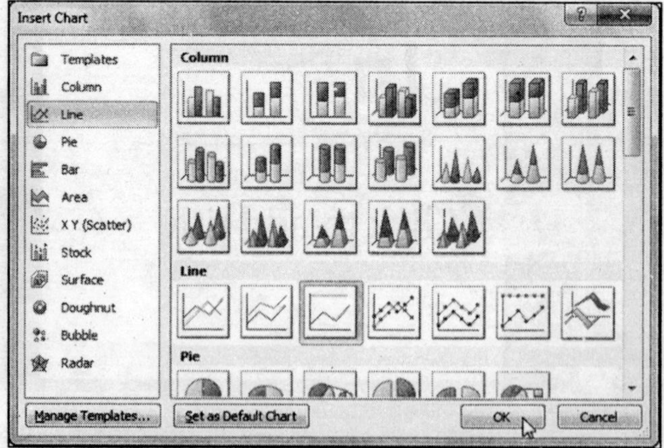

Figure-37: Click the OK button

The chart is inserted in the current slide, as shown in Figure-38:

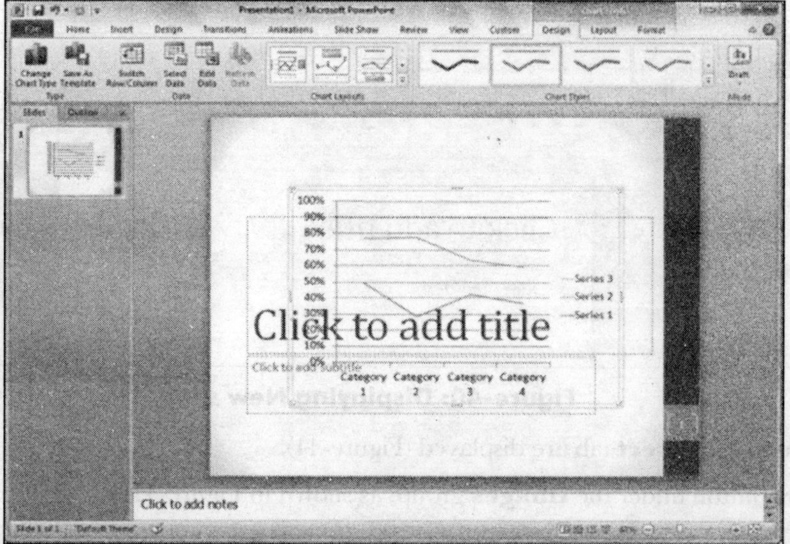

Figure-38: Displaying Chart in the Current Slide

Automatically, an Excel worksheet appears, displaying the default chart data, as shown in Figure-39:

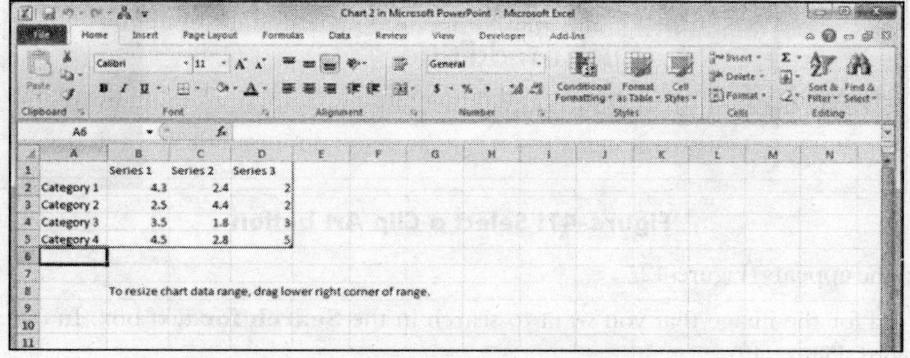

Figure-39: Displaying Default Chart Data

	Q1. What is the requirement of adding graphs to a slide in a presentation?

Let's now learn to work with clip arts.

4.7.2 Working with Clip Arts

A clip art refers to a vector-based image that is available in Windows Metafile Format (WMF). Clip arts are built-in images used to represent content in visual format. The clip arts can be resized without getting blurred or distorted. Microsoft PowerPoint 2010 provides you the ClipArt feature to insert clip art in your presentation. This feature contains thousands of images of different categories, such as arts, illustrations, borders, sports, education, animals, family, and art.

In this section, you learn how to insert clip arts into a slide and modify the inserted clip arts.

Inserting a Clip Art

As the clip arts are built-in graphics, you can use them to make your presentation more attractive. Nowadays, the clip arts are used at a large level in both personal and commercial presentations to attract the customers. Let's perform the following steps to insert a clip art in a slide:

1. Insert a new slide in an existing presentation (Figure-40).
2. Select the **Insert** tab (Figure-40).

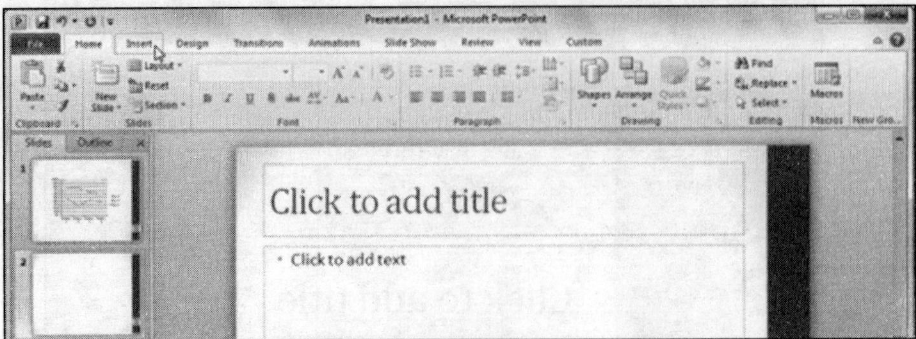

Figure-40: Displaying New slide

The groups present in the **Insert** tab are displayed (Figure-41).

3. Select the **Clip Art** button under the **Images** group, as shown in Figure-41:

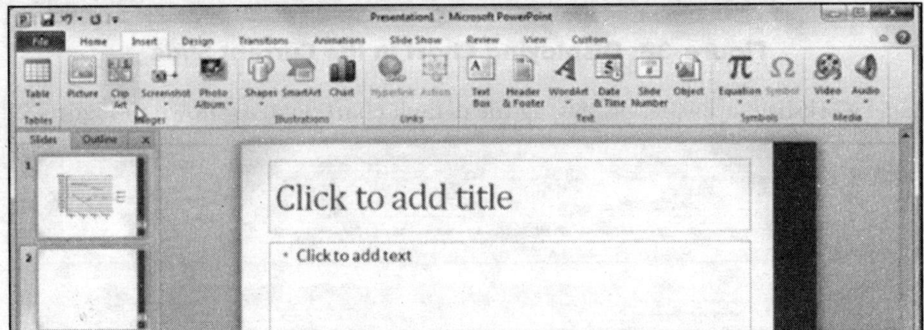

Figure-41: Select a Clip Art button

The **Clip Art** pane appears (Figure-42).

4. Type the keyword for the image that you want to search in the **Search for** text box. In our case, we have typed the **cloud** keyword (Figure-42).
5. Click the **Go** button (Figure-42).

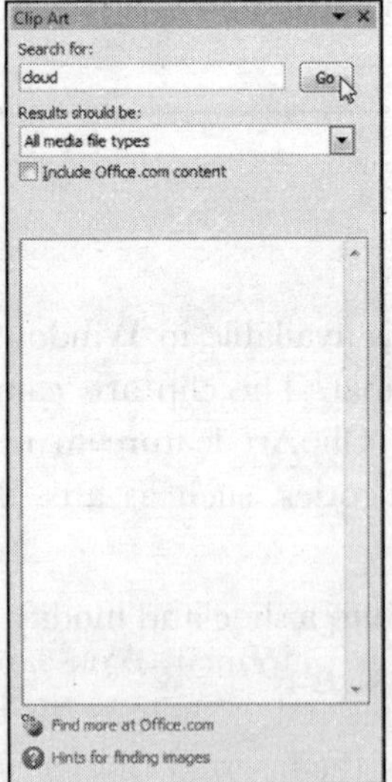

Figure-42: Clip art pane

Different images related to the **cloud** keyword are displayed (Figure-43).

6. Select the image that you want to insert in a slide (Figure-43).

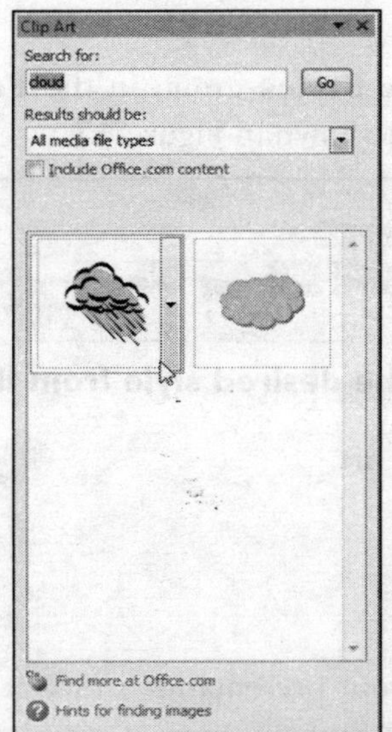

Figure-43: Images for cloud

The selected image is inserted in the slide.

7. Click the **Close** button of the **Clip Art** pane to close it, as shown in Figure-44:

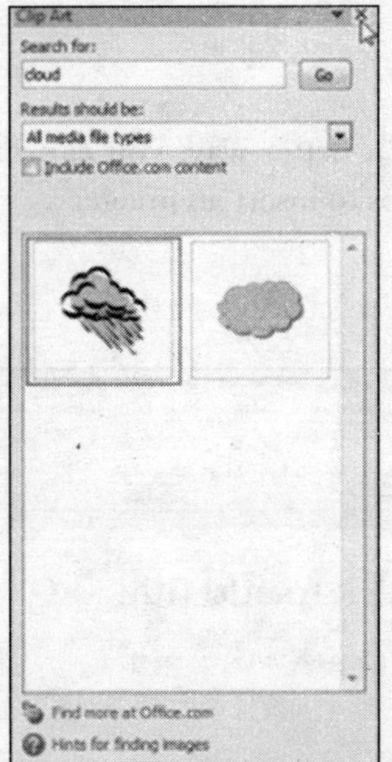

Figure-44: Closing Clip Art

Let's now learn how to modify the inserted clip art.

Modifying a Clip Art

PowerPoint 2010 lets you modify the inserted clip art according to your requirement. You can change the image's background, color, layout, and effect as per the requirement. You can also crop the inserted image and change its size and position. In addition, you can apply various styles, such as **Metal Frame** and **Simple Frame, White** to the image. In our case, we are modifying the style of the inserted clip art.

Perform the following steps to modify the clip art:

1. Select the clip art that you want to modify. In our case, we have selected the clip art inserted in the preceding section (Figure-44).
2. Select the desired style from the **Picture Styles** group in the **Format** tab. In our case, we have selected the **Reflected Rounded Rectangle** style, as shown in Figure-45:

Figure-45: Selecting the desired style from the Picture Styles group

The selected picture style is applied on the clip art.

Let's now learn how to work with images.

4.7.3 Working with Images

In PowerPoint 2010, you can add images in your presentation to make it interesting and expressive. PowerPoint 2010 provides images in various file formats, such as Bitmap (.bmp), Graphical Interchange Format (.gif), Joint Photographic Experts Group (.jpeg), and Portable Network Graphics (.png). The images may be your personal photos, diagrams, or the pictures that you use as wallpaper in your system.

In this section, you learn how to insert, recolor, crop, and rotate an image in a presentation. Let's first learn to insert an image in the presentation.

Inserting an Image

Since images help in representing an idea in a better way, you can insert the image in your presentation to make it more effective. Let's perform the following steps to insert an image:

1. Insert a new slide (Figure-46).
2. Select the **Insert** tab (Figure-46).

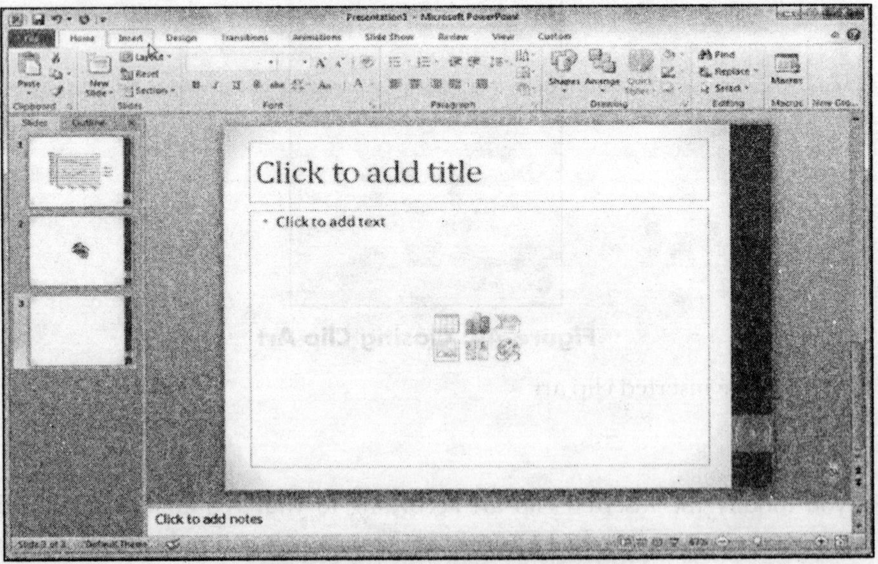

Figure-46: Inserting New slide

The groups present in the **Insert** tab are displayed (Figure-47).

3. Click the **Picture** button under the **Images** group, as shown in Figure-47:

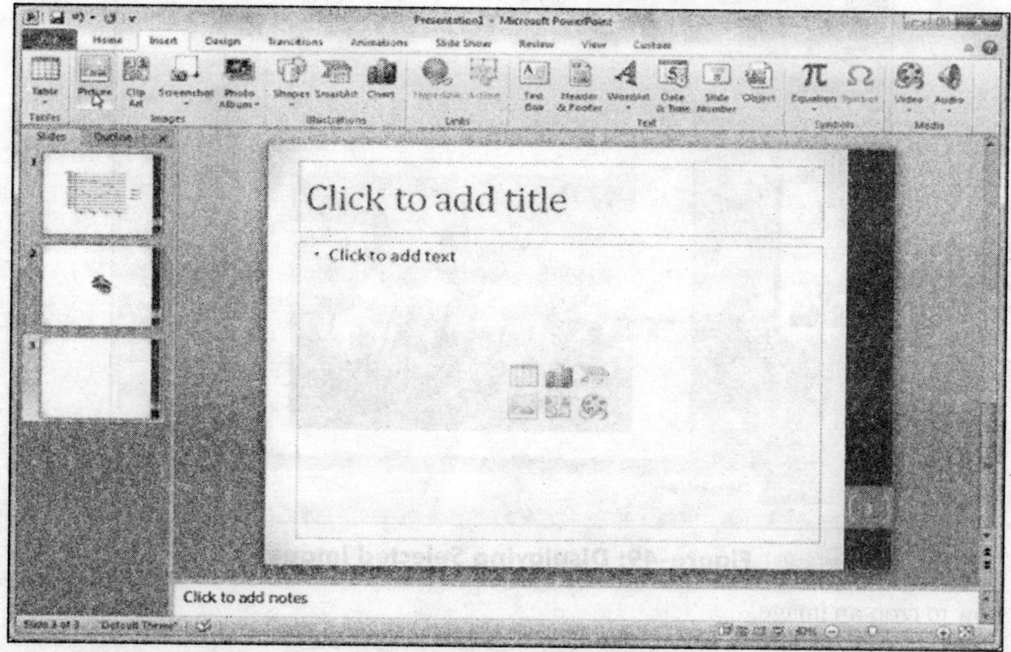

Figure-47: Displaying Picture button under the Images group

The **Insert Picture** dialog box appears (Figure-48).

4. Browse to the location where the image that you want to insert in your presentation is saved. In our case, we have selected the **Sample Pictures** folder (Figure-48).
5. Select the desired image. In our case, we have selected the **Tulips** image (Figure-48).
6. Click the **Insert** button (Figure-48).

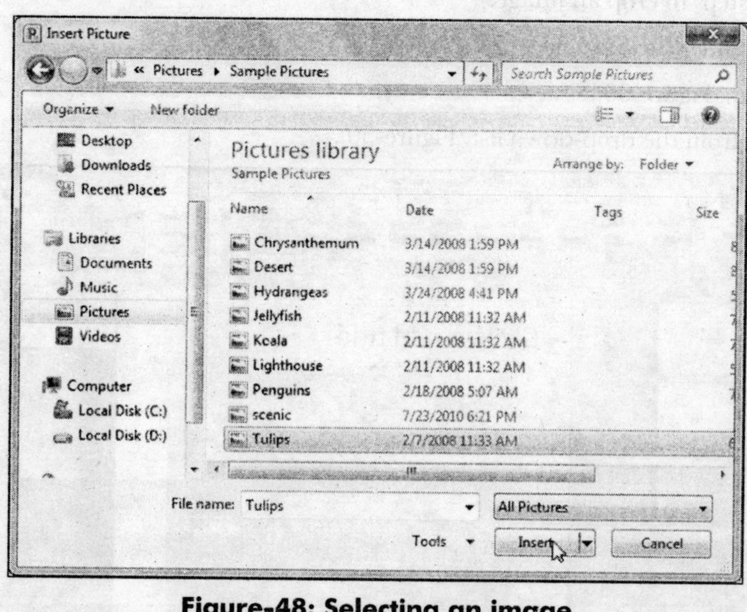

Figure-48: Selecting an image

The desired image is inserted in the current slide, as shown in Figure-49:

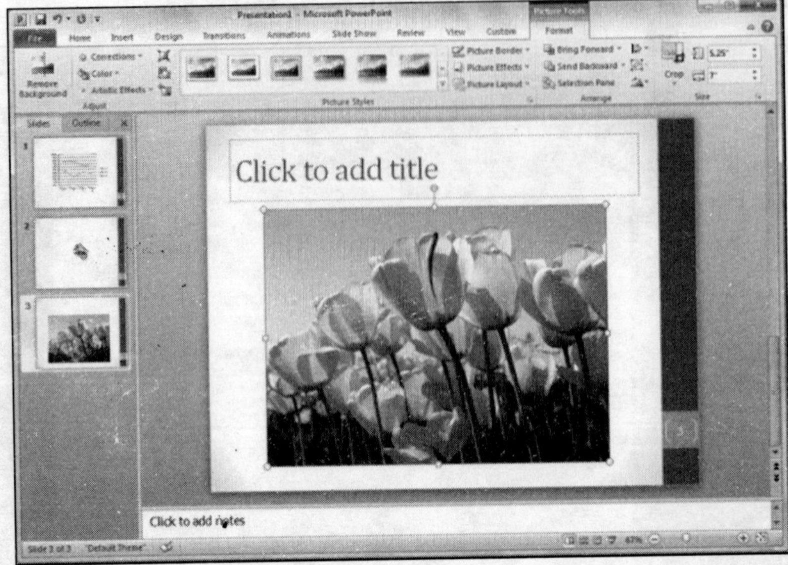

Figure-49: Displaying Selected image

Let's now learn how to crop an image.

Cropping an Image

Some images are of large size and do not fit in a slide when you insert them in your presentation. In addition, sometimes you may need to focus on some particular portion of an image. In such cases, you can crop the image by using the cropping feature of Microsoft PowerPoint 2010. This feature lets you remove the unwanted portions of the picture so that the picture accurately fits to the slide. You can crop the inserted image in different ways, such as cropping the image to a customized shape and size as well as to a predefined shape.

Let's perform the following steps to crop an image:

1. Click the **Crop** button under the **Size** group (Figure-50).

   A drop-down list appears (Figure-50).

2. Select the **Crop** option from the drop-down list (Figure-50).

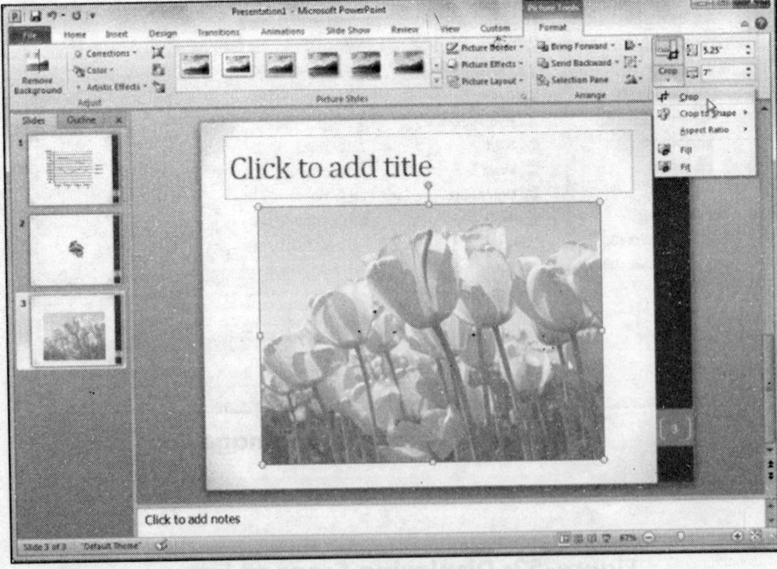

Figure-50: Selecting Crop option

The different cropping handles appear around the image, as shown in Figure-51:

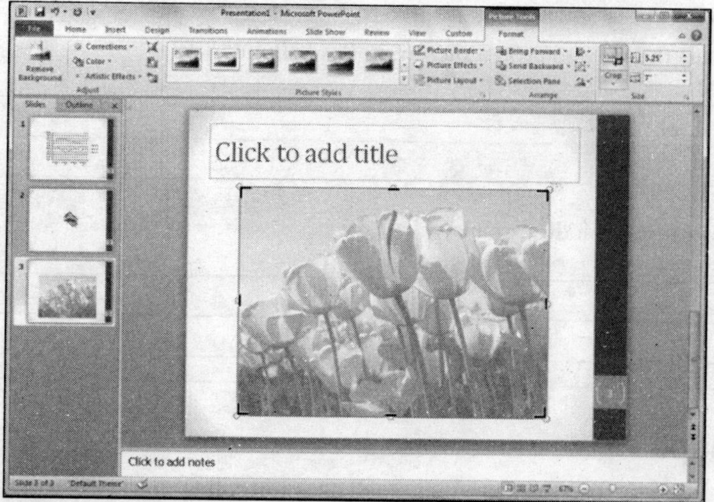

Figure-51: Cropping handles appear around the image

3. Click any cropping handle.
4. Drag the mouse pointer to the area to which you want to crop the image (Figure-52).

Figure-52: Selecting the Area to Crop

5. Release the mouse-button.
6. Click anywhere outside the slide.

The image is cropped, as shown in Figure-53:

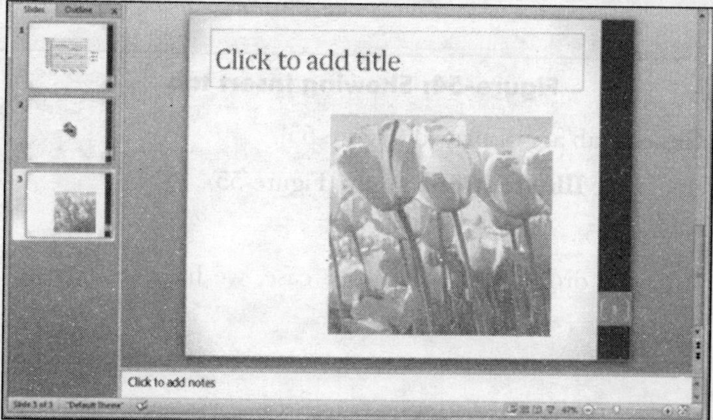

Figure-53: Displaying Cropped image

Let's now learn how to insert a shape in a presentation.

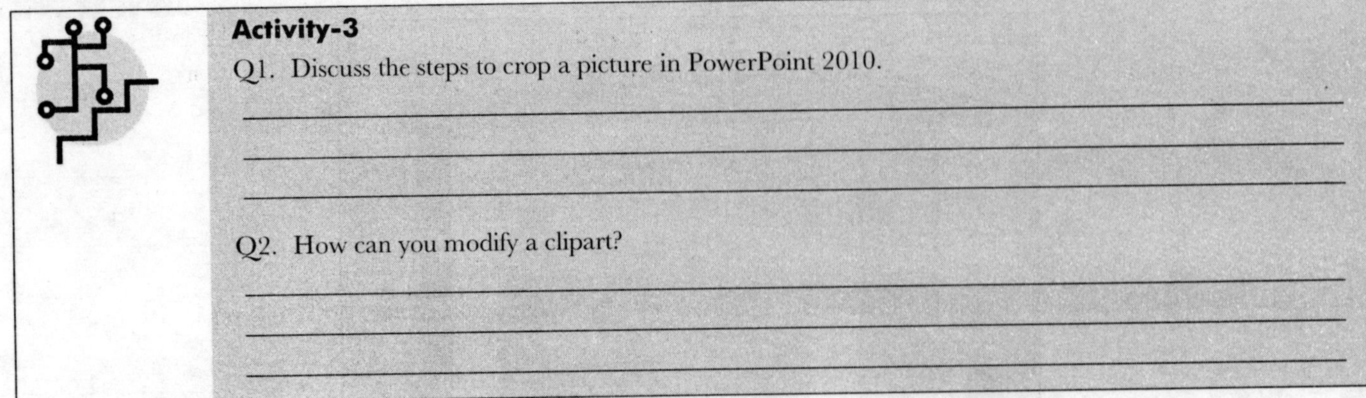

Activity-3

Q1. Discuss the steps to crop a picture in PowerPoint 2010.

Q2. How can you modify a clipart?

4.7.4 Inserting a Shape

Apart from inserting images, you can also insert shapes, such as square, line, and polygon in your presentation. You can insert shapes for various purposes, such as creating a presentation that needs some geometrical figures or representing the relationship between two entities while displaying the organizational hierarchy. Microsoft PowerPoint 2010 provides a wide variety of built-in Shape Style options, such as line, circle, rectangle, arrow, polygon, and clouds, which you can use in your presentation. After inserting a shape, you can also add text to it.

Let's perform the following steps to insert a shape in a presentation:

1. Select the **Insert** tab (Figure-54).

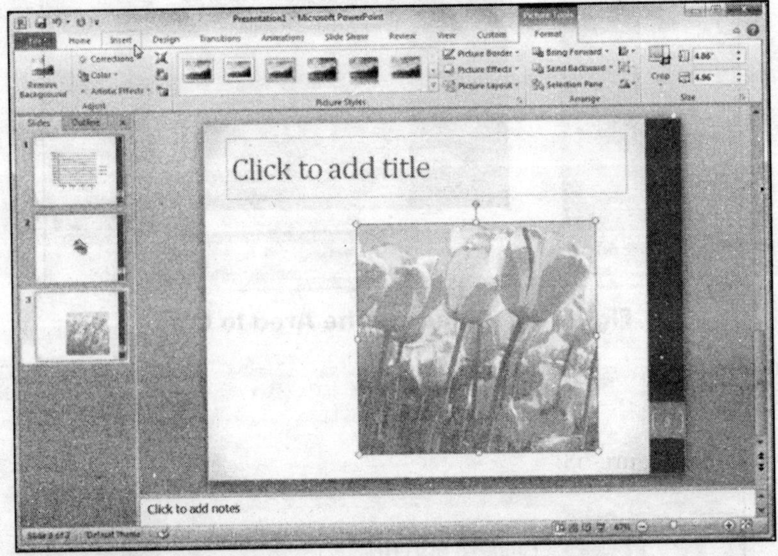

Figure-54: Showing Insert tab

The groups present in the **Insert** tab are displayed (Figure-55).

2. Click the **Shapes** button under the **Illustrations** group (Figure-55).

   A drop-down list appears (Figure-55).

3. Select the desired shape from the drop-down list. In our case, we have selected the **Wave** option, as shown in Figure-55:

Figure-55: Groups in Insert tab

4. Drag the mouse-pointer on the slide to draw the shape (Figure-56).

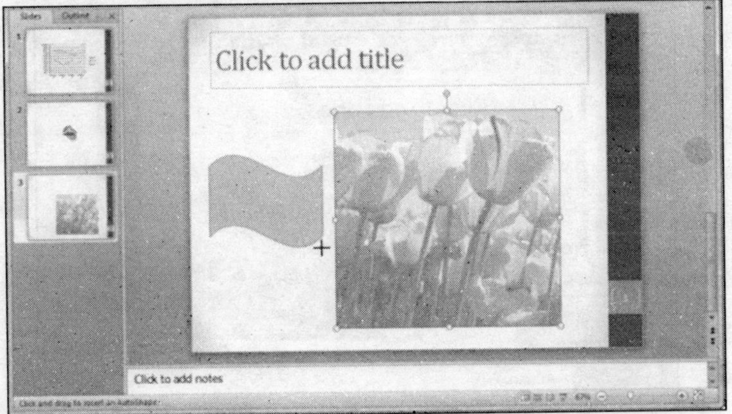

Figure-56: Draw the shape

The desired shape is inserted in the current slide, as shown in Figure-57:

Figure-57: Desired shape inserted

Perform the following steps to add text to the inserted shape:

1. Right-click the desired shape. A context menu appears (Figure-58).
2. Select the **Edit Text** option from the context menu (Figure-58).

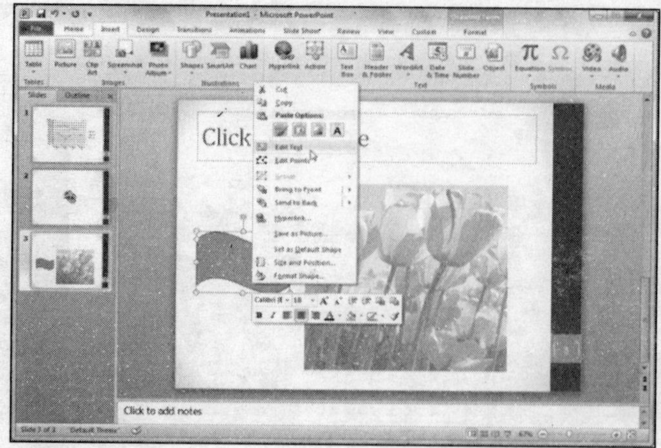

Figure-58: Context menu for desired shape

The cursor appears inside the shape (Figure-59).

3. Type the desired text in the shape. In our case, we have typed **Nature**, as shown in Figure-59:

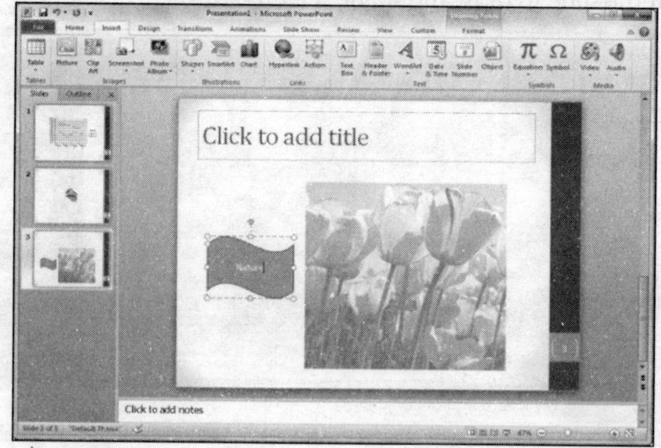

Figure-59: Writing text inside the shape

4. Click anywhere in the slide.

The text is inserted in the shape (Figure-60).

Figure-60: Text inside the shape

You can also customize the inserted shape, depending on the requirement, with the help of Shape Styles group (Figure-61) present in the Format tab. This group consists of options, such as shape fill, shape outline, and shape effects.

Figure-61: Shape Styles group

Let's now learn to insert WordArt in a presentation.

4.7.5 Inserting WordArt

WordArt is a collection of various text styles that are grouped together. Using the WordArt feature of PowerPoint, you can emphasize the text inserted in your presentation with decorative effects, such as shadowed or mirrored text. In addition, you can stretch a title, skew text, or apply a gradient fill on the text. Moreover, the text that you add as a WordArt acts as an object; therefore, you can move the text to any location according to the requirement.

Let's perform the following steps to insert a WordArt:

1. Select the **Insert** tab (Figure-62).

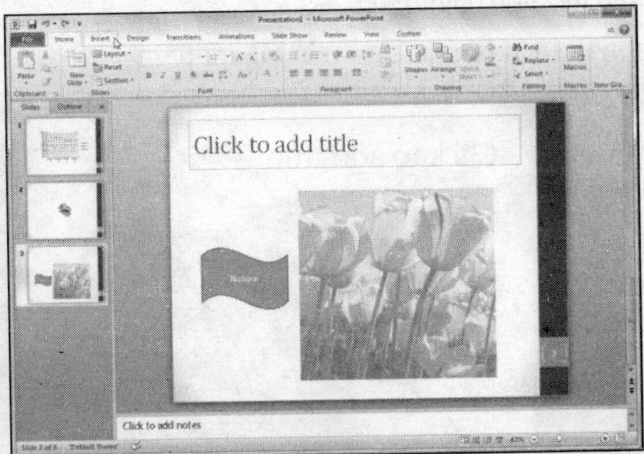

Figure-62: Insert tab

   The groups present in the **Insert** tab are displayed (Figure-63).

2. Click the **WordArt** button under the **Text** group (Figure-63).

   A drop-down list appears (Figure-63).

3. Select the desired WordArt style from the drop-down list, as shown in Figure-63:

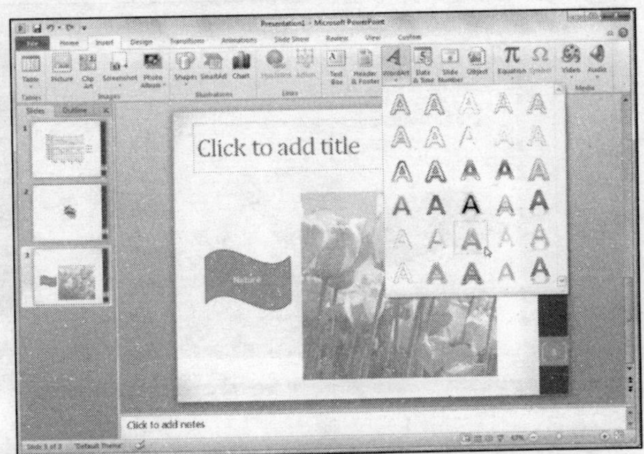

Figure-63: Groups in Insert tab

   The WordArt text box appears (Figure-64).

Figure-64: Word art text box

4. Move the text box to the desired location (Figure-65).
5. Select the default text present in the text box, as shown in Figure-65:

Figure-65: Default text present

6. Type the desired text in the text box. In our case, we have typed **Flowers** (Figure-66).

Figure-66: Typing the desired text

7. Click anywhere in the slide.

The WordArt is inserted in the current slide, as shown in Figure-67:

Figure-67: Word art is inserted

Let's now learn how to work with SmartArt graphics.

4.7.6 Working with SmartArt Graphics

SmartArt graphics are the stylish graphics used to design diagrams that represent a concept, relationship, hierarchy, cycle, or procedural steps. In other words, SmartArt graphics are professional looking and better designed shapes used to visually represent ideas. For example, you can also use the SmartArt graphics to design an organizational chart that depicts the management structure of an organization.

In this section, you learn how to insert a SmartArt graphic in your presentation and convert text into a SmartArt graphic.

Inserting a SmartArt Graphic

SmartArt graphics are generally used at a large level to design a set of presentation objects, such as flow charts, decision trees, and Venn diagrams. You can also include them into your document to leave a better impact on the end-users. When you insert a SmartArt graphic, the SmartArt Tools tab appears on the Ribbon. This is used to design and format SmartArt graphics.

Let's perform the following steps to insert a SmartArt graphic:

1. Insert a new slide (Figure-68).
2. Select the **Insert** tab (Figure-68).

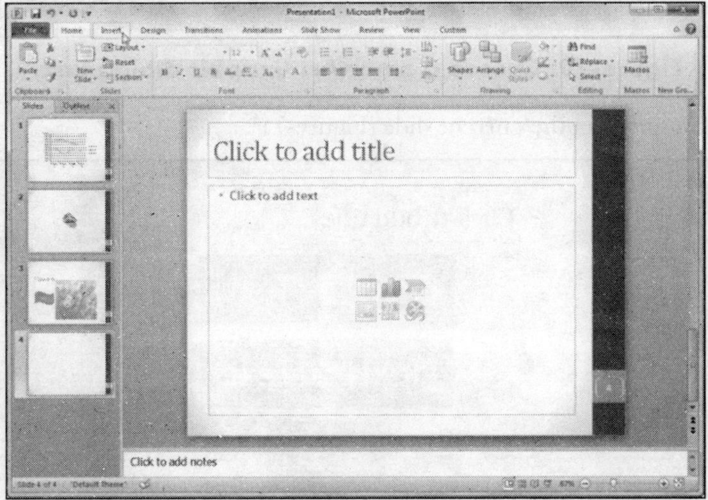

Figure-68: Insert tab

The groups present in the **Insert** tab are displayed (Figure-69).

3. Click the **SmartArt** button under the **Illustrations** group, as shown in Figure-69:

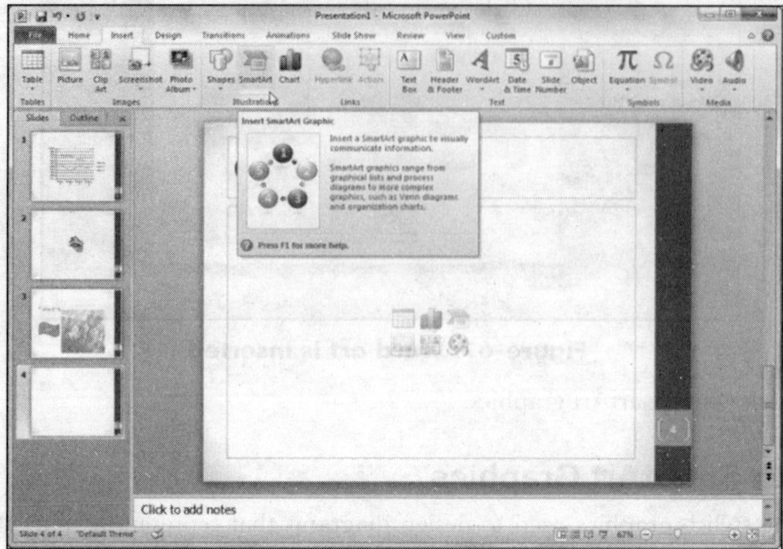

Figure-69: Groups in Insert tab

The **Choose a SmartArt Graphic** dialog box appears (Figure-70).

4. Select the desired shape from the middle pane of the **Choose a SmartArt Graphic** dialog box (Figure-70).
5. Click the **OK** button, as shown in Figure-70:

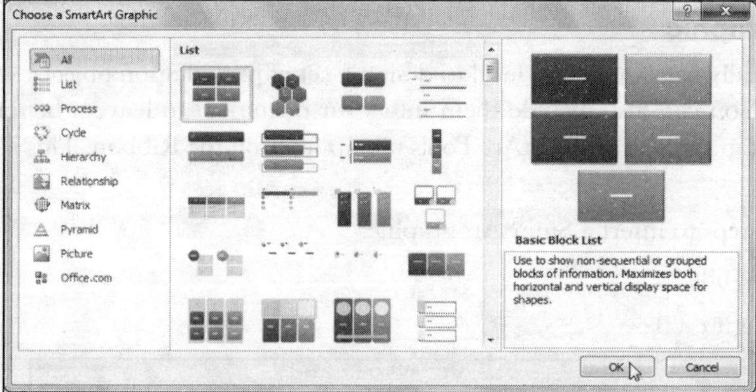

Figure-70: Choose a SmartArt Graphic dialog box

The **SmartArt** graphic is inserted in the current slide (Figure-71).

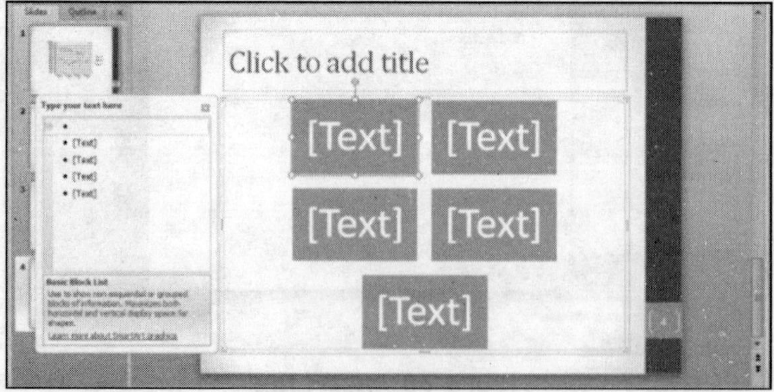

Figure-71: SmartArt graphic is inserted

6. Type the text that you want to insert in the first box of the SmartArt graphic in its corresponding text box that appears in the text pane, as shown in Figure-72:

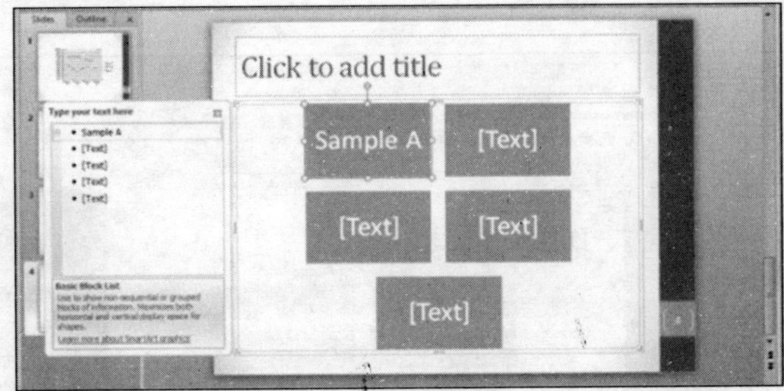

Figure-72: Text added to one text box

7. Similarly, you can add text for other boxes of the SmartArt graphic (Figure-73).

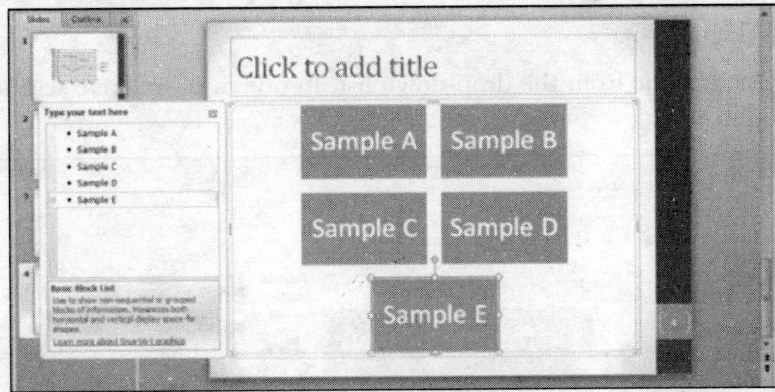

Figure-73: Adding text

8. Click anywhere in the slide.

   The SmartArt graphic appears with the desired text, as shown in Figure-74:

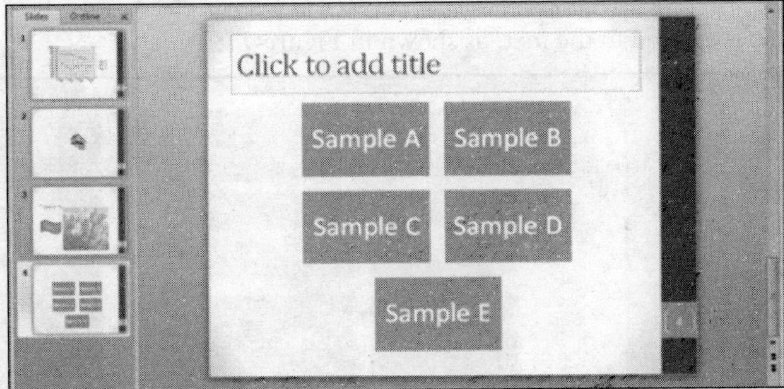

Figure-74: Desired text entered

Let's now learn how to convert text into a SmartArt Graphic.

Converting Text into SmartArt Graphic

Suppose you have a lot of text in your presentation and you need to view the text as graphics. In such case, you can convert the text into graphic by using the options present in the **Home** tab.

Let's perform the following steps to convert text into a SmartArt graphic:

1. Type the text that you want to convert into a SmartArt graphic in a slide. In our case, we have typed **Different samples** (Figure-75).

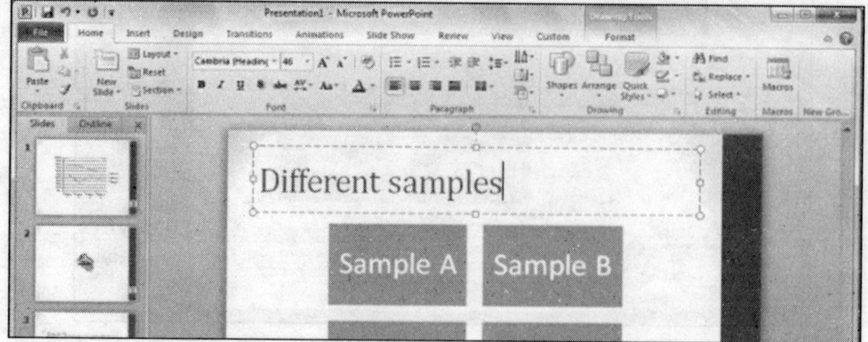

Figure-75: Type the text to convert into a SmartArt graphic

2. Click the **Convert to SmartArt Graphic** button under **Paragraph** group of **Home** tab (Figure-76).

   A drop-down list appears (Figure-76).

3. Select the desired SmartArt graphic from the drop-down list. In our case, we have selected **Vertical Bullet List**, as shown in Figure-76:

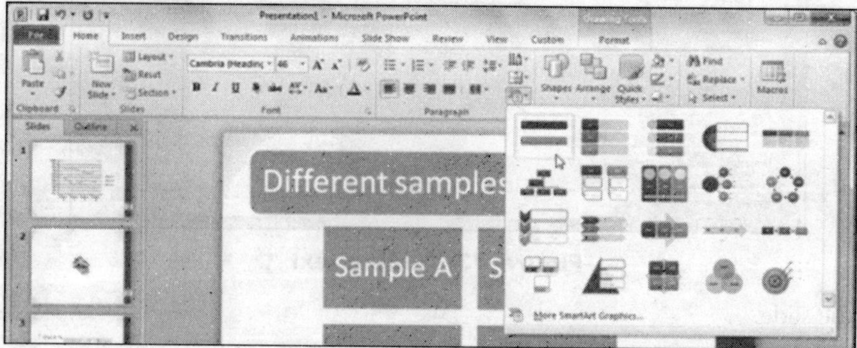

Figure-76: Select the desired SmartArt graphic

The selected SmartArt graphic is applied to the text, as shown in Figure-77:

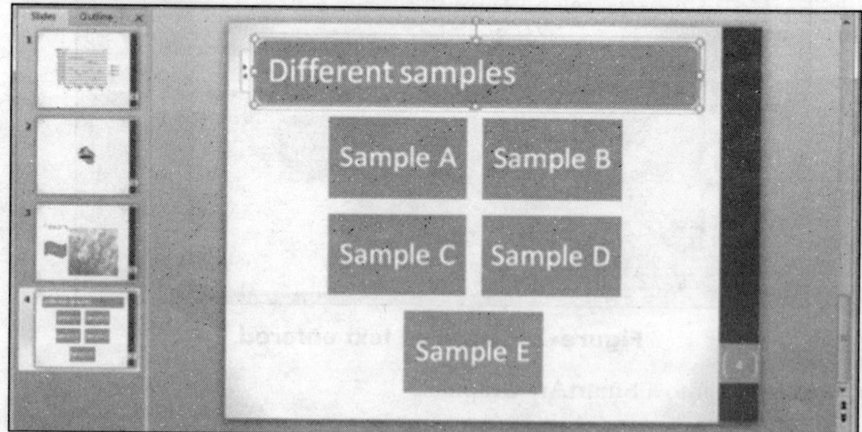

Figure-77: Selected SmartArt graphic is applied to the text

Let's now learn how to work with tables.

4.7.7 Working with Tables

Tables are the most effective way of presenting information in an organized way. The text you enter in a table appears in the form of rows and columns. The information given in the form of tables is easily recognized by the viewers compared to the information given in the form of simple text. In Microsoft PowerPoint 2010, you can create tables by using the Table command of the Insert tab. After creating a table, you can also edit or resize, modify, and delete the table.

In the following sections, you learn how to insert, modify, and delete a table.

Inserting a Table

You can add a table to a slide for a quick and easy reference of the data. In Microsoft PowerPoint 2010, you can either create a table manually or automatically; or draw a table. Let's perform the following steps to insert a table:

1. Insert a new slide.
2. Select the **Insert** tab. The groups present in the **Insert** tab are displayed (Figure-78).
3. Click the **Table** button under the **Tables** group (Figure-78).

   A drop-down list appears with grid of rows and columns (Figure-78).

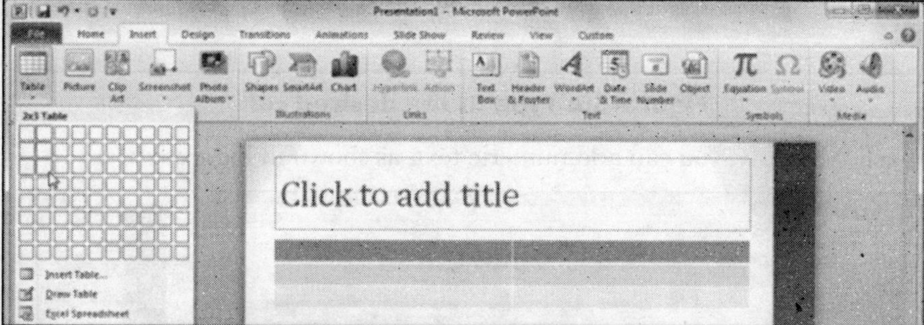

Figure-78: Groups in Insert tab

4. Move the mouse-pointer horizontally to define the number of columns, and vertically to define the number of rows to make a table. In our case, we have selected 2 rows and 3 columns, as shown in Figure-79:

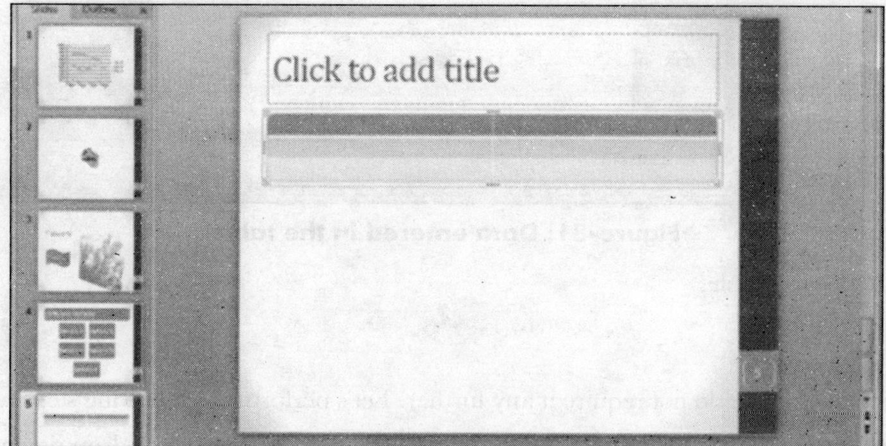

Figure-79: Table is inserted

The table is inserted in the current slide, as shown in Figure-79.

Let's now learn how to add text in a table.

Adding Text in a Table

When you create a table, it serves no purpose until it contains some data. Let's perform the following steps to add text in a table:

1. Click the cell where you want to insert the text. In our case, we have selected the first cell of the table.
2. Type the desired text in the cell. In our case, we have typed **Name** (Figure-80).

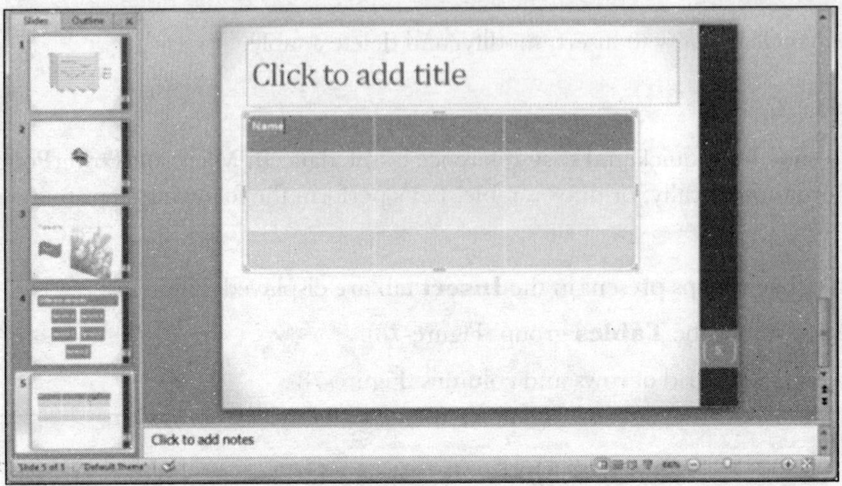

Figure-80: Type in the desired cell

The text is added in the cell. Similarly, you can add numeric text, as shown in Figure-81:

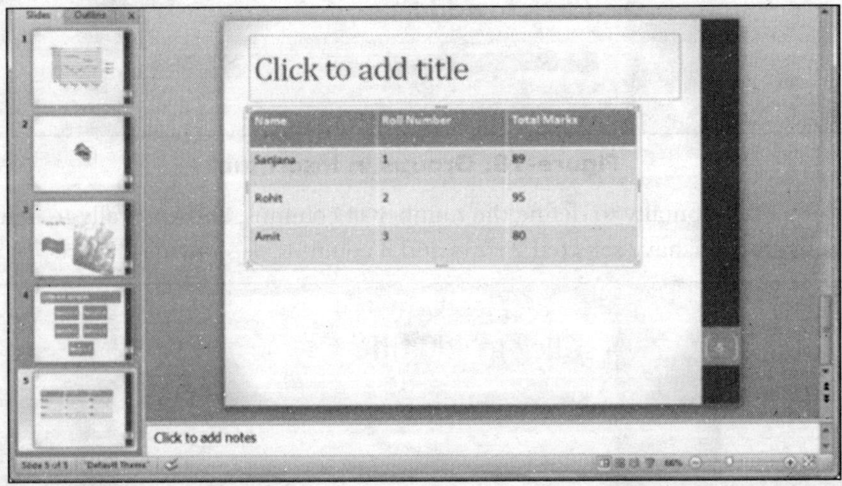

Figure-81: Data entered in the table

Let's now learn how to delete a table.

Deleting a Table

You can easily delete a table if you do not require it any further. Let's perform the following steps to delete a table:

1 Click the **Delete** button from the **Rows & Columns** group in the **Layout** tab. A drop-down list appears.

2. Select the **Delete Table** option from the drop-down list. The table is deleted.

Let's now learn how to add video and sound clip to a presentation.

4.7.8 Adding Videos and Sound Clip

In Microsoft PowerPoint, you can add videos and sound clips in your presentation to make the presentation more attractive. Media clips are the movie and sound clips that you use to view movies and listen to audios. You can insert video and sound clips available in your system as well as from the Internet. When you insert a movie or a sound clip from the Internet, note that only the link of the inserted video is embedded into the presentation, not the complete movie or the sound file. Therefore, if you e-mail only the presentation to the other user, the media file is not played. The media file will be played only when you e-mail both the presentation and the media file.

In this section, you learn how to insert a video and a sound clip in a presentation.

Adding a Video

Adding a video to a presentation allows you to play the video during the slide show. Movie clips add a certain amount of dynamism in the presentation; thereby, making it more lively and exciting to watch. Microsoft PowerPoint 2010 supports videos in various formats, such as Audio Video Interchange (.avi), Moving/Motion Pictures Group (.mpg), and Movie (.mov).

In the subsequent sections, you learn how to insert a video from a file saved on your computer.

Let's perform the following steps to insert a video from a file:

1. Create a new presentation.
2. Select the **Insert** tab. The groups present in the **Insert** tab are displayed (Figure-82).
3. Click the **Video** button under the **Media** group (Figure-82).

   A drop-down list appears (Figure-82).
4. Select the **Video from File** option from the drop-down list (Figure-82).

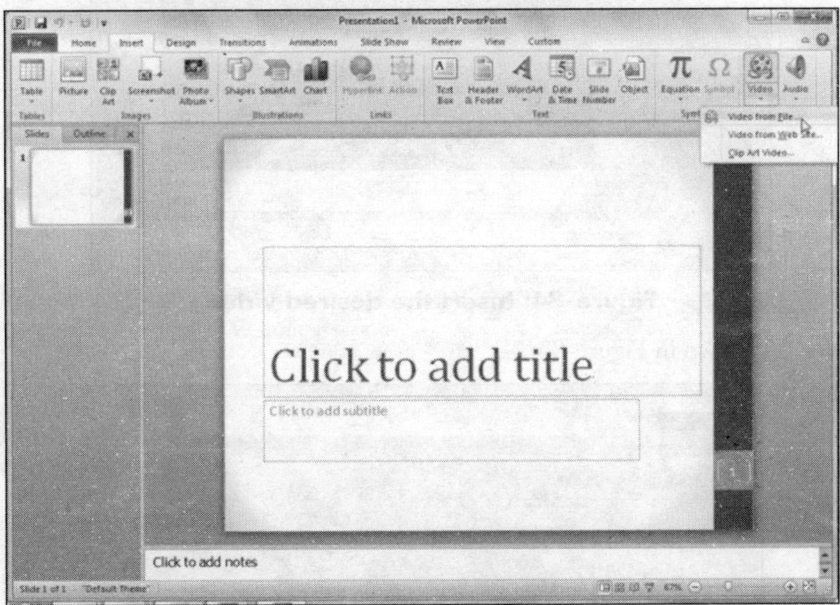

Figure-82: Groups in the Insert tab

   The **Insert Video** dialog box appears (Figure-83).

5. Browse to the location where the video is saved on your computer. In our case, we have selected the **Sample Videos** folder (Figure-83).
6. Select the desired video. In our case, we have selected the **Wildlife** video file (Figure-83).

7. Click the **Insert** button, as shown in Figure-83:

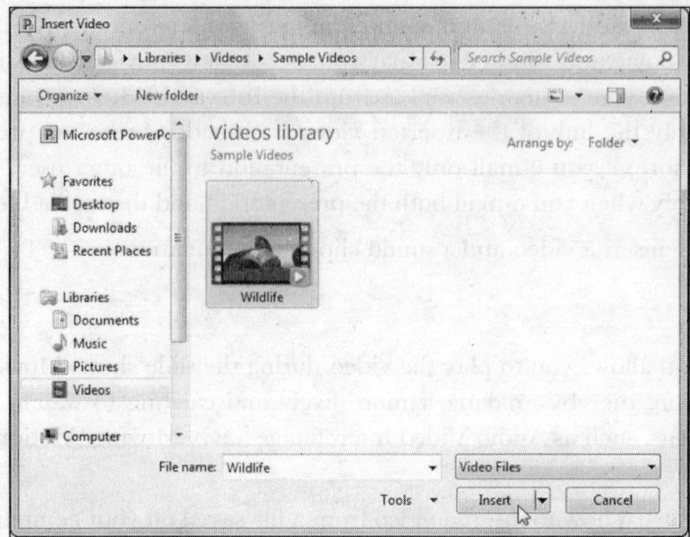

Figure-83: Insert Video dialog box appears

The desired video is inserted in the current slide (Figure-84).

8. Click the **Play/Pause** button to play the video file (Figure-84).

Figure-84: Insert the desired video

The video file is played, as shown in Figure-85:

Figure-85: Video played

Let's now learn how to add sound clips in a presentation.

Adding a Sound Clip

Similar to video clips, you can also insert sound clips and music in your presentation. The sound clips are also known as audio clips. Various sound clip formats, such as MPEG Audio-1 Media Player 3 (.mp3) and Musical Instrument Digital Interface (.midi) can be used in a presentation. Let's perform the following steps to insert a sound clip:

1. Select the slide in which you want to insert the desired sound clip. In our case, we have selected the first slide (Figure-86).
2. Select the **Insert** tab (Figure-86).

Figure-86: Insert tab

The groups present in the **Insert** tab are displayed (Figure-87).

3. Click the **Audio** button under the **Media** group (Figure-87).

   A drop-down list appears (Figure-87).

4. Select the **Audio from File** option from the drop-down list, as shown in Figure-87:

Figure-87: Audio button under the Media group

The **Insert Audio** dialog box appears (Figure-88).

5. Browse to the location where the sound clip is saved on your computer. In our case, we have selected the **Sample Music** folder (Figure-88).
6. Select the desired sound clip. In our case, we have selected the **Sleep Away** audio file (Figure-88).
7. Click the **Insert** button (Figure-88).

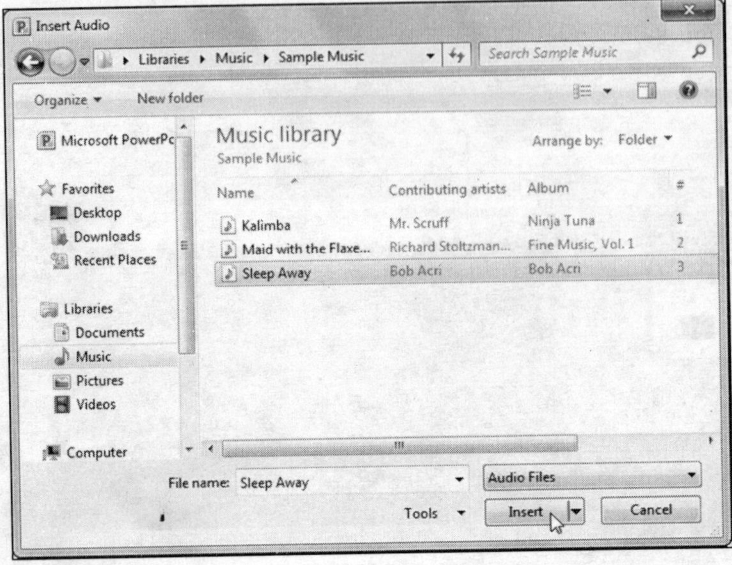

Figure-88: Select audio file

The audio file is inserted in the current slide, as shown in Figure-89:

Figure-89: Audio file inserted in the slide

4.8 Enhancing the Presentation

Apart from adding various objects, such as images, clip art, and videos, you can further enhance the appearance of your presentation by adding different types of effects, such as transition and animation effects, to the slides or the objects added in the slides of your presentation. These effects make the presentation dynamic by adding interactivity to it. Microsoft PowerPoint includes a wide range of transition and animation effects, such as Glitter, Cube, Flip, Fly In, and Fade. Using transition effects, you can specify how the slide will appear during the slide show and for how long will it be displayed on the screen. You can use animation effects to animate the images and other objects of your slides. In Microsoft PowerPoint 2010, you can use the Transitions and Animations tabs, respectively, to add transition and animation effects in your presentation.

4.8.1 Working with the Transition Effects

Transitions are special effects used to define a way in which the slides appear during a slide show. The transition effects allow you to specify how you want to navigate from one slide to the other. For example, if you move from one slide to another without any transition effect, the next slide appears instantly. When you add a transition effect, the next slide displayed after the initial slide appears animated, depending upon the type of transition effect you specify. It is important to note that transition effects can be only seen in the slide show.

In this section, you learn how to add a transition style and transition sound to a slide. You also learn how to set display time for a slide and apply same transition to all the slides.

Adding a Transition Style

The transition styles allow you to specify the appearance of the slides in the slide show. In other words, they determine how the slides appear in the presentation. Microsoft PowerPoint provides various types of transition styles, such as Dissolve and Fade Smoothly.

Let's perform the following steps to add a transition style to a slide:

1. Select the slide on which you want to apply the transition effect. In our case, we have selected the **first** slide (Figure-90).
2. Select the **Transitions** tab (Figure-90).

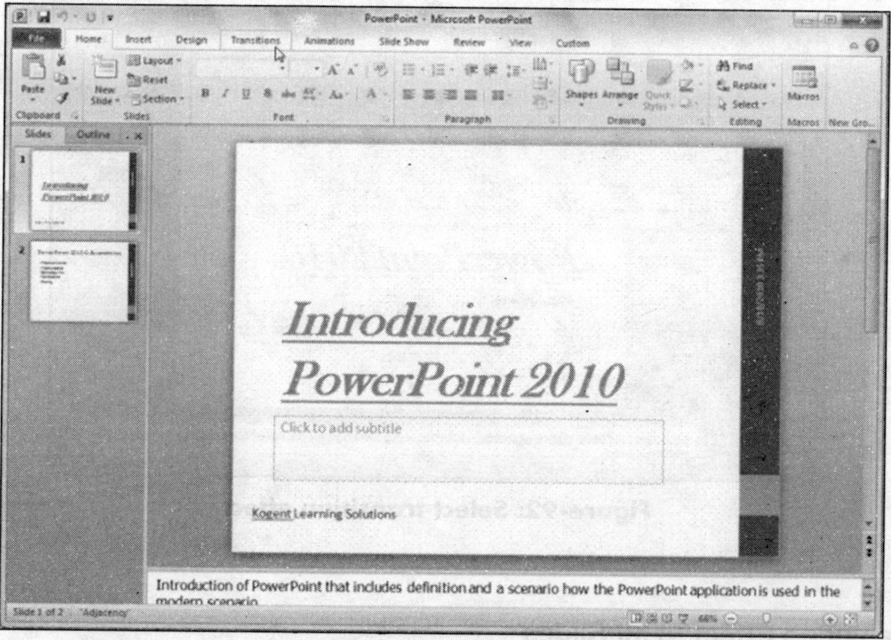

Figure-90: New slide

The groups present in the **Transitions** tab appear (Figure-91).

3. Click the **More** button, as shown in Figure-91:

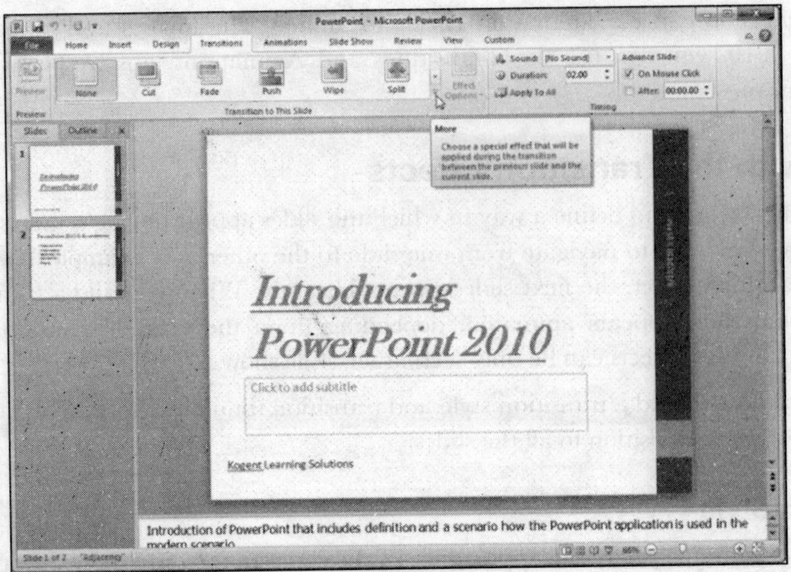

Figure-91: Transitions tab

A drop-down list appears (Figure-92).

4. Select the desired transition style from the drop-down list. In our case, we have selected the **Cube** transition effect, as shown in Figure-92:

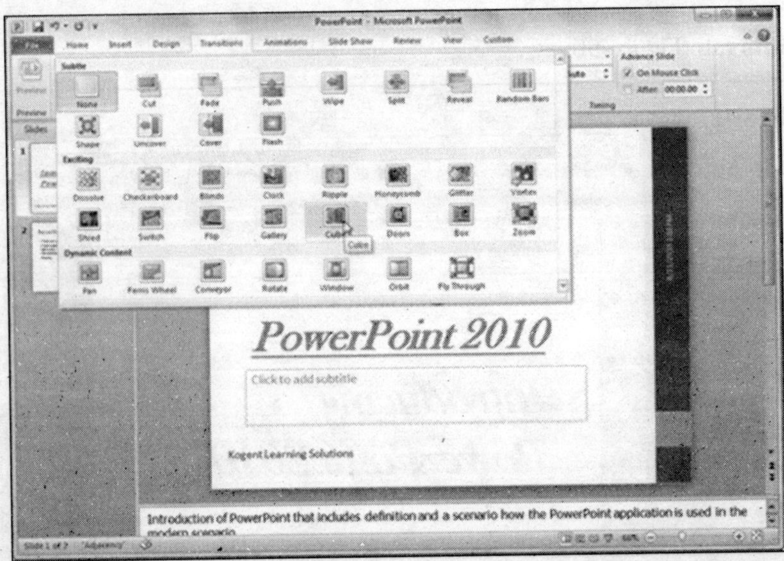

Figure-92: Select transition effect

The desired transition effect is applied to the slide.

Applying the Transition Effect to all Slides

In Microsoft PowerPoint 2010, you can either apply the same transition effect to all the slides or apply different effect to them. It is a best practice to apply the same effect to all the slides to maintain consistency in the presentation However, applying the same effect to all the slides one by one is a tedious and time consuming task. For this purpose you can use the Apply To All command to apply a single effect to all slides at once.

Let's perform the following steps to apply the same transition effect to all slides:

1. Select the slide, the transition effect of which you want to apply to all the other slides of the presentation. In ou case, we have selected the first slide (Figure-93).

2. Click the **Apply to All** button (Figure-93).

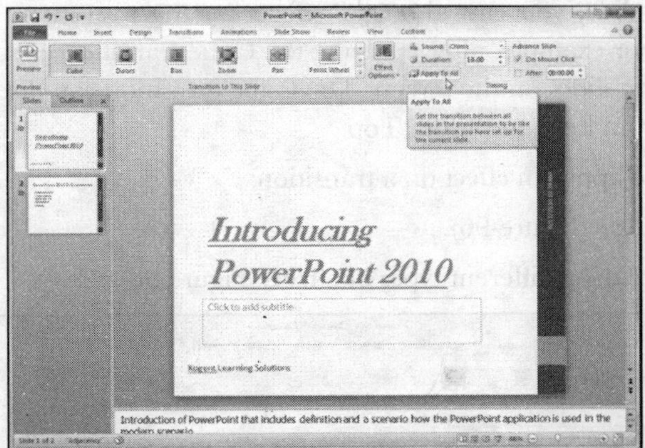

Figure-93: Select the slide where to apply transition effect

The **Cube** effect along with other effects, if any applied on Slide 1, are applied on all slides.

3. Click the **Preview** button, as shown in Figure-94:

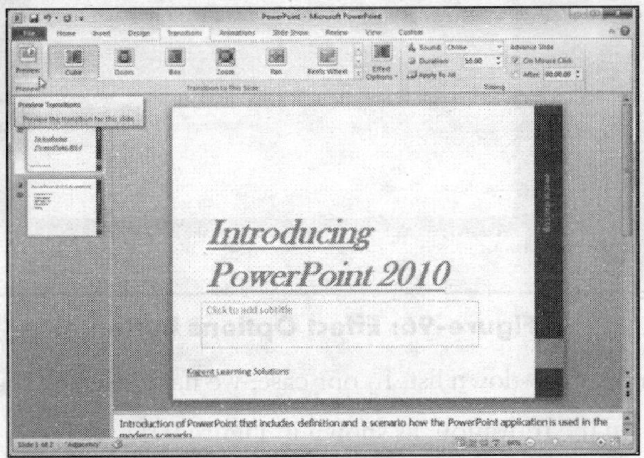

Figure-94: Click Preview button

The same transition effect is applied to all slides, as shown in Figure-95:

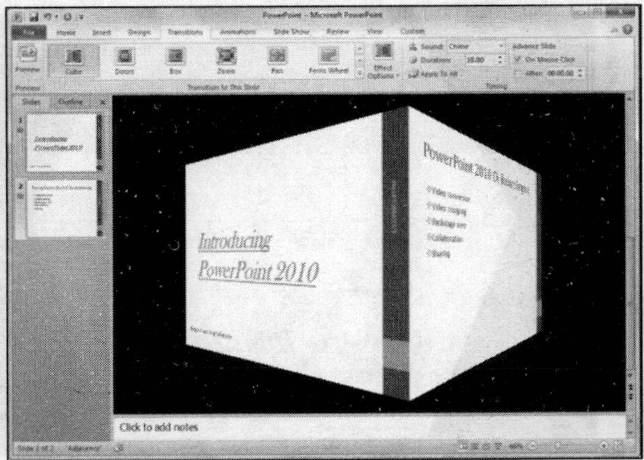

Figure-95: Same effect applied to all slides

Let's now learn how to apply effect on a transition.

Applying Effects on a Transition

After applying a transition to a slide, you can also add effects on the transition. You can customize these effects depending on the requirements. For example, after applying the Cube transition effect, you can set the directions from where the transition will display the slides on the screen. The Cube transition can display the slides in four ways, which are From Right, From Bottom, From Left, and From Top.

Let's perform the following steps to apply an effect on a transition:

1. Click the **Effect Options** button (Figure-96).

   A drop-down list appears, displaying different types of effects (Figure-96).

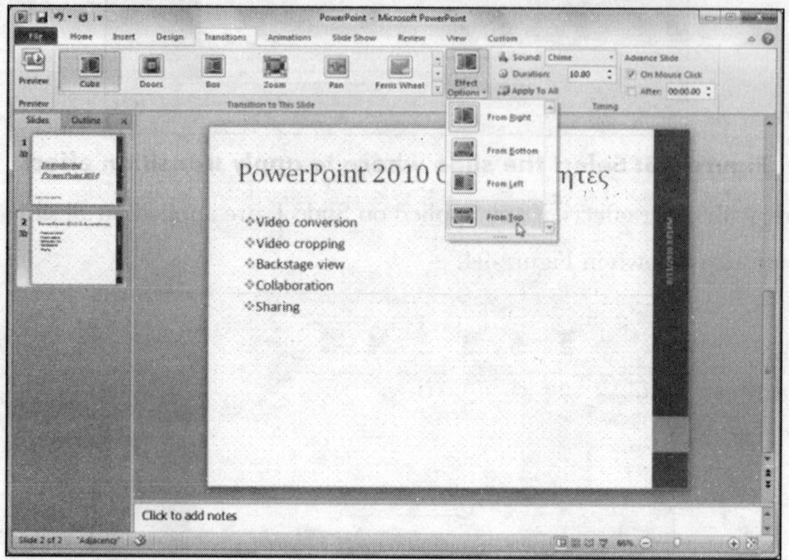

Figure-96: Effect Options button

2. Select the desired effect from the drop-down list. In our case, we have selected the **From Top** effect (Figure-96).

   The selected effect is applied on the transition, as shown in Figure-97:

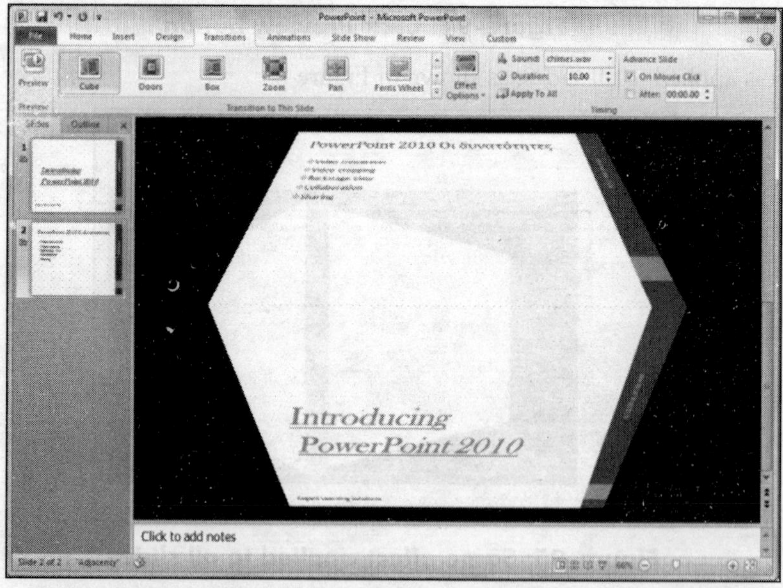

Figure-97: Selected effect is applied on the transition

Let's now explore the concept of animation in PowerPoint.

4.8.2 Working with Animation

Animation refers to the process of displaying images in sequence to create an illusion of movement. Animation allows you to specify how you want the objects of a slide to appear in the slide show. Using animation effects, you can control the objects' motion; for example, how the objects appear, move, and disappear. In Microsoft PowerPoint 2010, you can use the Animations tab to apply animations on objects.

In this section, you learn how to add animation, add effects to the animation, and modify the applied animation.

Adding Animation to an Object

Animation can be applied to different objects in a slide, such as text, shapes, clip arts, charts, and images.

Let's perform the following steps to add animation to an object:

1. Select the object on which you want to add animation. In our case, we have selected the Title of the first slide (Figure-98).
2. Select the **Animations** tab (Figure-98).

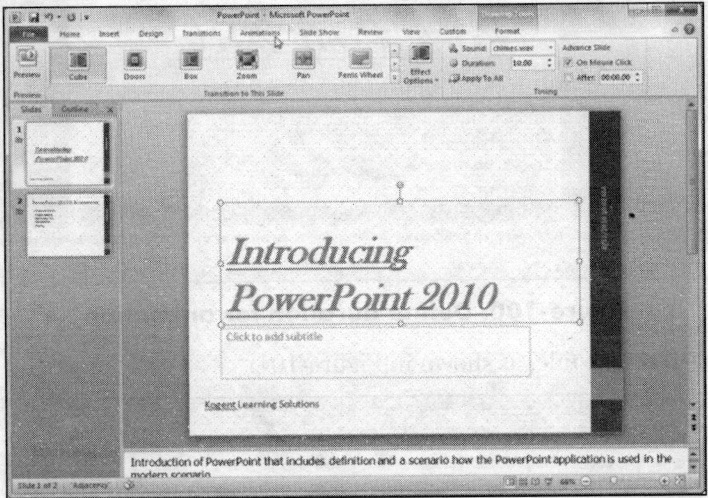

Figure-98: Select the object to add animation on it

The groups present in the **Animations** tab are displayed (Figure-99).

3. Select the desired animation. In our case, we have selected the **Fly In** option, as shown in Figure-99:

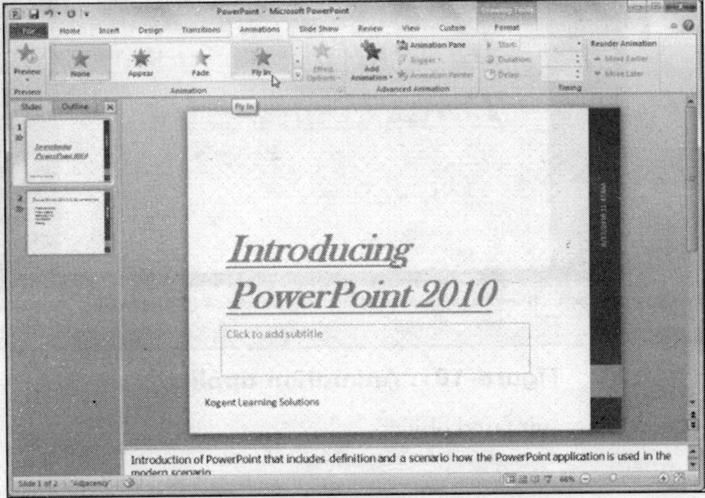

Figure-99: Groups in the Animations tab

4. Set the duration of the slide in the **Duration** spin box. In our case, we have set the duration as **1** second (Figure-100).
5. Set the time after which you want to play the animation in the **Delay** spin box. In our case, we have set the delay time as **5** seconds (Figure-100).
6. Click the **Preview** button (Figure-100).

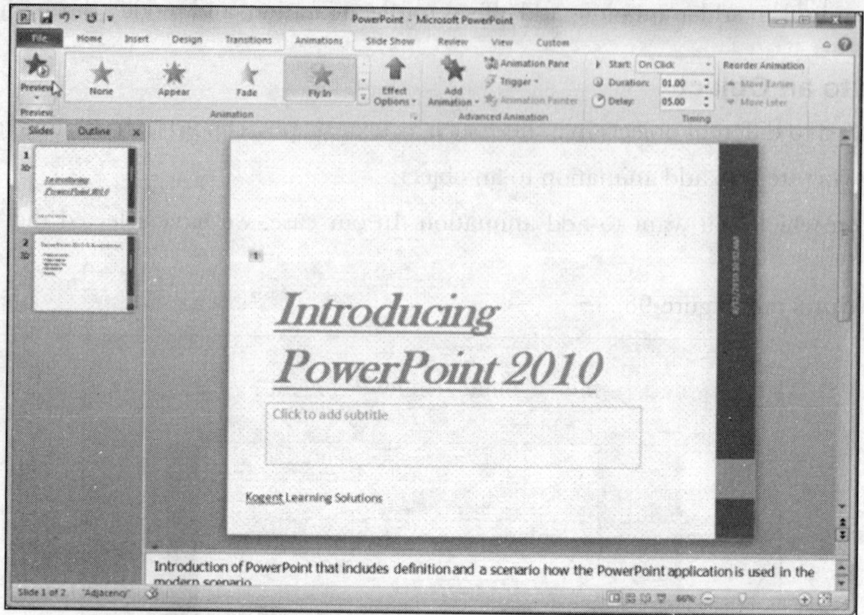

Figure-100: Define duration for animation

The desired animation is applied on the title, as shown in Figure-101:

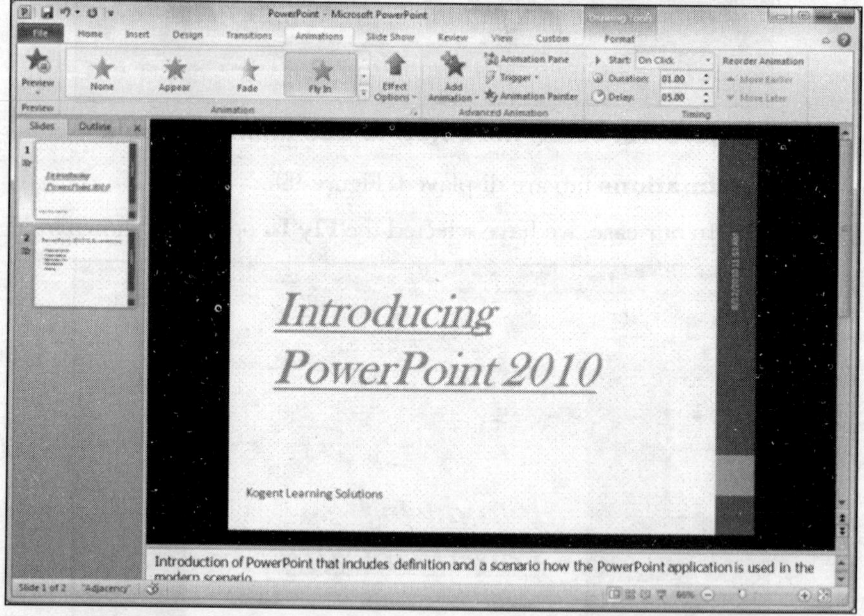

Figure-101: Animation applied

Let's now learn how to apply effect on an animated object.

Applying Effects to an Animated Object

After applying animation to an object, you can apply some effects based on that animation to the object. These effects allow you to customize the animated objects as per your requirements.

Let's perform the following steps to apply effect to an animated object:

1. Select an object in Slide and click the **Effect Options** button. In our case, we have selected text box in Slide 1 (Figure-102). A drop-down list appears as shown in Figure-102.

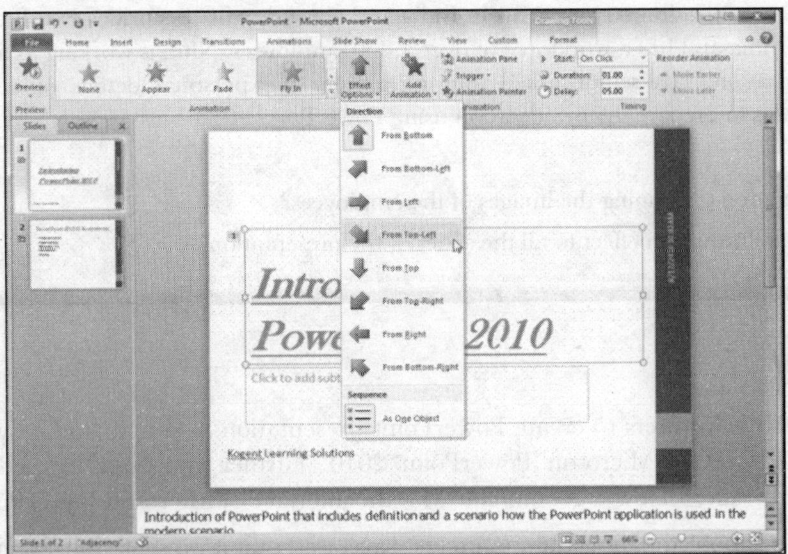

Figure-102: Apply Effect Options

2. Select the desired effect from the drop-down list. In our case, we have selected the **From Top-Left** effect (Figure-102).

   The selected effect is applied on the animated object, as shown in Figure-103:

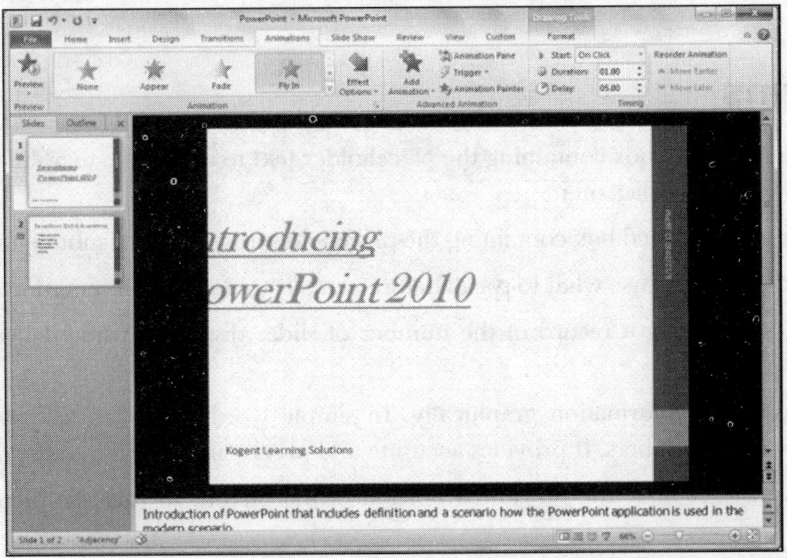

Figure-103: Effect applied on animated object

Case Study: Airlines Management Information System (AMIS)

ABC Securities Pvt. Ltd. is a Delhi-based organization that deals in the manufacturing and sales of security items.

Established in 1994, the organization serves clients in India and abroad. ABC Securities Pvt. Ltd. has become one of the largest organizations in India and has a workforce of over 4,000 employees. Nitin is working as a Human Resource (HR) manager in the organization. His senior asked him to present the personal details of all the employees in the organization. Nitin decides to prepare the presentation using PowerPoint 2010.

Questions:

Q1. Prepare the presentation containing the images of the employees?

Q2. Apply an appropriate transition effect to all the slides of the presentation.

*(*Case study presented is the proprietary information of the respective organization, and is used here specifically and only for educational purpose.)*

4.9 Summary

Microsoft PowerPoint 2010 helps users to create PowerPoint presentation in simple and easy process. In this chapter you have learned new features of Microsoft PowerPoint 2010. Further you have learned the procedure to start Microsoft PowerPoint 2010. After that you get familiar with the interface of Microsoft PowerPoint 2010.

This chapter also explained about the procedure to create, save, and quit a presentation. Next, you also learned about how to apply date, time and slide number to the slides. In this chapter, you have learned how to add charts to a presentation. You have also learned to work with clip art, which includes inserting and modifying the Clipart. Further, you learn to work with images, such as inserting, recoloring, cropping, and rotating images. In addition you have learned to insert shapes in a presentation and add a WordArt in a presentation. After that you learn to work with tables and add and format video and sound clips in a presentation. In the last, you learned about the ways of enhancing the presentation.

4.10 Key Terms

- **Title Box:** Represents a dotted box containing the placeholder text to add a title to a slide. The placeholder text in a title box disappears when you click on it.
- **Subtitle Box:** Represents a dotted box containing the placeholder text to add a subtitle to a slide.
- **Notes:** Help the speaker to rehearse what to speak before actually giving the presentation.
- **Slide Number**: Allows keeping a record of the number of slides displayed while delivering the presentation in front of the viewers.
- **Graph:** Represents data or information graphically. In simple words, you can also say that graph is a visual representation of a group of numbers. It provides accurate and precise information to the users.
- **Cropping:** Allows you to remove the unwanted portion of the picture so that the picture accurately fits to the slide.
- **Clip Arts:** Represent the images that can demonstrate any medium. PowerPoint contains a collection of clip arts, such as illustrations, borders, backgrounds, and auto shapes.
- **Movie Clip:** Represents video clips with the file formats, such as .avi, .mpg, and .mov. By inserting a movie clip in your presentation, you can play a movie in the slide show.

- **Sound Clip:** Represents the audio files the file formats, such as .mp3, .snd, and .midi. Inserting a sound clip in the background of your presentation makes the presentation more effective and the user does not get bored.
- **Animation:** Demonstrates the content of a slide in such a manner that the content of the presentation appears moving. Animations, when added to a slide in a presentation, quickly grasp the attention of its intended viewers.
- **Animation Effects:** Allow you to specify how you want the objects to appear in the slide show.
- **Transition Effect:** Allows you to specify how you want to navigate from one slide to the other during a slide show.
- **Transition Style:** Allows you to specify how the slide appears initially in the slide show.

4.11 Exercise

Multiple Choice Questions

Q1. The title of a slide is used:

a. To get the general idea about the slide
b. To give the viewers an idea about the Sensex
c. To guide viewers regarding the insertion of text in a slide
d. None

Ans. a

Q2. Notes are added to a slide for the purpose of:

a. Giving the general idea about the presentation to the presenter who has not created the presentation
b. Preparing documents for a presentation
c. Making a presentation more attractive
d. None

Ans. a

Q3. Slide numbers are inserted in the slides in a presentation:

a. To keep a record of number of slides displayed in a slide show
b. To mismanage the slides in a presentation
c. To fill the vacant space in a slide
d. None

Ans. a

Q4. Where the Quick Access Toolbar is displayed?

a. Top-right corner
b. top-left corner
c. bottom-right corner
d. bottom-left corner

Ans. b

Q5. The window that opens when you start PowerPoint is known as the _______ of PowerPoint 2010.

a. Interface
b. background
c. View
d. slide

Ans. a

Q6. Which navigation option allows viewing all the slides on a single screen?

a. Normal
b. Slide Sorter
c. Reading View
d. Slide Show

Ans. b

Q7. The slide number is added in the ______ of the slide.

a. Centre
b. bottom right
c. bottom left
d. top right

Ans. b

Q8. Choose the correct shortcut to save a file?

a. Ctrl + A
b. Ctrl + C
c. Ctrl + S
d. Ctrl + O

Ans. c

Q9. Which one of the following options is used to insert a sound clip in a presentation?

a. Audio from File
b. Restricted Access
c. From Drive
d. None

Ans. a

Q10. Which of the following tab is used to insert a table in a slide?

a. View
b. Insert
c. Organize
d. Table

Ans. b

Short Answer Type Questions

Q1. What is the default font, font size, and font color of the text on a slide?

Q2. Why the graph is inserted in a slide?

Q3. What are SmartArt graphics?

Q4. What is the purpose of adding notes to the slides in a presentation?

Q5. What are animation effects and their types?

Q6. What are transition effects?

Q7. What do you understand by command tabs?

Q8. What are the ways of creating a new presentation?

Q9. Differentiate between closing and quitting the presentation/application?

Q10. Imagine you are working as a sales representative in ABC Footwear Pvt. Ltd. You are asked to give presentation of a newly launched shoe at one of the client's site. How would you create this presentation in PowerPoint 2010?

Microsoft® Access® 2010

CHAPTER 5

Microsoft Access 2010

Office

CHAPTER STRUCTURE

CHAPTER OBJECTIVES

- Define a database
- Discuss the database objects
- Work on MS Access 2010

5.1 Introduction

Access is a database application that allows you to store data in the form of various objects, such as tables, reports, and forms. These objects allow you to access, manage, and update the data easily and effectively. For example, by storing data in tables, where the data is actually stored in the form of rows and columns, you can easily search a specific record from a large collection of data. Microsoft Access (MS Access) allows you to store simple data, such as name and address, as well as complex data, such as pictures, sounds, and videos). MS Access database can contain many tables, which may store information on different subjects. Each table can contain many fields of different types of data, such as text, numbers, dates, and hyperlinks. A field is a specific category of information in a table. A field name identifies the information in a field. You can use up to 64 characters to name a field. In a table, the data that you enter is called records. A record is a collection of information or a set of complete fields. When you save a table you give a name to a table. Access sets the primary key on the first field of the table that you create. A primary key is a key which is used to uniquely identify each record in a table. You must have a primary key in each table that you create. In MS Access, you can connect tables or establish links between tables by creating relationships between them using a common field that they share.

In this chapter, you learn about a database. Next, you learn about the database object of MS Access 2010. Further, you explore the new features of MS Access 2010. You also learn how to launch MS Access 2010, create a database, and open an existing database. You also learn about the user interface of MS Access 2010. Next, you learn about the table. You also learn about how to save a table and open a table in Design view. Further, you learn to work with the fields in a table. In addition, you learn to enter record in a table. Further, you learn to work with the keys in table and learn to create relationships between tables. Finally, you learn to close a database and quit MS Access 2010.

Let's start by learning about a database.

5.2 Introducing a Database

A database is used to store data in an organized format. It allows you to access, manage, and update data easily. In a database, data is stored in the form of tables. A database allows you to search a particular data in a large collection of data easily. In short, a database is a collection of data that can be accessed and manipulated easily and quickly. It can be divided into the following two main categories:

- **Flat-file database:** Refers to a database file that consists of a single table. This database file is also called sequential file.
- **Relational database:** Refers to a database that consists of multiple tables. You can access data from different tables by creating relation between them. To create a relation between different tables, there must be one common field in each table.

After learning about a database, let's now explore the database objects of MS Access 2010.

5.3 Exploring the Database Objects

A database contains various objects, such as tables, forms, and reports. The database object provides the structure to enter the data. You can use database objects to access and manipulate data easily. The database objects allow you to create an effective and efficient database. They allow you to manage a database easily. For example, by creating a database object, such as table, you can easily maintain the records of all the employees of your organization. The database objects of MS Access are as follows:

- Tables
- Forms
- Queries
- Reports

Let's discuss each database object in detail.

5.3.1 Tables

A table is used to store data in an organized form. In tables, data is stored in the form of rows and columns, where rows are known as records and columns are known as fields. A table is used to store related information. For example, you can store information of all the employees, such as employee id, name, salary, and contact details, in a table. The data stored in a table can be easily accessed and managed. Figure-1 shows the table-Kogent, which contains the details of employees of an organization:

Kogent

EmployeeID	Employee N	Address	Salary detail	Click to Add
012	meenakshi	New delhi	10000	
013	Kinshuk	chandni chowk	10500	
014	Heena	Laxmi nagar	11000	
015	Priya	Dhaula kuan	11500	
016	pooja	Gurgaon	12000	

Figure-1: A table

Each table of a database contains the following components:

- **Field:** Represents the vertical structure of information. It is also known as a column of a table. In table, every field has a specific name that represents the information about the particular subject. For example, the **Employee ID** field of the **Kogent** table contains the ID of employees.
- **Primary Key:** Refers to a unique key that does not allow you to insert duplicate information in a specific field of a table.
- **Row:** Represents the horizontal structure of information. In a table, a row is termed as a record, which contains a complete set of information. For instance, in the Kogent table, the first row contains the complete information of an employee such as employee id, name, address, and salary.
- **Relationship:** Allows you to retrieve data from multiple tables on the basis of a common field. For example, you have two tables, Kogent and Jetking, from which you want to retrieve the data. Now, to retrieve the data from both the tables, you need to create a relationship between the tables on the basis of a common field, which in this case is **EmployeeID**. Figure-2 shows the relationship between tables:

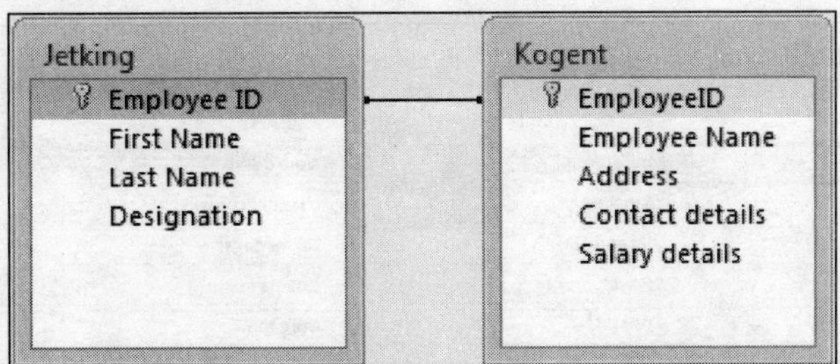

Figure-2: Relationship between tables

5.3.2 Forms

A form is a database object which presents the information of a table in an easily readable format. You can use forms to enter, edit, or display records of the table. A form usually shows one record at a time, instead of all records so that you can concentrate on that particular record rather than the entire set of records. For example, if you create a form for the Kogent table, then it shows you only the first record of the Kogent table. Figure-3 shows the structure of the Kogent form:

Figure-3: Form structure

5.3.3 Query

A query is the request sent to a database to retrieve specific data from a table. When you want to search records in a database, you can use query. For example, you can create a query to retrieve the employee name and salary from the Kogent Query table. This displays the specified information, as shown in Figure-4:

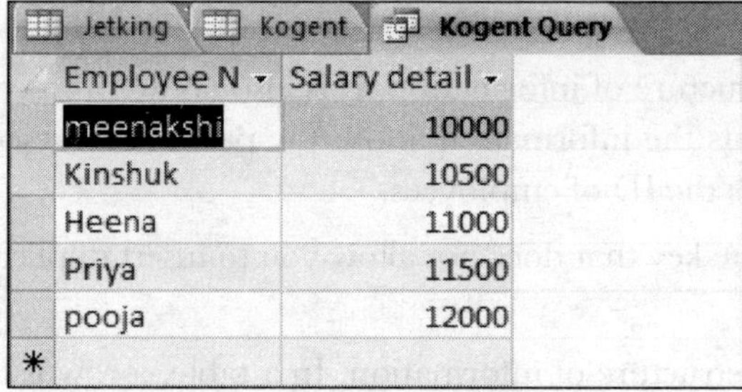

Figure-4: Specified information displayed

5.3.4 Report

A report refers to a database object that is basically display and summarizes data in an attractive manner. Using reports you can share your data by converting them to PDF or XPS files, or exporting to other file formats. Figure-5 shows the structure of the report:

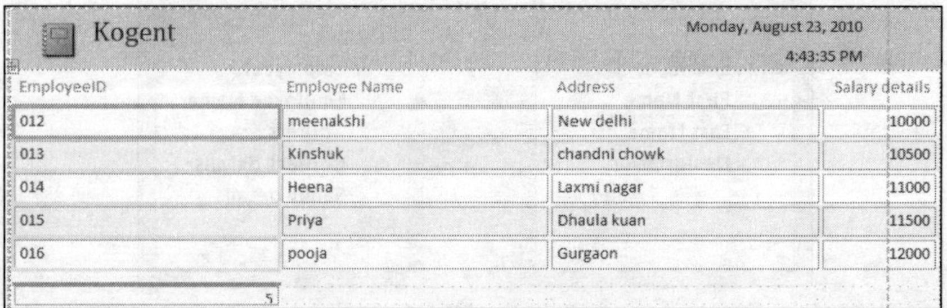

Figure-5: Report structure

After learning about the database objects of MS Access 2010, let's now learn how to start MS Access 2010.

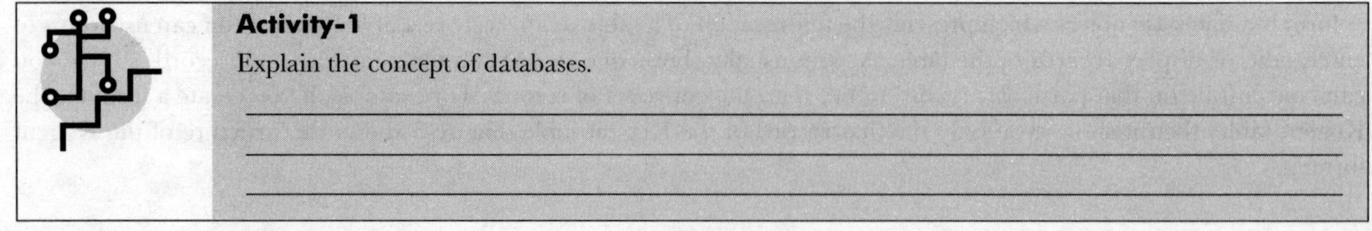

Activity-1

Explain the concept of databases.

____

____

____

5.4 Starting MS Access 2010

You need to start MS Access 2010 to create or open a database file. You can start MS Access 2010 by performing the following steps:

1. Click the **Start** button present on the **Taskbar**. The **Start** menu appears (Figure-6).
2. Place the mouse pointer over **All Programs** option in the **Start** menu. A list of programs installed on your computer appears (Figure-6).
3. Click the **Microsoft Office folder** (Figure-6). A list of applications of the **Microsoft Office** suite appears (Figure-6).
4. Click the **Microsoft Access 2010** option (Figure-6).

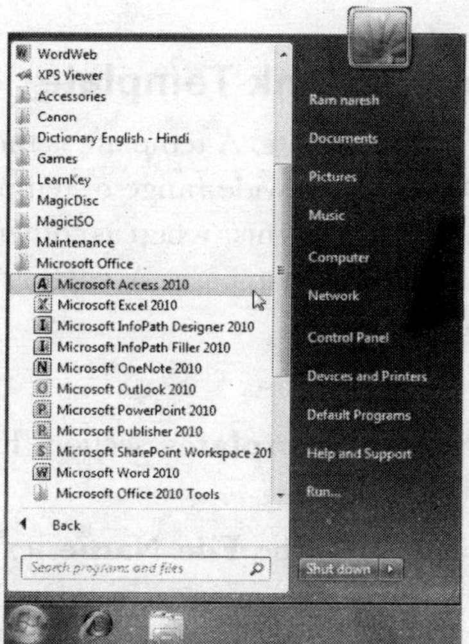

Figure-6: Accessing MS-Access 2010

The Microsoft Access window appears in the Backstage view, as shown in Figure-7:

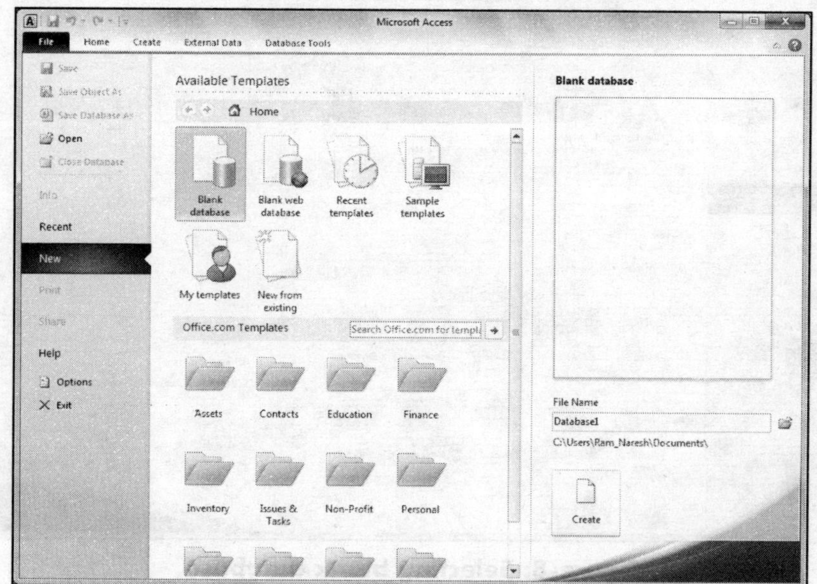

Figure-7: Backstage view of MS-Access 2010

The Microsoft Access window appears with the **File** tab opened and the **New** option selected (Figure-7). The left side of the Microsoft Access window contains various options, such as Save and Open. The middle part of the Microsoft Access window is divided into two sections. The top section displays the **Available Templates** category that contains sample databases. The bottom section displays the list of online templates, which you need to download to create a database using them. The right side of the Microsoft Access window shows a list of recently opened databases.

After learning how to start MS Access 2010, let's now learn about the Backstage view.

5.5 Creating a Database

As discussed earlier, Microsoft Access 2010 is an application that is used to create databases. Before creating a database, you must decide whether you want to create a blank database or create a database using a template or any predefined template. A properly designed database is easier to work with and modify. In MS Access 2010, you can create a database by using blank template and sample templates

Let's discuss these methods of creating a database.

5.5.1 Creating a Database using a Blank Template

Every database in MS Access 2010 is based on a template. A template is the basic model with which a database can be created easily and quickly. MS Access 2010 provides a wide range of templates with various layouts, fonts, styles, and colors. Some of the templates do not contain any elements; whereas, others contain well-arranged and pre-formatted elements. A blank template is used to create a blank database. A database with a single blank table, that is, a table without any data is known as a blank database.

Let's perform the following steps to create a blank database:

1. Select **Blank database** from the **Available Templates** section (Figure-8). The preview area above the **File Name** text box appears blank (Figure-8).
2. Type the desired name for the new database in the **File Name** text box. In our case, we have typed **Office Database** (Figure-8).
3. Click the **Create** button to create a blank database, as shown in Figure-8:

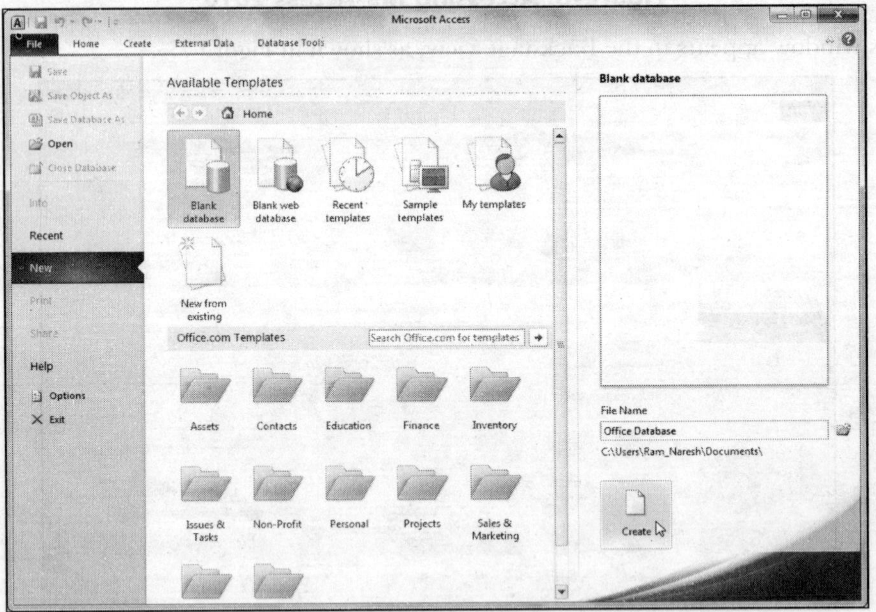

Figure-8: Selecting blank database

You can also create the blank database by double-clicking the Blank Database option in the Available Templates category.

When you click the **Create** button, MS Access 2010 opens the **Office Database** with a blank table, named **Table1** by default, as shown in Figure-9:

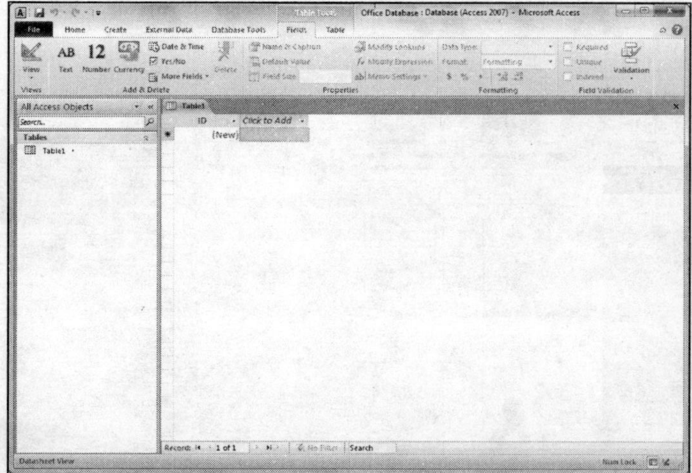

Figure-9: Displaying Blank database

Let's now learn how to create a database using sample templates.

5.5.2 Creating a Database using Sample Templates

You can use templates, which are already installed on your computer or available as sample templates in MS Access 2010 to create a database. With the sample templates, you can save a lot of time and effort to create a database as these templates provide a structure for a database.

Let's perform the following steps to create a new database using a sample template:

1. Select the **File** tab from the Ribbon. The Backstage view appears (Figure-10).
2. Select the **New** option from the Backstage view, as shown in Figure-10:

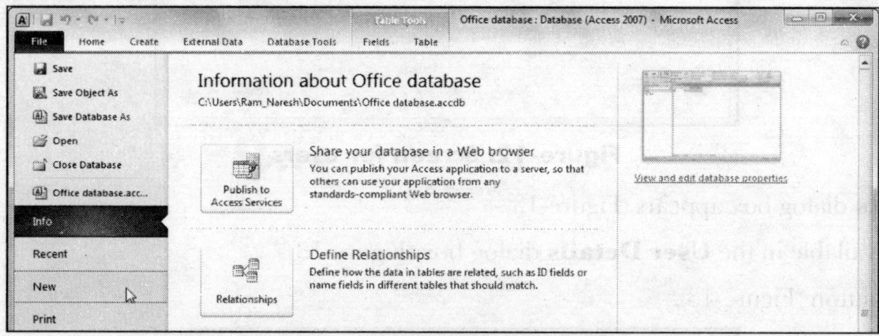

Figure-10: Backstage view

3. Select the **Sample templates** option under the **Available Templates** category (Figure-11). A list of sample templates appears (Figure-11).
4. Select the desired template. In our case, we have selected **Assets Web Database** (Figure-11).
5. Type the name of the selected template in the **File Name** text box. In our case, we have retained with the default name (Figure-11).
6. Click the **Create** button, as shown in Figure-11:

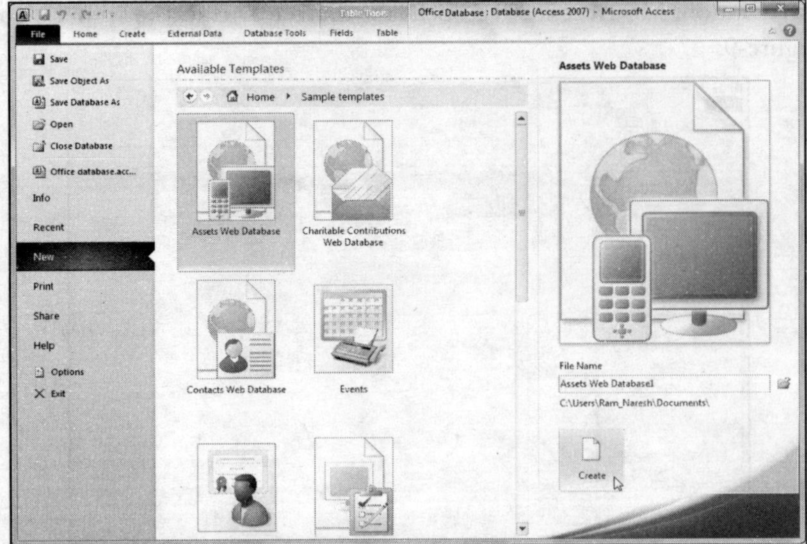

Figure-11: Selecting a desired template for the database

The **Preparing template** dialog box appears, asking you to wait till Microsoft Access prepares the template to use. As the progress bar completes, the **Login** dialog box appears with an empty list of users (Figure-12).

7. Click on the **New User** link in the **Login** dialog box, as shown in Figure-12:

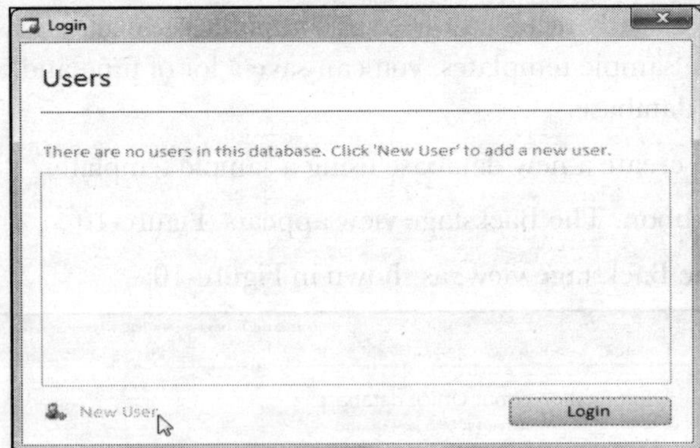

Figure-12: Screen for users

The **User Details** dialog box appears (Figure-13).

8. Fill all the fields available in the **User Details** dialog box (Figure-13).
9. Click the **Close** button (Figure-13).

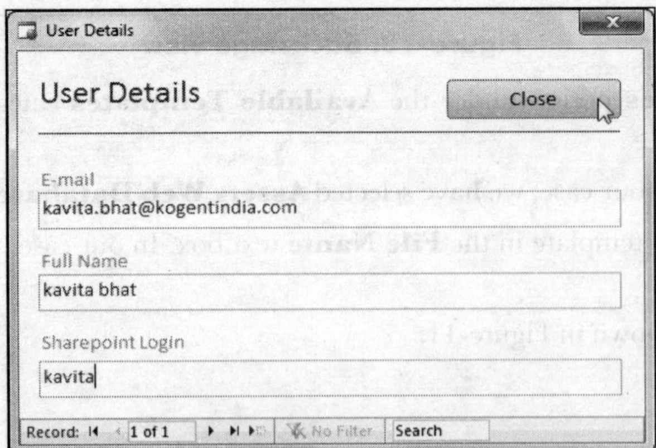

Figure-13: User details

The **Login** dialog box reappears (Figure-14).

10. Select the user name in the **Login** dialog box and then click the **Login** button, as shown in Figure-14:

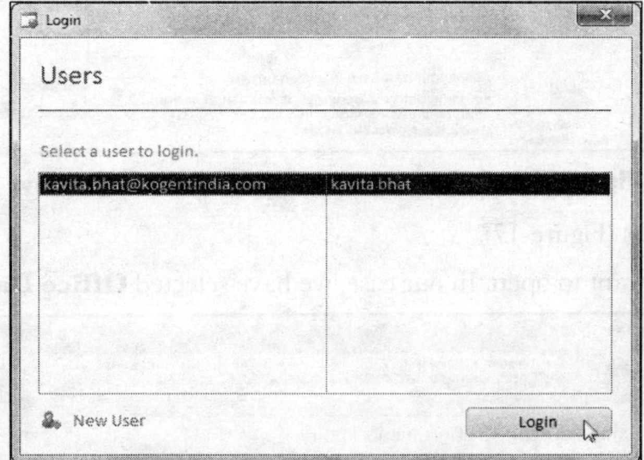

Figure-14: Login dialog box

The **Assets** database appears, as shown in Figure-15:

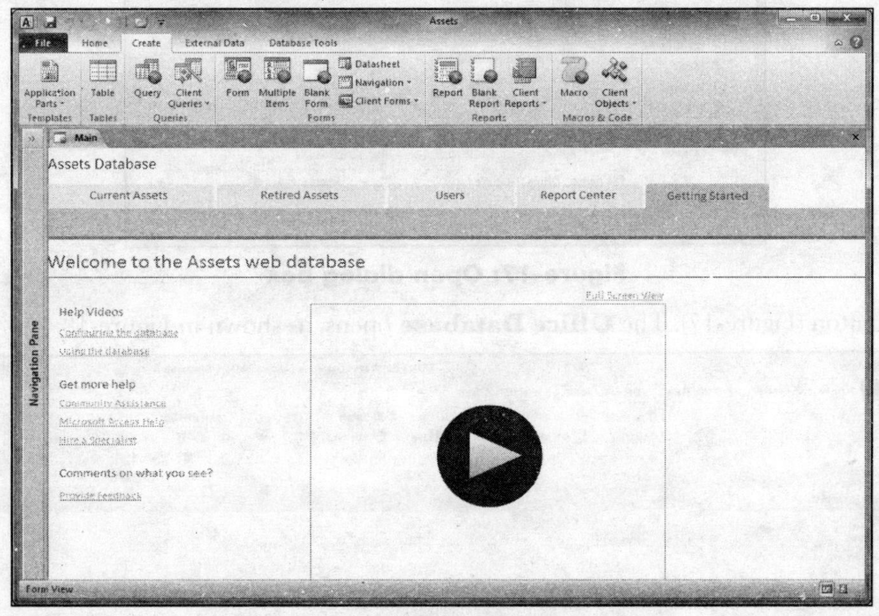

Figure-15: Assets database appears

After learning about various ways of creating a database, let's now learn to open an existing database.

5.6 Opening an Existing Database

Suppose you have a database that you had created earlier and want to open it now for further modifications or enhancements. In MS Access 2010, you can open an existing database, provided you know the location where it has been saved. After opening a database, you can modify its structure, insert records in it, or edit the records. You can use the Open command of the File tab to open an existing database.

Let's perform the following steps to open a database:

1. Select the **File** tab from the Ribbon. The Backstage view appears (Figure-16).
2. Select the **New** option from the Backstage view, as shown in Figure-16:

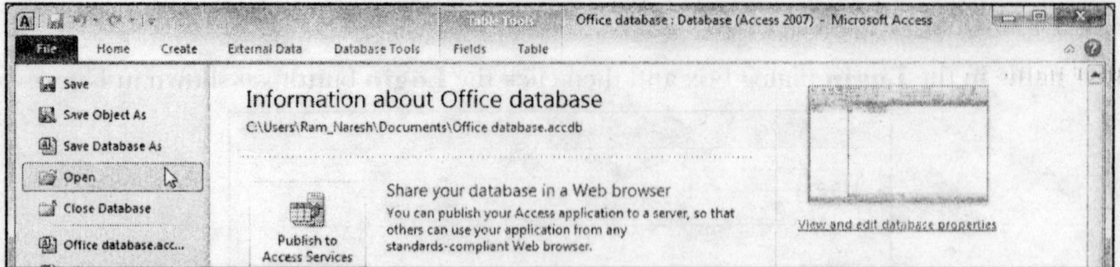

Figure-16: Selecting New from Backstage view

The **Open** dialog box appears (Figure-17).

3. Select the database that you want to open. In our case, we have selected **Office Database** (Figure-17).

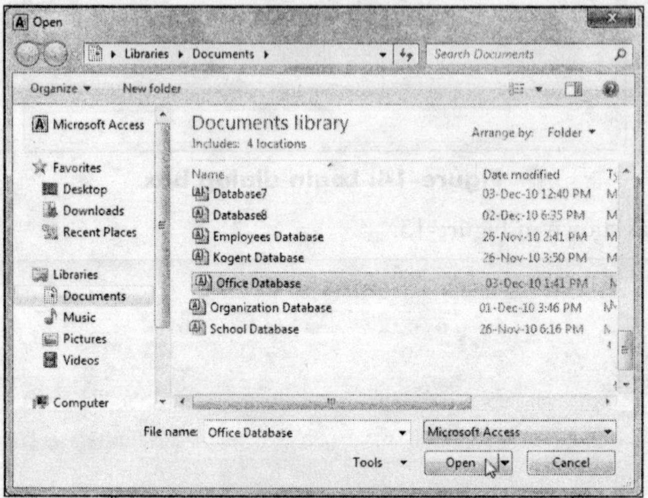

Figure-17: Open dialog box

4. Click the **Open** button (Figure-17). The **Office Database** opens, as shown in Figure-18:

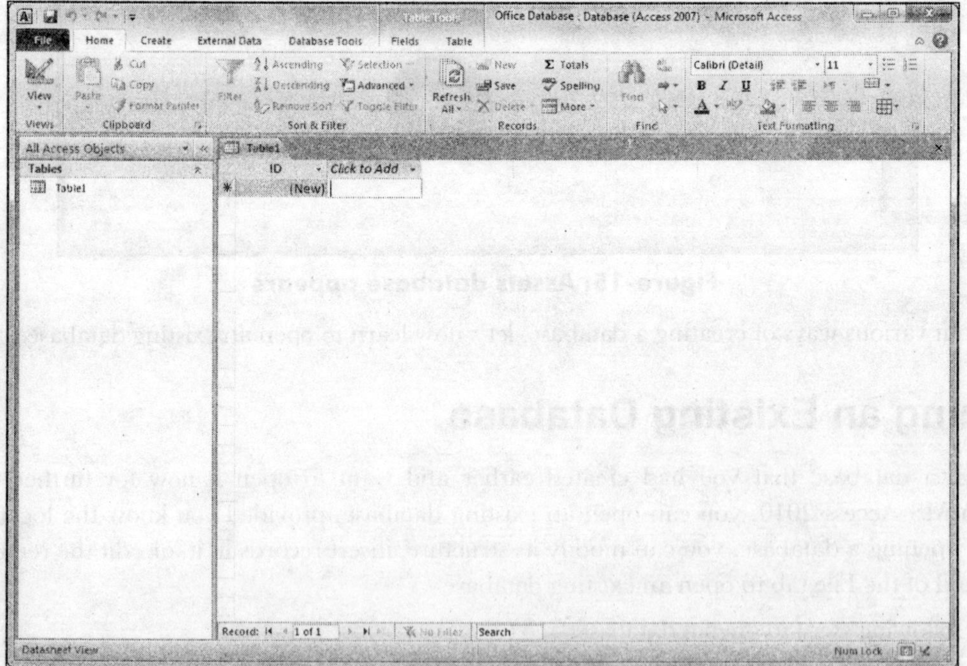

Figure-18: Office Database opens

After learning about opening an existing database file, let's now explore the user interface of MS Access 2010.

5.7 Exploring the MS Access 2010 User Interface

If you have worked with previous versions of MS Access, then you may be able to identify the change in the user interface of MS Access 2010. In previous versions of MS Access (such as MS Access 2007), the user interface primarily constituted different menus, submenus, and toolbars. Each menu, submenu, or toolbar, in turn, offered numerous options. Microsoft renewed the user interface and introduced a more compact and user friendly user interface in MS Access 2010. In addition, MS Access 2010 provides a Navigation pane that lists all the objects and allows easy access to all of the objects in a database that is currently open. The user interface of MS Access 2010 is shown in Figure-19:

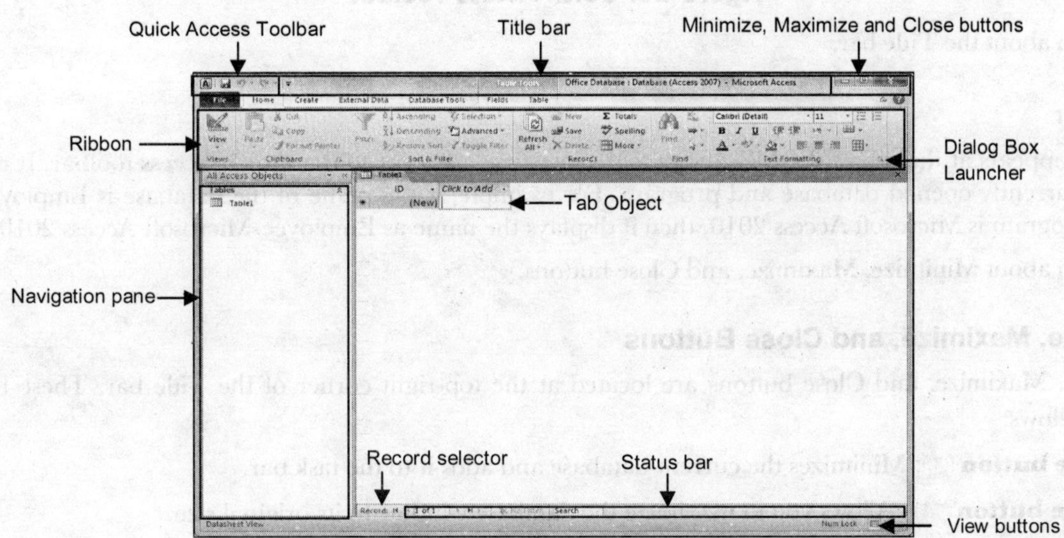

Figure-19: MS Access 2010 interface

As shown in Figure-19, the user interface of MS Access 2010 contains the following components:

- The Quick Access Toolbar
- The Title bar
- The Minimize, Maximize, and Close buttons
- The Status bar
- The View buttons
- The Record Selector
- Ribbon
- The Dialog box launcher
- The Navigation pane
- The Tab object

Let's discuss these components in detail, one by one.

The Quick Access Toolbar

The Quick Access Toolbar is located at the top-left corner of the MS Access 2010 interface. It contains a set of most often used options while working with MS Access. By default, it contains three options, Save, Undo, and Redo; however, you can also customize it to add more options. The Quick Access Toolbar is also available in the 2003 and 2007 versions of MS Access. The Quick Access Toolbar is shown in Figure-20:

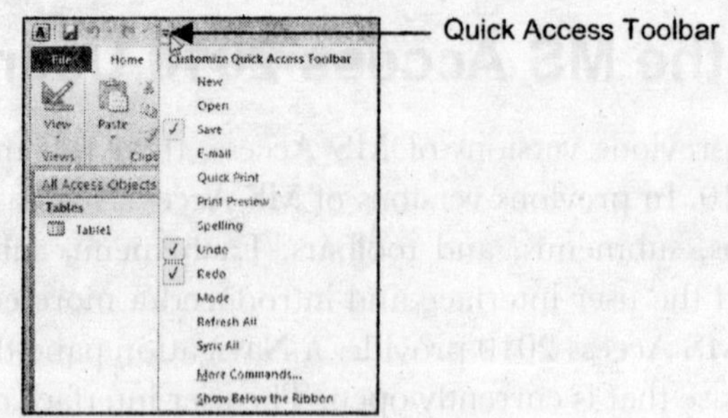

Figure-20: Quick Access Toolbar

Let's now learn about the Title bar.

The Title Bar

The Title bar appears at the top of the MS Access 2010 interface adjacent to the Quick Access toolbar. It displays the name of the currently opened database and program. For example, if the name of the database is Employee and the name of the program is Microsoft Access 2010, then it displays the name as Employee-Microsoft Access 2010.

Let's now learn about Minimize, Maximize, and Close buttons.

The Minimize, Maximize, and Close Buttons

The Minimize, Maximize, and Close buttons are located at the top-right corner of the Title bar. These buttons are described as follows:

- **Minimize button** (): Minimizes the current database and adds it to the task bar.
- **Maximize button** (): Allows you to maximize the database window to its original size.
- **Close button** (): Closes the current database. If you have performed any task in a database, it will show you a warning message to save the task before quitting.

Let's now learn about the Status bar.

The Status Bar

The Status bar is located at the bottom of the MS Access 2010 interface. It displays the information about the current database object or view. In MS Access 2010, the Status bar displays the view in which the current database object is opened.

Let's now learn about the Record Selector.

The Record Selector

The Record Selector is located at the bottom right of the MS Access 2010 interface. It displays the current record number of the opened database object. The Record Selector also allows you to navigate to other records. For example, if you are on the 1st record of a table and want to view the 115th record, then you can use the Record Selector to move to the desired record.

Let's now learn about the View buttons.

The View Buttons

View buttons enable you to display a selected object in a particular view. These buttons are basically locates in the bottom right corner of the MS Access 2010 interface. MS Access 2010 provides two buttons for a table- Datasheet view and Design view, if the table does not contain any data. These buttons allow you to switch from one view to another. For example, if you are viewing a table in a Datasheet view and want to view it in the Design view, then you can use the View buttons.

Let's now learn about the Ribbon.

Ribbon

The Ribbon is a pane which is located below the Title bar in the MS Access 2010 user interface. It contains a set of commands organized in the structure of tabs, such as Home, Create, External Data, Database Tools, Fields, and Table. These are the basic tabs that are also referred to as Command tabs. To reduce cluttering in the Ribbon, some tabs are shown only when they are needed, such as Format tab. These tabs are also referred to as Contextual tabs. The Ribbon is shown in Figure-21:

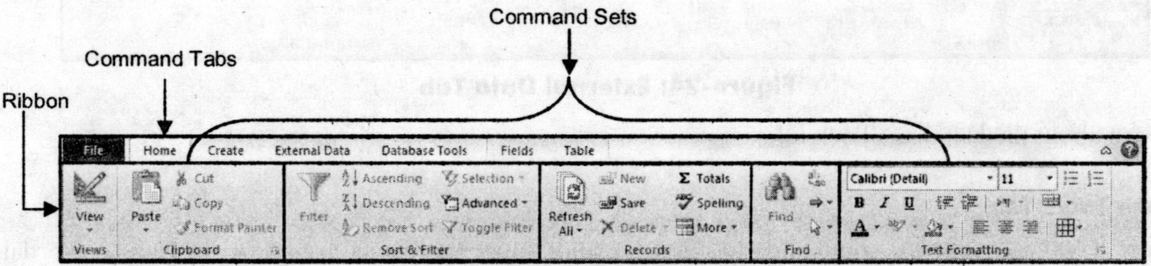

Figure-21: Ribbon

The tabs present on the Ribbon are as follows:

- The Home tab
- The Create tab
- The External Data tab
- The Database Tools tab

Let's discuss these tabs in detail.

The Home Tab

The Home tab consists of the basic commands, such as cut, copy, and paste, which are used to edit and format a data in a database. This tab is divided into six groups –Views, Clipboard, Sort & Filter, Records, Find, and Text Formatting. The Home tab with its various groups in MS Access 2010 is shown in Figure-22:

Figure-22: Home tab

Let's now learn about the Create tab.

The Create Tab

The Create tab contains commands to create and manage tables, forms, reports, and queries. This tab contains various groups, such as, Templates, Tables, Forms, Reports, and Macros & Code. The Create tab is shown in Figure-23:

Figure-23: Create Tab

Let's now learn about the External Data tab.

The External Data Tab

The External Data tab contains commands to import, export, and collect data. It also provides commands to work with SharePoint and offline data. This tab contains three groups, Import & link, Export, and Collect Data. The External Data tab is shown in Figure-24:

Figure-24: External Data Tab

Let's now learn about the Database Tools tab.

The Database Tools Tab

The Database Tools tab contains commands to create relationships, analyze tables and databases, move data, and restrict security on the data. This tab contains five groups, Macro, Relationships, Analyze, Move Data, and Add-Ins. The Database Tools tab is shown in Figure-25:

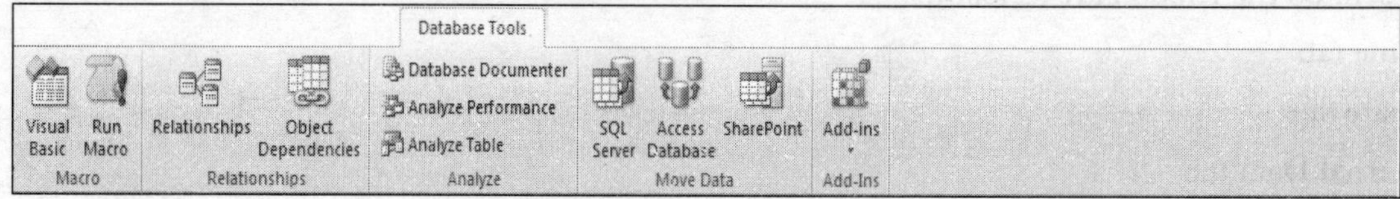

Figure-25: Database Tools Tab

Let's learn about the dialog box launcher in MS Access 2010.

The Dialog Box Launcher

The dialog box launcher is a button present in some groups on the Ribbon. Clicking this button opens a dialog box related to the specific group. This dialog box contains additional options that are not displayed as commands or options of the groups on the Ribbon. For example, when you click the dialog box launcher button under the Font group of the Home tab, the Font dialog box appears. The icon of the dialog box launcher is shown in Figure-26:

Figure-26: Dialog Box Launcher

Let's now learn about the Navigation pane.

The Navigation Pane

The Navigation pane is a pane that displays the database objects, such as tables, forms, reports, pages, and macros. When you create any object in a database, it is automatically added to the Navigation pane window, using which you can open the object directly by double-clicking it. The Navigation pane is shown in Figure-27:

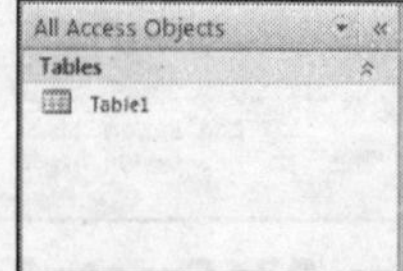

Figure-27: Navigation Pane

Let's now learn about the tab objects.

The Tab Object

The tab objects refer to objects that are located at the top of a Datasheet view. In MS Access 2010, the database objects, such as tables, forms, queries, and reports, appear as the tab objects. In case you want to rename a tab object, you have to first close it and then from the Navigation pane you can rename it by right-clicking it and selecting the Rename option from the context menu. The tab object is shown in Figure-28:

Figure-28: Tab Object

After learning about the user interface of MS Access 2010, let's now learn how to create a table in a Database.

5.8 Creating a Table

In MS Access a database stores information in the table which is a collection of information on a subject (such as Employees). A table stores data in a row and column format which are known as records and fields, respectively. A record is a combination of fields that you insert in a table. Using table, you can easily maintain a database in an organization or anywhere else you are require. You can create a table in Datasheet view and in Design view by using the Table Design option from the Create tab.

In this section, you learn to create a table in Datasheet view, in Design view and saving a table.

Let's now learn how to create a table in Datasheet view.

5.8.1 Creating a Table in Datasheet View

You can create a table in Datasheet view, adding new fields in a table by simply typing the field names in the columns.

Let's perform the following steps to create a new table in the Datasheet view:

1. Open a database in which you wish to create a table. In our case, we have opened **Office Database** (Figure-1).
2. Select the **Create** tab (Figure-29).
3. Select the **Table** option from the **Tables** group under the **Create** tab, as shown in Figure-29:

Figure-29: Create tab

A new table named as **Table1** appears in the **Datasheet** view with an **ID** field and **Click** to Add placeholder (Figure-30)

4. Click the **Click to Add** drop-down list. A drop-down list appears (Figure-30).
5. Select the desired field from the list. In our case, we have selected the **Text** field, as shown in Figure-30:

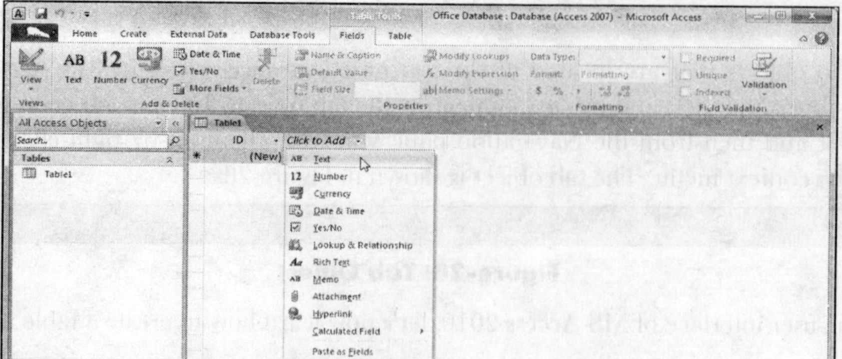

Figure-30: Select the desired field

The **Field1** text box appears, as shown in Figure-31:

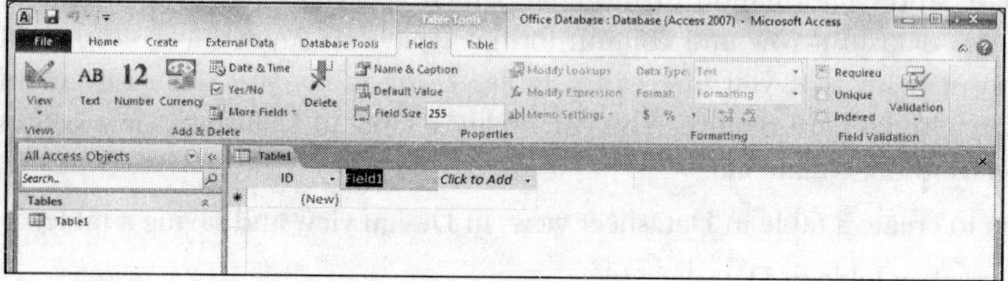

Figure-31: Text box appears

6. Type the desired name for the new field in the **Field1** text box. In our case, we have typed **First Name** in the text box, as shown in Figure-32:

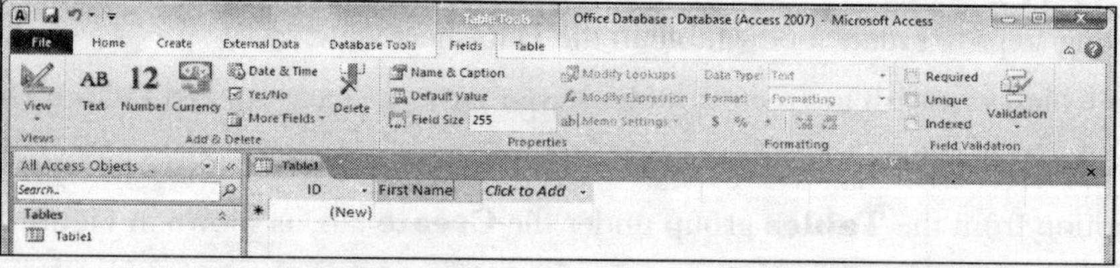

Figure-32: Typing in text box

7. Repeat the step 5 and 6 to add more fields. In our case, we have added the **Last Name, Designation, Address, and Mobile Number** fields in the table, as shown in Figure-33:

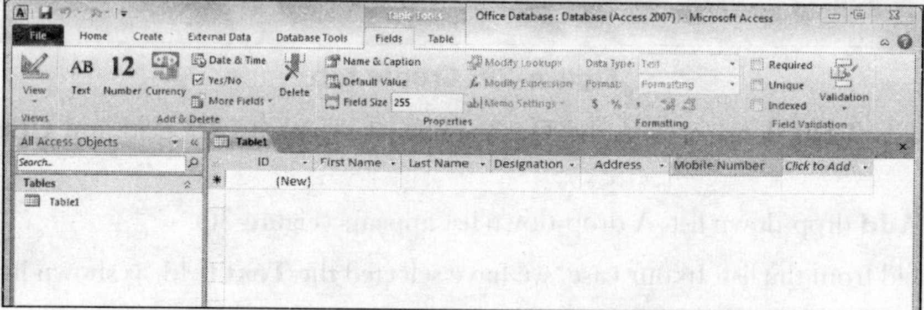

Figure-33: Add more fields to the table

Let's now learn to create a table in Design view.

5.8.2 Creating a Table in the Design View

You can create a table in the Design view to specify the exact field that you are required. The Design view has two sections-the upper section and the lower section. Using the upper section, you can enter a field and assign the relevant data type and description to it. In the lower section, you can specify the field properties, which are used to validate the property of a particular field. The main purpose of Design view is to create validation in the table. When we give data type and some other validation in the table then we use this Design view.

Let's perform the following steps to create a table in the Design view:

1. Select the **Create** tab (Figure-34).
2. Select the **Table Design** option from the **Tables** group, as shown in Figure-34:

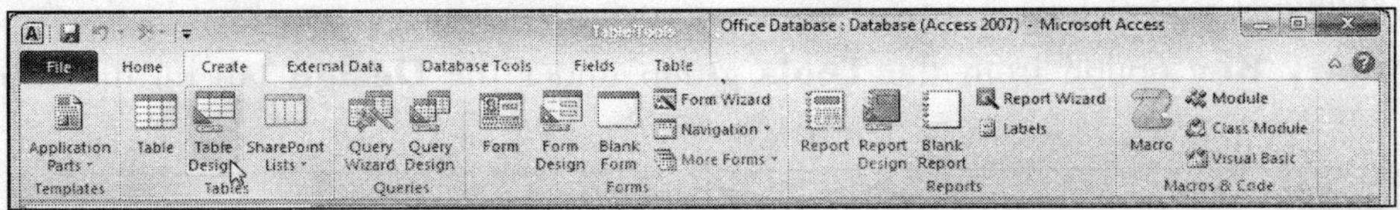

Figure-34: Table Design option from the Tables group

The **Design** view opens with a new table, named as **Table2**.

3. Select the first cell under the **Field Name** text box and **type** a desired field name. In our case, we have typed **EmpID** in the text box (Figure-35).
4. Press the **TAB** key on the keyboard to move to the next field.

   The **Data Type** column is highlighted and the **Text** data type appears, by default (Figure-35).
5. Click the down arrow button that appears beside the **Text** data type (Figure-35). A drop-down list appears (Figure-35).
6. Select the desired data type. In our case, we have selected **AutoNumber** data type, as shown in Figure-35:

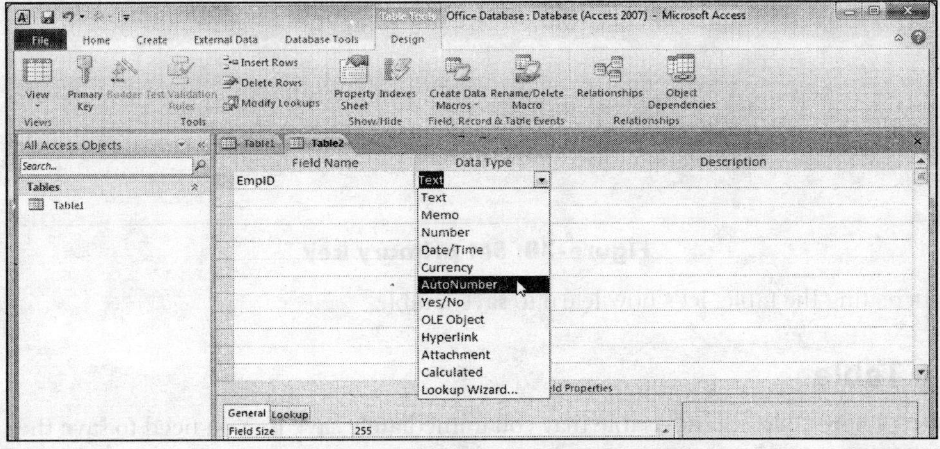

Figure-35: Working with first cell

You can also press the ENTER key on the keyboard to switch to another field or column in a table in both the Datasheet and Design views.

7. Press the **TAB** key on the keyboard to highlight the **Description** column (Figure-36).
8. Type the desired description of the field in this column. In our case, we have typed **This field is filled by autonumber**, as shown in Figure-36:

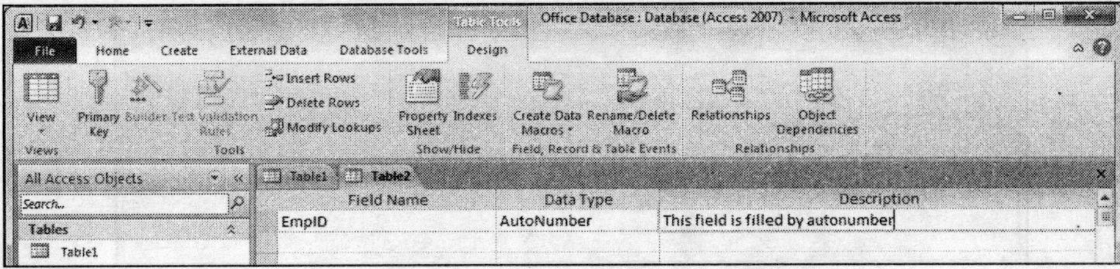

Figure-36: Description of the field

In the table Design view, the Description field is optional. This field is used when the purpose of the field is not clear from its name.

9. Repeat steps from 3 to 6 to more fields with its data type in **Table2**. In our case, we have added the **First Name, Last Name, and Salary** field (Figure-37).
10. Select the desired field in the row in which you want to set the primary key. In our case, we have selected the **EmpID** field (Figure-37).
11. Select the **Primary Key** option from the **Tools** group under the **Design** tab on the Ribbon, as shown in Figure-37:

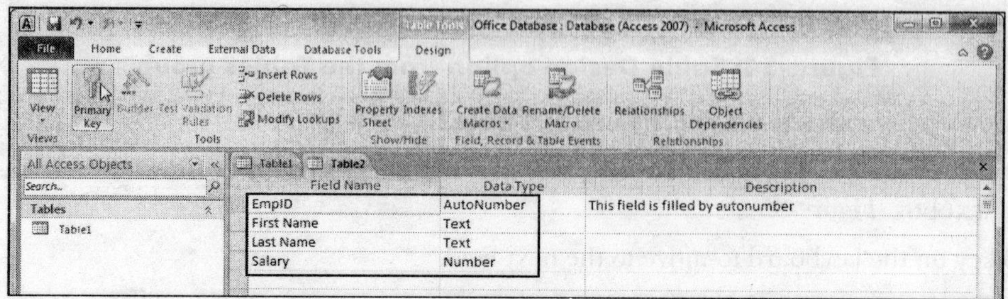

Figure-37: Add more fields

The primary key is set on the **EmpID** field, as shown in Figure-38:

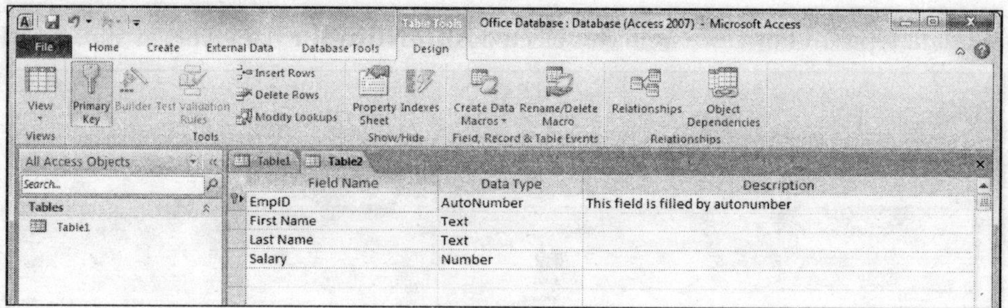

Figure-38: Set primary key

After learning about creating the table, let's now learn to save a table.

5.8.3 Saving a Table

After you have created a new table, it is advisable that you immediately save it. You need to save the table in a database as frequently as possible. Otherwise, due to any unexpected events, such as a power cut or system failure, you may lose the changes that you have made in the table.

Let's perform the following steps to save a table:

1. Right-click **Table2** in the **Document** tab (Figure-39). A context menu appears (Figure-39).
2. Select the **Save** option from the context menu, as shown in Figure-39:

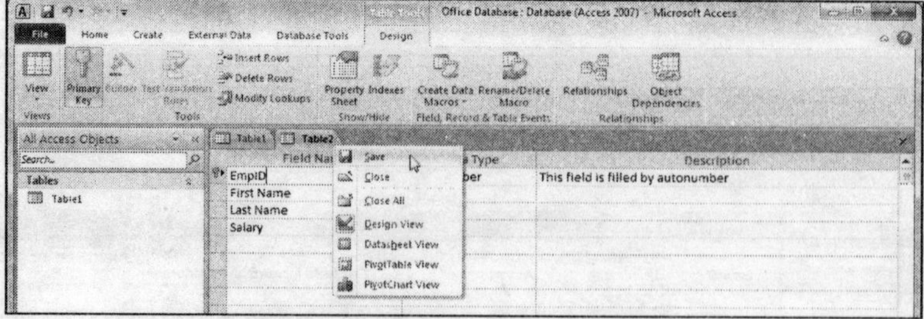

Figure-39: Context menu

The **Save As** dialog box appears (Figure-40)

3. Type the desired name in the **Table Name** text box. In our case, we have typed **Employees Salary** in the text box (Figure-40).
4. Click the **OK** button to close the **Save As** dialog box (Figure-40).

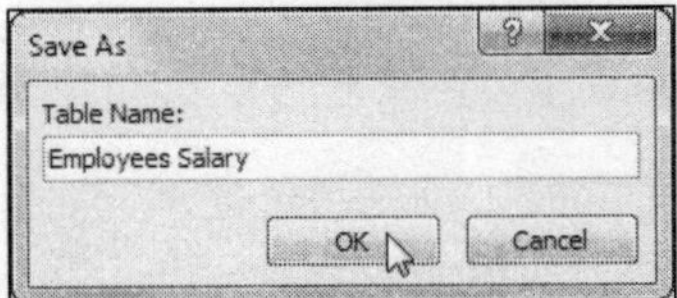

Figure-40: Save As dialog box

The table is saved as **Employees Salary**, as shown in Figure-41:

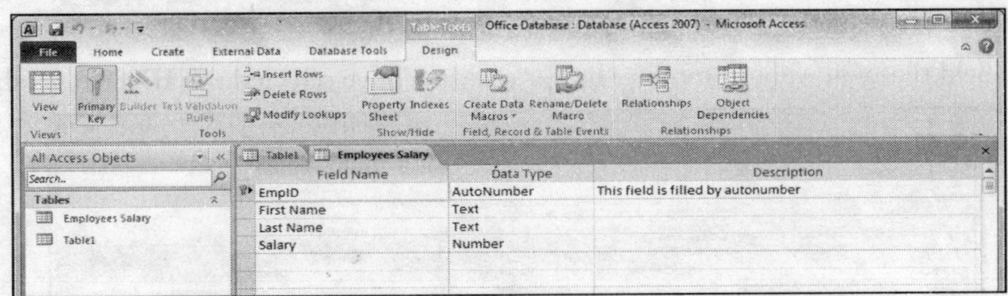

Figure-41: Table is named as Employees Salary

Similarly, you can save **Table1**. In our case, we have saved **Table1** as **Employees Details** table in **Datasheet** view.

5. Click the **Employees Salary** table which appears beside the **Employees Details** table in **Datasheet** view. The **Employees Salary** table appears in the **Design** view.
6. Click the **Close** button that appears beside the **Document** tab to close the **Employees Salary** table,

The **Datasheet** view reappears in which the **Employees Details** table is open (Figure-42).

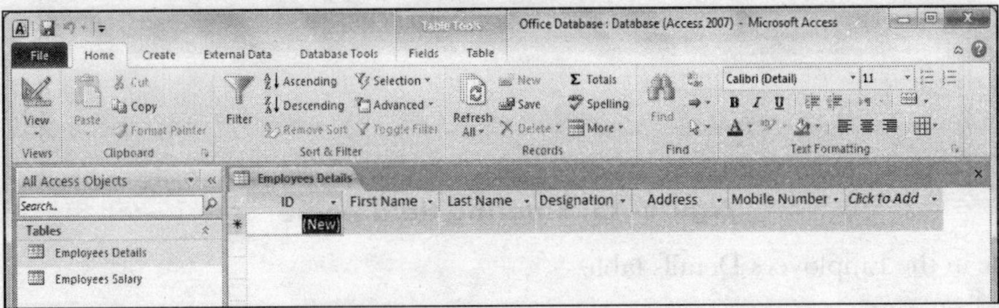

Figure-42: Datasheet view

Let's now learn to open a table in the Design view.

5.8.4 Opening a Table in the Design View

After creating a table, you can open it in the Design view to either add more fields in the table or modify the existing fields in the table. You can open a table in the Design view by performing the following steps to open a table in the Design view:

1. Select the desired table from the **Navigation** pane that you wish to open in **Design** view. In our case, we have selected the **Employees Details** table (Figure-43).
2. Right-click the **Employees Details** table. A context menu appears (Figure-43).
3. Select the **Design View** option from the context menu, as shown in Figure-43:

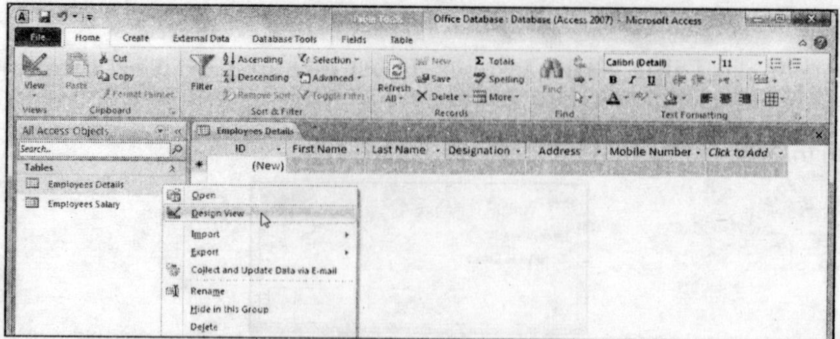

Figure-43: Design view

The **Employees Details** table appears in the Design view (Figure-44). In the Deign view, you can add a new field, modify a field such as change a field name, and delete a field.

4. Select the desired field that you want to modify. In our case, we have selected the **ID** field, as shown in Figure-44:

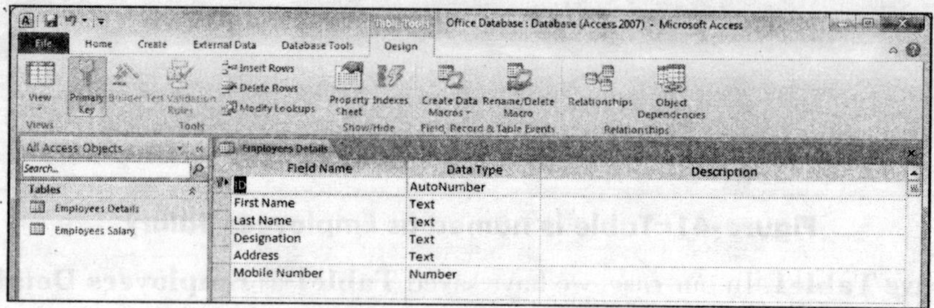

Figure-44: Modify the field

5. Type the desired name in the **Field Name** text box. In our case, we have typed **EmpID**, as shown in Figure-45:

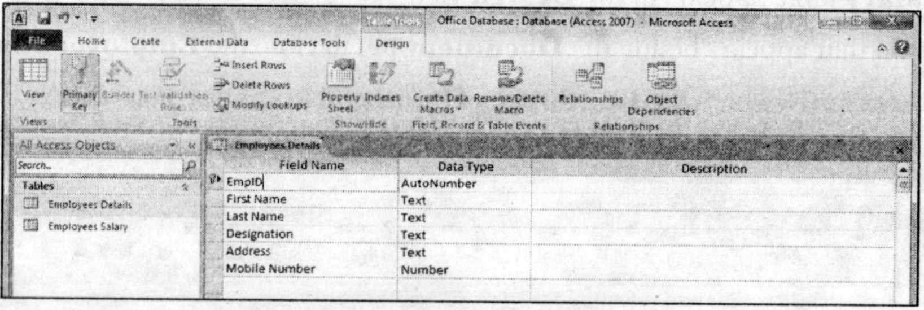

Figure-45: Entering field name

Save the changes made in the Employees Details table.

If you want to open a table in Design view that is already opened in the Datasheet view. Then, you need to right-click the table in the Datasheet view and then select the Design view option from the context menu.

Let's now learn to work with the fields in the table.

5.9 Working with Fields in a Table

In a table, fields are those essential characteristics, such as a name that uniquely identifies the data within a table, data type that defines the nature of the data, the field properties that defines the appearance or behavior of the data in a table. In MS Access 2010, you can add the fields in the table as per your requirement. You can hide fields if you do not wish to view the data that field contain. You can also freeze a field so that no one can stay in the same place while you scroll around the rest of the table. You can also rename and delete a field, if you do not require it.

In this section, you learn to insert a new field in a table, and delete a field.

Let's begin by inserting a new field in a table.

5.9.1 Inserting a New Field

You can insert a new field if you want to add more information in a table. When you insert a new field above the existing field, then the existing field or fields are push down. You can then enter information in a new field. For example, in our Employees Details table, we want to insert a new field above the Mobile field in a table.

Let's perform the following steps to insert a new field in a table:

1. Select the desired field from above you wish to insert a new field. In our case, we have selected **Mobile Number** field (Figure-46).
2. Right-click the **Mobile Number** field. A context menu appears (Figure-46).
3. Select the **Insert Rows** option from the context menu, as shown in Figure-46:

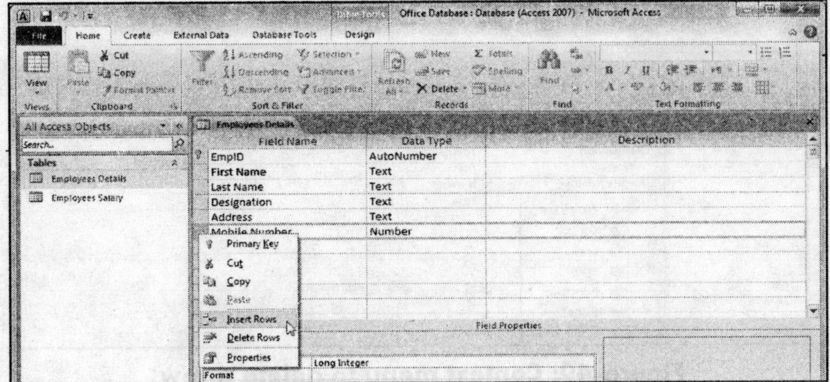

Figure-46: Inserting row

A new row appears above the Mobile Number field, as shown in Figure-47:

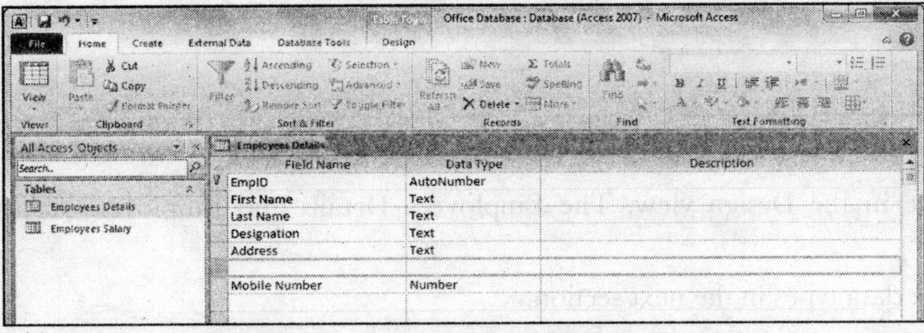

Figure-47: Give a name to the row

4. Type a desired field name in a new row in the **Field Name** column. In our case, we have typed **City** (Figure-48).
5. Press the **TAB** key. The **Data Type** field name gets highlighted (Figure-48).
6. Select the appropriate data type. In our case, we have selected **Text** as a data type, as shown in Figure-48:

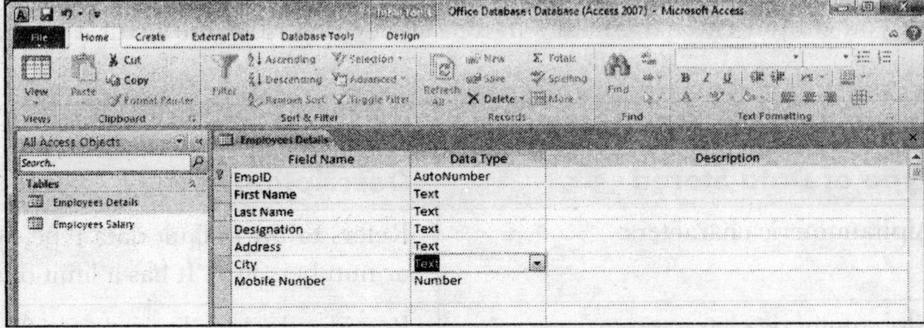

Figure-48: Define data type

Let's now learn to delete a field.

5.9.2 Deleting a Field

After creating a field in the table, you may realize that it is no longer required. You can delete the field that you no longer required.

Let's perform the following steps to delete a field:

1. Select the desired field that you wish to delete. In our case, we have selected the **City** field.
2. Right-click the **City** field. A context menu appears (Figure-49).
3. Select the **Delete Rows** option from the context menu, as shown in Figure-49:

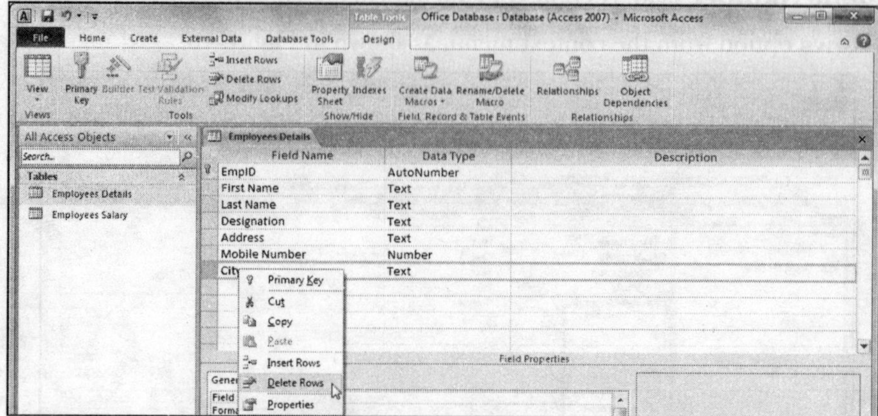

Figure-49: Context menu to delete a row

The selected field is deleted, as shown in Figure-50:

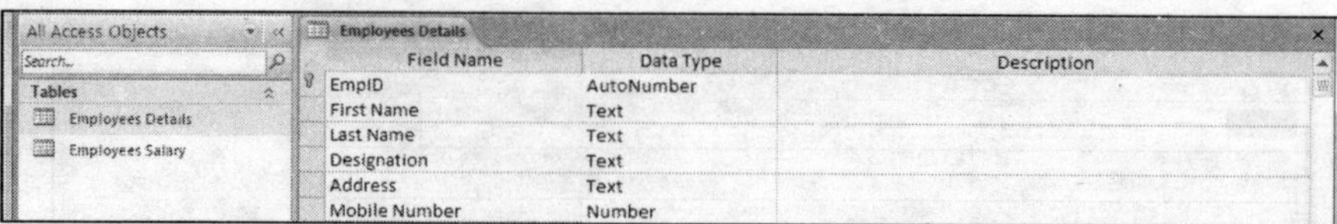

Figure-50: Selected field deleted

Save and close the table in the Design view. The Employees Details and Employees Salary table appears in the Navigation pane.

Let's now learn about the data types in the next section.

5.10 Understanding Data Types

When you create a table in the Design view, you need to assign the data types for each field in a table. These data types specify the type of data that each field will hold. In MS Access, you are provided with several data types field such as text, number, and autonumber that you can assign according to the data in the field. For example, if you have set the data types as number then you cannot enter the letters in it. Table-1 describes the Data Types available in MS Access 2010:

Table-1: Data Types available in MS Access

Data Type	Type of Data Stored	Description
Text	Alphanumeric characters	Refers to the default data type, which stores characters or numbers in it. It has a limit of up to 255 characters.
Memo	Alphanumeric characters	Provides the type limit of 65, 536 characters or less.
Number	Numbers only	Contains field size of 1,2,4,8 or 16 bytes. This data type also supports special characters, such as decimal points.

Table-1: Data Types available in MS Access

Data Type	Type of Data Stored	Description
Date/Time	Date and time data	Allows you to enter data and time in the table.
Currency	Related to money	Stores currency value as 8-bytes numbers.
AutoNumber	Automatically generated number increments	Stores Access generated values as 4-bytes numbers.
Yes/No	Boolean data	Represents the Boolean data in the table. The value 1 symbolizes Yes and the value 0 symbolizes No. In addition, the field can be formatted to display values, such as True/False.
OLE Object	Pictures, graphs, and other embedded OLE objects	Allows you to attach the external data, such as picture and graph in a table.
Hyperlink	Link to the external sources	Refers to the segment of text or a graphical item that serves as a cross-reference between different Web pages or different locations of the same Web page.
Attachment	Attach data files or any other external files	Allows you to attach data files, such as Word document and Excel Spreadsheet.
Lookup Wizard	Display data from another table	Creates look up list from data.
Calculated	Display data from another table	Allows you to view the calculated field in the table. This is the new feature in MS Access 2010 data types.

Let's now learn to enter records in a table.

5.11 Working with Records in a Table

In MS Access records refers to the data that we enter in the table. You can enter records in a table in a Datasheet view into a cell which is the intersection of a row and a column in spreadsheet format. Various operations can be performed over the records. These operations are insertion, deletion, navigation of the records. Let's explore these operations.

5.11.1 Entering the Records in a Table

Let's perform the following steps to enter a record in a table:

1. Select the desired table in which you want to enter the records. In our case, we have selected the **Employees Details** table. The table opens in the **Datasheet** view. The first column under the **EmpID** field is highlighted and appears as **New** is selected by default.

   The ID field (or EmpID field in our case) which appears as New is an AutoNumber field which is automatically filled by Access itself in a sequence such as 1 and 2.
2. Press the **TAB** key on the keyboard. The **First Name** field gets highlighted.
3. Type the desired name of the employee under the **First Name** field. In our case, we have typed **Monika**.
4. Press the **TAB** key on the keyboard. The next field named as **Last Name** is highlighted.
5. Type the last name of the employee under the **Last Name** field. In our case, we have typed **Sharma**.
6. Press the **TAB** key on the keyboard. The next field, **Designation,** is highlighted.
7. Type the designation of the employee under the **Designation** field. In our case, we have typed **Consultant**.
8. Press the **TAB** key on the keyboard to highlight the next field, **Address**.

9. Type the address of the employee under the **Address** field. In our case, we have typed **67, shivaji park**.
10. Press the **TAB** key on the keyboard. The **Mobile Number** field is highlighted.
11. Type the mobile number of an employee in the **Mobile Number** field. In our case we have typed **9947835276**.

Repeat the steps 3 to 11 to enter more records in the table and save it, as shown in Figure-51:

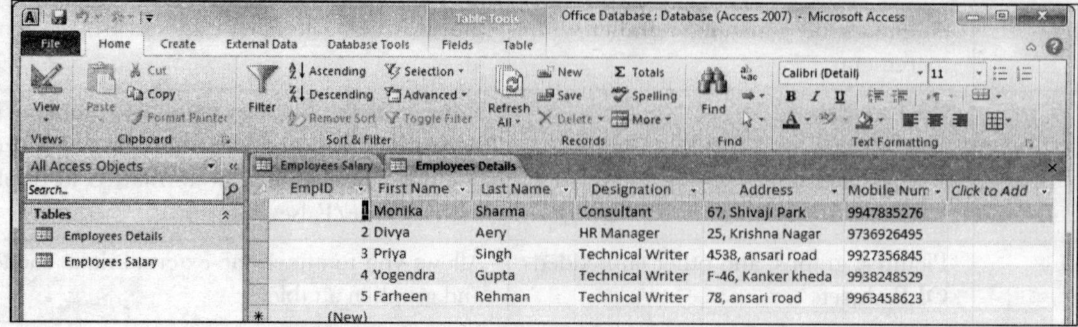

Figure-51: Records added to the table

After learning about entering records in the table, let's now learn to navigate between records.

Navigating between Records in a Datasheet View

After entering several records in a table, you may need to search for a particular record or relook at the entire record to make changes or evaluate the data that you have entered. You may navigate to the desired record that you wish by scrolling through the records and positioning your cursor on the desired record. Using these buttons, you can navigate between records, select the desired record, or start a new record. Let's now learn to edit records in a table.

5.11.2 Editing Records in a Table

Editing records mean changing or modifying records in a table, such as changing the record in a cell with a new data, updating records or deleting records. You can edit records in any objects such as in form, and reports in any view such as Datasheet, or Design view.

Let's now learn to select a record in a table.

5.11.3 Selecting a Record (Single or Multiple)

You need to select a record, before performing any tasks in the table. For example for changing a record or deleting a record you need to select that particular record to which you wish to change or delete. Whenever you select a single or multiple row of the table, it is highlighted on the tabular sheet. Selected data appear highlighted than the other records in a table.

Let's perform the following steps to select a record in a table:

1. Move the mouse pointer to the record which you want to select. In our case, we have moved the mouse pointer over the first record. The mouse pointer shape changed to an arrow, as shown in Figure-52:

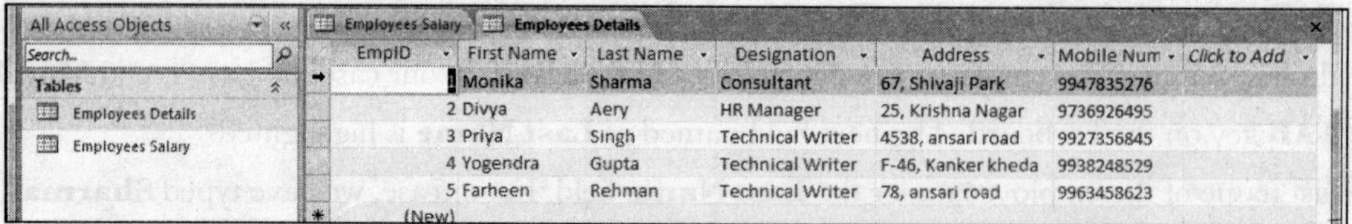

Figure-52: Choose the record which want to be selected

2. Click the record in a table which you want to select. The first record in a table is highlighted, as shown in Figure-53:

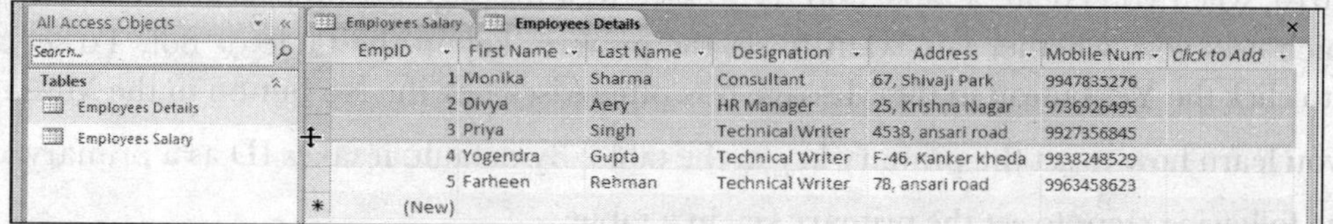

Figure-53: Selected record in a table is highlighted

3. Press the mouse button and keeping the mouse pointer till you reach the third row of the table to select multiple records from the table. Three records in a table are selected, as shown in Figure-54:

Figure-54: Selecting multiple records from the table

Let's now learn to delete a record in a table.

5.11.4 Deleting a Record

You can delete a particular record from the table whenever it is not required. Let's perform the following steps to delete a record in a table:

1. Select the desired record that you wish to delete. In our case, we have selected the **5th** record.
2. Select the **Delete** option from the **Records** group under the **Home** tab on the Ribbon.

   You can also delete a record by pressing the DELETE key on the keyboard. In addition, you can delete a record in a table by right-clicking the desired record and selecting the Delete Record option from the context menu.

   A **Microsoft Access** message box appears (Figure-55).
3. Click the **Yes** button, as shown in Figure-55:

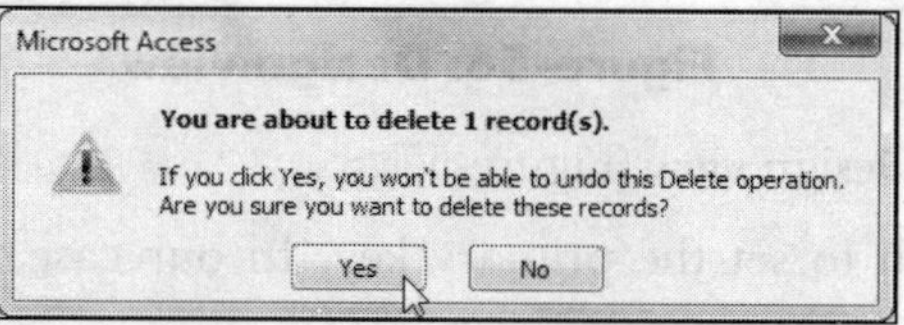

Figure-55: Message Box is confirming the deletion

Let's now learn to work with the keys in the database.

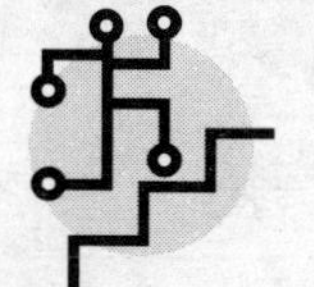

Activity-2

Create a database table named Books for a Library database. Insert, select, edit, and delete records from the table using MS- Access 2010.

5.12 Understanding the Concept of Creating Relationship between Tables

A key in a database refers to a field, which helps in sorting and identifying the data. In a database, there are two types of key, such as primary key and foreign key. A primary key is a key that is used to uniquely identify each record in a table. For example, EmpID, Bank account number, and student roll no. A primary key column does not contain a null and duplicate values. A foreign key is a key in a table, which is a reference of the primary key in the other table. A primary key can be used by multiple foreign keys in the other tables.

A relationship is a link between two or more tables. You can connect the two fields from two different tables with the help of the relationship. You can create relationships between tables to bring together related information. The relationships between tables are essential for creating a form, report, or query that uses information from more than one table in a database.

In this section, you learn about setting the primary key in MS Access.

5.12.1 Setting the Primary Key

In MS Access 2010, when you create a table and try to save it, a message box appears. The message box contains the information, which asks you, whether you want to set the primary key in the table or not. To set a primary key in a table, you have to click the Yes button in the Message box otherwise click the No button in the Message box.

In this section, you learn how to set the primary key in the table. By default, it takes ID as a primary key.

Let's perform the following steps to set the primary key in a table:

1. Select the desired table that you wish to open in the Design view. In our case, we have opened the **Employees Details** table (Figure-56).
2. Right-click the **Employees Details** table in **Navigation** pane. A context menu appears (Figure-56).
3. Select the **Design View** option from the context menu, as shown in Figure-56:

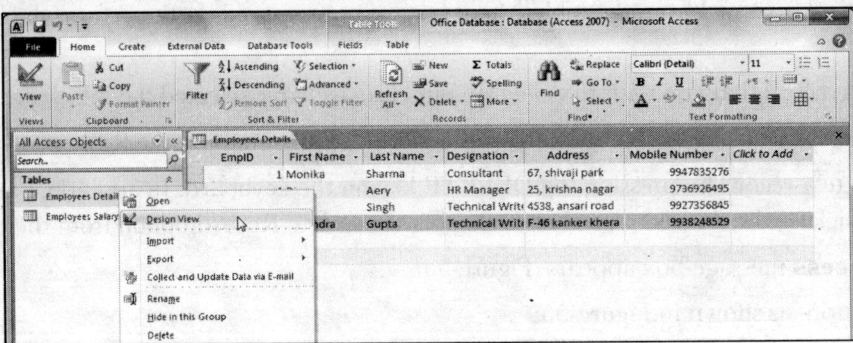

Figure-56: Design view

The selected table appears in the Design view (Figure-57).

4. Select the field at which you wish to set the primary key. In our case, we have selected the **First Name** field (Figure-57).
5. Select the **Primary Key** option from the **Tools** group in the **Design** tab, as shown in Figure-57:

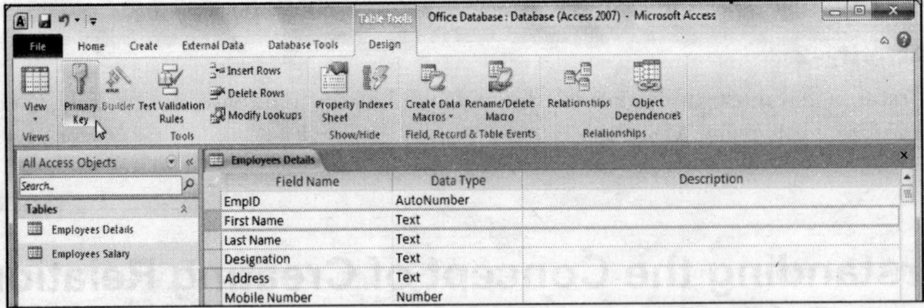

Figure-57: Selecting field to set the primary key

You can also set the primary key by right-clicking the selected field and selecting the Primary Key option from the context menu.

The primary key is set at the selected field, as shown in Figure-58:

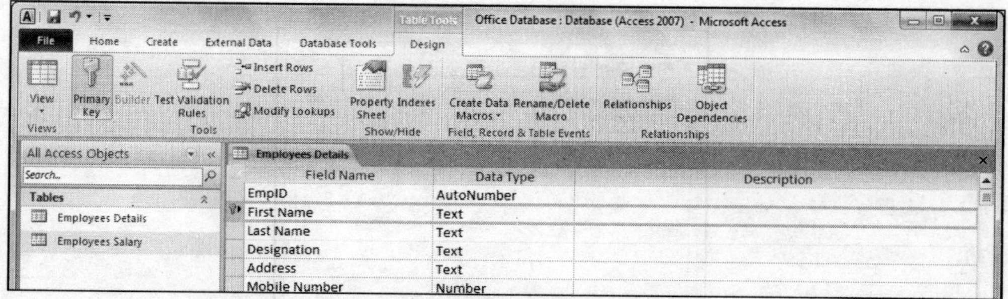

Figure-58: Primary key defined

Let's now learn to remove a primary key.

5.12.2 Removing a Primary key

You can remove the primary key from the field if you do not wish to apply it on the same field.

Let's perform the following steps to remove a primary key:

1. Select the field which is set as the primary key. In our case, we have selected **First Name** field (Figure-59).
2. Select the **Primary Key** option from the **Tools** group in the **Design** tab, as shown in Figure-59:

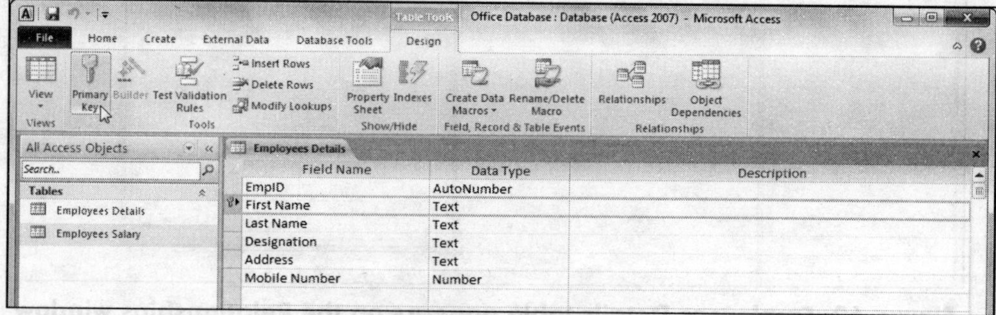

Figure-59: Primary key removed

The primary key is removed from the selected field.

Let's now learn to create relationship between tables.

5.12.3 Creating Relationships between Two Tables

Relationship defines relation between two or more table. You can create relationships between tables to bring together related information. When you create relationships between two tables then one table becomes the parent table which holds the primary key and another one is child table which hold foreign key.

Let's perform the following steps to create relationship between two tables:

1. Select the **Relationships** option from the **Relationships** group in the **Database Tools** tab, as shown in Figure-60:

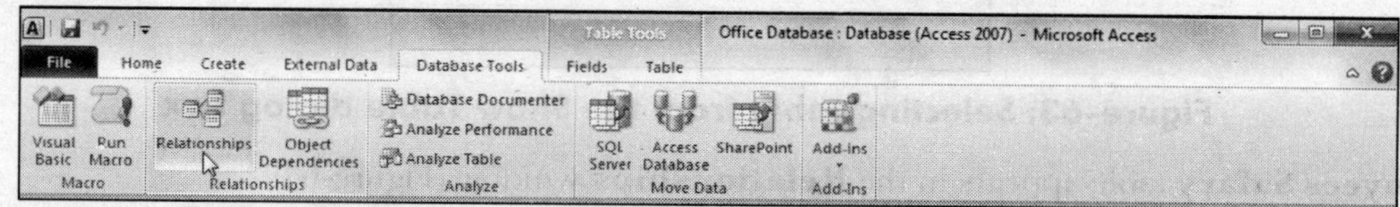

Figure-60: Relationships option from the Relationships group

The **Show Table** dialog box appears (Figure-61).

2. Select the **Employees Details** table from the **Show Table** dialog box (Figure-61).

3. Click the **Add** button (Figure-61).

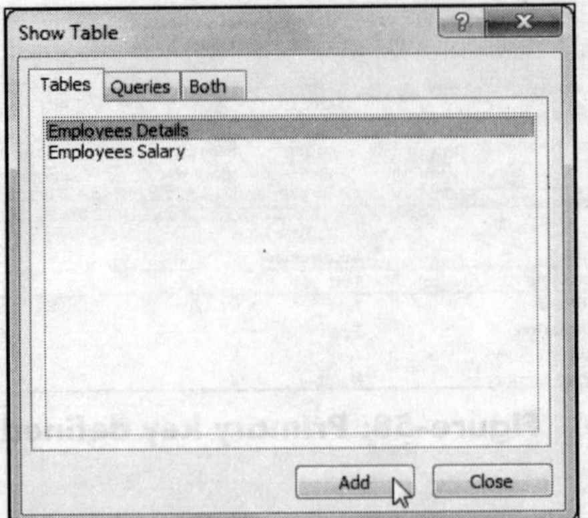

Figure-61: Show Table dialog box

The **Employees Details** table appears on the **Relationships** window appears, as shown in Figure-62:

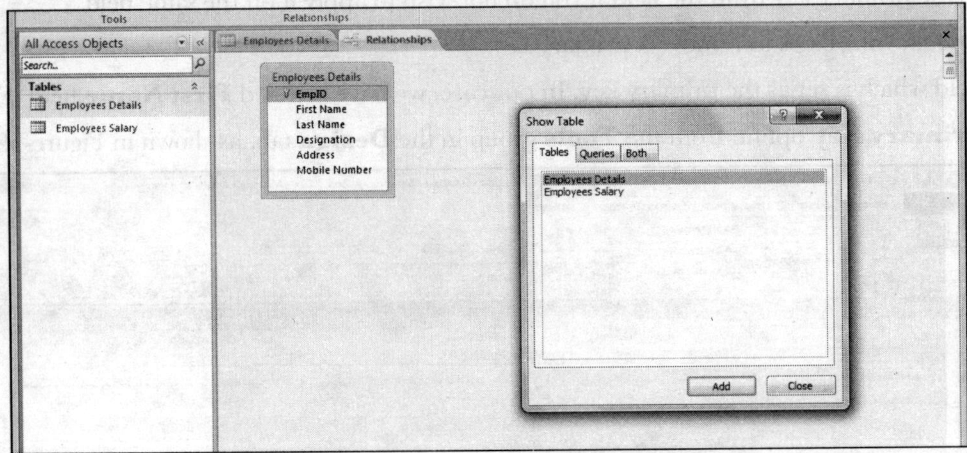

Figure-62: Employees Details table appears on the Relationships window

4. Select the **Employees Salary** table from the **Show Table** dialog box (Figure-63).
5. Click the **Add** button (Figure-63).

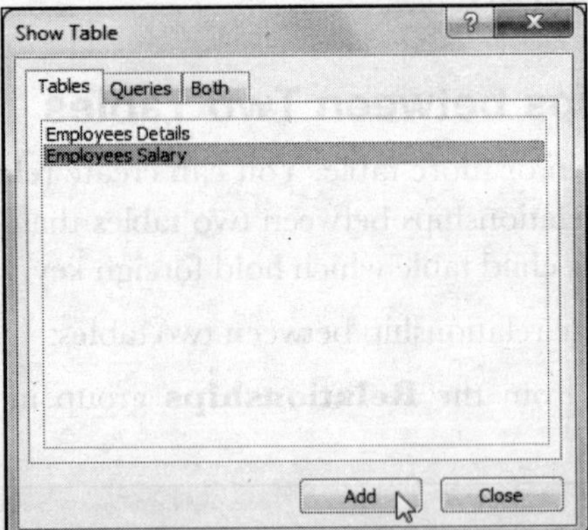

Figure-63: Selecting table from the Show Table dialog box

An **Employees Salary** table appears in the **Relationships** window (Figure-64).

6. Click the **Close** button to close the **Show Table** dialog box, as shown in Figure-64:

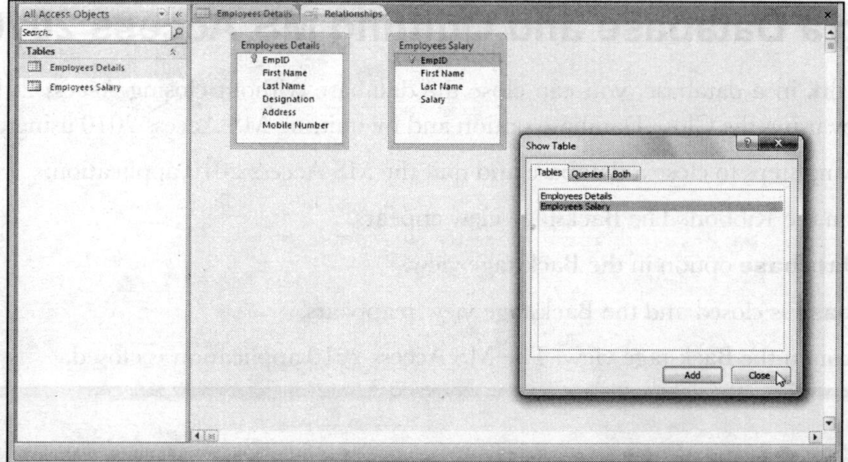

Figure-64: Employees Salary table appears in the Relationships window

7. Press the mouse button over the **EmpID** field from the **Employees Details** table and drag it inside the **Employees Salary** table, as shown in Figure-65:

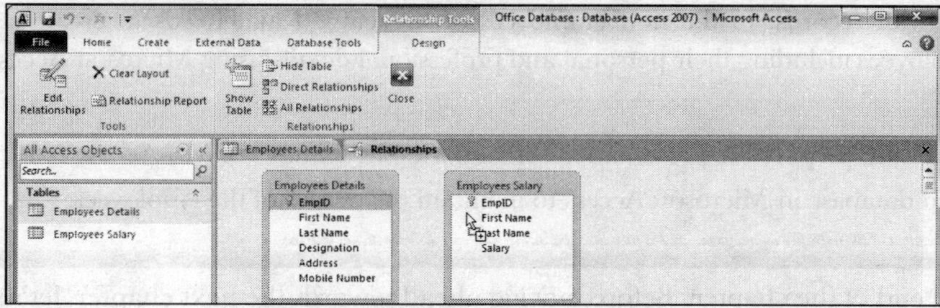

Figure-65: Setting relationship

8. Release the mouse button. The **Edit Relationships** dialog box appears (Figure-66).
9. Click the **Create** button, as shown in Figure-66:

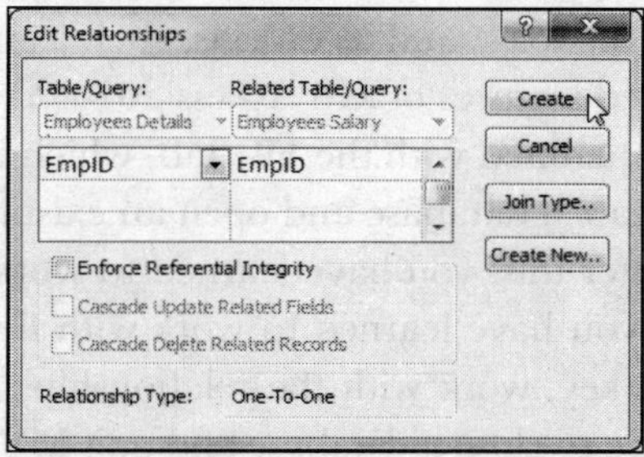

Figure-66: Create relationship

A connector appears which represents the relationship between the selected field in the **Employees Details** and **Employees Salary** tables, as shown in Figure-67:

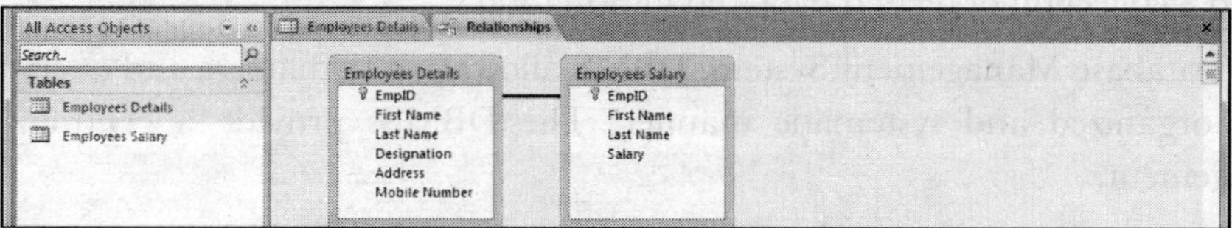

Figure-67: Relationship established

Let's now learn how to close a database and quit Access 2010.

5.13 Closing a Database and Quitting MS Access 2010

After completing the work in a database, you can close the database without closing Access 2010. You can close the database in two ways- by using the Close Database option and by quitting MS Access 2010 using the Exit option.

Let's perform the following steps to close a database and quit the MS Access 2010 application:

1. Select the **File** tab in the Ribbon. The Backstage view appears.
2. Select the **Close Database** option in the Backstage view.

   The **Office Database** is closed and the Backstage view reappears.
3. Select the **Exit** option in the Backstage view. The MS Access 2010 application is closed.

Case Study: Managing employee's data

Rajat is an operations manager in ABC organization. He has to give a presentation on Microsoft Access for creating databases and working with records, to the new employees of his team. Rajat needs to create a sample database to manage data about employees including their personal and professional details using Microsoft Access.

Question:

Q1. Assuming you are Rajat, prepare the presentation for exploring he features of MS-Access 2010.

Q2. Create the required database in Microsoft Access to maintain the details of the employees.

*(*Case study presented is the proprietary information of the respective organization, and is used here specifically and only for educational purpose.)*

With this, we come to the end of the chapter. Before moving ahead towards the next chapter, let's summarizes the main points of the chapter.

5.14 Summary

In this chapter, you have learned about the database and its objects, such as table, form, query, and report. After this, you have learned about the new and improved features of MS Access 2010. You have also learned about the procedure to start MS Access 2010. Next, you have acquainted with the File tab, which is also known as Backstage view. Further you have learned about the procedure to create a database and open an existing database. Then, the chapter discussed the user interface of the MS Access 2010.After this, you have learned to work with tables. Then, you have learned to open a table in the Design view. After this you have learned to work with fields and data types in a table. Next, you have learned to work with primary, foreign key, work with the relationships between tables. Towards the end of the chapter you have learned about the procedure to close a database and quit MS Access 2010.

5.15 Key Terms

- **Database:** Refers to a collection of related data and information.
- **DBMS:** Stands for Database Management System. DBMS allows you to manage and query the data stored within the database in an organized and systematic manner. The DBMSs provide a centralized control over data recording and management.
- **Entity:** Refers to the type of objects about which information is stored in the database.
- **Records:** Refers to the rows in a database table. Each individual record corresponds to a particular object in the database.
- **Field:** Refers to the columns of a database table. Field represents an individual data element within a table.

- **Relation:** Refers to an association between any two or more entities in a database.
- **Primary Key:** Refers to the field in the table that uniquely identifies the records in the table. It cannot have null or duplicate values. For example, in a Student table of a University database, the Student Enrollment Number field uniquely identifies each student record since the enrollment number of each student has a unique value.

5.16 Exercise

Multiple Choice Questions

Q1. A _______ is a collection of information or a set of complete fields

a. record b. entity

c. table d. database

Ans. a

Q2. You must have a _______ in each table.

a. record b. data

c. constraint d. Primary key

Ans. d

Q3. Identify the item which is not the part of MS-Access 2010 interface.

a. Tab object b. Dialog box launcher

c. Table viewer d. Navigation pane

Ans. c

Q4. Which of the following is the role of Record Selector?

a. displays the current record number of the opened database object

b. displays the first record number of the opened database object

c. displays the last record number of the opened database object

d. displays the last record number of the last opened database object

Ans. a

Q5. You can also press the ENTER key on the keyboard to switch to another field or column in a table in _______ view(s).

a. Datasheet view b. Design view

c. Description view d. Datasheet and Design

Ans. d

Q6. In the table Design view, the _______ field is used when the purpose of the field is not clear from its name.

a. Description b. Enter

c. Detail d. Data

Ans. a

Q7. A table stores data in a row and column format which are known as _______ and _______, respectively.

a. Fields, records b. Records, fields

c. Key, entity d. Data, attribute

Ans. b

Q8. The field that appears as New is a/an ______ field.

a. primary
b. default
c. AutoNumber
d. AutoLetter

Ans. c

Q9. To delete any record, access the ______ tab on the Ribbon.

a. Home
b. Fields
c. Table
d. Database tool

Ans. a

Q10. A ______ key is a key that is used to uniquely identify each record in a table.

a. Foreign
b. Candidate
c. Primary
d. Secondary

Ans. c

Short Answer Type Questions

Q1. What is MS- Access for you?

Q2. Write a short note on database.

Q3 Discuss the terms table, field, form, and relationship with reference to the database.

Q4. What is table and define different ways of its creation.

Q5. Describe the contents of a table.

Q6. Differentiate between a query and a report.

Q7. Give the two broad categories of the database?

Q8. What do you understand by key?

Q9. Write a short note on Dialog Box Launcher.

Q10. Name the tabs present on ribbon and describe any two of them.

CHAPTER 6

Introduction to Networking

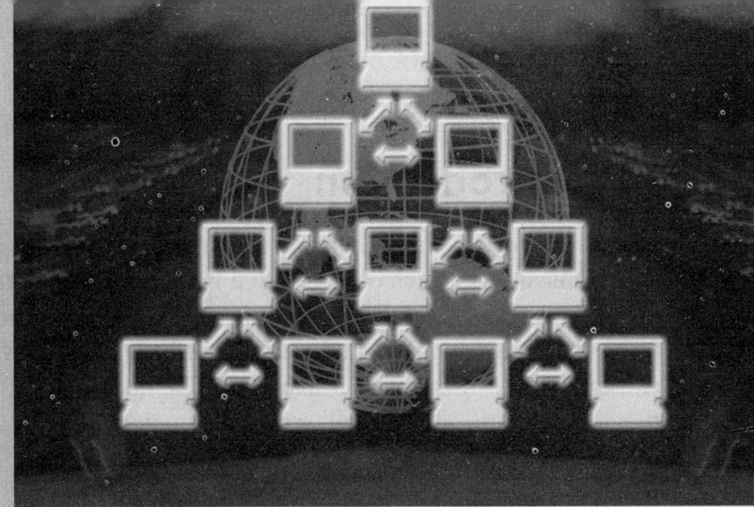

CHAPTER STRUCTURE

CHAPTER OBJECTIVES

- Provide a basic idea about networking and its types
- Discuss about various hardware and software used in networking
- Describe the need of security in networking
- Learn about security, different types of virus, antivirus, and firewall
- Explain the role of Internet in Information sharing

6.1 Introduction

A network is an arrangement in which two or more computers are connected in such a way that they are able to communicate with each other. With a network, computers can receive electronic mail (e-mail) as well as share files and messages instantly with each other. In an organization, networking plays a vital role as multiple files or resources need to be shared among the employees to perform daily activities. For example, a team member may need to get his/her work reviewed by the project manager. The document can be made available to the project manager either by sending the document through e-mail or placing the document at a shared location. In both the cases, the computer of the team member should be in a network.

In a network, computers are connected by network cables through which data is transferred in the form of signals. Today, communication between computers is not restricted to physical cables. Wireless networks allow computers to exchange information by radio signals. A network designer needs to use various networking hardware devices and software to connect various computers with each other.

In this chapter, you explore networking, its need, basic components, types, and characteristics of networks. You also learn the hardware and software requirements for networks. Apart from this, the chapter discusses about virus and its various types. The chapter also deals with various types of antivirus and the concept of firewall. Towards the end of the chapter, you learn about the Internet and its advantages. Let's begin by understanding the basics of networking.

6.2 Understanding the Basics of Networking

A network is a group of interconnected systems sharing services and interacting with each other through a shared communication link, as shown in Figure-1:

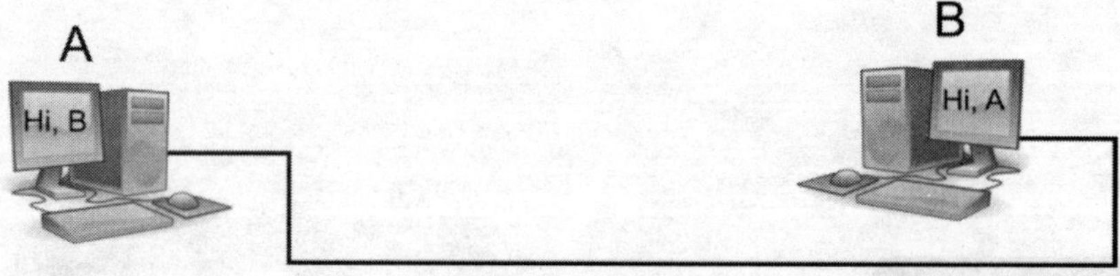

Figure-1: Displaying the Basic Network

In a network, a shared communication link can be established only if two or more individual systems have data to be shared. The individual systems must be connected through a physical pathway called the transmission medium. All the systems on the physical pathway must follow a set of common communication rules for data to reach its intended destination and for the systems that are sending and receiving the data to understand each other. The rules that govern computer communication are called protocols. In brief, all the networks must have the following:

- Data to share
- A physical pathway (transmission medium)
- Rules of communication (protocols)

Data communication is not possible just by having a transmission pathway; instead, there must be two entities that not only exchange data but also the data they receive from one another. Therefore, the goal of computer networking is not simply the exchange of data but to understand and use the received data. Figure-2 shows a network with three computers connected together with a network cable and also attached with a laser printer:

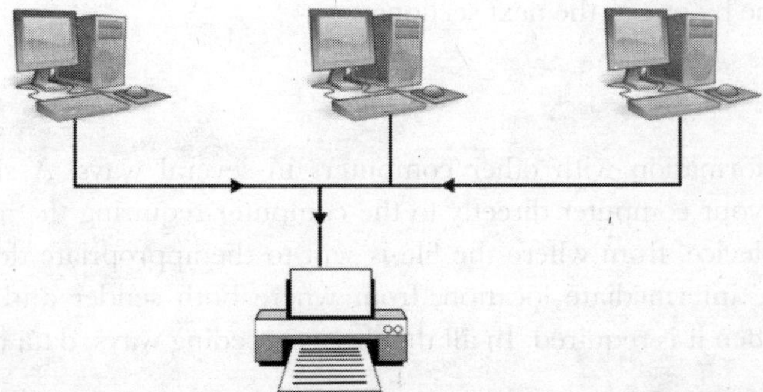

Figure-2: Printer Connected to Three Computers

In Figure-2, all the computers can use the laser printer because the printer gets connected to computers through a network.

Every computer connected to a network is said to be on the network. The technical term for a computer that is on the network is node or workstation. When a computer is turned on and users can access the network, the computer is said to be online. On the other hand, if the computer is unable for accessibility over the network, it is said to be offline. A computer could be offline for several reasons. For example, it could be turned off or the cable connecting it to the network could be unplugged.

After getting familiar with networking, now let us try to understand the need of networking.

6.3 Need for Networking

Today, computer has become an important part of our lives. Around the world, hundreds and thousands of computers exchange information with each other through different mediums, such as cables, microwaves towers, and satellites. Earlier, the information, used to take several days to reach to its destination, can now be read or heard in minutes through networking. Today, computer networks are not merely a circuitry of cables and computers; they had become the backbone of the human society.

Remember that the term network can be applied to human communication as well. For example, in a classroom, the students form a human information network. If the instructor speaks French and the students can understand only English, then the communication between the two parties would not be possible. Therefore, a common medium of communication is required which is easily understood by each party. Similarly, in networking, a common protocol is required to enable a successful transfer of data between server and network clients.

Now, let us look at some advantages of networking in the next section.

6.3.1 Exploring the Benefits of Networking

You can share files, resources, and programs on networks. You can also access your work from any computer connected to the network and easily exchange information with other users. The following are the advantages of computer networks:

- Sharing of files
- Sharing of resources
- Sharing of programs and backups
- Enabling enhanced communication
- Providing ease of connectivity
- Providing improved price/performance ratios
- Providing improved person-to-person communication

Let us discuss these advantages one by one in the next sections.

Sharing Files

Network allows you to share information with other computers in several ways. A simple way is to send the file containing the information from your computer directly to the computer requiring the information. Another way is to send the file to an intermediate device, from where the file is sent to the appropriate destination. The third way is to permanently store the file at the intermediate location, from where both sender and the receiver on the network requiring the file can retrieve it when it is required. In all the three preceding ways, data travels over a network through the cable.

Sharing Resources

A network allows users to share resources with others on the network. Files, programs, printers, and other devices can all be shared among multiple users on the network. A disk drive can also be a shared resource to share files with other users. Let us take an example to understand the concept of sharing of resources. Suppose, the user of computer No3 wants to share a file with the user of computer No4, and a shared disk drive has been set up on computer No2. The user of computer No3 has to first copy the file to the shared disk drive in computer No2 and inform the user of computer No4 about the location of the shared file. Then, the user of computer No4 can copy the file from the shared disk drive of the computer No2 to his/her computer.

You can also share other resources, such as CD/DVD drives or modems, which allow you to access other computers that are not on your network. These resources can be hardware devices, such as a printer or scanner; or software, such as database applications; or programs, such as word processors, as shown in Figure-3:

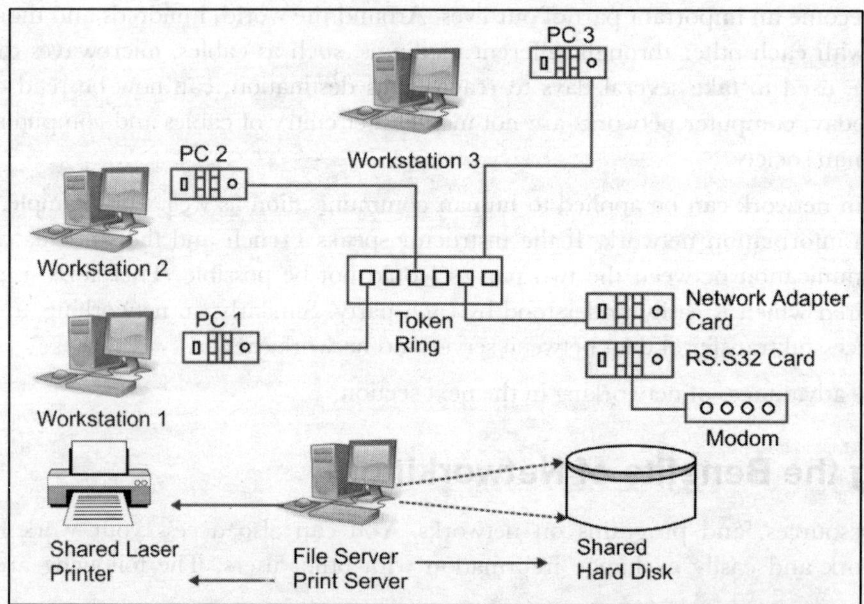

Figure-3: Displaying the Resource Allocation on Network

Now, let us discuss how programs and backups are shared in a network.

Sharing Programs and Backups

Sometimes, it is a good idea to share the programs that everyone uses on a shared disk, rather than keeping separate copies of programs on each user's computer. For example, if you have 10 computer users who use Microsoft Word, you can either store a copy of Microsoft Word on every computer or store just one copy of Microsoft Word on a shared disk. In the case of a shared disk, backing up critical data is easy and simple as all the data is stored on the server.

Enabling Enhanced Communication

One of the main advantages of networking is enhanced communication between users through e-mail and groupware applications. Through e-mail, members of a network can send messages and ensure the safe delivery of data to other members, even in their absence. Groupware applications allow users to collectively work on the same application.

Providing Ease of Connectivity

In the world of networking, each computer on a network is displayed as an icon displaying the name of the computer. The user of the computer, available on a network, can easily access another computer by double-clicking the network icon of the computer to be accessed. With high-speed connections, it becomes easy for users to access the resources of a computer on the network irrespective of its location. The amazing new world of computer connectivity through networking is sometimes called cyberspace.

Providing Improved Price/Performance Ratios

Generally, the entire network of workstations and servers, including the network hardware, is cost effective than a mainframe computer. The cost effectiveness is due to the rapidly decreasing cost of personal computers and related hardware.

Providing Improved Person-to-Person Communication

Networking has provided a quick and cost-effective means to people to communicate with each other. The following network services have led to improved person-to-person communication:

- **E-mail:** Provides faster message-sending service than postal mail
- **On-line Discussion:** Provides simultaneous textual discussion
- **Videoconferencing:** Provides face-to-face and real-time discussion

World Wide Web (WWW) is the best known example of the application of networks providing remote access to information for a variety of uses, such as interactive training, entertainment, and research opportunities, but other network applications, such as American OnLine, Gopher, and Wide Area Information Server (WAIS), have also existed for years.

Q1. What do you mean by networking?

Q2. What are the various benefits of using a computer network?

Q3. E-mail is the system for exchanging messages through a ---------

a. Client b. Program c. Network d. Backbone.

Q4. List the benefits of networking.

In the preceding section, you have learned about the need and advantages of networking. Let us now learn about the disadvantages of networking in the next section.

6.3.2 Disadvantages of Computer Networks

The rapid advancement in the technology of both the computer and networking fields led to need of data security and privacy. The laws controlling privacy and network infrastructure are yet to keep pace with these developments. Apart from this, networking has some disadvantages, which are as follows:

- Lack of data security and privacy
- Costly and complex wiring

- Complicated and expensive network software
- Crashing of the server

Let us briefly discuss these disadvantages in the next sections.

Lack of Data Security and Privacy

Data in a network is shared among many users. Therefore, there can be a risk of unauthorized users accessing confidential information if the network security is weak or poorly implemented. With so many users accessing a network, the lack of privacy is also an issue of concern, as a user having permissions to read or modify network privileges may read a private e-mail.

Costly and Complex Wiring

Getting a high-speed network connection at home is vital if you want to access online multimedia, but it is too expensive for a common person. Similarly, businesses must contend with the high cost of wiring in buildings, which was not thought of while designing buildings.

Complicated and Expensive Network Software

The cost of developing reliable network programs has increased due to the extra features that software must include to handle data inconsistencies, security, and network communications.

Crashing of the Server

One of the primary disadvantages of a computer on a server-based network is that, if the server is disrupted or crashes, users cannot access the resources and services from the server. Unless you have taken adequate precautions to ensure regular backups, the crash may result in irreparable loss of both data and time.

After discussing the advantages and disadvantages of computer networks, let us learn about the basic components of a network.

6.4 Basic Components of a Network

Connecting computers on a network allows users to share files and peripherals, such as modems, printers, tape backup drives, or CD/DVD drives. When networks at multiple locations are connected, users can send e-mail, share links to the Internet, or conduct videoconferences in real-time with remote users. The components of a network include protocol software (network), user interface software, Telecommunication Network (Telnet), OS software, and network hardware, such as Network Interface Cards (NICs), patch cables, and cross connect blocks.

Table-1 shows the important network components and their examples:

Table-1: Key Network Components with Examples

Network Component	Examples
Media	Twisted pair wire, coaxial cable, fibreoptics, microwave, satellites, Cellular radio, and transreceivers
Processors	Modems, multiplexers, concentrators, routers, bridges, gateways, front-end processors, and client and server computers
Software	Communication software, network OS, NetWare, Point-to-Point Protocol (PPP), Post Office Protocol (POP), SMTP, Internet Explorer or Netscape Navigator, and middleware

Table-1: Key Network Components with Examples	
Network Component	**Examples**
Channels	Analog/digital, switched/non-switched, circuit/message/packet switching, simplex/duplex, synchronous/asynchronous
Topology	Bus, star, ring, mesh, and Ethernet
Architecture	OSI, IEEE, Integrated Services Digital Network (ISDN), and Public Switched Telephone Network (PSTN)

Activity-1

Explain various network components with examples.

____

____

____

After learning various important components of a network, let us explore the types of networks.

6.5 Exploring the Types of Networks

There are many types of networks that are classified on the basis of various characteristics, which are used to connect computers on the network. The effectiveness of a computer network is measured by four characteristics: delivery, accuracy, timeliness, and variation. The different types of available networks are: Local Area Network (LAN), Wide Area Network (WAN), and Metropolitan Area Network (MAN).

In the next sections, you discuss LAN, WAN, and MAN.

6.5.1 Local Area Network

LAN refers to a privately owned network of an organization, which is used to connect a computer with other hardware, such as a printer in an office or at home. The range of LAN is restricted to a few kilometers only. This type of network is useful when you want to connect two different departments in a building. There are different technologies (such as Ethernet and Token Ring), each with its own advantages and disadvantages. The data transfer rate for LAN technologies is up to 10 Gbit/s. In case of LAN, the high data transmission rates are possible due to the short distances between various computers that are on network. This makes LAN a high-speed and fault-tolerant data network. LAN allows users to access shared devices and applications, exchange files, and communicate through e-mail and other applications.

LAN consists of:

- NIC, which is an expansion board allowing a computer to be on a network.
- A cable (or an equivalent wireless connection) to connect the computers together
- Protocol software to transfer data from one computer to another
- A user interface software to connect the user to the network
- An OS software to help a user to share resources, such as files and printers

You should note that the LANs having similar architectures are generally linked by bridges, which serve as transfer points. Networks with different architectures are linked by gateways, which convert data passed between systems on the network. Gateways may link computers with the help of cables, optical fibers, or satellites, but users commonly access the networks through a modem.

The following are the characteristics of LAN:

- LAN transfers data at high speed
- LAN's reach is limited
- LAN technology is generally less expensive as compared to MAN and WAN
- LAN is a transmission system that allows a large number and a variety of computing devices to exchange information at high speed over limited distances. These devices may range from large mainframe systems to personal computers and peripherals (devices). The OS used by LAN interprets the input and instructs the networked devices, allows users to communicate with each other, share printers and storage devices, and simultaneously access centrally located processors, data, or programs (instruction sets). Due to the complexity of computer communications, LAN protocols are divided into several hierarchical levels, which is known as a protocol stack. LANs have become popular because they allow users to share vital computing resources electronically including expensive hardware, such as printers and CD/DVD drives, and application programs. Nowadays, LAN inter-networks are powerful, flexible, and easy to use, but they incorporate several technologies that must work together flawlessly.

6.5.2 Wide Area Network

WAN is a type of network used to cover a wide geographical area or region, which can be interconnected with LANs. This type of network links different metropolitans, countries, and national boundaries; thereby, enabling easy communication. Several protocols, such as X.25, Transmission Control Protocol/ Internet Protocol (TCP/IP), and Frame Relay, are available for WAN. The transfer rate of these protocols is around 1 Mbit/s or less and they often use public telephone networks or leased transmission lines.

The following are the characteristics of WAN:

- WAN exists in an unlimited geographical area
- WAN is more susceptible to errors due to the increased distance as compared to LANs
- WAN interconnects multiple LANs
- WAN is more sophisticated and complex than LAN
- WAN technology is expensive

WAN can further be classified into two categories:

- **Enterprise WANs:** Connects computer resources of a single organization that are located at great distance. An organization that needs to perform computer operations at several distant sites can employ an enterprise WAN to interconnect the sites. An enterprise WAN can use a combination of private and commercial network services, but is dedicated to the needs of a particular organization.
- **Global WANs:** Interconnects the networks of several corporations and organizations.

It has been noticed that WANs are often a natural choice when connecting geographically separated LANs into a single network. Much of the complexity and expense of operating WAN is due to the great distance that the signal must travel to reach the interconnected sites. WAN links are often slower and typically depend on a public transmission medium hired from a communication service provider. The most common example of WAN is the Internet.

Q1. List the advantages of LAN, WAN and the Internet.

Q2. Distinguish between LAN and WAN.

6.5.3 Metropolitan Area Network

MAN provides a network coverage between LAN and WAN. In other words, MAN covers an area that is larger than the area covered by LAN but smaller than the area covered by WAN. MAN generally connects two or more LANs or Campus Area Networks (CANs). It usually acts as a backbone connecting several LANs owned by an organization, as well as provide Internet services to users. MAN contains several protocols, such as Fiber Distributed Data Interface (FDDI) and Distributed Queue Dual Bus (DQDB), which have their own topology and may have a higher data transfer rate. MAN typically uses wireless infrastructure or optical fiber connections to link its sites. It is generally owned by a group or combination of users or by a single network provider providing the service to the users. It adopts technologies from both LAN and WAN. Protocols, such as Asynchronous Transfer Mode (ATM), FDDI, DQDB and Switched Multi-megabit Data Service (SMDS), are used in MAN. You should note that MAN acts as a high speed network that allows the sharing of regional resources. Figure-4 shows the MAN architecture:

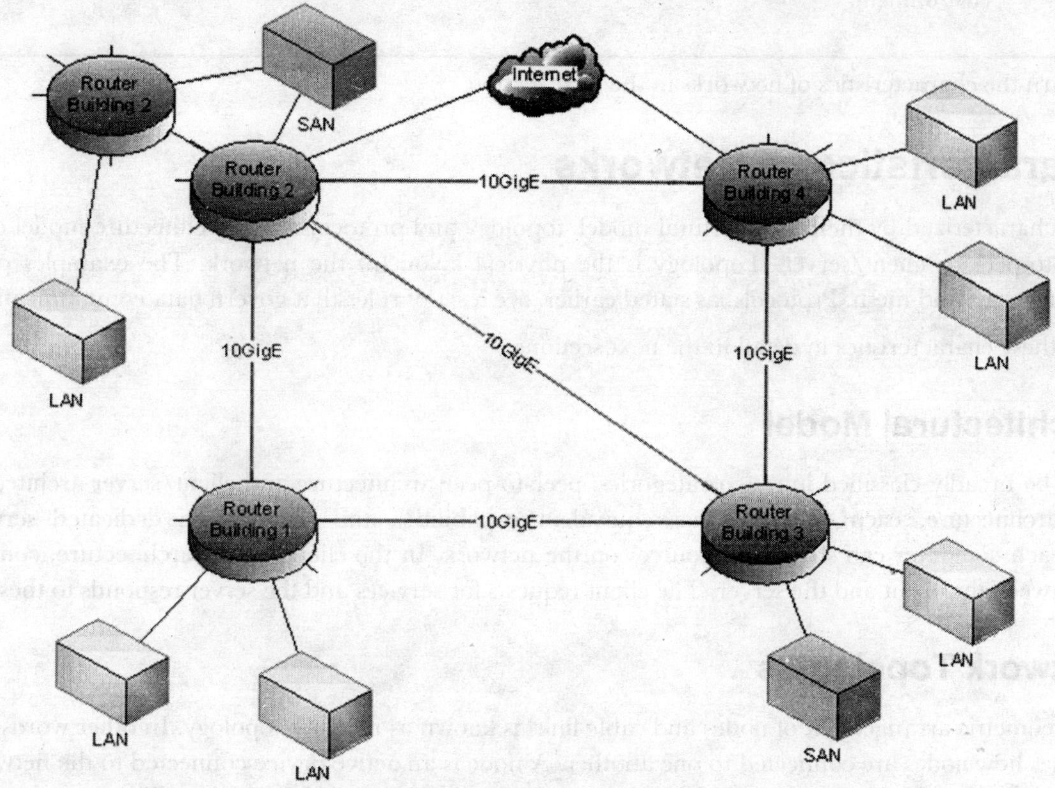

Figure-4: Displaying the MAN Architecture

Apart from the three main types of networks namely, LAN, WAN, and MAN, other types of networks are also available, which are as follows:

- **Personal Area Network (PAN)/Home area network (HAN):** Refers to the network that allows communication between a person's digital devices, such as fax machines, telephones, and Personal Digital Assistant (PDA).
- **Campus Area Network (CAN):** Refers to the network that spans within a limited geographical area, such as a campus or military base.
- **Global Area Network (GAN):** Provides support for mobile applications across a number of wireless LANs, such as satellite coverage areas.
- **Value-added Network (VAN):** Refers to a type of network where a communication channel is hired by an organization either to facilitate Electronic Data Interchange (EDI) or to provide other network services.
- **Virtual Private Network (VPN):** Provides links between various nodes with the help of open connections or virtual circuits.
- **Wireless/Mobile Network:** Refers to the transmission media, such as infrared light, radio channels, microwave radio, cellular telephone systems, and satellite relays. The transmission rates vary with the media, from 1 Mbit/s to 1Gbit/s range for satellite relays.

- **Intranet:** Refers to a network specific to an organization. It serves the needs of the employees of the organization. Intranet cannot be accessed outside the office or for browsing the Internet.
- **Extranet:** Refers to a network owned by an organization. The employees can access extranet even when they are outside the office for official task.

Talk to Teacher

Discuss the situations in which LAN, WAN, and MAN can be implemented in the networking environment.

Now, let us learn the characteristics of networks in the next section.

6.6 Characteristics of Networks

Networks are characterized by their architectural model, topology and protocols. The architecture model of a network is either peer-to-peer or client/server. Topology is the physical layout of the network. The examples of topologies include bus, ring, star, and mesh. Protocols, as stated earlier, are a set of rules that govern data communication.

Let us discuss these characteristics in detail in the next sections.

6.6.1 Architectural Model

Networks can be broadly classified into two categories: peer-to-peer architecture and client/server architecture. In the peer-to-peer architecture, each computer has equivalent capabilities and there is no dedicated server. In this architecture, each computer can share its resources on the network. In the client/server architecture, communication takes place between the client and the server. The client requests for services and the server responds to these requests.

6.6.2 Network Topologies

In LAN, the geometric arrangement of nodes and cable links is known as network topology. In other words, this type of topology defines how nodes are connected to one another. A node is an active device connected to the network, such as computer or printer. It can also be networking equipment, such as a hub, switch, or router. The three most often used topologies are bus, ring, and star. Users can use a combination of topologies according to their requirement. Different network topologies offer different advantages and disadvantages in terms of cost, complexity, and robustness.

Let us now discuss various types of network topologies in the next sections.

The Bus Topology

In the bus topology, each machine on the network is connected to the other using a long single cable, as shown in Figure-5:

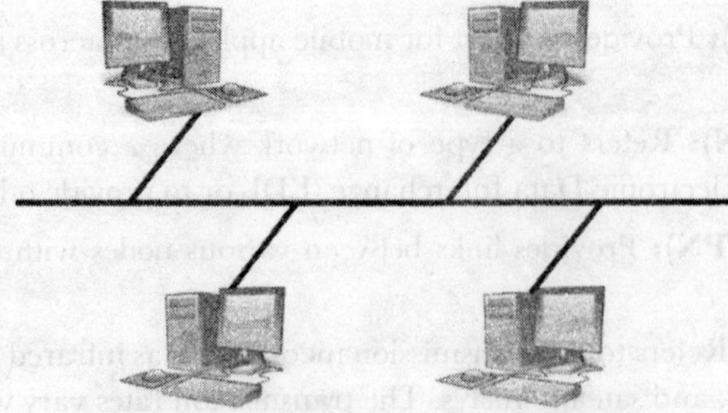

Figure-5: Displaying the Bus Topology

This type of topology is ideal for a small classroom or lab and becomes unmanageable when spread over large areas. This is the most common topology as it has no switches and no repeaters (in its simplest form), but simply shares a common and linear communication medium. In this topology, each node requires a tap (hardware that attaches the computer to the cable), which must be capable of delivering the signal to all the nodes.

Note: *Switches are netwcrk devices used to connect multiple computers on a network. Repeaters are network devices used to regenerate signals.*

Data is sent in packets, which are recognized by each node on the network. The nodes check the packets to determine whether or not the packets are intended for them. If a packet is meant for a node, the node claims it, and if not, the packet is ignored.

Note: *A data packet is a basic unit of communication on a network.*

Bus topologies have the advantage of being passive, implying that all the active components are in the nodes and the failure of any component in a node affects only that node. In this type of topology, generally only one node at a time can transmit data; therefore, results in the problem of network traffic.

Besides the difficulty of connecting large networks, a big weakness of a bus topology is the lack of robustness in the network. It uses only one connection between all the machines so the damage caused to the network at a single point makes some or all the machines unable to communicate with each other.

Note: *Robustness of a network is its ability to continue functioning even if the damage occurs to any part of the network.*

The Ring Topology

In the ring topology, a series of devices are connected to one another by unidirectional transmission links to form a single-closed loop. The ring topology is very similar to the bus topology, except that the two ends of the network connect to form a complete ring, as shown in Figure-6:

Figure-6: Displaying the Ring Topology

The main advantage of the ring topology over the bus topology is that if a break occurs in the ring, the nodes are still able to communicate by transmitting the data through the other side of the ring. Generally, in the ring topology, it is difficult to bring both the ends of the network together. Moreover, the cost incurred in wiring the ring topology is very high. The main disadvantage of the ring topology is that every node in this topology is involved in the transfer of data; therefore, one failure of a repeater brings the whole ring to halt. Another disadvantage of the ring topology is that it needs to determine the node that starts the ring and prevents the same packet from going round the ring repeatedly because of a node fault.

These problems faced in the ring topology are overcome by Token Rings. Similar to the bus topology, the Token Rings also use a single cable whose ends are looped to form a complete logical circle or ring. In the Token Rings, each workstation is connected directly to the central device called Media Access Unit (MAU). Figure-7 shows the Token Rings:

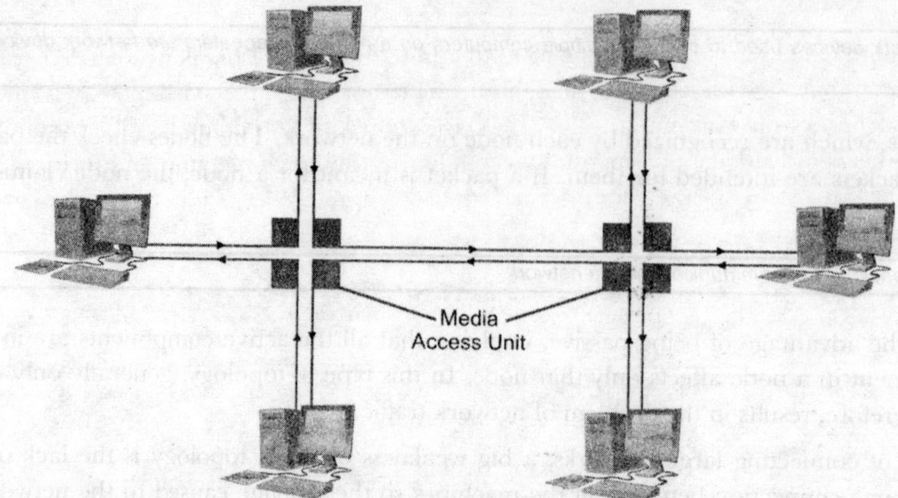

Figure-7: Displaying the Token Rings

In the Token Ring, an electronic signal called a token circulates on the ring. When a node sends some data to another node on the network, the sending node has to first capture the free token. The sending node then writes the data as well as the recipient's address onto the token and sends it on the network. When the token passes to the next node, the node checks the recipient's address. If the address stored in the token matches with the address of the node, the node receives the token; otherwise, the token is forwarded to the next node. When the token reaches the correct destination, the destination node sends an acknowledgement to the originator of the token informing the sending node that the data has been received.

The Star Topology

The star topology is a LAN architecture in which the computers or nodes on a network are connected to a common central hub or switch by dedicated links. Figure-8 shows the star topology with each computer connected to a central hub or switch by a dedicated physical link:

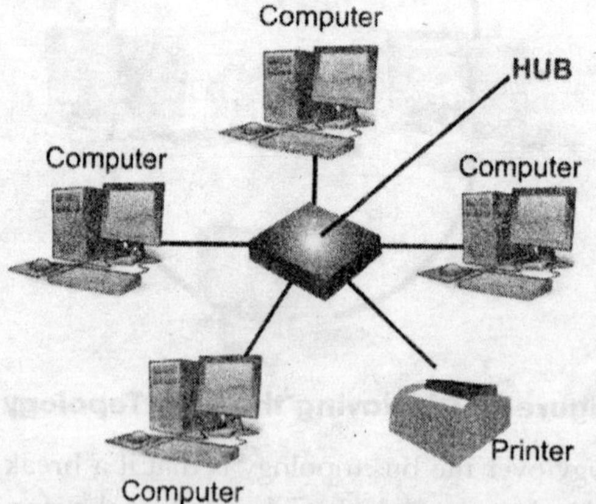

Figure-8: Displaying the Star Topology

In the star topology, a switch provides a path between any two devices that communicate to transfer data, either physically in a circuit switch or logically in a packet switch.

The main advantage of the star topology is that the decision on when a node can or cannot transmit data, is under central control. The star topology is easy to install and configure. Another advantage is that of robustness, which means that if one link fails, only that link is affected and all other links continue working.

In the star topology, all machines are directly connected to a hub; therefore, a break in a single network cable does not allow a machine to communicate with the other machines. The major risk in the star topology is that the failure of hub prevents any of the machines from communicating. However, the risk of hub failure can be minimized by selecting an appropriate hub. Another disadvantage of using the star topology is that the large amount of wiring required to connect machines with the hub. If the network designer places the hub far from the machines then the cost of wiring increases. The designer can minimize the cost of wiring by selecting an appropriate central location for the hub.

The Mesh Topology

In the mesh topology, each computer is connected to the other computer with a separate physical link on a network, as shown in Figure-9:

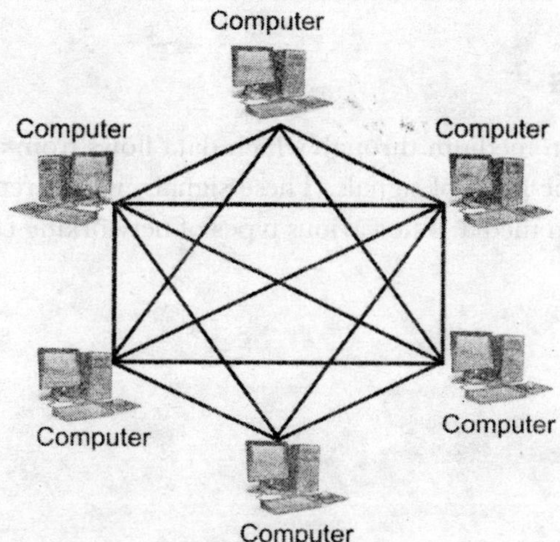

Figure-9: Displaying the Mesh Topology

The mesh topology provides several advantages over other topologies. It can send data from one computer to several other computers simultaneously. It minimizes the problems related to network traffic because each connection carries its own load. The main disadvantage of this topology is that a large number of cables and Input/Output (I/O) ports are required.

Hierarchical Star

Apart from the four basic topologies, a network designer can create a combination of two or more topologies, called a hybrid combination. The most common of these combinations is the hierarchical star. You can understand this topology with an example. Suppose, the computers of a department are connected to a hub and a network designer runs only one line of network from this hub to the second hub, to which the computers of another department are connected. In this example, the combination of two topologies, star and bus, reduces the amount of wiring needed to create a true star.

Q1. Explain various network topologies.

Q2. Name the topology that is ideal for a small classroom.

After learning about various network topologies, let us now discuss the protocols that govern the communication process in a network.

6.6.3 Protocols

A protocol defines a common set of rules and signals that computers on the network use to communicate with one another. One of the most popular protocols for LANs is called Ethernet. The Token Ring is another popular LAN protocol.

Now, you are familiar with the various characteristics of a network, let us discuss the hardware and software required to establish a network.

6.7 Hardware and Software Used for Networking

While designing a network, various hardware and software are required. The hardware includes network interface card (NIC); networking cables, such as the coaxial cable, twisted pair cable, or fiber-optic cable; and network devices, such as hub, switches, bridges, and repeaters. The software includes protocols as well as the network OS.

Let us discuss about the usage of these software and hardware in the next sections.

6.7.1 Networking Cables

Networking cables are the transmission medium through which data flows from a source to the destination. The data is transmitted through these cables in the form of signals. These signals, which represent data, are propagated from one device to another through transmission media. The various types of networking cables are:

- The twisted pair cable
- The coaxial cable
- The fiber-optic cable

Let us discuss these cables in detail.

The Twisted Pair Cable

The twisted pair cable contains two cable wires that use copper as a conductor. These wires have plastic insulation and are twisted, as shown in Figure-10:

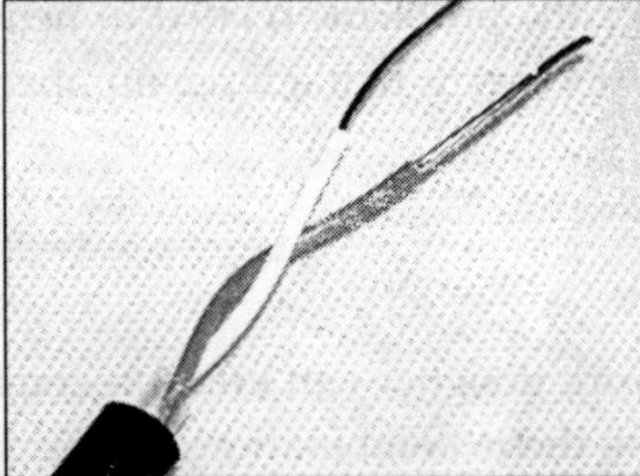

Figure-10: Displaying the Twisted Pair Cable

As shown in Figure-10, there are two twisted cables: one twisted cable wire carries the signal to the receiver and the other cable wire acts as a ground reference. At the other end, the receiver obtains the difference in the values of the signals between these two cable wires. The twisted pair cables are used for voice and data communication; therefore, the cable wires are twisted to provide protection against crosstalk and noise.

***Note:** Crosstalk is the disturbance caused when an electric or magnetic field of one signal affects the adjacent signal.*

The twisted pair cable is of two types: Shielded Twisted Pair (STP) and Unshielded Twisted Pair (UTP). Let us discuss each of them in detail in the next sections.

The Shielded Twisted Pair Cable

STP is a form of the twisted cable created by IBM, which has a metal shield covering each pair of insulated cable wires. This type of shielding protects the cables from external electromagnetic interferences and crosstalk. The STP cable is shown in Figure-11:

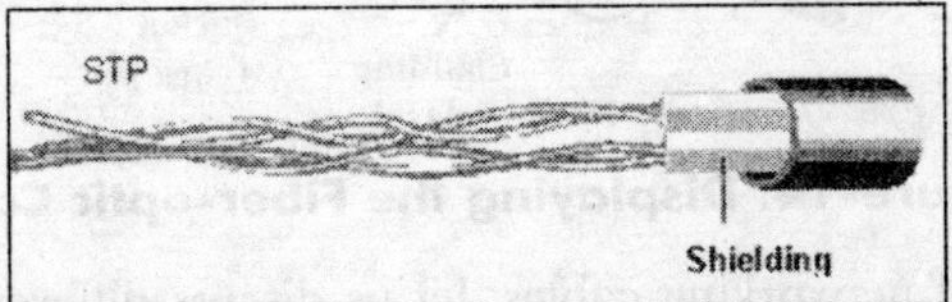

Figure-11: Displaying the Shielded Twisted Pair Cable

The Unshielded Twisted Pair (UTP)

UTP is the most commonly used cable in communication. It is used in Ethernet networks and telephone systems. The UTP cable is easy to install and its installation charges are also very less. The UTP cable is shown in Figure-12:

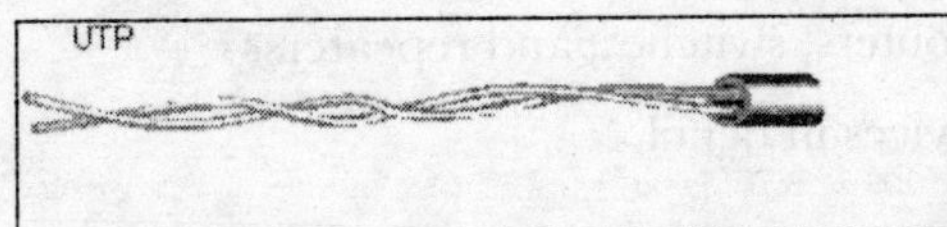

Figure-12: Displaying the Unshielded Twisted Pair Cable

The Coaxial Cable

The coaxial cable consists of two conductors: one is the inner conductor made up of solid copper (also called the core conductor) and the other is the outer conductor. The outer conductor serves as a shield against noise. There is an insulating plastic between the conductors and the whole cable is covered with a plastic jacket. The coaxial cable can carry signals of higher frequency ranges than the twisted pair cables. The coaxial cables are used in cable television network and traditional Ethernet LANs. Figure-13 shows the coaxial cable:

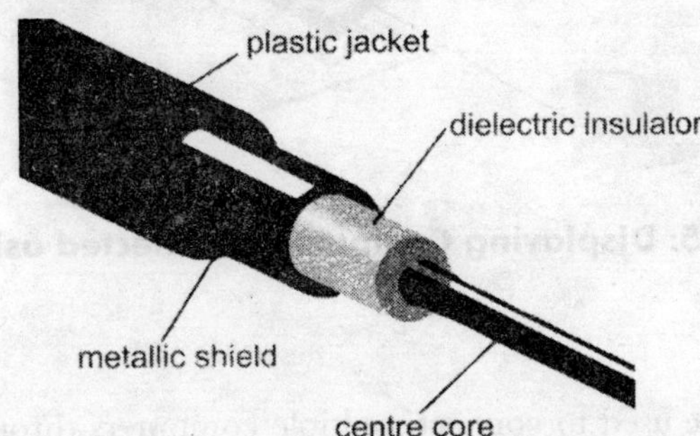

Figure-13: Displaying the Coaxial Cable

The Fiber-Optic Cable

The fiber-optic cable is made up of glass or plastic and the signal propagates in the form of light. The inner core of the fiber-optic cable is surrounded by a cladding of glass or plastic that is less dense than the outer core. The fiber-optic cable contains greater bandwidth than metallic cables, due to which, these cables can carry more data. The fiber-optic cables are thinner and lighter than metallic cables. The main disadvantage of the fiber-optic cable is that it is very expensive. Figure-14 shows the fiber-optic cable:

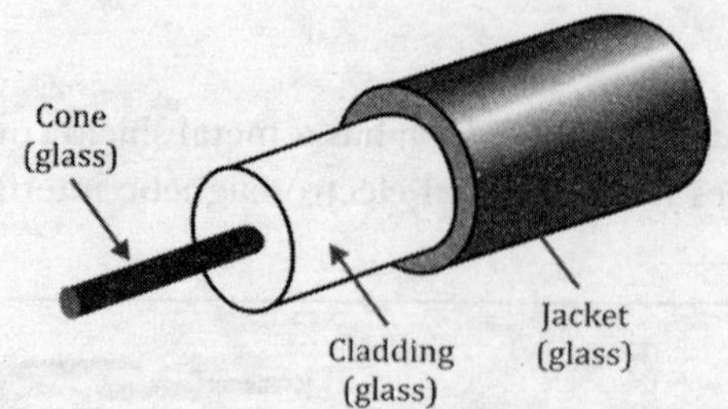

Figure-14: Displaying the Fiber-optic Cable

After discussing about various types of networking cables, let us discuss different networking devices used to design a network.

6.7.2 Networking Devices

The devices that are used to transfer data in a network are known as networking devices. These devices are also known as networking equipment, Intermediate Systems (IS), or InterWorking Unit (IWU). Some of the commonly used networking devices are hubs, bridges, routers, switches, and repeaters.

Let us now discuss these networking devices in detail.

Hubs

A hub is a network device used to connect multiple computers together to form a small network. A hub contains a number of ports, which allow you to connect different computers. Figure-15 shows a number of computers connected through a hub:

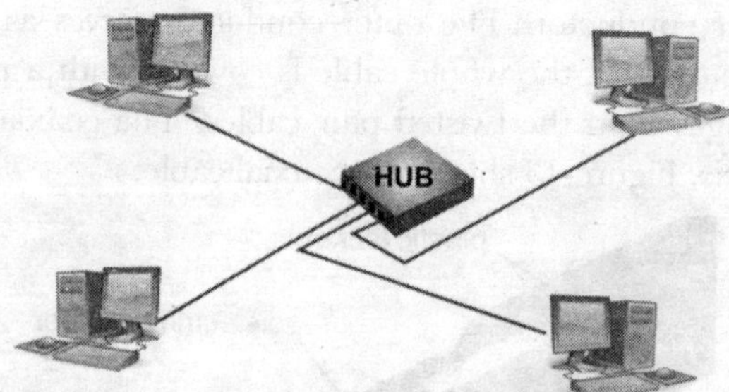

Figure-15: Displaying Computers Connected using Hub

Switches

A switch is a network hardware device used to connect multiple computers through LAN. Switches are identical to a hub and efficient in transporting data. They are normally used in areas of high network traffic. Figure-16 shows computers connected through a switch:

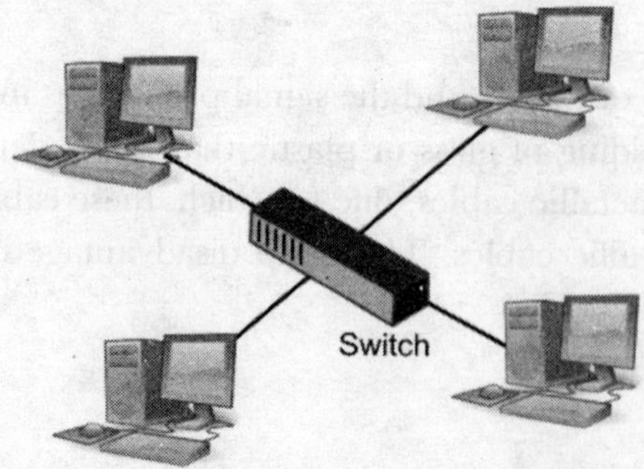

Figure-16: Showing Computers Connected through a Switch

When a computer connected through a hub sends data to other computers on a network, the hub broadcasts the data as packets to all the computers on the network, without determining the source and destination devices of the data. On the other hand, a switch is able to inspect the received data packet, determines its source and destination devices, and forwards the data accordingly. Therefore, on a busy network, a switch performs better than a hub.

Repeaters

A repeater is a networking hardware device that operates at the physical Layer of the OSI model. It connects the two segments of the same LAN. Signal carrying information can travel a limited distance before its quality weakens. When a repeater receives a weak signal, it regenerates the signal to the original bit pattern.

Figure-17 shows the functioning of a repeater:

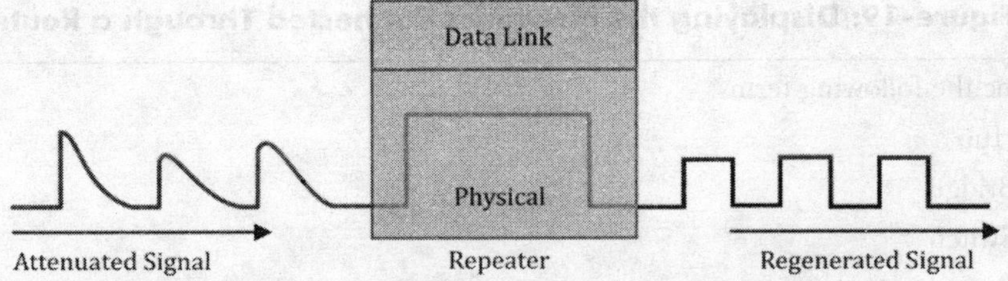

Figure-17: Displaying the Functioning of a Repeater

In Figure-17, you can see that a weak signal is passing through the repeater and regenerated to its original strength in the process.

Bridges

A bridge is a hardware device that works in the physical as well as the data link layers of the OSI model. As a physical layer device, the function of a bridge is to regenerate the weak signals and as a data link layer, its function is to check the physical address of the source and destination nodes. This physical address in the data frame includes information, such as data bits and the physical address of the source and destination nodes.

Note: *Physical address is an address of a device defined by its LAN or WAN.*

Figure-18 shows a bridge connecting two segments of a network:

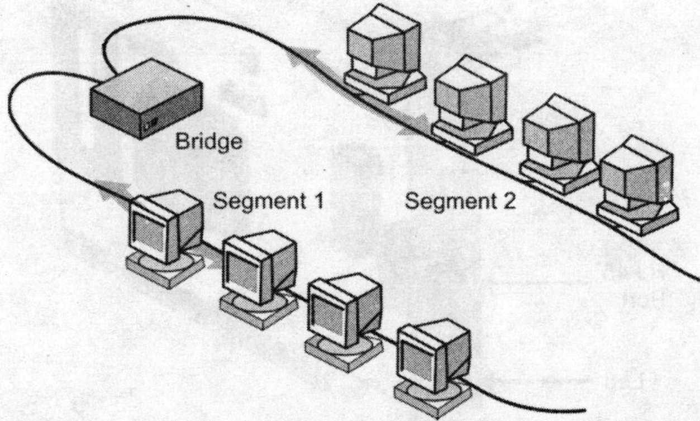

Figure-18: Showing the Bridge Connecting Segments of Network

Routers

A router is a networking hardware device that connects LANs and WANs on the Internet. It works at the network layer of the OSI model. A router contains a routing table that decides the route of a data packet. The routing table contains the IP address of the source and destination nodes. The router receives a packet from a network (source), checks the IP address of the destination, and then sends the packet to the appropriate destination.

Figure-19 shows three networks connected through a router:

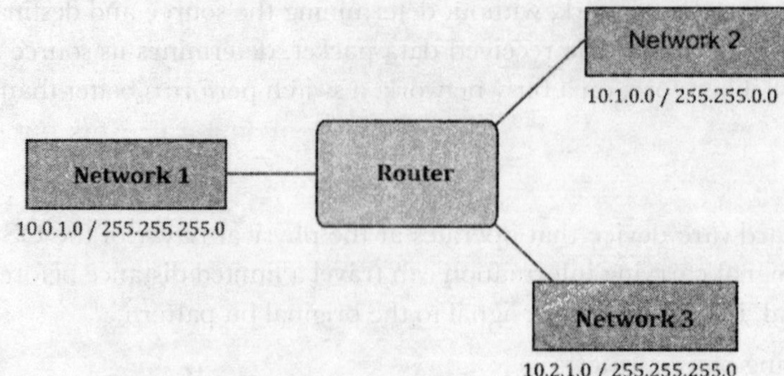

Figure-19: Displaying the Networks Connected Through a Router

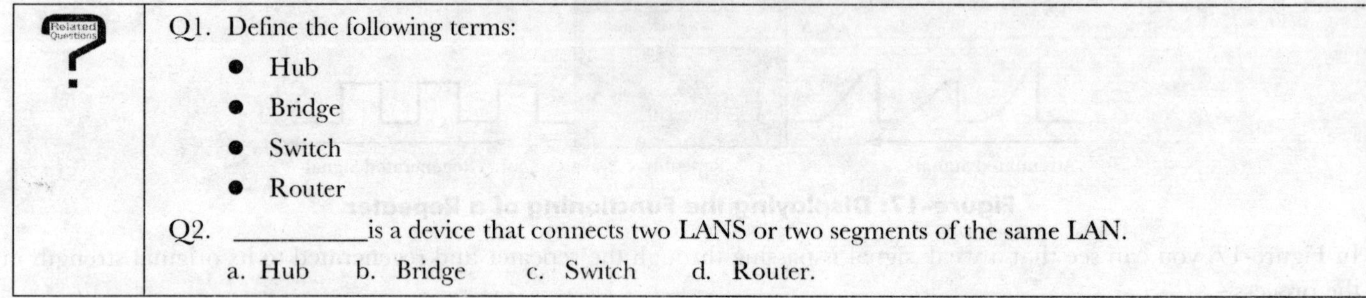

Q1. Define the following terms:

- Hub
- Bridge
- Switch
- Router

Q2. __________ is a device that connects two LANS or two segments of the same LAN.

a. Hub b. Bridge c. Switch d. Router.

6.7.3 Network Interface Card

NIC enables a computer to send and receive data across a network. It provides an interface between a data bus (a pathway inside the computer that carries data between the hardware components) and the network medium. Every NIC has a MAC address, which is a binary address unique to a single network. This MAC address is 48-bit long and used to uniquely identify each node of a network. NIC is integrated into the system's motherboard, which is shown in Figure-20:

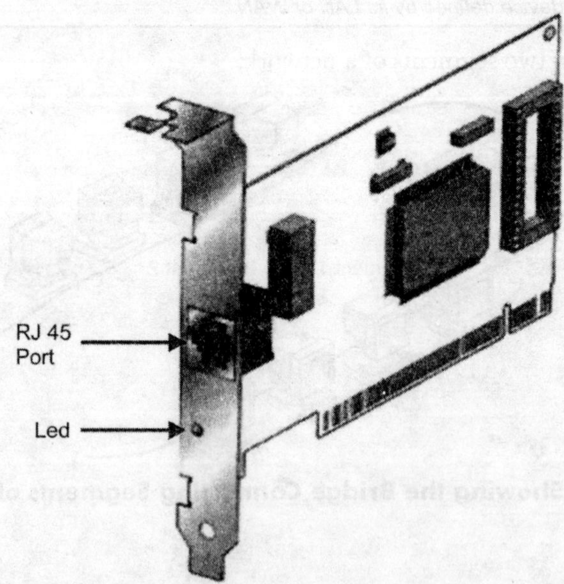

Figure-20: Displaying NIC

After learning about the networking hardware, let us now discuss the software used in networking.

6.7.4 Protocols

A network protocol is a set of rules that allows two or more computers to communicate with each other on a network. Protocols govern the format of data, timing (when the data should be sent and how fast it can be sent), sequencing, and error control. Without these rules, the computer can only be connected on a network but cannot communicate with other computers or devices.

A protocol is a software that resides either in a computer's memory or in the memory of a transmission device, such as NIC. Protocols are required when the data is ready for transmission. The protocols help in preparing the data for transmission and setting the transmission process. At the receiving end, the protocols help in accepting the data from the cable wire and preparing it for the computer by removing the information added at the transmitting end.

Some common network protocols are given as follows:

- **TCP/IP:** Provides communication protocols required for the communication of host machines over a network. It basically consists of two protocols: TCP and IP. The TCP/IP suite is a set of protocols that implement a protocol stack on which the Internet runs. This suite can be described by the layers included in the OSI model. The OSI model is a reference model, which is used by IT professionals to describe networks and network applications. In a protocol stack, each layer solves the problems related to the transmission of data and provides a well-defined service to the higher layers.
- **Internetwork Packet Exchange/Sequenced Packet Exchange (IPX/SPX):** Works on the Novell NetWare OSs. IPX is a network layer protocol, which is the third layer of the OSI model; while SPX is a transport layer protocol, which is the fourth layer of OSI model. Both of these protocol layers are used in Novell Netware networks. The SPX transport layer resides on the top of the layer of the IPX protocol (the third layer of OSI model). IPX is a datagram protocol that is used to maintain communication between the connectionless devices. However, the SPX protocol provides connection-oriented services between the nodes on a network. This protocol is used by the client/server applications. The IPX/SPX protocol works similar to the TCP/IP protocol, in which the IPX protocol is similar to the IP protocol; and the SPX protocol is similar to the TCP protocol.
- **Network Basic Input/Output System (NetBIOS):** Allows you to design Application Programming Interfaces (APIs) for local network communication. NetBIOS is a protocol, which was developed by IBM and Sytec in early 1980s. It is used over various other protocols, such as IPX/SPX and TCP/IP, and many types of software can be used with NetBIOS only. This NetBIOS protocol over the Token Ring or Ethernet is known as NetBIOS Enhanced User Interface (NetBEUI). The NetBEUI protocol is an enhanced version of the NetBIOS protocol, which is used by network OSs, such as LAN Manager, LAN Server, Windows for Workgroups, Windows 95, and Windows NT. NetBIOS and NetBEUI are only used on local networks.

6.8 Security

Security can be defined as the process or procedure to ensure the integrity, availability, and confidentiality of data and resources against threats, viruses, bugs, and vulnerabilities. The main components of a computer that are most sensitive to attack are the software, hardware, and data. Security is divided into two categories: computer security and network security. Computer security refers to the protection of a single or standalone computer; while network security refers to the protection of computers in the network. Security is the major concern in an enterprise network, as the data and resources of the enterprise are distributed through a network. Therefore, the network administrator needs to ensure the security of the network resources by configuring various security settings and technology.

The hardware and software components of a computer are highly vulnerable to many threats. In IT, a threat is an illegal activity that can cause damages, such as loss of information and data corruption to the network of an organization. There are two basic types of threats—accidental threat and intentional threat. Accidental threat is an activity that occurs accidentally and its occurrence is not dependent on any entity. It can occur due to the exposure of confidential information and unauthorized modification in information. On the other hand, intentional threat is an activity that is performed by an entity to violate the security of the computer and network.

6.8.1 Virus and Its Types

Virus is a computer program that gets copied on a computer and infects the computer by giving erroneous results on various operations. In a network, if one computer is infected by a virus, there is an acute possibility of other computers to get infected by that virus. The following are the types of computer viruses:

- **Boot Sector Virus:** Infects the master boot record of the hard disk. It is executed during the booting process.
- **File Infector Virus:** Attaches itself to executable files. It is executed when the program runs.
- **Macro Virus:** Attaches itself with the document and gets activated when the document is opened.
- **Multipartite Virus:** Combines the boot sector virus with the file infector virus.
- **Polymorphic Virus:** Gets activated when the virus starts replicating themselves over the network.
- **Worm:** Refers to the type of virus that can execute independently and travel from one computer to other in the network. It can spread all over the network by creating its copies.
- **Trojan Horse:** Refers to the program that appears safe but can be harmful for the computer and network. It can steal password, delete data, and format hard disk.
- **Logic Bomb:** Refers to the type of virus that embeds with some programs. It can be executed only at a particular date or day.
- **Bacteria/Rabbit:** Refers to the piece of codes that do not damage the files but deny access to the resources by consuming all disk space or memory space.

6.8.2 Antivirus

Antivirus refers to software that is designed for preventing, identifying, and removing malware, including malicious codes and computer viruses. The computer virus is a sequence of code that is inserted into other executable code or program, so when the program runs, it is automatically executed. These types of viruses modify other programs and insert copies of themselves in the computer or program or network.

The antivirus has a catalog of several thousand known viruses that can be detected and removed. It can also recognize the types of changes that viruses make to files present in the computer. Therefore, there are fewer chances that the virus would not be detected.

The following are several approaches to deploy antivirus software on your network:

- Placing antivirus client software on each client computer in your network and then an antivirus server automatically updates the antivirus client's software on a regular basis.
- Installing antivirus software on your mail server to scan all incoming mails for viruses and remove them before your network users ever see them.

The following is the list of some of the top antivirus software:

- Norton Antivirus 2010
- McAfee VirusScan Plus 2010
- Trend Micro Antivirus Internet Security 2010
- ESET NOD32 Antivirus
- BitDefender Antivirus 2010
- Kaspersky Antivirus 2010
- CA Antivirus Plus 2010
- Shield Deluxe 2010 Antivirus & Antispyware
- Webroot Antivirus with Antispyware 6.0

Let us now discuss about firewall.

6.8.3 Firewall

When you are connected to the Internet or some other network, you need to protect your computer from harmful programs (for example, viruses) and hackers from causing any damage. You should have a firewall to avoid any serious damage to your computer. A firewall prevents any unsafe data from entering your computer. The firewall acts as a virtual wall that stands between your computer and the outside world (the Internet or a network).

Windows XP is shipped with firewall software, known as Windows Firewall, to protect your computer against threats from the outside world. Windows Firewall supports the filtering of both incoming as well as outgoing data and allows or blocks a particular program.

Let's now learn about Internet.

6.9 Internet

The Internet uses Transmission Communication Protocol/Internet Protocol (TCP/IP) to transmit or exchange data. The Internet does not have any centralized governing body for its technical implementation or defining policies to access or use its services. The general idea of introducing the Internet was to allow people to share information from their computers across the world. J.C.R. Licklider was the first person who proposed the development of global network of computers, in 1962. Later, he moved to Defense Advanced Research Projects Agency (DARPA) to develop the network of computers in late 1962. In addition, Leonard Kleinrock developed the theory of packet switching, which was used as a basis for Internet connections. In 1969, the scientists in DARPA succeeded to network two computers, known as ARPANET, which was based on packet switching. Initially, ARPANET was developed for communication among United States military services but by the end of 1971, almost 15 sites from different organizations were connected to ARPANET. Earlier, the ARPANET implemented host-to-host connectivity and was traversed on the Network Control Program (NCP). The NCP, developed by Internet Engineering Task Force (IETF), provided the middle layers of the protocol stack that runs on the host computers of ARPANET.

For the rapid growth of network and to connect more and more locations, the TCP protocol was developed in 1973 and the first description of the TCP protocols was released in 1974. The Internet was not publically used until 1991. It was the effort of Tim Berners-Lee who invented the Web in 1989, and published the Internet in 1991. With the passage of time, the popularity of the Internet grew day-by-day, as a result, the Internet accommodated almost all private networks.

6.9.1 Functioning of Network

Internet is defined as the network of networks, which was initially evolved from the ARPANET. In other words, Internet can be defined as the interconnection of large and small networks across the globe. Internet consists of many networks each of which belongs to different organization and is interconnected at some peering points. There are some Internet standards that enable a user connected to one network to easily communicate with the user connected to some other network. To facilitate exchange of information (or communication) over a network, all the computers connected to Internet need to use a common set of rules known as protocol. The set of protocols that the Internet uses is known as Transmission Control Protocol/ Internet Protocol (TCP/IP).

Working of an Internet: Computers on the Internet are connected to each other with the help of various small networks. These networks are in turn connected through the gateways to the Internet backbone. Figure-21 represents a backbone connecting various LANs:

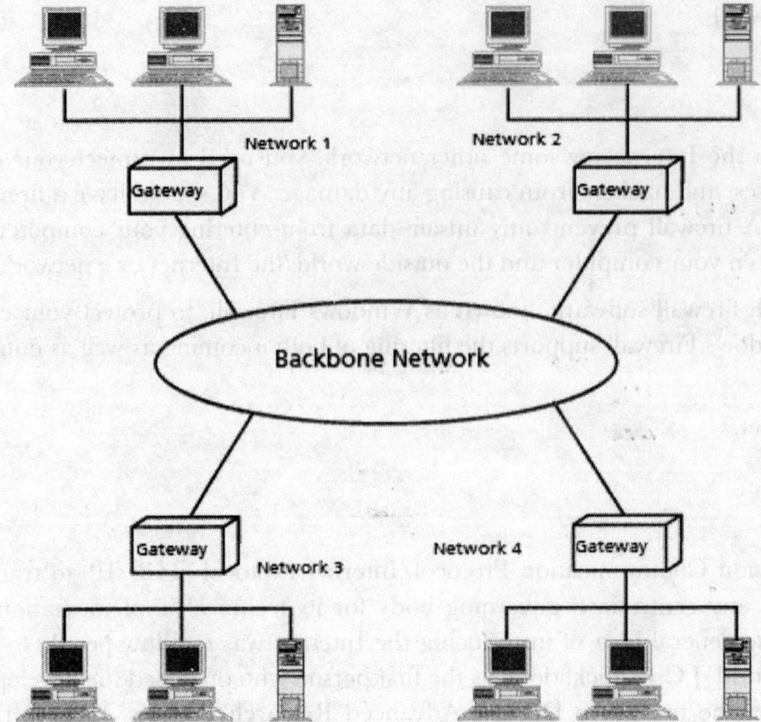

Figure-21: A Backbone Connecting Various LAN's

The following steps discuss how Internet functions:

1. The source computer (the computer that is sending the data) prepares the data to send to the destination computer (the computer that receives the sent data) by dividing the data into small portions known as packets.
2. Each packet is given a serial number, such as I, II, III, and so on.
3. The packets are sent to the destination computer.
4. The destination computer receives the packet in random order. If a packet is lost during transfer then it is requested again.
5. The packets are reassembled in the order of their serial numbers and the original data is obtained.

All computers on the Internet communicate with one another using the Transmission Control Protocol/Internet Protocol suite, abbreviated as TCP/IP, which is the basic communication protocol of the Internet. The TCP part of the TCP/IP suite breaks the data into small packets to be transmitted over the Internet. It is also responsible for assembling the packets at the destination computer. The IP part handles the address of the destination computer so that the data is sent to the correct address.

6.9.2 Internet Protocols

The architectural design of the Internet software system is performed by the IETF. IETF creates several work groups for setting the Internet standards, which discusses about different aspects of the Internet architecture. The results of discussions and the different standards for the Internet architecture are published as Request for Comments (RFC) that is available on the website of IETF. In the Internet standards, a framework is defined, which is known as the Internet Protocol Suite.

The Internet Protocol suite is a collection of Internet protocols, such as TCP, IP, and User Datagram Protocol (UDP). TCP is one of the important protocols among the Internet Protocol suite. It is a reliable service provider for exchanging data between two computers connected with a network. It transfers the data between two different programs of two computers in the form of byte streams. Today, most of the Internet applications, which require a secured way of exchanging data over the Internet, use TCP protocol.

The IP is a part of TCP/IP, which is used to exchange data (datagrams/packets) between computers on a packet switched network. IP is an important protocol of the Internet Layer of the TCP/IP model and is responsible for delivering packets from the source computer to destination computer. The IP protocol contains the IP addresses of the source and destination computer. Each packet contains a header, which has address information about the host and destination computer. Due to this, IP defines an addressing and datagram encapsulation approach. The Internet Protocol Version 4 (IPv4) was the first major version for defining addressing structure and the current version for defining addressing structure is Internet Protocol Version 6 (IPv6). Both of the TCP/IP protocol works together in sending failure, receiving notification, and giving the pending notification over the network.

UDP, another important protocol of the Internet Protocol suite, transfers the user data in the form of packets. The additional overhead for giving notification for receiving, sending, and pending data led to the development of the UDP protocol. UDP provides an unreliable data exchanging service and as a result the packets may arrived out of order, duplicated, and may not delivered without any notification.

Q1. What is TCP/IP protocol?

Q2. What is UDP?

Q3. What is protocol?

6.9.3 World Wide Web(WWW)

WWW consists of a large collection of servers that support various types of communication protocols for exchanging information over the Internet with the help of Internet browsers. These protocols permit you to access any file available on the Internet by using the naming system called Uniform Resource Locators (URL). In addition, WWW also specifies a way in which HTTP should send a file over the Internet. The terms Internet and WWW are often used interchangeably without any difference. However, Internet and WWW are not same. The internet is the global system of different connected networks whereas WWW is one of the services provided by the Internet. Before the development of WWW, Internet was primarily used for receiving textual information. However, after the development of WWW, popularity of the Internet increased rapidly. This happened because WWW provided the support for the graphical content, which is easily understood. Thus, WWW can be credited for increasing the popularity of the Internet.

6.9.4 HyperText Transfer Protocol (HTTP)

HTTP is a generic, stateless, and object-oriented protocol that helps in performing several tasks, such as naming servers and management of distributed systems. It defines that how messages are formatted and transmitted and what actions should be taken by the Web servers and browsers to generate response with respect to the commands issued. For example, when you enter the address of a Web page in the browser, it sends the HTTP command to the Web server thereby asking to fetch and transmit the requested Web page. HTTP makes use of a set of methods to understand the purpose of a request. HTTP builds on the reference provided by the Uniform Resource Identifier (URI), as a location (URL) or name (that is, Uniform Resource Name, URN), for indicating the resources on which a method needs to be applied.

6.9.5 File Transfer protocol (FTP)

FTP is an acronym for File Transfer Protocol. As the name implies, FTP is a protocol that is used to transfer files among users over the Internet. File transfer simply means sending a copy of a file from one computer to another. As most of the information on the Internet is available in the form of files, you can use the FTP protocol to access this information. In FTP terminology, the computer on which you are working is called local host and the other computer is known as remote host. When you copy a file from a remote computer to your computer, it is known as downloading the file. On the other hand, when a file is copied from your computer to a remote computer, it is known as uploading the file. Following are the benefits provided by FTP:

- Useful in quick transferring of files from one network to another in an organization
- Helpful for the geographically dispersed group to work on a project

6.9.6 Telnet and Gopher

Telnet is a program that allows you to connect to the remote computers (called hosts) over the Internet. A Telnet program provides you with a character-based terminal window on the remote computer. Before start working on the remote computer, you need to login to that computer from your computer. After successful login to remote computer, you can work on that computer and you would feel as if you are sitting next to the remote computer. Generally, Telnet is used by people to carry out some sort of crucial work. However, nowadays, Telnet is also used for some other purposes, such as connecting to the libraries around the world, which helps the people involved in research.

On the other hand, gopher can be regarded as a tool that is used to browse through files and directories across Internet. It is basically a menu-driven text based tool that searches and displays the file appropriately. For example, the gopher automatically uncompresses a compressed file.

6.9.7 IP Addresses

A network may consist of several computers as well as peripherals (collectively called devices). It is important that each device should have a unique address to identify it on a TCP/IP network. This unique address is known as the IP address. To carry out effective communication between various networks, IP address is an essential requirement. Just as a person can be identified through his/her identity card or Permanent Account Number (PAN) card, each device on the TCP/IP network is uniquely identified by its IP address. An IP address contains a set of four numbers, each separated by a period or dot (.). Some examples of IP addresses are: 192.168.1.2, 10.324.1.3, and 109.134.2.2.

6.9.8 Internet Service Provider (ISP)

As you already know, the Internet is a network that can be accessed from anywhere in the world. However, before you access the Internet, you need to have an Internet connection. You can subscribe for an Internet connection from an Internet Service Provider (ISP) which is an organization that provides Internet connections. The ISP provides you the settings, such as user name and password, which you need to configure the Internet connection on your computer. Two factors that you should consider while selecting the means to connect to the Internet are: connectivity and speed. Some popular ISPs of India are:

- VideshSanchar Nigam Ltd. (VSNL)
- Mahanagar Telephone Nigam Ltd. (MTNL)
- Airtel
- Vodafone
- Reliance

6.9.9 Uniform Resource Locator (URL)

A Web site is hosted on a computer, which is known as server. You can access a particular Web site by accessing its server, that is, the host computer. For accessing the host computer, you need its IP address. Since an IP address is comprised of a set of unrelated numbers; therefore, it is difficult to remember it. An easier way of remembering a Web site is by its Uniform Resource Locator (URL), which is a simple string of characters used to represent and identify a

Web page or Web site. Unlike the IP address, the URL consists of text, which makes it easier to remember. The URL actually represents the domain name of the Web site, which is a unique name of that Web site.

The general form of URL is as follows:

```
type://address/path
```

where,

- **type:** Specifies the type of a server on which a file is located
- **address:** Refers to the address of server
- **path:** Refers to the location of a file located on a server

Consider the following example:

```
http://en.wikipedia.org/wiki/World_Wide_web.html
```

In the preceding example:

- http refers to the type of server
- en.wikipedia.org is the address of the server
- wiki/World_Wide_Web.html is the path of the file World_Wide_Web.html

The browsers, such as Internet Explorer and Netscape Navigator are considered as intelligent browsers as they can display files in any format and on any common types of servers.

6.9.10 Domain Name System (DNS)

Domain Name System (DNS) refers to the domain name resolution mechanism, which allows using domain names, instead of IP addresses, to access a domain. For example, you can use http://dreamtechpress.com instead of the http://207.106.22.8/ IP address to access the Dreamtech Press website. In this example, http://dreamtechpress.com is the DNS name provided for the http://207.106.22.8/ IP address. Prior to the introduction of DNS in 1983, the computers on a network retrieved the hosts.txt file from the network information center. The hosts.txt file is used to provide the names of the domains mapped to their IP addresses. The basic limitation of this mechanism was that whenever the IP address of a computer changes, the computer had to communicate with the network information center to update the hosts.txt file. The updating process of the hosts.txt file became very time consuming and error prone with the increase in the number of domains in a network. This led to the emergence of the DNS mechanism, in which the other hosts are automatically informed about the updates.

DNS helps to identify the service locations based on the name records, as it helps in assigning names to computers or services in a hierarchical form. These name records can be inscribed either manually or automatically on the DNS servers. The primary DNS server provides read and write services to manually inscribe the name records. You must note that only the administrators have the privilege to inscribe records manually. The records can also be inscribed automatically with the help of dynamic DNS servers that accept name records from devices, such as computer running editions of Windows 2000, Windows XP, Windows 2003, Windows Vista, or Windows Server 2008. DNS consists of the following three elements:

- **DNS namespace:** Comprises hierarchical tree structure of domain names. Each node in the tree has resource records to store the information related to a domain name.
- **DNS servers:** Manage the DNS database hosted by the DNS server. The computer on which the DNS server service runs is known as the DNS server. The DNS server can be primary, secondary, or caching-only.
- **DNS resolvers:** Use DNS queries to request records (information) from the DNS servers.

The DNS domain acts an administrative identity comprising groups of hosts as well as computers, routers, printers, and various other TCP/IP-enabled devices.

Figure-22 shows the DNS domain hierarchy:

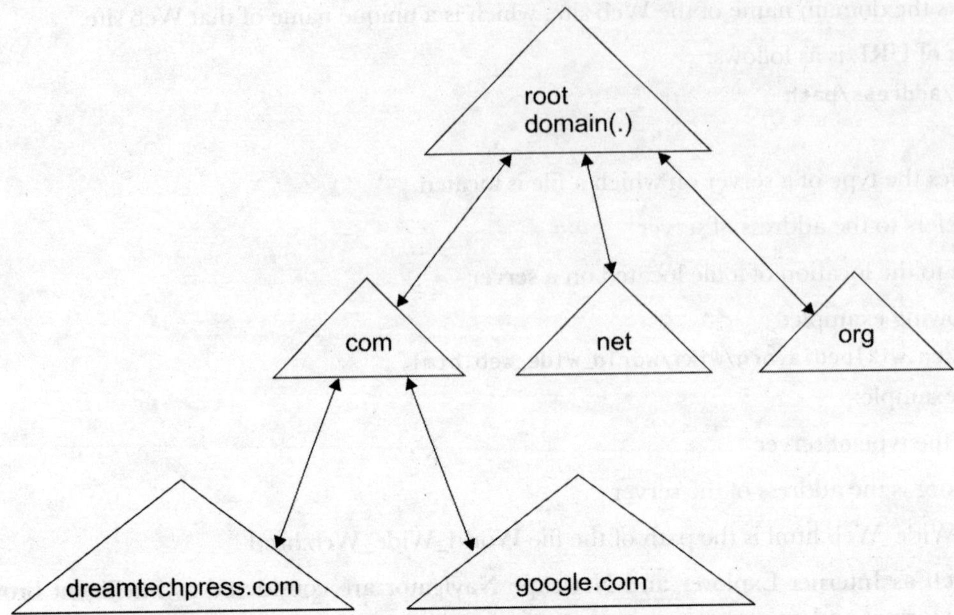

Figure-22: Displaying the DNS Domain Hierarchy

Figure-22 shows that the root domain (.) is the top-level domain, containing the com, net, and org domains. The further two subdomains under the com domain are dreamtechpress.com and google.com.

A DNS domain name comprises two or more labels separated by a dot(.). The right-most label depicts the top-level domain and each label towards left depicts the subdomains. For example, in the www.dreamtechpress.com domain name, the dreamtechpress label is separated from the com label by using dot. Moreover, the top-level domain is com and dreamtechpress.com is the subdomain of the com domain. When you access the www.dreamtechpress.com domain name, the domain name automatically resolves into an IP address. The most crucial task is to understand how the domain name resolves into the IP address and various terminologies associated with DNS.

The most commonly used top-level DNS components of the DNS hierarchy are listed in Table-2:

Table-2: Listing the Commonly Used Top-level DNS Components

Top-Level Name Components	Description	Examples
.com	Represents the domain name for the websites of commercial businesses	google.com
.edu	Represents the domain name for the websites of educational institutions	amity.edu
.gov	Represents the domain name for the websites of government agencies	defence.gov
.mil	Represents the domain name for the websites of military	army.mil
.net	Represents the domain name for the networking websites	rtmx.net
.org	Represents the domain name for the websites of non-profit organizations	peta.org
.in	Represents the domain name for the official Indian website	registry.in

6.9.11 E-mail

Electronic mail or e-mail is the most significant service of the Internet. It has become the most widely used tool for communication. This service allows users to send and receive electronic messages from all over the world. E-mail is an electronic message sent from one computer to another through the Internet. Earlier, e-mail was used to send text messages but today different types of files, such as images, graphics, or sound and video clips, can be sent along with e-mail messages.

Following are the basic advantages of e-mail:

- Saves paper processing and provide ease of editing message
- Transmits messages faster
- Sends messages as per sender's convenience
- Enables the user to transmit single e-mail to multiple users
- Provides space to store incoming and outgoing messages for future reference

6.9.12 Web Browser

Web browser is a software application that is used to retrieve, traverse, or represent information resources on WWW. An information resource can be a video, textual information, or Web page. These resources are identified using Uniform Resource Locator (URL) over the Internet. Web browser is specifically designed for accessing WWW, but it can also be used to access resources on local intranet or files in a file system. Some of the commonly used web browsers are Internet Explorer, Mozilla Firefox, Netscape, Google chrome etc.

The main function of the Web browser is to bring information resources. The process of bringing the information resources starts when a user types the URL in a Web browser. Consider a URL, http://kogent.com/, which is navigated by a user in the Web browser. In this URL, the prefix, http, identifies the protocol that is used by the Web browser to communicate with the Web server. Some examples of other prefixes are: https that works on HTTP with Secure Socket Layer (HTTPS) and ftp that works on File Transfer Protocol (FTP) for transferring files. In the URL, the name of the protocol is followed by :// and the next part of URL is the name of the server that stores the file that you need to display in the Web browser. In our example, the name of the server is kogent. The last part of the URL is the domain, which is com in our case.

6.9.13 Surfing and Searching

Surfing refers to the process of exploring and finding information from Web pages or websites on the Internet using a Web browser. Internet Explorer is one of the most popular Web browsers provided by Microsoft. For example, you can surf the website of Delhi University to know whether the results of the distance learning MBA course have been announced or not.

On the other hand, searching is a process of finding information on a particular topic from different websites. For example, if you want to get information on universities that provide MBA course, you can search your information using a search engine, where you can type your query.

6.9.14 Search Engines

A search engine is an application that is used to search for information on the Internet according to a specified criterion. Without search engines, finding the desired information from the colossus Internet would be a painstaking and cumbersome task. To use a search engine, you just need to go to its home page, type a keyword or a search criterion in the search box, and click the search button. The relevant information is displayed on your screen instantly.

A search engine hunts for the specific information from its own database. Different search engines have different databases. For this reason, it is advisable to use more than one search engine when searching for information on the Internet. Some popular search engines are Google, Yahoo, MSN, AltaVista, Look Smart, and Bing.

6.9.15 Uploading and Downloading from Internet

The process of uploading or making a website on the Internet is called Web hosting. The organizations that provide Web hosting services are called Web hosts. Web hosting services may vary from a simple Web page hosting to file transfer or uploading e-commerce on the Internet. Simple Web page hosting refers to the process of uploading a single Web page on the Internet. The other form of Web hosting is to upload files using FTP. Web hosts provide various types of services, which are as follows:

- **File hosting service:** File hosting service is used for uploading static content, such as large files on the Internet.
- **Image hosting service:** Image hosting services are used to upload an image on a website. There is an image host that stores the image on the Web server and provides different types of codes to other users to view the image.
- **Video hosting service:** Video hosting services are used to upload video clips and video files on a website. The video hosting websites are also known as video sharing website.

When you type the URL of a particular Web page in the Address bar of the browser and press the Enter key on the keyboard, the browser retrieves the Web page from the Internet and stores its content. The process of retrieving and storing the content of a Web page by the browser is known as downloading. A very common example of downloading is retrieving your favorite videos, songs, books, forms etc from Internet and storing them in your computer.

6.9.16 Applications of Information Technology (IT)

Information technology has changed the way we used to look at our world. Earlier, it was troublesome to do business from one country to another country predominantly because of distance issues. Information technology has provided solution to this mammoth problem by providing global access and usability of information through technology. Information technology has been defined as the use of technology for managing information. The task that required time of days or weeks is a work of just few clicks today. Internet has undoubtedly facilitated real time information sharing around the world that supports business operations worldwide.

According to the Information Technology Association of America (ITAA), "IT (Information technology) is the study, design, development, implementation, support or management of computer based information system particularly software applications and computer hardware."

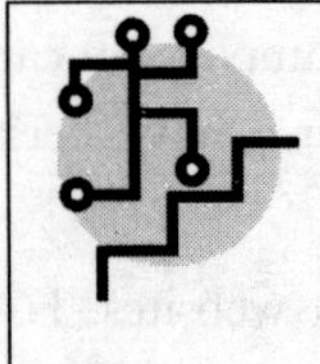

Activity-2

Assume yourself as a general manager of a multinational organization and prepare a list of daily business functions. Find out the activities that require the help of IT.

____

____

____

Business requires an interaction among stakeholders so that they can share information necessary to run the business effectively. Technology has brought revolutionary changes in the way business communication used to take place in the past. Earlier, sharing information between countries was a matter of one or more days, but now, it is possible in few minutes.

IT has itself become an industry, which is expected to grow and become worth 225 Billion US Dollar by 2020. It has made information a scientific product and has materialized the field of Information Technology Enabled Services, also known as ITES. Besides its application in business, IT has contributed significantly in various other spheres, such as education, manufacturing, banking, and telecommunication. In India, the industry has a significant contribution in the country's GDP. Figure-23 shows the contribution of IT in various fields:

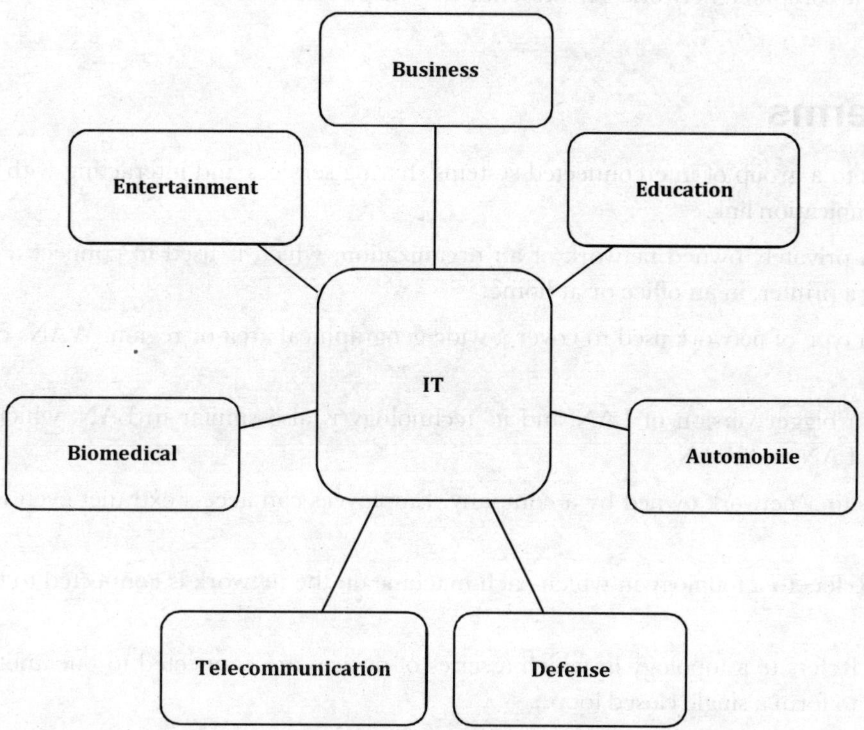

Figure-23: Contribution of IT in Various Fields

As shown in Figure-23, IT contributes significantly in business, education, automobile, defense, telecommunication, bio-medical, and entertainment. In business, it provides information systems, while in education sector, it provides e-learning. Apart from this, in automobiles, it helps in running efficient engines. The field of telecommunication and entertainment has been enriched with communication networks and many other devices.

Case Study: Detecting and Removing Virus from Network

Imagine you are a network administrator in an organization and have constructed the entire network for the organization. Now, a virus has infected your network due to which there is threat of loss of data across networks. The virus is attached to the executable files on the network. You need to install an antivirus on your network to detect and remove the virus infected files or programs.

Questions:

Q1. Which virus has affected your network as only the executable files have been infected?

Q2. As the network administrator, which antivirus would you install on the network?

*(*Case study presented is the proprietary information of the respective organization, and is used here specifically and only for educational purpose.)*

6.10 Summary

In this chapter, you have learned about the networking and its need. Apart from this, the chapter explored the various components of computer networks, such as protocols, and NICs. In addition, you have learned about various types of networks that are categorized on the basis of their characteristics in detail. The chapter has also discussed the hardware and software used in a computer network. At the end, the chapter described security, virus, antivirus, firewall and Internet.

6.11 Key Terms

- **Network:** Refers to a group of interconnected systems sharing services and interacting with each other by means of a shared communication link.
- **LAN:** Refers to a privately owned network of an organization, which is used to connect a computer with other hardware, such as a printer, in an office or at home.
- **WAN:** Refers to a type of network used to cover a wide geographical area or region. WANs can be interconnected with LANs.
- **MAN:** Refers to a bigger version of LAN and its technology is also similar to LAN, which provides a network coverage between LAN and WAN.
- **Extranet:** Refers to a network owned by a company. Employees can access extranet even when they are outside the office premises.
- **Bus topology:** Refers to a topology in which each machine on the network is connected to the other using a long single cable.
- **Ring topology:** Refers to a topology in which a series of devices are connected to one another by unidirectional transmission links to form a single closed loop.
- **Star topology:** Refers to a topology in which a LAN architecture in which the computers or nodes on a network are connected to a common central hub or switch, by dedicated links.
- **Mesh topology:** Refers to a topology in which each computer is connected to the other computer with a separate physical link on a network.
- **Protocol:** Defines a common set of rules and signals that computers on the network use to communicate with one another.
- **Router:** Refers to a networking hardware device that connects LANs and WANs on the Internet.
- **NIC:** Provides an interface between a data bus (a pathway inside the computer that carries data between the hardware components) and the network medium.
- **Search Engine:** Refers to an application that is used to search for information on the Internet according to a specified criterion.
- **Web browser:** Refers to a software application that is used to retrieve, traverse, or represent information resources on WWW.

6.12 Exercise

Multiple Choice Questions

Q1. Which of the following topology is highly reliable?

a. Star
b. Bus
c. Fully connected mesh
d. All of the above

Ans. c

Q2. Which of the following topology is not broadcast type?

a. Star
b. Bus
c. Ring
d. Tree

Ans. c

Q3. Identify the odd term among the following group.

a. Coaxial cable
b. Optical fiber
c. Twisted pair wire
d. Microwaves

Ans. d

Q4. What is the name of the network topology which has bidirectional links between each possible node?

a. Ring
b. Star
c. Tree
d. Mesh

Ans. d

Q5. Transreceivers is the example of the ______________ network component.

a. Media
b. Processors
c. Software
d. Channels

Ans. a

Q6. Which of the following virus attaches itself with the document and gets activated when the document is opened?

a. Boot sector virus
b. File infector virus
c. Macro virus
d. Multipartite virus

Ans. c

Q7. What is the protocol for transferring a file?

a. FTP
b. TCP
c. IP
d. UDP

Ans. a

Q8. What is the purpose of UDP?

a. Transferring data on the Internet
b. Transferring the file
c. Transferring the packets on the Internet
d. Transferring the images on the Internet

Ans. c

Q9. WWW stands for:

a. World Wide Wealth
b. World Wide Word
c. World Wide Width
d. World Wide Web

Ans. d

Q10. Which one of the following is a search engine?

a. www.google.com
b. www.yahoo.com
c. www.indiatimes.com
d. www.rediffmail.com

Ans. a

Short Answer Type Questions

Q1. What is difference between LAN and WAN?

Q2. Briefly explain network interface card (NIC).

Q3. Explain bus topology.

Q4. Write a short note on firewall.

Q5. List some of the top antivirus software.

Q6. Explain the mesh topology.

Q7. What do you understand by HTTP?

Q8. What is a search engine? Name different types of search engines available on Internet.

Q9. What is the difference between surfing and searching on the Internet.

Q10. What is a Web browser? Name some commonly used Web browsers.

CHAPTER 7

Introduction to Management Information System

CHAPTER STRUCTURE

CHAPTER OBJECTIVES

- Understand the concept of information system
- Elaborate on the components of information system
- Explain various trends in information system
- Describe various types of information system
- Explain the framework of information system in an organization
- Elaborate on different aspects of management information system

7.1 Introduction

Every business area such as operations, management, decision-making, and marketing is influenced by technology, which in turn contributes highly in productivity, efficiency, effectiveness, and overall growth of various organizations with the help of resourceful tools and technologies. An information system is one such resourceful tool, which has become an indispensable element of organizational decision-making. It has emerged as a highly effective combination of information technology and people activities that support operations, management, and decision-making. Although, in the past such tools used to be quite expensive and sophisticated, with continuous innovations in information technology, business enterprises started using economical and user-friendly information systems. Management Information System (MIS) is one of them. The primary function of MIS is to keep business management updated with well-structured information to achieve organizational objectives, efficiently. It utilizes the business concepts of defect free production, quick and logical decision-making and strategic business environment.

This chapter presents a comprehensive understanding of MIS. It explains the concept of information systems, the components of an information system along with its framework. The chapter also presents a developmental trend of information systems and its classification, and the relationship of business organization with information system. It also compares a human body with an information system, to clearly explain the concept. Having described information system in detail, the chapter then moves on to explain the nature, scope, need, role, and functions of MIS.

7.2 Concept of Information System (IS)

Information System (IS) was derived from information technology; however, it is no longer just a part of information technology. Now, IS has become more efficient and gives extremely high productive results. Essentially, an IS provides necessary information for business operations. It has been designed to support all business functions. Currently, complex business functions have been equipped with various types of IS to sustain and grow in the everyday changing business environment.

To understand an IS, it is logical to first understand the terms it is made up of, namely: information and system. Information can be defined as a well-structured data with a specific meaning. A system is an arrangement that takes input and provides output after completing the required process. In other words, IS can be defined as an arrangement that processes data and provides meaningful information. Essentially, it is a set of several components that process data to derive information. It can also be defined as a set of interrelated components that collects, stores, processes, generates and disseminates information for effective business functioning. This information supports decision-making and helps in performing control on various organizational departments and their functions. An IS can be useful for individual departments and collectively for all departments. This interrelationship between the components of an IS, is shown in Figure-1:

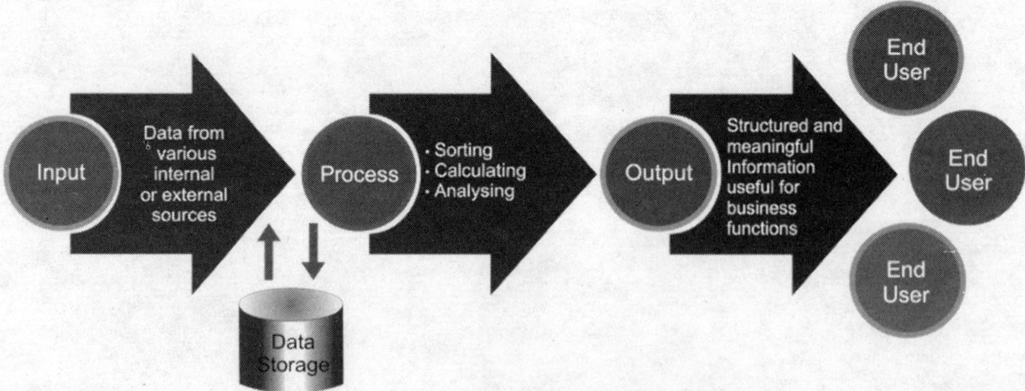

Figure-1: Displaying IS Model

The data for an IS can be collected from various inter-organization and intra-organization sources such as employees' personal details and competitors' performance. This data can be stored in paper or electronic format. The processing of this data includes calculations, logical analysis and other statistical methods, depending upon the information to be derived. Once data is processed, it is transformed into information. This information is disseminated to various end users to support their decision-making, problem solving, strategy forming and controlling functions in an organization.

For example, data about individual sales by each sales associate in a month, the general sales target for each associate and market sales trends for that month can be put to use. This data can be sorted, classified, calculated and analyzed to produce information. This will provide information about the sales trends for that time period, gaps between target and actual sales for individual associates and aggregate sales based on teams. The same data can be utilized to predict the next month's sales, target setting for the next month, strategy building for future sales and the expected production level.

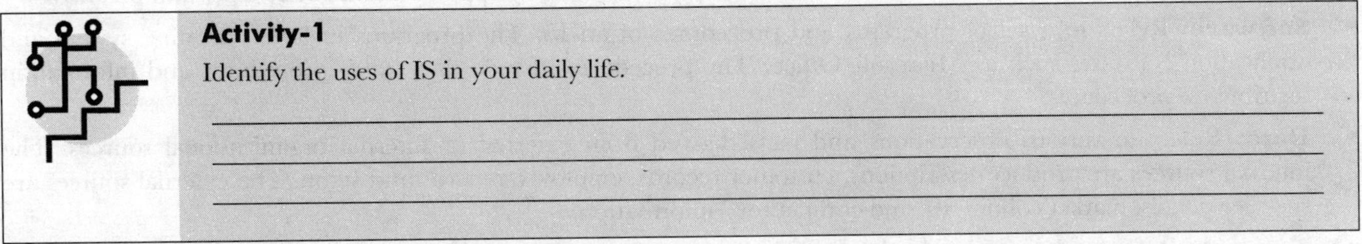

7.2.1 Computer Literacy and IS Literacy

Literacy means having a basic knowledge on any subject matter. IS literacy refers to the knowledge about accessing, organizing, evaluating and using data from various resources. However, computer literacy refers to the knowledge about various computer peripherals, computer software, and usage of a computer.

Let us now understand the differences in the scope of computer and IS literacy. IS cannot become part of a computer system, though computer science (CS) helped in updating IS with more user friendly and quick systems. The scope of computer science is quite different from the scope of IS. CS is a discipline, while IS is an application. An IS might not be always computer-based. The scope of IS is wider than that of CS.

Nonetheless, it is an undeniable fact that the use of computer system increases the efficiency of IS. Any information system can be installed on a computer system. The accuracy of calculation and time saving technology of a computer system helps in increasing the efficiency of a computer. File maintenance and data storage is also easy with a computer system.

Therefore, both the subjects have their own scopes and when integrated, that system becomes more efficient for business functions.

7.2.2 IS Components

An IS has various components mainly grouped under two heads. The first head is system resources and the other is system activities, as shown in Figure-2:

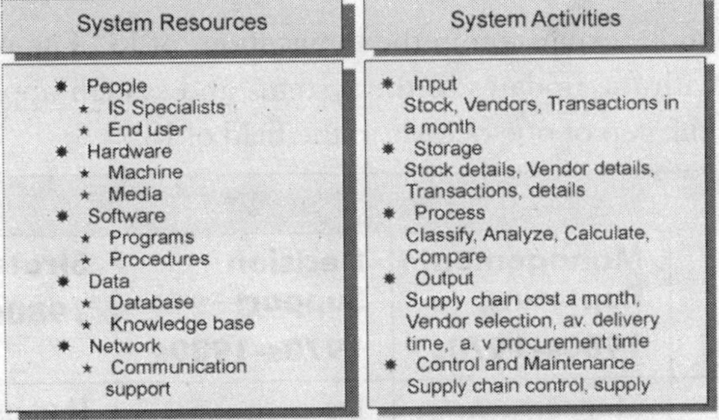

Figure-2: IS Components

Let us discuss the components of IS (Figure-2) in detail in the next section.

Information System Resources

System resources are those resources, which comprise a system. An IS consists of five major resources, which are as follows:

- **People:** Refers to the humans associated with an IS. This resource can be divided into two categories. The first category includes IS specialists, such as system analysts, software developers, and system operators. The second category includes the end users of information, anybody who uses the information derived from an IS.
- **Hardware:** Refers to the machine and media components of an IS. The machine components include computers, monitors, printers and scanners, while the media components include floppy disks, magnetic tapes and pen drives.
- **Software:** Refers to a set of programs and procedures of an IS. The programs include operating system and application software, such as Microsoft Office. The procedures include data entry procedures and information distribution procedures.
- **Data:** Refers to various observations and facts derived from external or internal organizational sources. The internal sources are product descriptions, customer records, employee records and so on. The external sources are supplier details, market conditions, and competitors' information.
- **Network:** Refers to the communication and media components of an IS. For example, network access and control software.
- **Information:** Refers to the reports and results derived after data processing. For example, management reports and business documents including text, graphics, audio and paper reports.

Information System Activities

System activities involve the components that belong to a particular system activity. It includes the following:

- **Input:** Involves data entry activities such as recording and editing. Generally, data is entered into a computer system or reordered in a paper form.
- **Data Storage:** Involves maintaining and organizing records, such as details related to customers, employees, and various other parties. Data is generally stored in file folders and hard disk.
- **Processing:** Involves those activities performed to process the data to produce information. For example, calculating, classifying, and summarizing.
- **Output:** Involves communicating the processed information to the end users. For example, presenting sales performance of an organization in the form of videos and reports is an output activity.
- **Control and system maintenance:** Refers to the feedback at every activity level to maintain the standard of performance and ensure the flexibility of a system.

7.2.3 Trends in IS

Over the years there has been continuous expansion in the applications of IS. The roles that it has taken up in business functioning is also upgraded along with the updates in the systems and system applications. Table-1 provides a list of the major trends, which occurred at the gap of one decade in the field of IS:

Table-1: Trends in IS

Trends (in ascending order)	Data Processing 1950s-1960s	Management Reporting 1960s-1970s	Decision Support 1970s-1980s	Strategic Support 1980s-1990s	E-Business 1990s onwards
Major Contributions	Electronic data processing systems	Management Information system	Decision Support systems	End user support, Executive support systems, Expert systems, Strategic IS	Internet based e- business and e-commerce

Table-1: Trends in IS

Trends (in ascending order)	Data Processing 1950s-1960s	Management Reporting 1960s-1970s	Decision Support 1970s-1980s	Strategic Support 1980s-1990s	E-Business 1990s onwards
Functional contributions	Transaction processing; record keeping and traditional accounting applications	MIS; Management reports of pre-specified information to support decision making	Decision Support; Interactive ad-hoc support of the managerial decision-making process	End user's computing; Direct computing support for user, Executive support; Critical information for top management Expert system; Knowledge based expert advice for users, Strategic support; Strategic products and services for competitive advantage	Internet based electronic-business and electronic-commerce; Web-enabled enterprise and global e-business structure, operations, e-commerce with internet, intranet, intranet and other networks
Forming concept	Era of efficiency	Era of effectiveness	Era of effectiveness	Era of competitiveness	Era of E-business

As you see in Table-1, major trends became evident from 1950s till 1960s—the first decade of IS; as electronic data processing (EDP) was popular. This trend brought transaction processing systems that performed record keeping and traditional accounting functions electronically.

Until the 1970s, Management Support Systems assumed managers as the end users. This provided managers with pre-specified reports and supported their decision-making. However, the pre-specified information did not prove to be effective for decision-making and thus, decision support systems emerged. It was an interactive ad-hoc support system for decision-making in business functions.

By the end of 1990s, several new contributions popularized. The updates in technology provided microprocessors, new software packages and end-user support concepts. All this provided end users with their own computing systems to support their functions instead of centralized services. As a second contribution in the same decade, Executive Support Systems emerged; this enabled the top management to access critical information in their preferred format. Yet another contribution was of expert systems—artificial intelligence. With the introduction of artificial intelligence, the business functions became more user-friendly. A number of functions developed as expert systems and replaced human efforts. They were knowledge-based systems that could advice the end-user on limited subjects.

Simultaneously, the concept of strategic support for competitive advantage was developed. Systems based on this concept were called Strategic Support Systems. At this point, information technology had become a global business concept. A significant trend of this decade was the Enterprise Resource Planning (ERP) system.

Since 1990s, there has been astounding growth in the field of internet and other networks for business information sharing and business promotion. Electronic business and web-enabled enterprises emerged in a big way. Simultaneously, there has been growth in the information systems field. They have not only become effective, but an essential part of business functions. If IS continue to grow and develop faster, it can play an immensely important role in organizational success.

7.2.4 Classification of IS

An IS system can be classified into several categories based on its application, as shown in Figure-3:

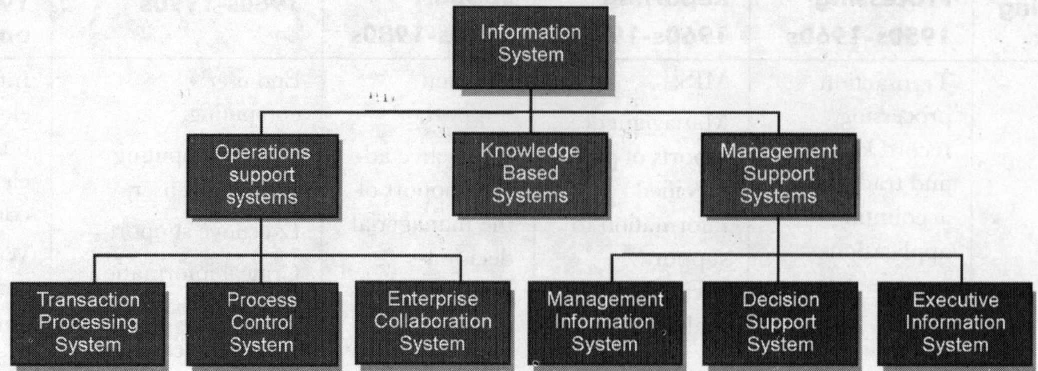

Figure-3: Classification of IS

In the next few sections, let us learn about the different categories of IS.

Operations Support Systems

IS has been supporting various business operations such as accounting and production. Those systems that support some business operations are grouped under Operations Support Systems (OSS). There are three main divisions of OSS, which are as follows:

- **Transaction Processing System:** Helps in processing various business transactions and retrieving information from them. There can be two ways of processing a transaction, namely: batch processing and online or real time processing. In batch processing, transactions are stored over a period and then processed, while in real-time processing, transactions are processed at their occurrences. For example, at retail stores, the cash receipts or card payments is registered and processed simultaneously.
- **Process Control System:** Helps in monitoring and controlling physical processes in an organization. This system helps in making day-to-day decisions and controlling operational processes. This system automates the adjustment of a production process. For example, in an underground mining plant, electronic sensors can monitor the pressure and send automated warnings, if the pressure is about to reach the danger level. It can also identify water sources in a particular range in the mining field.
- **Enterprise Collaboration System:** Helps in sharing information amongst employees. A proper flow of information helps in increasing the productivity of an organization. For example, use of electronic mail to share information by one team member to the other and a team leader addressing a meeting with the team through video conferencing.

Management Support Systems

A management support system (MSS) provides useful information to managers for decision-making and control. The following are the different types of MSS:

- **Management Information System (MIS):** Provides information on various business aspects to managers. It generates information for monitoring performance and maintaining coordination. For example, a production manager can check the report of cost and time of production for the previous year, so that he/she can take effective production decisions for the current year.
- **Decision Support System (DSS):** Supports managerial decision-making. For example, a sales manager can set sales targets for the coming year by considering current market conditions.

- **Executive Information System (EIS):** Provides critical information to the executive and top-level managers for making strategic decisions. It provides statistical representation of information. For example, an executive can check for a brand image, by looking at the graphs representing customers' preferences and the sales of competitive brands in the last five years.

Knowledge Based Systems

A knowledge-based system provides information to users in different business areas, when required. The following are the two types of knowledge-based systems:

- **Expert System:** Provides adequate knowledge and expert advice for making various managerial decisions. An expert system is composed of two main components, namely: knowledge base and software modules. It not only helps in management decision-making, but also enables non-management employees in taking job-related decisions.
- **Knowledge Management System (KMS):** Provides knowledge and expertise for making various management-level decisions. For sharing knowledge, KMS uses a group of collaboration systems such as the intranet. It provides two types of knowledge, namely: explicit and tacit knowledge. Information that is documented, stored, and coded with the help of an information system, is known as explicit knowledge. Information based on processes and procedures stored in the human mind falls under tacit knowledge. The following are the major benefits of using KMS:
    - ⇨ Allows free flow of ideas in an organization by innovation and creativity
    - ⇨ Improves the productivity and performance of an organization
    - ⇨ Achieves high level of customer satisfaction

7.2.5 Framework of IS in an Organization

IS has been made of many complex technologies and applications. Five essential areas you must learn to understand the framework of IS are:

- **Foundation in IS:** Refers to the fundamental concepts of an IS, which includes fundamental business environment, basic components and managerial concepts. For example, the basic system has developed result-oriented systems.
- **Information Technology in IS:** Refers to the technical components and concepts for an IS, which involves hardware, software and networks. For example, internet-based information sharing developed e- business.
- **Business Applications in IS:** Refers to application of IS in various business functions making it suitable for them. The cross functional application such as customer relationship management is an example of business application of IS.
- **Development in IS:** Refers to more professional and effective system development for a business function. This was basically to gain a competitive advantage. More specific and advanced systems were produced to support a business.
- **Challenges with IS:** Refers to various ethical and social issues arising out of IS applications in a business. For example, security issues and cyber-crimes.

7.2.6 IS and Business Organization

IS has become an integral part of business organizations today. For example, those organizations involved in share trading are highly dependent on IS. Figure-4 shows how IS integrates various functions and users of an organization:

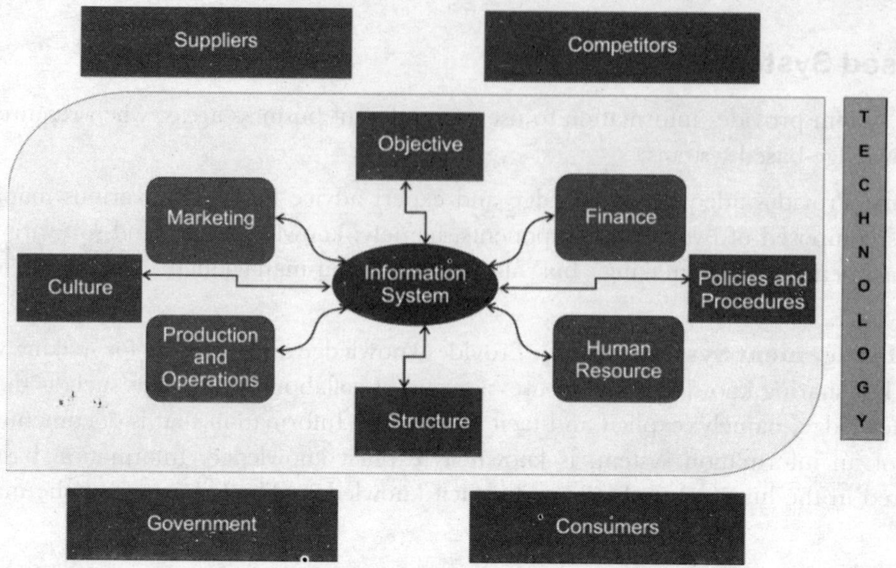

Figure-4: IS and Business Organization

As you can see in Figure-4, IS has become a core component of a business organization. It plays a vital role in coordinating between internal and external organizational factors. The internal organizational factors include various departments and organizational behavioral factors, such as, culture, objectives, structure, policies and procedures. The external organizational factors include suppliers, competitors, consumers and the legal system.

IS supports the following business processes:

- **Operations Support Process:** Use of IS in various business processes at operational level. For example, running of plant and machinery for production and purchase of material. Organization certainly depends on IS for productive business processes.
- **Decision Support Process:** Use of IS for business decision-making. IS provides useful and relevant information after processing data from various inter and intra organizational sources. This information helps in effective decision-making and logical functioning of a business.
- **Strategic Support Process:** Gaining competitive advantage by providing critical information to management at the top level. With the help of information on various inter and intra organizational factors, management can work on various business strategies to improve productivity and profit. For example, quick delivery of orders by Domino's pizza without unnecessary delay.

7.2.7 Human Body as an Information System

Human body is the most effective and elaborative information system ever created. It has senses that help in data collection. The memory part works as a storage device and information is stored in our minds, which is reflected in our actions. The IS in an organization resembles a human body. Hence, a human body is believed to be a perfect information system, as depicted in Figure-5:

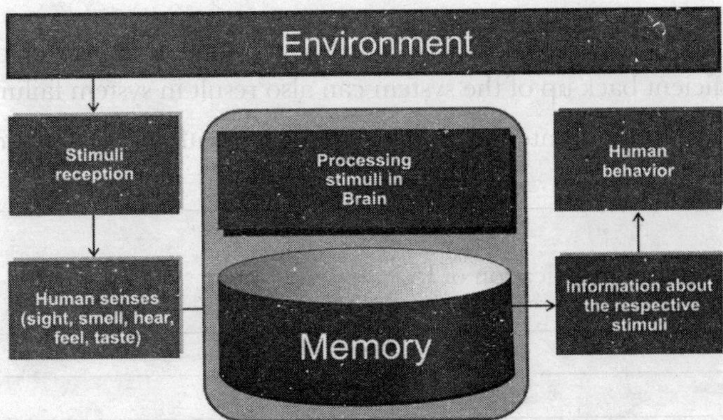

Figure-5: Human Body as an IS

Figure-5 shows the functioning of a human body as an IS. It has the following steps:

- **Stimulus Reception through Senses:** Stimulus is any change arising in the surrounding environment that can be heard, seen, smelled, tasted or felt through human senses. This action serves as an input in the information system of a human body.
- **Human Brain:** Involves two main functions 'as a system' which are as follows:
  - ⇨ **Memory:** Refers to the memory power in the human brain that can save the pervious stimulus. It can also save information from the previous process and learning from the past. This serves as a storage device in the human body.
  - ⇨ **Processing Stimulus Received:** Refers to the analytical and reasoning capacity of a human brain.
- **Information about the Respective Stimuli:** Refers to the production of information related to the collected stimulus from the environment after processing it in the human brain.
- **Human Behavior:** Refers to the response of that stimulus by the human body as a reaction of understanding the information processed in the brain.

There are other views that assume each function in a human body is an information system such as the nervous system and digestion system.

7.2.8 IS Failures and Causes

System failure refers to system stoppage and accidents that do not allow a system to run correctly. For correct functioning of the information systems, it is essential to provide timely, accurate, and relevant information. Any failure in adequately performing its functions, is an IS failure. The results of IS failure prove fatal for productivity and may lead to a significant drop in the organizational success curve. For example, any problem in the server of an organization results in the waste of productive working hours.

There are several reasons that can lead to a system failure, which include the following:

- **Incorrect Requirement Realization:** Refers to the incorrect assumptions about the system requirements. A system required for quality management should be able to evaluate quality on all the set parameters. At times, the software developed does not match the requirements and results in a system failure.
- **Insufficient System Development Practice:** Refers to the inefficiency of system developers. At times, system development lifecycle fails to perform a proper system testing, which results in failures such as system stoppage or slow processing.
- **Untrained or Poor System Usage:** Refers to an improper user interface. Any untrained user can harm or produce undesirable results using an IS. Poor usage may cause internal or external system damage.
- **System Damage:** Refers to harming the system physically or with the help of software. This can be intentional or unintentional that can result in unproductive functioning or non-function of the IS. For example, a mouse may cut the wiring in the local area connection causing system damage.

- **Other Causes:** Refers to any unforeseen situations such as network failure of network congestion. Improper electricity support and inefficient back up of the system can also result in system failure.

Thus, we find that proper back up and maintenance is required even with an information system along with avoiding the obvious causes of system failure.

Activity-2

Write a short note on classification of IS.

____

____

____

7.3 Management Information System (MIS)

MIS provides information to the management, which helps in decision-making and effective business management. It is one of the fastest growing concepts in the business environment. It has influenced the decision-making patterns and strategic business concepts significantly. To understand MIS, you need to learn management and information systems.

Management is the process of planning, organizing, directing and controlling the resources to obtain business objectives effectively. Some of the popular definitions of MIS are as follows:

*According to **Schwartz**, "MIS is the system of people, equipment, procedures, document and communication that collects, validates, operates on, transforms, stores, retrieves and presents data for use in planning, budgeting, accounting, controlling and other management processes."*

*According to **Coleman and Ritley**, "An MIS*

i. applies to all management levels;

ii. is linked to an organizational subsystem;

iii. functions to measure performance, monitor progress, evaluate alternatives or provide knowledge for change or collective action; and

iv. is flexible both internally and externally."

*According to **Davis and Olson**, "MIS is an integrated user-machine system designed for providing information to support operational control, management control and decision making functions in an organization. ISs make use of resources such as hardware, software, men, procedures as well as suppliers."*

IS refers to a set of interrelated components that collect, store, process, generate and disseminate information for effective business decision-making. MIS collects data from various resources, processes it, and transforms the data into meaningful and useful information. Figure-6 shows the structure of MIS:

Figure-6: Structure of MIS

This data is collected from various internal and external resources. Technical and analytical measures are utilized to process this data. After processing, data is transformed into meaningful information. This information helps various levels of decision-making and in improving organizational effectiveness.

7.3.1 Nature and Scope of MIS

As discussed in the previous section, MIS has become an important tool in the business environment. It provides useful information to managers for making various business decisions. The nature of MIS is explained as follows:

- **System Approach:** Involves the approach of input, process and output involved for the management decision-making.
- **Technology-based Concept:** Utilizes various technologies for data processing in the system.
- **Interdisciplinary Concept:** Encompasses all business disciplines, such as accounting, computer science, operational research, statistics, behavioral science and management.

MIS helps in analyzing and organizing unstructured data collected from various resources. The conversion of such data into meaningful information creates an opportunity for the management to make best productive decisions at various levels. Information technology has significantly broadened the scope of MIS.

7.3.2 Characteristics of MIS

The following are the characteristics of MIS:

- **Management Oriented:** MIS deals with managerial processes, such as decision making, production planning, and goal setting.
- **Need Based:** MIS fulfills the information needs of managers.
- **Integrated:** MIS integrates various processes and resources and provides integrated information, when required.
- **Growth Oriented:** MIS facilitates growth through effective planning and control of the production processes.
- **Flexibility of Process:** Implies that various processes followed in MIS are flexible in nature.

7.3.3 Need of MIS

MIS provides support to management functions at all levels of an organization. The various benefits that create a need for MIS in an organization are as follows:

- Fulfills the information requirements of an organization in setting goals
- Facilitates effective decision-making measures
- Organizes data from various resources
- Ensures the efficiency of planning in an organization
- Provides an effective control on operational functions
- Facilitates the flow of information amongst employees of different levels

7.3.4 Role of MIS

MIS plays a vital role in today's managerial working as it serves various needs of managerial functions. It serves to perform the complicated managerial functions with ease efficiently.

The role of MIS can be explained as follows:

- **Increased complexity of business:** Refers to the level of complexity in performing business operations. With revolutionary updates in technologies, a rapid change in the business environment occurred. This change increased the complexity of functions to be performed by every department. MIS serves as a necessary tool in such complex business environment. Calculation based and logical analysis is quicker and accurate with the use of MIS that saves time and increases efficiency of business. For instance, in today's business environment most organizations have different branches at different locations worldwide. MIS serves for information sharing from one branch to another and helps management to have control on all the functions of all branches.

- **Increased competition:** Refers to the level of competition that has increased in the changing business environment. Currently, the challenge is not only about becoming the most profitable business, but also to remain successful. MIS provides critical information to sustain in the competitive environment. For competitive business, various strategic decisions depend upon the information provided by MIS. For instance, in constantly changing market conditions, MIS keeps the management informed about the prevailing market conditions and demand trends to help them take production related decisions.
- **Increased complexity and burden on management:** Involves sharing the liability of management to serve managerial functions efficiently. Currently, there has been evolution of strategic management. The decision making functions have become more complex and need better analytical approach and expertise. With the use of MIS, these decisions can be made more productive. It also shares the management functions by performing the most logical actions. For instance, management has to handle strategic, tactical or operational decisions, for which relevant information is served by MIS.
- **Information technology:** Impacts business with high degree of result orientation. The emergence of Electronic Business requires an organization to be updated with IT revolutions. MIS utilizes this technological change for the growth of an organization, being able to perform with less effort yet derive more efficient information. For instance, various new technologies help management to work fast and be perfect. Introduction of online training helps in improving productivity.

7.3.5 Functions of MIS

As discussed earlier, MIS serves the information needs of managers to make various management decisions. Figure-7 shows the functions of MIS:

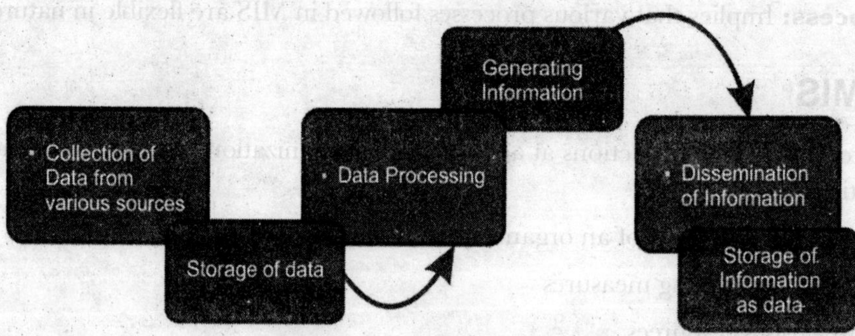

Figure-7: Functions of MIS

The various functions of MIS are discussed as follows:

- **Collecting Data from Various Sources:** Involves gathering data from various internal and external sources. The external sources include suppliers, competitors, customers, newspapers, magazines and so on. Internal sources include financial reports, sales records and so on. This data is collected in both paper and in electronic forms.
- **Storing Data:** Storing all records and retrieving, when required.
- **Processing Data:** Involves functions, such as calculating, sorting, classifying, analyzing, comparing, and summarizing the collected data.
- **Generating Information:** Involves transforming the collected data into useful and meaningful information after processing. This information is well structured and organized.
- **Disseminating Information:** Involves distributing information produced to users or managers to help them in performing their functions efficiently. For example, report generation.
- **Storing Information:** Involves saving information again in the database for future references. If required, the same information can be further processed.

7.3.6 Adopting MIS in Organizations

MIS has been successfully adopted by most business organizations. This is because MIS is helping improve efficiency of organizational functions. According to Goodman (1993), there is a positive correlation between success of an organization and assessing the requirement of information, gathering information and information usage. Organizations are required to acquire the skills of creating, organizing and sharing knowledge to enable to adapt to changes in knowledge and such organizations are referred to as intelligent learning organizations. The usage of information strategically is considered as a critical success factor for the success of an organization.

The following table shows this trend of adopting IS with time by organizations:

Table-2: Adoption of MIS in organizations

Time frame	Major Adoptions	Skills required to be acquired or developed
1970s	Main focus was to automate existing processes Use of Mainframe computers Centralization of computers and data Systems tie up with few business functions: payroll, inventory, billing	Programming in COBOL
1980s	Main focus was on automating existing processes Installation of PCs and LANs Set up of separate computer systems for separate Departments End-user computing with Word Processors and Spreadsheets making individual departments less dependent on the IT department	PC support, basic networking
1990s	Main focus was on central control and corporate learning Adopting Wide Area Networks (WANs) as corporate standards System integration and data integration efforts by Senior management Reduction in stand-alone systems	Network support, systems integration, database administration
2000s	Main focus is on efficiencies and speedier business processes in inventory, manufacturing, distribution Expansion of Wide Area Networks to the Internet Introduction of global enterprises and business associates for more efficient supply chain and distribution practices. Senior management looks for data sharing across systems.	Global Network support, systems integration

7.3.7 Future of MIS

Future is always uncertain, but we can set our expectations based on the trend analysis of the past. While predicting the future of MIS, it puts forth a question as to how else an MIS can be made more efficient and useful. A group of predictors including R Watson possess a pessimistic view in this context. They postulate that MIS has already been modified to serve its best for management functions. However, there are those who believe that the dynamism of business world would definitely require MIS to present another successful trend. With the hope to make it more useful, expectations are set to create more interactive and user-friendly systems. There can be another generation of systems that will be able to lead to even further shortening of hectic management functions. This will be updated with contemporary business requirements. It will be more skilled apart from being knowledgeable. The next generation of the system is believed to be more automated. It can also improve in terms of time effectiveness and its overall experience for users. It should be more responsive towards changes and developments in the environment to help generate new knowledge for designing new products, services and improving organizational processes.

It is also expected that in future management challenges and system failure issues will be eliminated. With all these big hopes, we believe that the future MIS will definitely be better than the current.

7.4 Structure of MIS

There is no rigid structure of MIS. However, MIS comprises four elements, as shown in Figure-8:

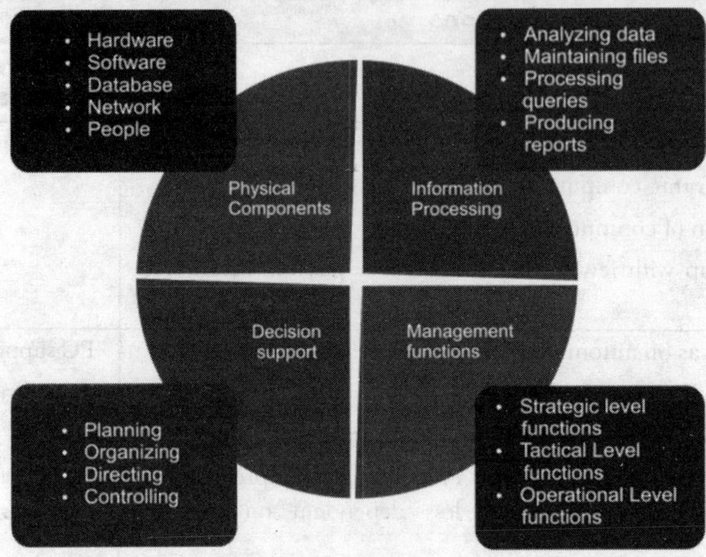

Figure-8: MIS Structure

The four elements of MIS (Figure-8) are discussed in the next few sections.

7.4.1 Physical Components

The components of MIS that can be physically examined fall under this category. These include:

- **Hardware:** Refers to various physical devices used in MIS. It includes machine equipment; for instance computers, as well as media devices, such as compact disks, key board, and monitor.
- **Software:** Refers to a set of programs and procedures required to process data.
- **Database:** Refers to the collection of observations, documents, reports, and findings kept in a documented or electronic form.
- **Network:** Include Intranet, Extranet and Internet, which are used to maintain the flow of communication at different levels in MIS.
- **People:** Refers to end-users working on MIS in an organization.

7.4.2 Information Processing

The structure of MIS can also be explained through the elements required in processing the data. Information processing includes the following activities:

- **Data Analysis:** Refers to activities such as calculating, sorting, classifying, comparing data.
- **Management of Files:** Refers to creating and maintaining records of data and information obtained in previous processes in folders or files for future reference.

- **Processing of Queries:** Refers to extracting data and analyzing it for required operation to produce information for the query.
- **Report Generation:** Refers to preparing reports in a paper or electronic form for the reference of managers. Since MIS generates reports regularly, it is also known as management reporting system.

7.4.3 Management Functions

Based on the activities performed, management is divided into three levels in an organization. The components of MIS can be explained with the help of management functions at each level, as shown in Figure-9:

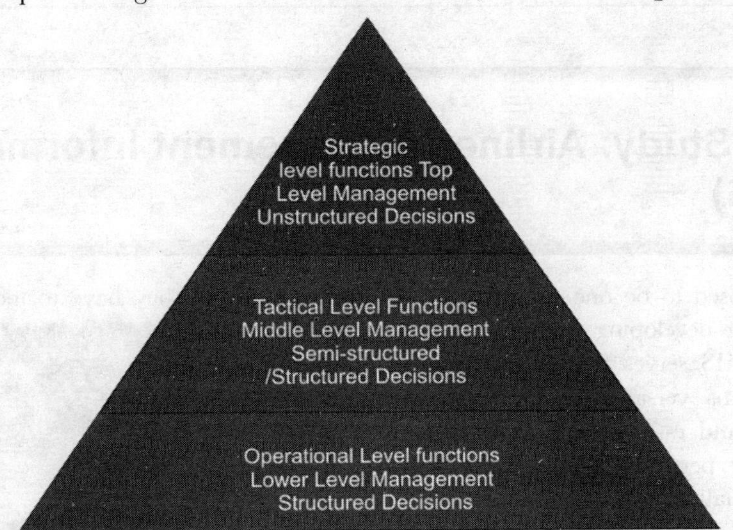

Figure-9: MIS Structure at Different Levels of Management

The following are the three types of management functions:

- **Strategic-level Functions:** Include top-level management functions, which are not affected by other managerial functions. It includes acquisition and mergers, entry into new market segments, and launching of new product lines. The decisions taken at strategic level are called unstructured decisions.
- **Tactical-level Functions:** Include middle-level management functions. It includes acquisition of resources, efficient management of available resources, organizational budgeting, and formulation of work policies and so on. The decisions taken at this level are semi-structured/structured decisions.
- **Operational-level Functions:** Includes lower-level management functions. Operational-level functions include deciding the production and inventory level, selecting vendors, supervising production processes and so on. The decisions taken at operational level are structured decisions.

7.4.4 Decision Support

MIS supports various managerial decisions in an organization. A decision can be of two types, namely: structured and unstructured. Unstructured decisions are those that do not relate to any previous decisions and are administrative in nature, whereas, structured decisions are dependent on previous decisions and operational in nature. Unstructured decisions are unique and the information needed for decision-making is unpredictable.

An organization needs to take a number of decisions for performing management functions such as planning, organizing, directing, and controlling. Planning is generally a structured decision, which is taken by the top management. Organizing, directing and controlling are unstructured decisions. Organizing is a function of middle-management, whereas, directing and controlling are dealt by operational-management. Apart from these two categories, there can be semi-structured decisions, which are taken by middle-management; but, are indirectly related to top management.

Table-3 shows the examples of structured, semi-structured, unstructured decisions:

Table-3: Examples of Management Decisions

Unstructured Decisions (Planning)	Semi-structured Decisions (Organizing)	Structured Decisions (Directing and Controlling)
• Financial planning • Portfolio management • Ratio analysis	• Financial forecasting • Financial budgeting	• Cash management • Purchase decisions

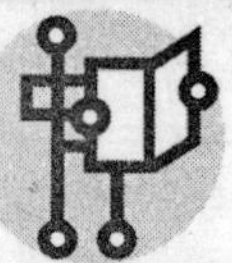

Case Study: Airlines Management Information System (AMIS)

Airlines industry is supposed to be one of the early adopters of MIS, as they have to incur heavy costs on human resources. The reason for developing this system was cost cutting and improving efficiency. AMIS serves for all management activities. The system efficiently performs versatile functions, such as finance and accounting, reservation and e-ticketing, inventory management, flight operation and engineering, personnel and payroll and marketing statistics. The system works individually on these functions along with an integrated approach.

AMIS is a web-based browser that supports all operating systems such as Linux, Netware, Windows 95/98/ME, Windows XP/2000/NT. It is an easy-to-use system. The system involves four levels of security to ensure restriction on unauthorized usage. Many controls have also been implemented that can identify fake-ticket or passengers without ticket. It can check random booking, overstaffing, under staffing, earned or unearned revenue, daily transactions, expense records and many such functions. It can also be easily customized as required. The cost of such system ranges from 20,000 to 100,000 in rupees.

Questions:

Q1. Do you think installation of AMIS would prove cost-effective for an aviation organization?

Q2. List the functions performed in aviation business and match them with functions served by AMIS.

*(*Case study presented is the proprietary information of the respective organization, and is used here specifically and only for educational purpose.)*

7.5 Summary

In this chapter you have learned about the concept of information system (IS), which included computer literacy and IS literacy, IS components, trends in IS, and classification of IS based on its application. In addition to that, you have also learned about Management Information System (MIS), as a concept that helps in decision-making and effective business management. With respect to MIS, you have learned about the following: nature and scope of MIS, characteristics of MIS, need of MIS, role of MIS, functions of MIS, and future of MIS. Towards the end of the chapter, the structure of MIS is also explained in the chapter, which includes physical components, information processing, management functions, and decision support.

7.6 Key Terms

- **Acquisition and Mergers:** Refers to the purchase of one company or business enterprise by another as part of a growth strategy. This can be with or without the mutual consent of both companies.
- **Portfolio Management:** Refers to the process of decision-making related to investments such as investment policy, investments objectives, asset allocation for individuals and institutions, and balancing risk against performance.
- **Programs and Procedures:** Refers to various set of instructions for a computer system. Set of operation instructions are programs, whereas, set of information processing instructions are procedures.
- **Securities Management**: Refers to financial securities like assets and investments.
- **Inventory:** Refers to the raw material, work in progress and the finished goods in a production process.
- **General Ledger:** Refers to a type of accounting record for a business.
- **Vendor:** Refers to suppliers related to production process in an organization.

7.7 Exercise

Multiple Choice Questions

Q1. What does MIS stands for?

a. Managerial Information System
b. Management Information System
c. Market information system
d. Management Integrated System

Ans. b

Q2. MIS is ------- based concept.

a. Money
b. Technology
c. Product
d. Entertainment

Ans. b

Q3. According to Coleman and Ritley," An MIS applies to all ----------levels.

a. Management
b. Educational
c. Financial
d. Material

Ans. a

Q4. Until the__________ Management Support Systems assumed managers as the end-users managerial functions.

a. 1960s
b. 1970s
c. 1980s
d. 1990s

Ans. b

Q5. MIS is the system of people, equipment, procedures, document and--------.

a. Communication
b. Commitment
c. Concentration
d. Collection

Ans. a

Q6. Which of the following are functions of MIS?

a. Data collection
b. Dissemination of Data
c. Data Processing
d. All of them

Ans. d

Q7. EDP stands for________.

a. Electronic Data Processing
b. Electrical Data Processing
c. Elementary Data Processing
d. Economical Data Processing

Ans. a

Q8. ERP stands for______.

a. Enterprise Resource Planning
b. Enterprise Recruitment Planning
c. Engineering Resource Planning
d. Elementary Resource Planning

Ans. a

Q9. Which of the following is an Operation Support Systems?

a. Transaction Processing System
b. Management Information System
c. Decision support System
d. Executive Information System

Ans. a

Q10. What do MIS relate with?

a. Provision of information to management
b. Provision of confidential information to competitors
c. Provision of unnecessary information
d. Provision of monetary funds

Ans. a

Short Answer Type Questions

Q1. What do you mean by information system?

Q2. Differentiate between computer literacy and IS literacy.

Q3. What do you mean by system resources of IS?

Q4. What do you mean by system activities?

Q5. What are the main divisions of operations support systems?

Q6. What is management support system?

Q7. What do you mean by knowledge based system?

Q8. Briefly discuss the framework of IS.

Q9. What do you mean by strategic support process?

Q10. Discuss the nature of MIS in brief.

CHAPTER 8

System Development and Design

CHAPTER STRUCTURE

CHAPTER OBJECTIVES

- Elaborate on system approach
- Explain the development of information system
- Describe the traditional system of development lifecycle
- Understand the concept of system analysis
- Explain system design
- Elaborate on the alternative system development methods
- Discuss on system development and organizational change

8.1 Introduction

Organizations either build or buy a system to support their business functions. The development of a system is one of the crucial tasks, since most organizational development processes depend upon systems. Developing a system by system programmers and IT experts is a part of the whole system development process. This process requires system requirement analysis, user support, proper implementation of the system, and system evaluation. These functions are as necessary as building a system. Non-performances in these phases may prove to be a non-beneficial cost and may cause discomfort to users. There is a cost involved in developing or buying a system; the system analyst has to make sure that this cost is less than the utility derived by that system over a period of time. The use of a system in an organization not only depends on its capabilities; but, also on people in the organization adopting the newly installed system. Apart from development and evaluation, proper maintenance is also required. For a business professional it is necessary to be familiar with the basics of a system. This helps professionals in adopting the systems well and improving the efficiency of their work.

This chapter helps in understanding the system approach and the concept of system. The chapter then provides an overview of system analysis. It also elaborates on the traditional system development lifecycle. The chapter further explains the aspects of system design and the system development methodologies.

Let us first understand the systems approach in problem solving.

8.2 The System Approach

The systems approach is involvement of systems to solve a problem. A systematic approach is cause-effective. The steps involved in the system approach are shown in Figure-1:

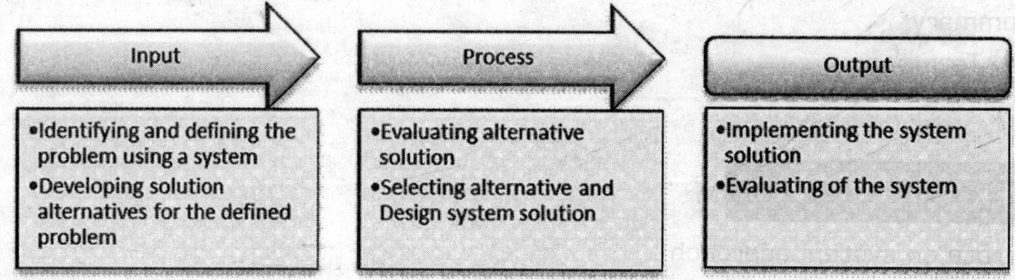

Figure-1: System Approach to Problem Solving

The system approach involves the following steps:

1. **Identify and Define a Problem using a System:** Utilizes data resource and managerial skills to anticipate and identify a problem. Certain authors believe this approach is a thinking approach, which identifies interrelationship amongst several systems and examining the scope of change among them.
2. **Develop Solution Alternatives for the Defined Problem:** Involves environmental analysis and organizational analysis to find all possible solutions to check the identified problem.
3. **Evaluate Alternative Solution:** Performs a what-if analysis with each alternative solution of the problem. The aim is to find out the best amongst them.
4. **Select Alternative and Design System Solution:** Selection of the best solution and designing it to meet the requirements of the system solution.
5. **Implement the System Solution and Evaluate:** Implementation of the designed system solution and analyze with the level of expected advantages.

The above mentioned five steps form a system approach to problem solving. Now, let us understand the system concept.

8.2.1 The Concept of System

The word 'system' originated from the Latin term 'systema', which means a set of interacting entities to form an integrated whole. A system represents a set of relationships between the elements of a set that forms a relational regime.

*According to **Cleland** and **King**, "a system may be defined as an assemblage or combination of things or parts forming a complex whole".*

As clear from the above definition, a system is an assembly of various components. This assembly serves a specific purpose or a goal. Amongst these components, there is always a relation of input-process-output which forms the basis of a system. A system has the following key features:

- A system is a combination of interrelated components.
- A system has a specific goal.
- It involves a process that transforms the inputs into outputs.
- The output in the system is more valuable than the combination of inputs.

Let us take an example of a computer system. It has input devices such as keyboard and CPU as its processor. Every input given to the computer is processed and the output is provided through its output devices such as monitor. It is a combination of various input and output devices. It shares the human burden in work. It has its CPU as the processor to transform the input into the required output and adds value in the process. Shortly, a system is a collection of components working together to achieve certain objectives of a system. There are three parts of a system namely: input, processing and output.

Now, let us understand the characteristics of a system.

8.2.2 Characteristics of a System

Following are the basic characteristics of a system:

- Systems consist of interrelated components (a relationship exists between parts and the whole).
- Systems are arranged in a hierarchy (subsystems and super-systems).
- Synergies among system components create a whole that is more than the sum of its parts.
- System boundaries are artificial: systems are components of another larger system. Systems can be opened (influenced by their environment) or closed (not influenced by their environment).
- Systems have inputs, processes, outputs, and feedback loops.

Let us now understand the types of system.

8.2.3 Types of Systems

Systems can be categorized based on its operation and features. Table-1 shows the categories:

Table-1: Types of Systems

Relativeness to Environment	Visibility	Operation
• Open Systems • Closed Systems	• Virtual Systems • Physical Systems	• Automated System • Semi-automated System • Manual System

The categories are explained as follows:

- **Open and Closed Systems:** Depends on the effect of the surrounding environment. Most systems are closed due to less possibility to remain unaffected by the surrounding environment. Best example of an open system is a human being. Human beings react as per changes in their surrounding environment. There is no perfectly closed system, but being emotionless, computer system is regarded as closed system, as it is least affected by the surrounding environment.
- **Virtual and Physical Systems:** Depends on the visibility of a system. There can be systems which are abstract and do not exist physically. These are virtual systems. The example of a virtual system is the thought system of a human mind. On the contrary, the system with physical appearance is a physical system. Examples of physical systems are machines.
- **Automated, Semi-automated, and Manual Systems:** Depends on the system operation. If the system is self-operating, it is an automated system; whereas, those systems that need manual operation are manual or user systems. There can be systems which are neither fully automated nor fully manual; such systems are called semi-automated systems. Example of an automated system can be an electrically operating machine. Most systems require manual interaction such as a computer system. Earlier, machines were manual systems.

8.2.4 Elements of a System

The components essential for a system are the elements of a system. The basic components of a system are input, process and output, which are discussed as follows:

- **Input:** Refers to the basic ingredients provided to the system for obtaining the desired output. There can be one or more input for a desired product.
- **Process:** Refers to the transformational events with the input or combination of inputs.
- **Output:** Refers to the result of transformational process upon the input. Output should match with the desired product in a good system. Figure-2 displays the elements of a system:

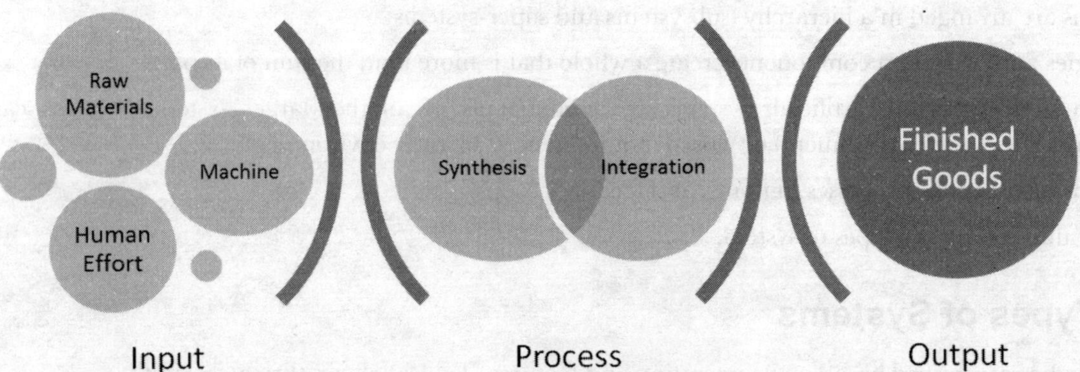

Figure-2: System Elements

In Figure-2, the illustration shows a production process of goods. In this process, raw materials, machine, and human efforts are the inputs. Synthesis of raw materials and its integration with human efforts produces the finished goods as the output. Now, let us understand the approaches of decomposition and integration of a system.

8.2.5 Decomposition and Integration of a System

The major elements of a system are called the subsystems. Dividing a system into subsystem is the decomposition of a system, while integrating the subsystems to compose a system is integration of a system.

Figure-3 shows the decomposition of a system:

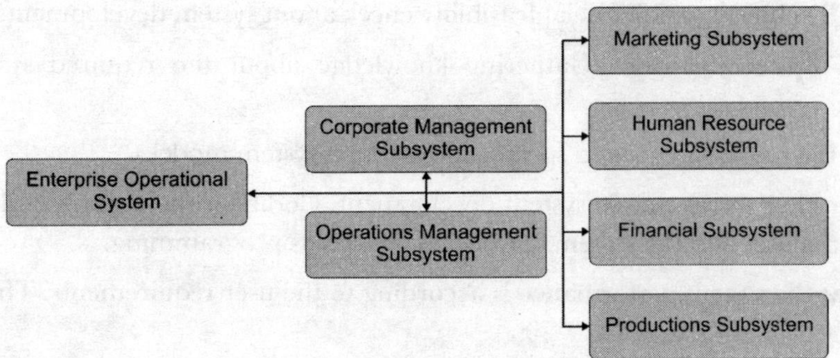

Figure-3: Decomposition of a System

As you can see in Figure-3, enterprise operational system is divided into composite subsystems of respective functional areas such as marketing, finance, and production. The two management subsystems, one at corporate level and other at operational level are also subsystems of the enterprise wide system.

Now, let us study the system development approaches.

8.3 Developing Information System

There are various approaches developed for effective system development. The main approaches are listed as follows:

- Waterfall Model
- Prototyping
- Evolutionary Model
- Spiral Model
- Incremental Model

In the next few sections, let us discuss these approaches in detail.

8.3.1 Waterfall Model

Waterfall model is the basic model of system development. This model follows a flow of steps beginning from feasibility check until system maintenance in a sequence. This is method is also called linear sequential model. The steps in the waterfall methods are shown in Figure-4:

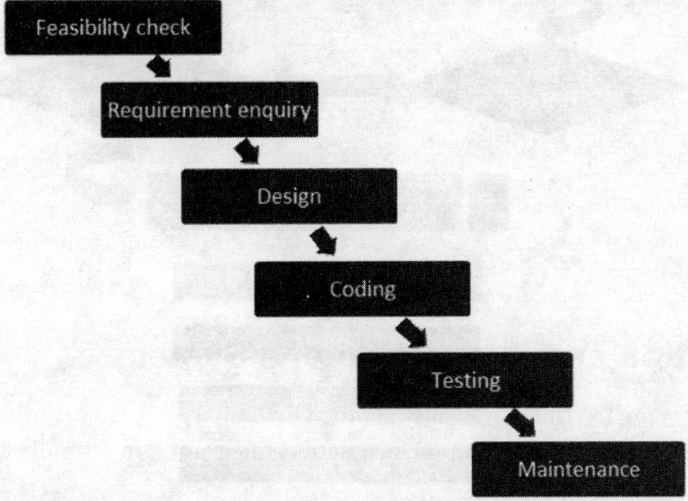

Figure-4: Waterfall Approach in System Development

Brief discussion about these steps is given as follows:

- **Feasibility Check:** Technical and financial feasibility check about system development.
- **Requirement and Specifications:** Gathering knowledge about the required system and developing the specifications needed.
- **Design:** Converting the requirements and specifications into a system model.
- **Coding:** This is a very important step in system development. Coding is the process of designing a bridge between the understanding of the user and the system. This is also called as programming.
- **Testing:** Ensures that the system performance is according to the user requirements. This is done after a system is set for use.
- **Maintenance:** Changes in the system after testing or use to correct the shortcomings or further requirements.

Waterfall method is a simple and an easy to understand model; however, it suffers from certain drawbacks. These drawbacks are given as follows:

- It approaches feasibility analysis before requirement analysis, which is not practical.
- It tests the system after implementing and designing, therefore, any change required after testing can be hard to be introduced.
- Any feedback to the previous process has not been approached.

Note: *The error of providing feedback has been corrected in the model and the corrected model has been named iterative waterfall method.*

8.3.2 Prototyping Approach

Prototyping approach is an effort to improve the drawbacks of waterfall model. A prototype is similar to the model or blueprint of a system before the actual development is done. This model first performs requirement analysis and develops a prototype or draft of the whole development process. This approach helps in understanding the shortcomings before the actual design is built and implemented.

This helps in system evaluation. Hence, any specification or further improvement can be done easily at a much less cost. This can be done with the support of prototype software and physical design modeling. After finalizing the prototype, the actual system building is done similar to that in the waterfall method. Figure-5 represents the prototype approach to system development:

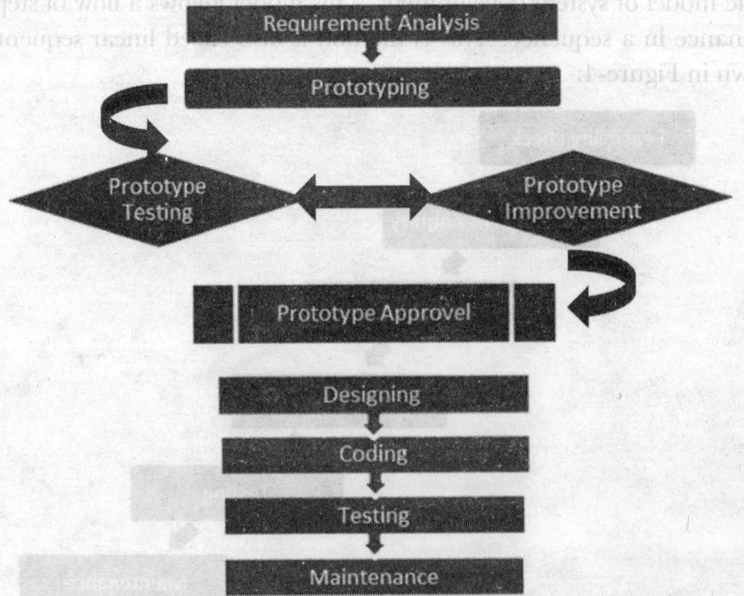

Figure-5: Prototype Approach to System Development

This model helps in matching the client requirements for system development, as any suggestions can be easily incorporated in the prototype. Also, any constraint in the system development process can also be identified and improved upon.

8.3.3 Evolutionary Model

Evolutionary model approaches to improve the classic waterfall model by providing scope of feedback and improvement at every stage of the system development. This model tries to develop a realistic view that client can change the requirements in the system at any stage of the system development; therefore every stage should be taken as a separate evolutionary phase. There is scope of improvement in design and software.

8.3.4 Spiral Model

This model is a further improvement in the system development. It is a combination of the features of the waterfall and prototype models. This idea was given by Boehm, a computer professional. Similar to the evolutionary model, this model also adapts to repetitive improvement, as shown in Figure-6:

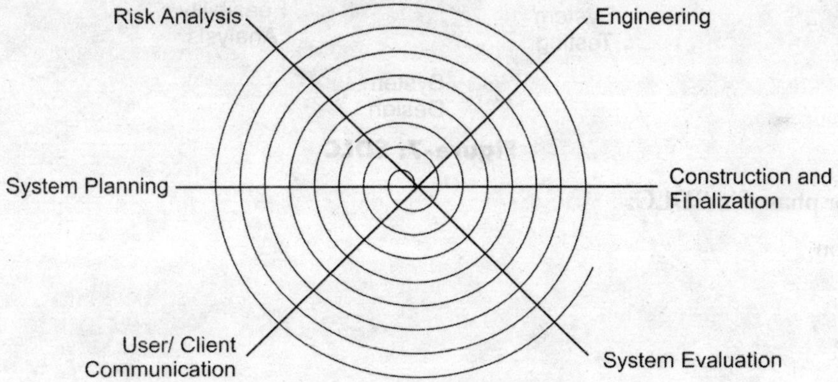

Figure-6: Spider Model

Following phases are included in the spider model of system development:

- **User/Client Communication:** Interaction with the client or users of the system to identify the requirements and specifications in the system.
- **System Planning:** Planning the system to be developed and preparing a rough draft and schedule of the development process.
- **Risk Analysis:** Identifying the problems in the plan and developing solutions to check them.
- **Engineering:** Involves system hardware and software design, coding, and testing the system.
- **Construction and Finalization:** Involves system building and testing to release it for use.
- **System Evaluation:** Evaluation by user or client to use the system.

All these phases are repeated in the process of system development, until users approve the system.

8.3.5 Incremental Model

Incremental model approaches system development through various incremental steps, where every step tries to add more functions in the system development process. Every step of system development is a separate group of activities. This model can also be called as continuous improvement model.

In this model, the phases are listed in the development process, and then go back to the same list to improve the steps involved. At every stage an incremental development takes place.

8.4 Traditional System Development Lifecycle

In system development lifecycle model (SDLC), he system approach involves developing a system solution, which is a multistep process. Since proper update and maintenance to check the problem in the existing system is also required, the development of a system becomes a cyclic process that involves seven steps mainly. These steps are as shown in Figure-7:

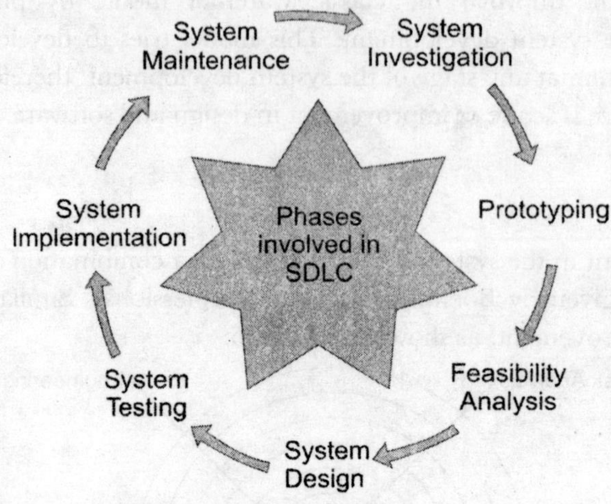

Figure-7: SDLC

Following are the major phases in SDLC:

a. System Investigation
b. Prototyping
c. Feasibility Analysis
d. System Design
e. System Testing
f. System Implementation
g. System Maintenance

In the next few sections, let us discuss these phases in detail.

8.4.1 System Investigation

The process of system development begins with system investigation. In an organization the IS experts perform an investigation before they develop any system. This investigation is generally followed by system requirement by management or other users.

The objectives at this stage include:

- Understanding the system requirement
- Distinction between existing and proposed system
- Determining the requisites in the system requested

This phase is important since system developers should have a clear idea about the desired system. Else, there is a possibility of mismatch in the required system by users and system developed by developers.

The next step is prototyping.

8.4.2 Prototyping

Building a prototype system with required specifications is called prototyping in SDLC. A prototype is the model form or blueprint of the required system. Prototypes clarify the development process and reduce obstacles in it.

The prototyping process involves the following steps:

- **Formulating System Objectives:** Determining the system requirements for the new system.
- **System Analysis:** Involves filling the gap between the specifications of the existing and the required system.
- **Designing the Prototype of a System:** Designing of the model of the proposed system is called the prototype of the system.
- **Feasibility Analysis of Prototype:** Checking the prototype of the system based on the technology and resource availability.
- **Testing the Prototype:** Testing the model of the actual system by using it. This helps in identifying the drawbacks in the prototype system that needs to be improved.
- **Improving the Prototype:** Determining and implementing improvements, if required and testing again.
- **Finalizing the Prototype:** Getting approval from the system users and experts on the prototype system that represents all specifications required in the system to be developed.

Prototyping helps in reducing waste and saving cost in system building, as it can be improved easily on less cost as compared to the actual system building.

8.4.3 Feasibility Analysis

Feasibility refers to suitability. After determining the required system through prototyping, it needs to be analyzed, if building such a system will be beneficial for the organization. Feasibility of a system involves comparing its development with its alternatives based on the following:

- **Technical Feasibility:** Assesses the availability of required hardware and software and technical specifications along with technical reliability and accessibility.
- **Economic Feasibility:** Performs the cost-benefit analysis. The expected tangible and intangible costs involved in the system development and implementation should be less than the sum of the tangible and intangible benefits it derives.
- **Operational Feasibility:** Checks the availability of the required skills and labor, suppliers of material, and customers' point-of-view.
- **Feasibility of Time:** Assesses the time duration required for the development and the target timelines given.
- **Environmental Feasibility:** Analyses the pros and cons of the system for environment and legal aspects of the system development.

After identifying the feasibility of the system, the developers can start actual system designing. If the system does not prove feasible, the idea is either modified or abandoned.

8.4.4 System Design

The next phase of the SDLC is the system design. In this phase, the objective of the system is accomplished. The design brings in action the overall plan for the system. It involves composition of the system, which consists of all the specifications that deliver the functions identified during the system analysis phase. These specifications deal with requirements of the system solution. The essentials to be designed for developing an information system are:

- User interfaces
- Databases and files in physical structure

- Data processing and logical structure
- Storage of data and information
- Acquisition of hardware and software
- Preparation and communication of reports

The user interface determines the interaction between the system and the user, which also involves input and output device designing. The logical view requires proper coding of each input through suitable software. Adequate solution for data storage has to be developed. Traditional file approach or database approach can be followed for this purpose. This design is generally similar to the prototype designed in the earlier phase. The developer should ensure to build a user-friendly system.

8.4.5 System Testing

Exhaustive tests are conducted to ensure that the system produces the right results. It involves testing the performance of the whole information system. It is generally performed with testing unit and user. Testing is done for each program individually in the system. System testing is a type of evaluation by users, which is reviewed by the management. Once they are satisfied with the performance of the designed system, it is formally accepted for installation.

Following are the objectives of this phase:

- To test, if distinct modules are functioning as planned and any differences exist between the actual working of the system and the proposed system.
- To test hardware, software, and process.
- To test the codes at various levels in software testing.
- To provide the final approval for a production setting.

8.4.6 System Implementation

This phase aims at successful implementation of the system, which is one of the major responsibilities of system experts and developers. Any failure in this phase ruins all previous efforts and results in a financial loss for an organization.

System implementation involves the following:

- **System Installation:** Getting the system equipment or machinery installed at the right location and again testing its functions.
- **Training Personnel:** Imparting the required knowledge and training about the system usage. The aim is to prevent from damages of ignorant usage and undesirable practices.
- **Change Management:** Managing the change in the operations and functions of an organization with the new system. It basically involves system conversion and employees adopting the new system.

8.4.7 System Maintenance

Maintaining the system is an important aspect of SDLC. As key personnel change positions in an organization, new changes are implemented, which requires system updates. The system is reviewed by both users and technical specialists, to determine if the new system has met the objectives initially proposed. Any revisions or modifications to be done are also analyzed. In certain cases, a formal post implementation audit document is prepared. Once the system is fine-tuned, it has to be maintained to meet the following objectives:

- Correction of errors
- Meeting the requirements such as formatting, cleaning, and upgrading
- Improving the efficiency of the existing system

All these seven steps contribute to the lifecycle of the system development. Let us learn about the advantages and disadvantages of SDLC.

8.4.8 Advantages of SDLC

The major advantages are as follows:

- Provides proper guidelines and steps of the system development, to support users
- Helps the less experienced or fresh staff in using the system and produce required output
- Trains the junior staff in the SDLC
- Reduces the cost of continuing support and promotes consistency amongst projects
- Allows the staff to be transferred from one project to another

In a typical SDLC, coding techniques are not specified. However, the extensive documentation that is an intrinsic part of most methodologies simplifies ongoing maintenance. It reduces dependency on developers by providing information about the system development and the functions included in each program modules.

8.4.9 Disadvantages of SDLC

Although, SDLC is the best way to understand system development in a totally unstructured environment, there are few disadvantages, which are as follows:

- Complete dependency results in unnecessary documentation. Various methodologies have forms for every possible situation. Inexperienced staff may believe that all are required and may, for example, insist on three levels of customer sign-off, when only one is needed.
- This complicates the process and extends the project schedule unnecessarily. To prevent this, most organizations view SDLC as a set of guidelines and use only those steps and forms specific to the size and type of project under development. Many even provide templates to their staff outlining the steps required for specific types and sizes of projects. An 18-month mainframe development project might require different processes than a two-week Web front-end.
- It is difficult for customers to identify all requirements early in the project; however, the sequential "river of no return" approach dictates this. SDLC means that there are no easy ways to mitigate this problem and still remains true to the methodology.
- Customers are involved only periodically, rather than being an active participant throughout the project. This can result in misunderstandings on both sides: IT and customers.
- The combination of incomplete specifications, infrequent communication, and long elapsed time increases the probability that the system will be "off track", when it is finally delivered. As highway engineers are aware that an error of a few degrees, if left uncorrected for thousands of miles, results in the road going to the wrong destination.
- With a long development cycle, SDLC increases the possibility of business changes invalidating the initial design or the project champions leaving the company or reassigned.

The purpose of SDLC is to establish understandable procedures, guidelines, and practices of system development. This approach is helpful in planning, analyzing, designing, developing, integrating, testing, implementing, and maintaining information systems within an organization. This approach requires concurrence with the existing policy and guidelines. This methodology is used in the development of most information systems and is applicable across all environments such as mainframe, client server and so on. The participants in the life cycle process review will differ from project to project.

Activity-1

Discuss the steps involved in SDLC.

____

____

____

In the next section, let us understand the concept of system analysis.

8.5 Concept of System Analysis

When a new information system is developed, it has to be analyzed in any organization. The system is developed based on the requirements, goals and objectives of an organization. System analysis is the analysis of the problems related to information systems. The steps involved are defining the problem, identifying the causes, specifying the solution and identifying the information requirements. It is a feasibility study to establish that the proposed system is practical from technical, financial and organizational views.

System analysis is the primary task of the system development once it is decided that a new system is to be developed. It helps to understand the efficacy of the existing system and to identify the information requirement of the users. The organization must have a clear understanding of its information requirements to develop an information system. Analysis involves a detailed study of the current system, which leads to the development of specifications of the proposed system. It is a detailed study of a variety of operations performed by a system and also the relationship within and outside the system. The information on the files available, decision points and transactions of the present system is obtained. The various techniques used for collecting this data are interviews, on-site observations and questionnaire. The system analysis shoots up from the objective, scope of the information system. The objective of the information system supports the overall objective of the business. The scope of information system depends on the information requirements of an organization.

Following steps make it easy to draw the exact boundary of the new proposed system:

- Assessing the problems and requirements of the proposed system
- Working on the advantages and disadvantages including new areas of the system

The procedures and requirements are analyzed and documented in the form of data flow diagrams (DFDs), data dictionary, and logical data structures. Data analysis involves these tools to perform a structured analysis. In the next few sections, let us discuss these tools.

8.5.1 Data Flow Diagram

Data flow diagram (DFD) is a technique used in requirement analysis process. It shows the data flow between the functions of each program. This approach in system analysis was first used by Larry Constantine. DFD approach is also used at the start of system designing.

There are two types of DFDs, discussed as follows:

- **Physical DFD:** Representation of physical characteristics of system implementation such as user name department.
- **Logical DFD:** Representation of the flow of data in business operations such as business events.

Physical DFD depends on logical DFD, as it provides lower level details. This approach analyses the system requirement using only four symbols. A graphical representation helps in identifying the loopholes and requirements in the existing system of an organization. These four symbols are shown in Figure-8:

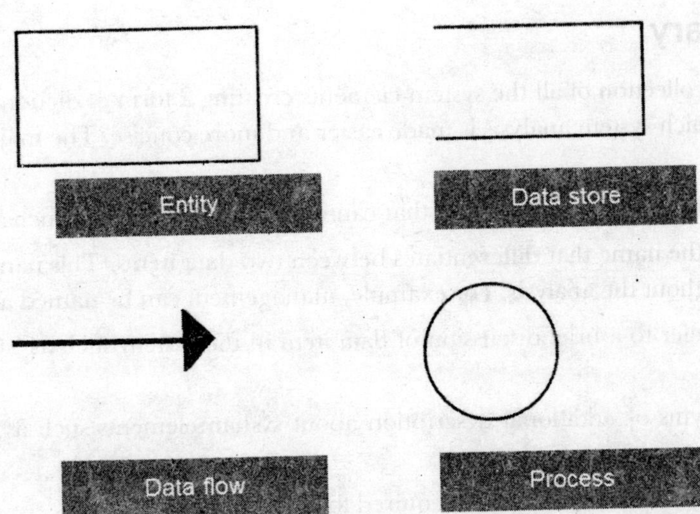

Figure-8: Four Symbols used in DFD

The symbols are discussed as follows:

- **Entity:** Defines the limitations of the system. It represents external components of a system such as a person, a department, and other organizations. An entity is represented by a rectangle in DFD. Each entity is given its appropriate name.
- **Data Store:** Refers to storage of data, which is represented by an open rectangle. It shows such an accumulation of data that allows addition as well as retrieval of data in the system. If there are more than one data stores used in the system analysis, they should be named uniquely to be easily understood by the analyst. Any temporary data store is not represented in a DFD.
- **Data Flow:** Refers to the transmission of data represented by an arrow in the direction of flow. This arrow shows the movement of data in the DFD.
- **Process:** Refers to the work or action performed in the system represented by a circle. It shows the change or transformation in data. This transformation is the result of an activity performed in the system.

In this technique, the system analyst prepares a graphical representation of data processes in an organization. A pictorial representation is developed with the logic underlying the system development. A DFD is required to be presented in a sequential manner. This representation helps in finding system requirements and organizational resources that can satisfy those requirements. This also helps in understanding system boundaries.

8.5.2 Context Diagram

A context diagram approaches system analysis in a single process. The diagram has a flow from general elements to specific elements. For example, if the first diagram gives the basic idea of structure, the next diagram gives its general nature and limitations, and the following gives its uses. Therefore, the initial context diagram provides an overview. In a context diagram, process is represented by circle, while inputs and outputs are represented by rectangles.

As a major difference from DFD, context diagrams do not have any data store. Hence, only three symbols are used. Another difference is that the context diagrams are generally two dimensional, while DFDs are only one dimensional. A context diagram can be subdivided to show resulting processes. In such cases, the base diagram is called the parent diagram and the resulting diagram is called the child diagram. As seems logical, a child diagram cannot take any input or produce any output that parent diagram does not take or produce. Context diagrams are helpful in understanding the characteristics of the system. This approach identifies the processes involved in system implementation and then analyses it by creating a context diagram.

8.5.3 Data Dictionary

As the name suggests, it is a collection of all the system elements creating a form of dictionary. It consists of a catalogue of different elements using which system analysis is made easier and more concise. The major items of this catalogue are discussed as follows:

- **Data Element:** Refers to the unit of data items that cannot be further classified such as a reference number.
- **Data Name:** Refers to the name that differentiates between two data items. This name should be meaningful and logical as it is used throughout the analysis. For example, management can be named as MGT.
- **Data Descriptions:** Refer to a brief discussion of data item in the system such as SOFT represents the software solution in the system.
- **Aliases:** Refer to synonyms or additional description about system elements such as software can be application software or system software.
- **Data Length:** Refers to the number of spaces required for a data item.
- **Data Values:** Refer to the criteria for the data items. For instance, an order number cannot exceed 6 characters.
- **Data Structure:** Refers to the logical structure of data flow in the system, such as a size can be in bit, byte, kilobyte, and gigabyte.
- **Data Flows:** Represent the transmission of data from one place to another. Data dictionary provides a unique identity to every data flow.
- **Data Stores:** Refer to the data storage system. Data dictionary sets a unique name to every class of store such as data from marketing department is named as MKT file.

Data dictionary items are case sensitive and reduce the complexity of system analysis.

8.5.4 Entity-relationship Diagram

The entity-relationship diagram (E-R Diagram) approach is helpful in analyzing data models. The various components in a system analysis are called entities. The relationship between these entities forms the structure of the E-R diagram. Entities can be of different types such as input, output, storage, and process. These entity types are uniquely represented in such diagrams. The attribute of each entity type needs to be identified initially.

Let us now understand the role of a system analyst.

8.5.5 System Analyst

System development being a critical process requires enough care and expertise throughout the process. Each step of SDLC involves thorough study of aspects it relates with. It also involves upgrading the technological trends and performing the conventional task of system development in simultaneous technological developments. This task is assigned to a competent person in the organization designated as the system analyst.

Apart from programming, the system analyst has to handle the successful system implementation. Following are the major roles of a system analyst:

- **Study of System Requirement:** Involves a detailed study of a system requirement with respect to its required specifications. This helps in understanding the scope of the system to be developed and system analysis. Analysis of existing systems and proposed system is also done.
- **Design and Building of System:** Involves analysis of logical and physical design along with careful analysis of system building. The system built should meet the requirements of the proposed system.
- **Analysis of Existing System:** Involves analysis of the traditional and old system development methodologies. This is generally done through study of reports and documents of the last system development process.

Technological Updates: Upgrade with recent technological developments. When a proposed system is implemented, technical aspects may change because of rapidly changing technical scenario. System analysts are responsible to meet with technical updates in the system development.

The role of a system analyst is wider than just programming. While programming is a skill-based process, system analysis is knowledge-based process. System analysis is a holistic approach, while programming is an individualistic approach. Let us now learn about system design.

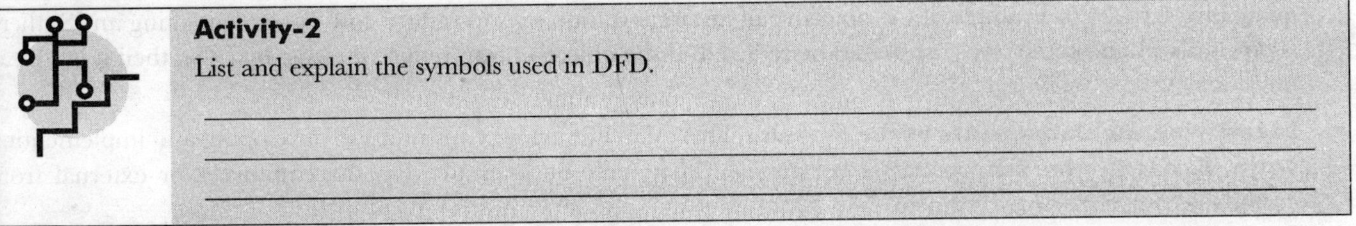

Activity-2

List and explain the symbols used in DFD.

____

____

____

8.6 System Design

This is another important phase in the system development process. The objectives of the proposed system are achieved using the system design, which is the overall plan for the system. The information required by an organization is obtained using system analysis, which leads to a system design. Practicality, flexibility, efficiency, and security are the objectives of the system design. Systems are designed as user-friendly and capable of handling the information requirement of users. As the business environment is dynamic, the system should be designed to accept any changes. A system becomes efficient, if it fulfills the requirements of users and handles any situation, responds to the user request, can complete the job within the stipulated time. System design ensures the reliability of the hardware and physical security of the data.

System designing is done at two levels, namely: conceptual and physical. Conceptual design is required in the development of any information system and is generic; whereas, physical design is used in the development of information system in an organization and is also known as detailed design. Let us now understand more about these two designs.

8.6.1 Conceptual Design

In conceptual design, a study on the available information systems designs is done and the best that suits the information requirements of the organization is chosen. The physical design is based on this. The steps involved in the conceptual design are shown in Figure-9:

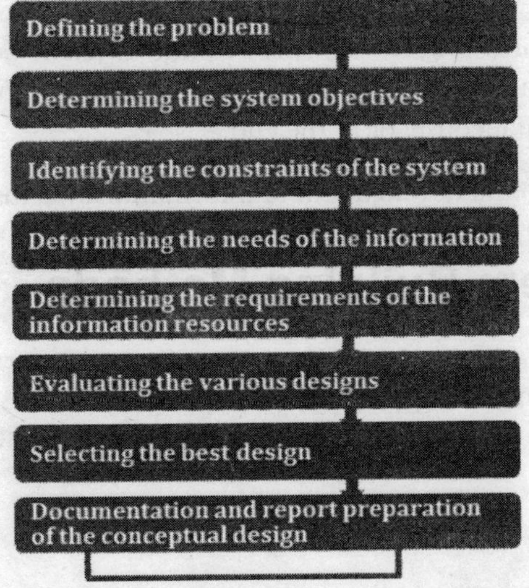

Figure-9: Steps Involved in Conceptual Design

These steps are discussed in brief as follows:

- **Defining the Problem:** Deals with problems in the current scenario. The system has to ensure that these problems do not occur in future; therefore, it is necessary for organizations to plan long-term information systems. This has to be examined in both short-run and long-run.
- **Determining the System Objectives:** Ensures that the objectives of the information systems are drawn based on the long-run objectives of an organization. Objectives should be clear and expressed in quantitative instead of in qualitative terms. For example, if the objective of an organization says to reduce cost by implementing an IS, there is no clarity on the extent the cost should be reduced. If the objective is to reduce the cost by 13%, then it is a clear objective.
- **Identifying the Constraints of the System:** There can be various constraints in developing and implementing an IS. Knowledge on the constraints is essential. They may be internal from the employees or external from customers, suppliers, or government.
- **Determining the Need of Information:** Analyses about the information required for system design development to finalize the system design.
- **Determining the Requirement of the Information Resources:** Identifying the resources of information required for designing a system. This information generally deals with internal and technological information. Market analysis and suppliers information is also required. It also ensures the availability of required resources and finalizing the resources elements.
- **Evaluating of the Various Designs:** Analyzing each alternate design of the proposed system based on the feasibility and requirement.
- **Selecting the Best Design:** Selecting the design that is most feasible for an organization.
- **Documentation and Report Preparation of the Conceptual Design:** Preparing reports and documents for reference of the selected design. This is through study material for subsequent systems and system improvement.

8.6.2 User Interface Design

The conceptual design offers the requirements of the system in general, which is the input for the user interface design. The requirements are further redefined in this design such as project planning and control. This involves users' definition of the elements of the system, designing input and output, user's feedback, designing the database, and documentation. A prototype user interface is designed and modified several times till the user is satisfied with it.

8.6.3 Designing Methodology

The system designing methodology works towards an effective and efficient design. It has been divided into two sub tasks, namely: system planning and control. Documentation is required to complete the designing process to give clarity to the process, which can be done simultaneously or at the end.

Now, let us discuss the aspects related to the development of information systems.

8.7 Alternative System Building Methods

System development cannot be a rigid approach, as it depends on user requirements and technological aspects. There are other alternative methods of system development. These approaches have proved to be less time consuming and more feasible for organizations. Hence, most organizations are adopting them. Outsourcing and end-user development are some of these methods.

Let us now discuss few of these methods.

8.7.1 End-User Development

In this approach, an organization seeks end-users to build the system. This has been made possible with fourth generation computer technology. Fourth generation software are developed to support end-user requirements. This allows users to enquire about various software tools, select a suitable one and configure it. After this online configuration, the system experts deliver it to the user.

Fourth generation software are user-friendly and do not require knowledge of any procedural language. The procedural languages need all the specifications to be in a sequence. Fourth generation languages are non-procedural; they need specifications of what is to be done instead of how it is to be done or in which order it is to be done.

Following are the benefits of this method:

- Ensures development of systems that are faster than the traditional SDLC
- Involves users in the development process and allows them to select their own specifications
- Ensures user satisfaction and accurate in meeting system requirements

However, there are certain disadvantages of this system. There is a risk involved in this method, as the actual development is still not done inside the organization. The success of such systems depends on the ability of users in actualizing the system of their requirement. It is quite possible that users might not have a clear idea about the system specifications. System testing can be inadequate in this method. However, this approach is quite time saving and is proving to be more beneficial for immediate requirements.

8.7.2 Outsourcing of System

In this modern business world with high competition, organizations strive to specialize in their core area of business. A modern day business organization believes in applying its best practices and all its efficiency in its core field; whereas, the traditional business approach believed in allocating efficiency in all the fields. This new strategy in business has given birth to outsourcing of capacities, where the organization does not specialize. Organizations are using this strategy to gain advantage in the competition. With this aim to streamline the business processes, organizations now outsource the services that are not its core business functions. In many organizations, system development is a non-core activity. Outsourcing involves contracting with outside consultants, system development or system solutions to perform system analysis, programming or other system development activities. The outsourcer should be evaluated as a long-term asset and a source of ongoing value to the company. Outsourcing reduces the burden on the organization and lets it focus on its core business area. This method is beneficial for such organizations that do not have system development as their core business area. Outsourcing is economical than self-development, when compared with the sum of tangible and intangible costs of system development.

There are some challenges in outsourcing the availability of reliable outsourced firm and differences in the work culture of the contractor may be difficult to be adopted.

8.7.3 Rapid Application Development

The technology advancement has brought up the idea of building information system in a short duration. This is called rapid application development. Fourth generation language tools, prototyping, and object-oriented software are some of these technologically advanced tools. These tools help system builders in creating a system in short duration.

8.7.4 Component-based System Development

This approach provides software components for a whole system. The system is developed by assembling these components. The objective is divided into sub objectives of component development for the system. The system is developed by integrating these sub objectives. It enables one application to communicate with the other without any customer programming for data sharing.

Web-based services such as reusable software and use of extensible markup language are the key development measures. This technique has proved to be less difficult and less expensive than the other techniques.

8.8 System Development and Organizational Change

In the global business environment, organizations compete fiercely in the market and strive to gain competitive advantage by resource optimization and technology integration. For this, an organization needs to take several decisions. IS helps in the process of decision-making from the strategic level to the operational level.

Every business environment is subject to constant changes. Therefore, IS of organizations should be capable enough to meet these changes. The change in organization is always a factor of return on the investment. Once the system is developed in an organization, there can be four phases of change in the organization, which are shown in Figure-10:

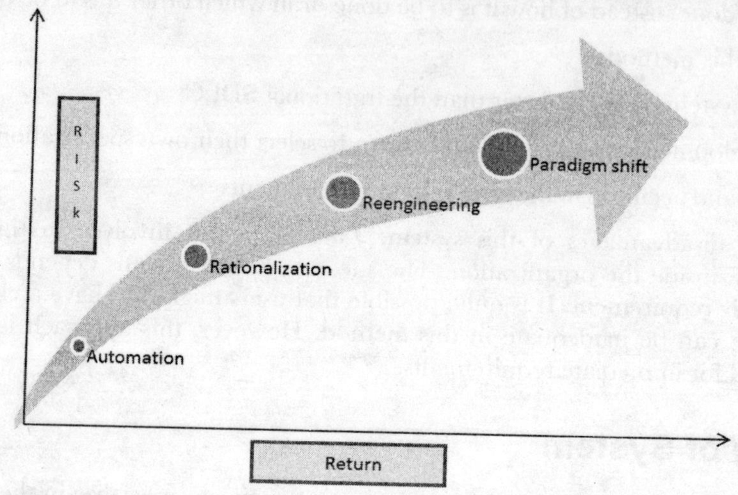

Figure-10: System Development and Organizational Change

Let us discuss these phases as follows:

- **Automation:** Involves automated calculations, record keeping, payroll, transactions, and logical analysis. These functions have been automated with the development of IS in an organization. This is the most common form of change caused by the system development. For example, online ticket booking facility in airlines.
- **Rationalization:** This form of change quickly follows automation. It involves rational approach to problem identification and problem solving. For example, web service software.
- **Reengineering:** Analyzing business processes on certain standards and redesigning them as per the required standards. It is more ambitious as compared to the previous levels. It deals with discarding the old system and developing a more useful and advanced system. For example, invoice less processing at Ford Motors.
- **Paradigm Shift:** Effect of reengineering in various parts of an organization. The ultimate effect of change is paradigm shift, which involves redesigning of the nature of business in the organization.

8.8.1 Business Process Re-engineering

While implementing a system, the organizational change should be managed with great care and concern. As per the philosophy of BPR, the business process that does not add value needs to be removed, which means all business processes should add value. As the term re-engineering means building up again, BPR also asserts demolition of the process that does not add value and building up a fresh process to replace it. The approach encompasses rethinking and redesigning. Michael Hammer and James Champy are regarded as the developers of the reengineering approach. According to them, BPR is "the fundamental rethinking and radical redesign of business processes to achieve dramatic improvement in critical, contemporary measures of performance such as cost, quality, service and speed". BPR eliminates unnecessary work processes and develops of new and more effective practices.

While organizations prefer to build information systems for improving their business processes and competitive advantage, they are confronting the phase of radical restructuring and redesigning. These processes of radical restructuring and redesigning the processes lead to BPR. As discussed earlier, reengineering is the phase that involves igh risk and high return. This high risk requires organizations to effectively implement the reengineering approach in he organizational change. Following are the steps for effective reengineering:

- **Understanding the Need for System Implementation:** Identifying the problem area, where implementation of change has to be performed.
- **Analyzing and Measuring the Performance of the Existing System:** Evaluation of performance of the existing or unchanged system.
- **Implementing the Change:** Appropriately implementing the improved system that serves the requirement in the problem area.
- **Evaluating Improvement:** Comparison of the performance of the changed system with the performance of the unchanged system evaluated before.

Such systematic BPR leads to reduction in risk and increase in return on the investment of system development.

8.8.2 Restructuring

The restructuring process involves an organization in determining its core competencies and identifying opportunities. This process identifies the sector an organization should diversify and the market factors it should focus on. Restructuring occurs based on this. Restructuring and re-engineering seem to be similar; however, restructuring is one of the possible outcomes of re-engineering.

8.8.3 System Conversion in Organization

Conversion is to bring the change from an existing system to the newly built system. There are four basic approaches in conversion from old system to new system in an organization. Figure-11 represents the different system conversion approaches in organization:

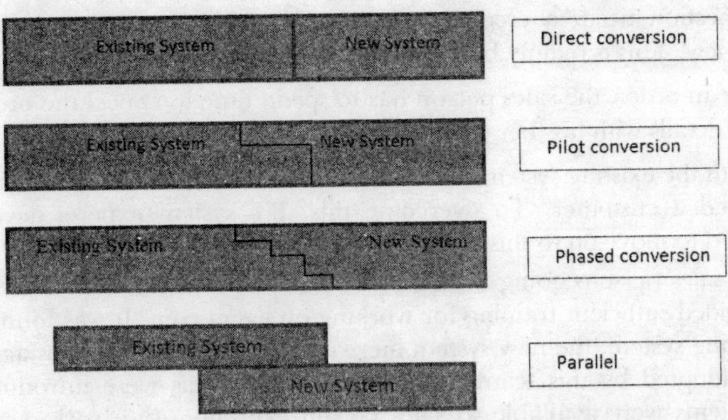

Figure-11: System Conversion Methods

These approaches are discussed as follows:

- **Direct Conversion:** Bringing change by abandoning the old system and adopting the new system completely. The existing system is abandoned (Figure-11) when a new system comes into use. This approach is not very popular amongst organizations, as employees are not trained and productivity can be harmed.
- **Parallel Conversion:** Bringing change by working with both the existing system as well as the new system simultaneously. This approach rationalizes the conversion process as productivity is not harmed. There is a drawback, employees usually choose to work on the existing system and easily not accept the new system.
- **Phased Conversion:** Refers to a special type of parallel conversion. In this approach, the existing and the new systems are used independently. This is repeated till the employees become comfortable with the new system. This approach has been criticized as it does not let employees concentrate on their work and such changes may affect their productivity.

- **Pilot Conversion:** Refers to a more rational approach in system conversion. In this approach, a batch o employees is made to work on the new system, when they become comfortable the rest of the employees are als given the new system. This approach does not harm the productivity and also makes change mechanism easy.

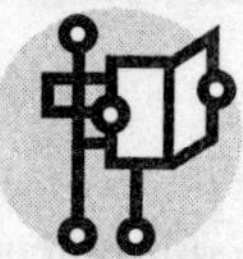

Case Study: British Telecom PLC and System Implementation

British Telecommunication Private Limited Company, popularly known as BT, is a global telecommunication service provider. It is one of the largest telecom service providers and provides services in about 170 countries. The BT Group deals with a number of telecommunication services while its BT retail division serves for telephone, broadband, and television services. BT retail has its specially built systems for its employees to assist them in providing services to the customers. It has huge customer data to be collected and recorded. These systems are specially required to access customer data as and when required.

BT has its team of system experts to develop and maintain these systems. The company has recently developed an advance system for placing orders for new connections. These new connections can be of telephone, broadband, television or any combination of these three services. In its existing system called 'Oneview' the order placing process has the following shortcomings according to its sales team:

- Oneview is slow in updating the records, till the update is completed, the order placement cannot proceed.
- Oneview has a record sheet type appearance; no other information is available if the customer wants the sales person to repeat it for confirmation.
- Bundled order, that is a combo of two or more services, consumes more time, as all information has to be updated simultaneously for various back-office operations.
- Giving a postpaid connection needs a credit history checking for the customer, which becomes the most time consuming case in Oneview. This is mainly because the credit referral team of BT is based in Philippines.
- If the customer modifies an order, the sales person has to spend time to cancel the order. There is no option for the customer to confirm the details with his/her partner or family.

These are the discomforts with the existing system that created a bad impression of service in the first interaction between the company sales agent and a customer. To overcome this, BT system experts developed a new system named 'agent.com'. And then decided to move on to this system.

BT prepared a team of best sales persons going through the sales records. This team was properly introduced with the new system. They were provided sufficient training for working on agent.com. It was found that along with overcoming the shortcomings of the existing system, the new system increased the efficiency of sales agents and the sales percentage. After being approved and adopted by this team rest of the sales persons were introduced with the new system. In operations both of these systems were available so sales person can choose to work on any of them. Because of the effectiveness of the new system, most of them never got back to the old system.

Questions:

Q1. Identify the benefits of the new system for sales agents of BT retail.

Q2. Describe the system conversion approach adopted by BT retail in the case.

*(*Case study presented is the proprietary information of the respective organization, and is used here specifically and only for educational purpose.)*

8.9 Summary

In this chapter, you have learned about the system approach, which includes the concept of system, characteristics of system, and decomposition and integration of system. Next in the chapter, you learned about the different models used for effective system development: waterfall, prototyping, evolutionary, spiral, and incremental. The traditional system development lifecycle (SDLC) is also discussed in the chapter, which includes the following: system investigation, prototyping, feasibility analysis, system design, system testing, system implementation, and system maintenance. Later n the chapter, system analysis is discussed, which includes the following tools: data flow diagram, context diagram, data lictionary, entity-relationship diagram, and system analyst. A discussion about system design is also included in the chapter, which includes the following two designs: conceptual design and user-interface design. The various system building methods such as end-user development, outsourcing of system and rapid application development is also included in the chapter. Towards the end, a discussion about business process re-engineering is included in the chapter.

8.10 Key Terms

- **Relational Regime:** Refers to a logical establishment
- **Homeostasis:** Refers to the capacity of a system to maintain internal process
- **Tangible:** Refers to those costs and benefits that are available in material form which can be physically examined
- **Prototyping:** Refers to a sample of a concept or process
- **Sub-systems:** Refers to decomposed part of a system
- **Super-system:** Refers to a system that is built through integration of two individual systems

8.11 Exercise

Multiple Choice Questions

Q1. The word 'system' has originated, as a term, from which Latin term?

a. Systema
b. Simon
c. Systeme
d. Systematic

Ans. a

Q2. A system consists of which type of components______________?

a. Integrated
b. Interrelated
c. Inter organizational
d. Intelligent

Ans. a

Q3. On the basis of relativeness to environment what are the types of systems?

a. Virtual and physical system
b. Automated and manual systems
c. Open and closed systems
d. Cannot be categorized on this basis

Ans. c

Q4. How many basic elements are there of a system.

a. Two
b. Seven
c. Three
d. Five

Ans. c

Q5. A ______________ is the model form or blueprint of the desired system.

a. Requirement analysis
b. Prototype
c. Process
d. System Design

Ans. b

Q6. Which of the following is not a phase of traditional SDLC?

a. System Investigation
b. Prototyping
c. Coding
d. System Maintenance

Ans. c

Q7. Which of the following is an objective of system investigation?

a. Understanding the system requirement
b. Clarifying distinction between existing and proposed system.
c. Determining the requisites in the system requested.
d. All of them

Ans. d

Q8. Feasibility Analysis does not involve __________

a. Technical Feasibility
b. Financial Feasibility
c. Competitor's Feasibility
d. Operational Feasibility

Ans. c

Q9. Environmental feasibility of system involves __________

a. Global Warming
b. Plantation of trees
c. Legal aspect of system
d. Raining

Ans. c

Q10. Which of the following refers to an aspect of system implementation?

a. System Installation
b. Training Personnel
c. Change Management
d. All of them

Ans. d

Short Answer Type Questions

Q1. What are the steps involved in system approach?

Q2. What is the evolutionary model?

Q3. Describe waterfall model of system development.

Q4. What do you mean by a system?

Q5. What are the main characteristics of a system?

Q6. Explain in brief about different categories of systems.

Q7. What are the main components of a system?

Q8. What is prototyping?

Q9. Briefly explain the incremental model.

Q10. What is system investigation?

CHAPTER 9

Knowledge Management and Artificial Intelligence in Business

CHAPTER STRUCTURE

CHAPTER OBJECTIVES

- Elaborate on the role of knowledge in business
- Discuss on various dimensions of knowledge
- Elaborate on knowledge culture
- Discuss on knowledge concept
- Elaborate on various aspects of knowledge management
- Describe knowledge support system
- Clarify strategic advantages of knowledge management
- Explain the measures of protecting corporate knowledge
- Discuss the concept of intelligence
- Elaborate on evolution and applications of artificial intelligence
- Describe the techniques of generating artificial intelligence

9.1 Introduction

The business environment is getting more competitive day by day. Every organization is implementing TQM (total quality management) and BPR (business process re-engineering) for competitive advantage. Innovations in business processes are also taking place more frequently. In such a scenario, organizations have to be updated with continuously changing business situations.

For continuous updates, a fast and constant flow of information is a must. This information need is well served by various information systems. Management takes help from an organization's knowledge base to understand business concepts with their pros and cons. Huge amount of facts and figures get appended to this knowledge base and it becomes increasingly difficult to remember all of it. The concept of Knowledge management overcomes this hurdle and maintains records of previously explored concepts in business. These are helpful in business decision making as well as in improving operational efficiency. Primarily because of this, effective knowledge management is the need of the hour.

In addition to knowledge, intelligence is also a necessary pre-requisite for better decision-making. Intelligence is such a quality that has always been regarded to be a unique characteristic of human beings. However, recently science has proved that intelligence can be created and transferred to machines. Science is now making fast strides in the evolution of artificial intelligence. The relation of man-machine has got further strength with the development of intelligence technologies. Managers need to know about these technologies as they utilize artificial intelligence in managerial decision making.

This chapter brings an insight of knowledge management with information systems. The chapter analyses scope of knowledge in business and explores the concept of knowledge management in organizations. It discusses about acquisition of knowledge, sources of knowledge, and knowledge base. The chapter explains about knowledge management systems with its types and strategic advantages with it. It also discusses about knowledge networks. Later the chapter explains the concept of artificial intelligence along with its application, evolution, and the components that generate this technology. The chapter also describes the expert systems that are being developed with the use of artificial intelligence technology.

9.2 Knowledge in Business

Knowledge, in general sense, refers to a state of being aware of something or having information about something. This awareness, when relates to any specific topic, is called as dimension of knowledge. Knowledge about any specific dimension enables the knowledge bearer to answer who, what, why, when, how, and where about that subject. In the words of a layman, to know something is knowledge. Knowledge is of the following two types:

- **Explicit Knowledge:** Refers to the knowledge that can be expressed verbally such as, in words and numbers. It is easy to communicate the explicit knowledge. Scientific formulae, general principles, and theories are some of the examples of explicit knowledge.
- **Tacit Knowledge:** Refers to the knowledge that is hard to be expressed in verbal form such as, in words or numbers. It is not easy to communicate tacit knowledge as it is inexpressible. Examples of this type of knowledge include the intuitions and insights of people.

In business environment, knowledge is the outcome of understanding and evaluating the information. This understanding helps in innovating, and decision making in business. This is done through a process of analyzing the hidden patterns of information and generating new business concepts and principles. Knowledge about two phases of a concept helps business professionals evaluate them in terms of their effectiveness. Innovation is based on the knowledge of business environment. All these aspects of knowledge help in effective decision making by management of an organization. Unless the management has knowledge about the requirements, resources, opportunities, and threats for the organization, adequate and rational decisions cannot be taken.

Effective knowledge management is considered as one of the important factors for the success of business organization. In fact, knowledge is the key to success in terms of it being the eyes of organization. Adequate knowledge allows an organization to explore innovative business practices. Competitive advantage can be created by collecting, sharing, and updating knowledge. Knowledge is not only a collection of information processed through the information systems; it is also the knowledge of employees of the organization. An employee can share his/her knowledge in the organization that is helpful in improving the efficiency of business process of the organization.

9.2.1 Dimensions of Knowledge

Knowledge is divided into different areas which are called the dimensions of knowledge. The significant knowledge for business has been divided into different dimensions as shown in Figure-1:

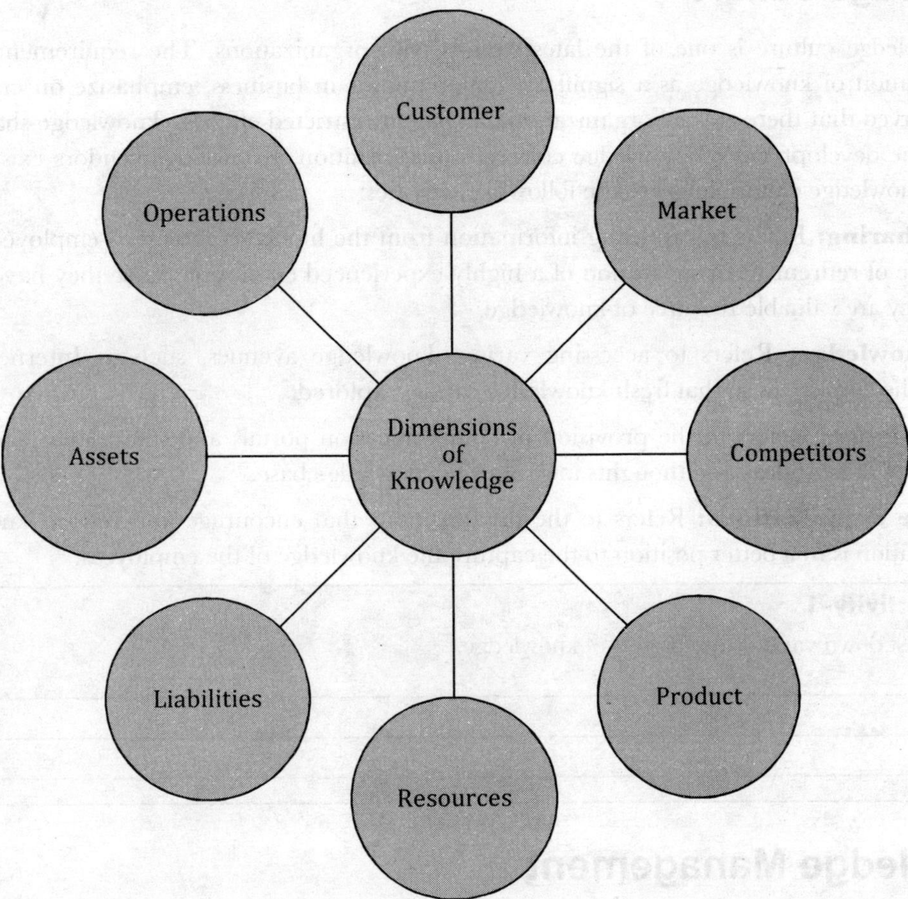

Figure-1: Dimensions of Knowledge in Business

The various dimensions of knowledge in business shown in Figure-1 are discussed as follows:

- **Knowledge of Customer:** Involves knowledge of consumer behavior, customers' feedback, and customers' tastes and preferences.
- **Knowledge of Market:** Involves knowledge about market trends, market regulations, market segments, and opportunities arising in the market.
- **Knowledge of Competitors:** Involves knowledge about other organizations in the same business, the scope of competitive advantage, competitors' best practices, and competitors' position in the market.
- **Knowledge of Product:** Involves knowledge about existing and upcoming products, the features and benefits of product, and stage of product in the product life cycle.
- **Knowledge of Operations:** Involves knowledge about business policies and practices, how the business operations are conducted, and operational efficiencies and challenges.
- **Knowledge of Assets:** Involves knowledge about the goodwill, brand image, financial assets, and resources.

- **Knowledge of Liabilities:** Involves knowledge about the financial burden, employee development, and expectations of the stakeholders.
- **Knowledge of Resources:** Involves knowledge about human resources, suppliers, financial resources, and technological resources.

Now let us now understand knowledge culture.

9.2.2 Knowledge Culture

Developing a knowledge culture is one of the latest trends with organizations. The requirement of knowledge and increasing consideration of knowledge as a significant differentiator in business, emphasize on creating a knowledge culture. It was observed that there existed organizational bias that restricted effective knowledge sharing. This problem was overcome by the development of knowledge culture in organization. Knowledge vendors exist from grapevine to data mining. The knowledge culture involves the following activities:

- **Experience sharing:** Refers to capturing information from the highly experienced employees. This is generally done at the time of retirement or separation of a highly experienced employee. Since they have spent long time in the industry, they are valuable resource of knowledge.
- **Exploring knowledge:** Refers to accessing various knowledge avenues, such as Internet and openness to experience for the employees so that fresh knowledge can be explored.
- **Sharing knowledge:** Refers to the provision of communication portals and information sharing opportunities among employees. Their ideas and thoughts improve the knowledge base.
- **More Flexible organizations:** Refers to the organizations that encourage and reward knowledge sharing. A flexible organization is in a better position to the capture the knowledge of the employees.

Activity-1

List down various dimensions of knowledge.

____

____

____

9.3 Knowledge Management

With the continuous development of information, business has to deal with huge information on daily basis. The aggregate of information on some specific subject develops knowledge on that subject. Organizations store information with themselves for future reference in business activities. This stored information when organized, creates a knowledge base for them, which is updated on continuous basis so that any obsolete information does not confuse or misdirect the management. Management refers to the knowledge base whenever they require understanding of the concepts inherited by information.

Knowledge management is the effective and adequate management of communication of knowledge in an organization. Efficient knowledge management helps in acquiring, sharing and updating knowledge across the organization. The process of knowledge management involves sourcing the internal and external information that is explicit as well as tacit and transforming it into valuable knowledge for the organization. This knowledge is made available for all the employees with a learning objective. In this way knowledge management deals with communication and learning.

Knowledge management deals with acquiring knowledge from various knowledge sources, and developing a knowledge base that fulfills communication and learning for the organization.

9.3.1 Shift from Information Age to Knowledge Age

In the last one decade, the business environment has noticed a shift from mere information age to a knowledge age. Knowledge age is the new concept of industrial economy where knowledge stands as a major contributor of economic growth. It has been experienced that knowledge is more productive resource for an organization than other resources, such as land, labor, capital, and entrepreneurship. Therefore, knowledge has been regarded as an asset for an organization. Competition required organizations to go beyond information need and this led them to the doorstep of knowledge age.

By 1987, organizations had started setting up separate systems for separate departments and provided coordination among the system users. By 1991, policies and procedures regarding use of data began to be formulated for the development of network database. The fulfillment of information needs arrived to the need of understanding the relationships of data and information. This understanding helps in identifying rules and patterns hidden in that data and information. These patterns and rules helped in creating knowledge with establishment of principles and rules of thumb. While with information, managers had to spend more time for knowledge creation; knowledge is already in this form. Gradually expert systems were developed to give more interactive user support. Soon after that, it was realized that knowledge is less in documents and more in the minds of people. Thereafter, the concept of knowledge management came with the objective of collecting, creating, storing, and disseminating knowledge in an organization. Various organizations implemented this as a strategy and gained advantage in terms of profit.

9.3.2 Knowledge Sources

There can be different sources of knowledge for an organization. Some of the sources are discussed as follows:

- **Written Sources:** Include books, reports, blogs, portals, and newspapers.
- **Unwritten Sources:** Include observations, procedural attitudes, and perceptions of people.
- **Experts:** Include experience sharing and other expert advices.

Among these sources written sources are the most required and trusted sources. These sources contain less ambiguous information. Expert sources are developed as they are not any conventional sources. For unwritten sources the information is required to be collected in the written format so that is easily understandable. The knowledge managers need to discover these sources and explore information from them so that knowledge can be developed.

9.3.3 Knowledge Acquisition

Acquisition of knowledge is the very first step in knowledge management. The process of knowledge acquisition is named as knowledge engineering and people involved in this task are called knowledge engineers. The flow of knowledge in an organization can be in two directions; top to bottom and bottom to top. Knowledge engineers adopt different approaches while acquiring knowledge in these two directions.

The methods generally followed in knowledge acquisition from top level to bottom are as follows:

- **Interview method:** Involves general interviews, personal interviews, object oriented interviews, and structured interviews.
- **Questionnaire method:** Involves open and closed ended questions to be answered.
- **Group Discussion Method:** Involves a knowledge sharing discussion on some topic. The ideas and thoughts of participants help in knowledge creation.

The methods generally followed in knowledge acquisition from bottom to the top level are as follows:

- **Observation method:** Involves observation of process and employees' performance in the process.
- **Protocol method:** Involves identification of general formulae while solving any problem in organization. This information helps in creating thumb rules in problem solving.

- **Expert Opinion:** Involves expert or group of experts to share their ideas and opinions about a particular situation. This information also helps in forming principles of solving that type of problems.

Some important aspects about knowledge engineers that must be kept in mind are pointed out as follows:

- Method selection and knowledge acquisition is a skill.
- Paper work and documentation is important however, it should not be a time consuming process in knowledge acquisition.
- Continuous improvement in knowledge acquisition methods with the feedback of participants in necessary.

9.3.4 Knowledge Base

Similar to database, knowledge base represents the organized storage of knowledge with or without the use of computer. Knowledge base facilitates in accessing to knowledge whenever required. The knowledge it contains includes rules, principles, theories, best practices, and other forms of organized knowledge.

Knowledge for organization is a vast source of efficiency improvement. If we compare the knowledge in an organization to water resource in our nature, it helps in understanding the need of knowledge base. Water is although necessary for life but it needs to be managed and stored properly. There should be tap to control and avoid waste of water. Similarly, in organizations knowledge base is also required to manage the existing knowledge and avoid wastage of it. A knowledge base is generally managed through computers. There are a number of knowledge based software that an organization can develop to support its knowledge base. Knowledge management requires developing a knowledge base to effectively manage knowledge in an organization.

9.4 Knowledge Support System

Knowledge Support System (KSS) or Knowledge Collaboration System (KCS) is a computer based knowledge management application. This application supports effective and efficient knowledge management. This system consists of knowledge base software that is updated automatically whenever system engineers acquire new knowledge. The knowledge seeker has to enter the keyword of the dimension of knowledge he/she is searching and the system will provide link to all the related documents and knowledge.

Technological advancement in business has conceptualized the KSS. These systems have smarter search systems that provide easy access to the desired knowledge whenever required. Google, Yahoo, and Mozilla are some popular search engines. These are based on KSS technology and provide information on searched topics through internet. Another access mechanism is creation of knowledge portals. A knowledge portal is a web based portal that facilitates knowledge sharing through its knowledge base generally among the members of a community. Wikipedia is an example of web based knowledge portal. Creation of knowledge portal creates a brand image of the organization's knowledge management.

A KSS has following components:

- **Software:** Refers to the knowledge based software.
- **Hardware:** Refers to the parts building the physical structure of KSS.
- **Programming:** Refers to the physical data design of KSS and the coding. The physical design is responsible for converting the user language knowledge into computer language knowledge.
- **User interface:** Refers to the interaction between user and computer. This is responsible for converting computer language knowledge into user language knowledge after digging the knowledge from the knowledge base.

Figure-2 shows a model structure of a KSS, as follows:

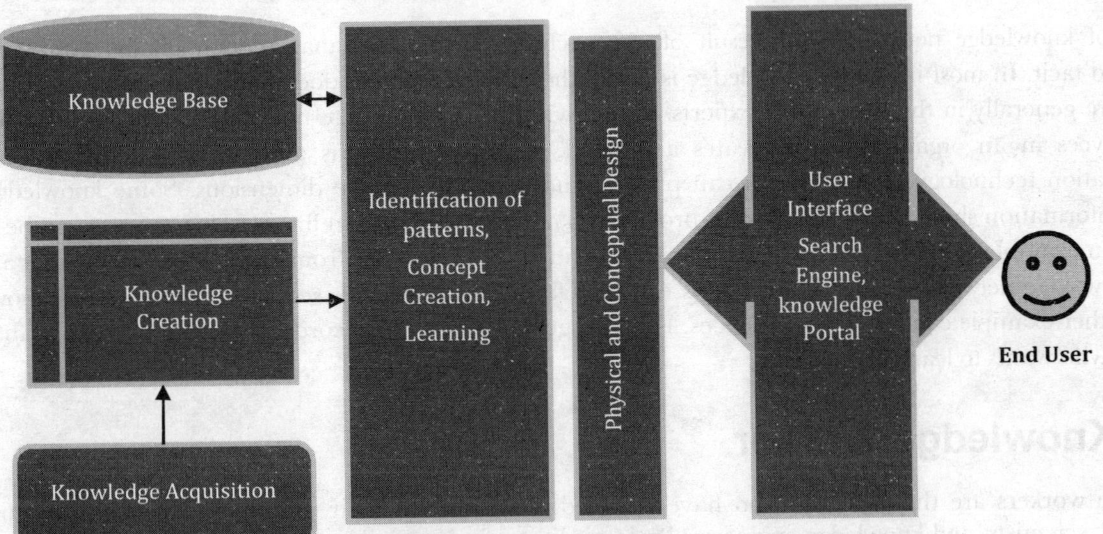

Figure-2: Knowledge Support System

In this system (Figure-2), knowledge is acquired and created to be stored in the knowledge base. For the user a user interface has been developed for interactive support with knowledge. The physical design is the system coding for understanding the input by the user. On the other hand, conceptual design is designing of language which is understandable by the user. Whenever user wants to get knowledge of some dimension, he or she can search for that. The knowledge base shows the user all the knowledge that relates with his/her search. User can see the results and pick the knowledge he/she wants to go through. This knowledge is continuously updated with new acquisitions to prevent storage of any incorrect knowledge.

9.4.1 Types of KSS

Knowledge support systems are categorized into two types. These are explained as follows:

- **Manual Support Systems:** Refer to such a category of KSS that help users with any knowledge support for effective deployment of their work. Such systems provide all type of support in decision making; however, ultimate decision is based on user's rationale. After acquiring the available knowledge, user can take decision more efficiently.
- **Intelligent Systems:** Refer to such a category of KSS that is able to take decisions based on a rational approach developed through the knowledge it contains. These are called intelligent support systems. The knowledge base and system specifications let the system apply a logical thinking in decision making. This technology is called artificial intelligence and such systems are called expert systems.

9.4.2 Scope of KSS

There is an increasing trend in the recognition and adoption of KSS by organizations. The scope of KSS covers the following aspects in business:

- Learning of business concepts, best practices, and business trends.
- Sharing valuable knowledge to build organizational competencies.
- Doing right thing at right place in right time.
- Innovation in business process and procedures.
- Intelligent support through knowledge base.

9.4.3 Knowledge Network

Creation of knowledge network is the result of approaching document management digitally. Knowledge can be explicit and tacit. In most instances, knowledge is not in the form of a digital document. The experience and cognitive learning are generally in the memory of experts and individuals. A knowledge network is a well-defined directory for the employees in an organization. It creates a network among the experts and the knowledge seekers by using communication technology. This network can provide knowledge in definite dimensions. Some knowledge networks store the information shared by the experts to provide as knowledge support in future. This concept can be understood well with an example of creating FAQs. FAQs are frequently asked questions from knowledge seekers that are recorded by the knowledge network system. These FAQs can be referred by knowledge seekers for the quest of knowledge they want. Another example can be of best practices. Knowledge networks keep record of best practices that can be referred by person who wants to learn about them.

9.5 Knowledge Worker

Knowledge workers are those people who have knowledge creation as their primary work. This category includes researchers, scientists, and knowledge engineers. Basic qualities of a knowledge worker include high level of educational qualification, judgment ability, logical ability, and reasoning abilities. Knowledge workers in an organization have their primary job of generating knowledge from information and updating knowledge base with newly explored knowledge.

To support knowledge workers in performing their job, organizations develop knowledge work systems. These systems are equipped with advance processing capabilities and graphics. These systems are capable of performing complex calculations and providing access to external database. A knowledge worker needs to locate, access, and present information quickly. So these knowledge work systems are to serve their needs. Most of the knowledge work systems are computer based. For example, a system for scientist is capable of performing complex calculations desired for their work.

9.6 Strategic Advantage with Knowledge Management

Knowledge management supports organizations with an easily assessable knowledge base and encourages learning. Learning is the base of continuous improvement in processes that ultimately provides competitive advantage to the organizations. Every organization has to adopt a learning approach so that it can keep updated with every moment changing business environment. Success is the ultimate objective of every business for which organizations develop strategies. There are some specific types of strategies adopted by organizations developed on the basis of KSS. These strategies include development of learning organization, knowledge creating company, and building value chain via knowledge management. Let us discuss about them in detail.

9.6.1 Knowledge Creating Company

In the competitive environment of today's business world, knowledge is the only weapon with which an organization can beat the competitors. The uncertainties prevailing in the market can make any product obsolete overnight and can make another product the leader in the same time. A knowledge creating company engages itself in continuous creation of knowledge. This knowledge needs to be disseminated throughout the company so that it can be implemented in business operations and decision making as quickly as required. The main objective of a knowledge creating company is continuously updating the knowledge to create new knowledge and innovation.

Knowledge management develops methods that support sharing knowledge, creating new knowledge, and applying this knowledge at workplace. Honda, Cannon, and Sharp are some of those companies who have quickly created knowledge and implemented it in their business.

9.6.2 Learning Organization

A learning organization believes in continuous learning and improving business practices and its activities by its learning. In his book '*Building a Learning Organization*', ***David A. Garvin*** *has defined a learning organization as "A learning organization is an organization skilled at creating, acquiring, and transferring knowledge, and at modifying its behavior to reflect new knowledge and insights"*

Similar to human beings organizations have also adopted a learning approach to development. An organization learns through industry experience. By following a knowledge management system it can create knowledge that guides its future operations. Organization adjusts its functions according to what it learns from the market. The knowledge gained by the organization helps it in making strategic decisions. These decisions are based on market knowledge and organization's learning about market practices; therefore, this approach leaves less possibility of strategy failure.

A Learning organization has five main characteristics:

- System approach to problem solving
- Innovation of new concept and approaches
- Learning from concepts and experience
- Learning from experts and best practice
- Creating knowledge and disseminating it efficiently throughout the organization.

9.6.3 Value Chain with KSS

A value chain advantage has also been attained along with other strategic advantages of knowledge management. The value chain model discussed in previous chapters, visualizes an organization as a chain of business processes which add value as margin of effective functioning. The business value chain with knowledge management visualizes the knowledge management processes in an organization. With each step of this process, organization moves forward towards improvement in its core services. A modeled form of value chain developed with knowledge management is shown in Figure-3:

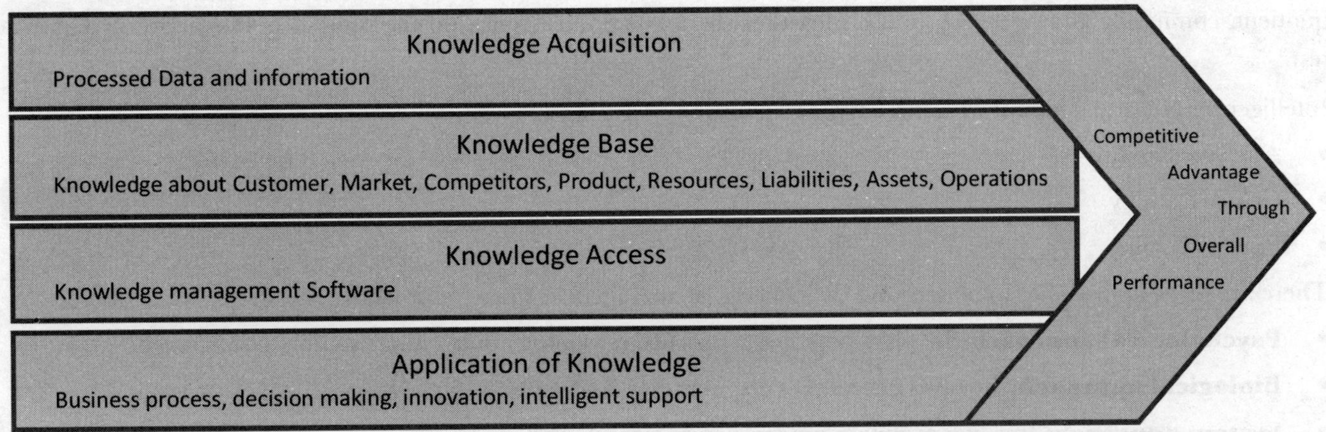

Figure-3: Value chain with Knowledge Support Systems

As shown in Figure-3, in the knowledge management process an organization acquires knowledge and develops a knowledge base which provides easily available knowledge for the management of the organization. This knowledge, accessed by management, is applied in various business processes and decision making. Management also gets an intelligent support with its knowledge base and attains innovation making capabilities. The knowledge acquisition gradually develops knowledge culture in organization. It can develop KSS for the support of its management. This knowledge support helps in improving customer relationship management, supply chain management, and production operations management. All these functions ultimately result in overall performance improvement that creates competitive advantage for the organization.

9.7 Protection of Corporate Knowledge

We have discussed so far that an organization should convert data into information and derive knowledge from this information to gain strategic advantage. This knowledge is as precious as all other assets of an organization. It is counted among the corporate assets; therefore, it needs to be secured. Protection of knowledge also means prevention of misuse of organizational knowledge. As a threat to an organization, knowledge theft and misuse of knowledge can certainly cause security concerns. To check this, organizations make an agreement with their employees about preventing unauthorized usage of knowledge. Employees who have access of organization's knowledge base are restricted from using organizational asset as their personal asset. Organization also considers knowledge as an intellectual property and applies legal aspects of security such as patents and copyright.

There are three types of protection measures taken by an organization for knowledge protection. These are discussed as follows:

- **Legal measures of knowledge protection:** Involves agreements and contracts which are enforceable by law.
- **Instrumental measures of knowledge protection:** Involves conversion of knowledge into intellectual property such as, patents and copyrights.
- **Strategic measures of knowledge protection:** Involves secrecy maintenance, lead time and password protection.

By adopting any individual measure or a combination of measures, an organization can protect its knowledge.

9.8 Concept of Intelligence

It is noteworthy that intelligence has no separate definition that does not relate to human intelligence. The term intelligence generally refers to human ability. It basically relates to the development of thinking machines. The level of this ability is measured on cardinal tools. One can measure intelligence between two intelligence bearers on the basis of greater than, equals to, and less than. Another measurement approach of intelligence is by calculating intelligent quotient, commonly known as IQ. It also measures the relative intelligence on the basis of performance in a standard test.

Intelligence is basically inbuilt with three types of ability:

- Analytical ability
- Creative ability
- Practical ability

There are three approaches to understand the concept of intelligence. These approaches are discussed as follows:

- **Psychological approach:** Involves perceptual process, reasoning ability, and emotion management.
- **Biological approach:** Involves neural process, impulses, and sense.
- **System approach:** Involves cognitive system, neural system, and communication system.

After understanding the concept of intelligence, let us now understand artificial intelligence.

9.9 Artificial Intelligence

Artificial is something that is not natural or provided by nature. Intelligence refers to an individual's ability of understanding, analyzing, evaluating, and observing a particular situation and making appropriate decisions. AI can be defined as a technology that facilitates the application of computers to the fields that require knowledge, reasoning, and cognitive abilities. In other words, it is a technology of building machines with human intelligence. Intelligence in human beings is a biological feature that relates to human brain. On the contrary, intelligence in machines is a technological feature that relates to science. In fact, AI is an intellectual ability that is not humane but created by human-beings.

Undoubtedly, Artificial intelligence is regarded as a field of science. This field relates with information technology, engineering and computer science. In this field of science, researchers wanted to develop a machine that could have the ability to think and finally developed the machines that are able to think. These machines were mainly computer systems. Artificial intelligence not only developed ability to think, in machines, it also successfully developed reasoning, problem solving, and learning abilities in machines. Artificial intelligence technology is widely used in business to improve decision making. Information systems are artificially intelligent in data mining, data processing, and information retrieval. The product development, designing and development, resource management, and order management are the areas of organizational functions where artificial intelligence technology has been implemented. Various machines are being developed with artificial intelligence.

The following are the popular definitions of AI:

According to ***Kurzweil****, "Artificial intelligence is the art of creating machines that perform functions that require intelligence when performed by people."*

According to ***Charniak*** *and* ***McDermott****, "Artificial intelligence is the study of mental faculties through the use of computational models."*

Undoubtedly, AI is regarded as a field of science. This field encompasses various other fields, such as information technology, engineering, and computer science. The AI technology is widely used in business to improve decision making.

9.10 Evolution of Artificial Intelligence

The development of AI has its roots in the myths of such technology to be developed over the years. Passing through many different phases (where researchers have been facing no fund for research issues), artificial intelligence has become the base of upcoming generation. These phases are shown in Table-1, as follows:

Table-1: Development of Artificial Intelligence

Year	Invention	Contributors
1943-1956	Digital computers, Neural networks that can learn,	McCulloch and Pitts
	Development of	Minsky
	Logical theorem of Principia Mathematica,	Newman, Simon , McCulloch, Minsky
	Artificial Intelligence (AI) name was given	
1952-1969	New theorems for artificial intelligence	Robinson, Gelerneter, Rosenblatt, John McCarthy
	Perception development	
1969-1979	Development of knowledge based system, expert systems	Mycin, Dentral, Prospector
1980-1988	Development of AI industry, Robotics	Fifth generation computers
1988-till now	User interactive intelligent systems and machines	Learning, Knowledge, Reasoning, Interacting

As given in Table-1, the early development of AI belonged to development of neural networks in computer science. Various seminars were organized that contributed towards the development of artificial intelligence. Such a seminar was organized in 1956 at Dartmouth College in New Hampshire. In this seminar a research report of 10 researches was presented which brought out some logical theorems. The contribution of John McCarthy for the development of logic was very valuable. Researchers had to face problems of fund and criticism of their work for AI development. Slowly and gradually with the development of expert systems and robots, artificial intelligence was realized for common people. Today we have machines with intelligent capacities, computers that can perform intelligent tasks and further development in this field is going on as it will create fifth generation computers.

9.11 Applications of Artificial Intelligence

The applications of AI can be categorized into three major fields of technological development. These fields are broadly categorized as field of cognitive science, field of robotics, and field of user interface developments. Each of these areas includes the machines or technology developed with the applications of AI. Among the most recognized applications there are expert systems and robots. Figure-4 shows these areas along with the major applications:

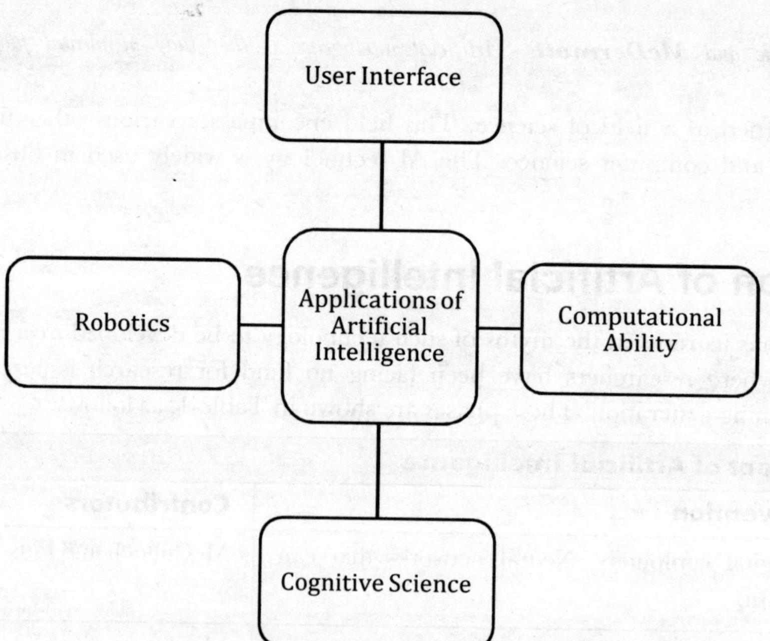

Figure-4: Applications of Artificial Intelligence

Let us discuss about these application categories.

9.11.1 Applications in Computational Ability

Computation is the very first area of computer intelligence development. In this early stage, computers were made to solve complex calculations to assist human intelligence. It was named as computational intelligence in machines. There has been continuous enrichment in this early intelligence with the development of new technologies and tools. This ability was set as basic intelligence required in computer systems.

9.11.2 Applications in Cognitive Science

The area of cognitive science integrates biological and psychological approaches to AI. It follows the idea of how the human brain works for learning and thinking. There are various computer-based applications of AI developed through human information processing. The applications of AI in the field of cognitive science include expert systems and knowledge-based systems. It also includes the development of adaptive learning systems that adopt to behave according to the information provided. Fuzzy logic implemented in AI systems made them able to perform reasoning with incomplete information.

9.11.3 Applications in Robotics

The area of robotics integrates the fields of engineering and psychology. This field basically involves the development of robots. Robots are the machines that are artificially designed to look and act similar to human beings. The design and development of robots includes application of neural network, logical reasoning, and learning. The development in this field includes visual and sensor capabilities, navigational ability, and sense for recognition.

An area of application that aims at building human like cognitive capabilities in robots is called cognitive robotics. These cognitive capabilities include perceptual ability, reasoning, and forestalling. Human cognitive principles form the basis for development of robotics algorithms in this technology. This enables robots to express knowledge in the manner similar to those of human beings.

9.11.4 Applications in User Interface

User interface is an ability of the system to interact with the world. One of such developments is the development of speech recognition technology through which a computer can understand the verbal commands of users. For this purpose, multisensory devices and linguistics were developed in computers. This field has evolved virtual reality systems. These systems have multisensory parts that can understand the words as well as the actions of the user.

Let us now discuss how artificial intelligence is generated.

9.12 Generating Artificial Intelligence

An AI system is a type of information system that is able to perform intellectual actions. This task was far more complex than the development of knowledge-based and expert systems. This is mainly because an AI system involves expert information and knowledge intelligently for the purpose of decision making. The feature of intelligence enables the AI system to deal with real world situations logically. The development of AI system is an outcome of research conducted for a long period of time. After testing various hypotheses, an information system that involves intelligence of human brain was developed. Different researchers found different systems and technologies, which are neural network, fuzzy logic, generic algorithms, and virtual reality. Let us these systems and technologies in detail in the next sections.

9.12.1 Neural Network

Neural networks are developed by following neurology, which is a science of human brain. These networks are basically developed to solve computing problems. The elements in neural network are called neurons. The structure of human brain is supposed to be the most complex one. The complex structure of neural network is far less complex than the structure of human brain. A neural network contains neurons that are connected to one another for processing any information like human brain. It is enabled to learn and recognize the patterns of data. A neural network is so fast to learn and store information. Human brain might forget but a neural network always keeps the information stored until it is deleted. A neural network keeps on feeding information and learning, until it shows a high level of accuracy.

9.12.2 Fuzzy Logic

The fuzzy logic is basically a logical reasoning that enables processing on the basis of proximity of solutions. Any incomplete or ambiguous data can lead to correct information on the basis of proximity. Although the term fuzzy logic relates to certain doubtful technology, but there is no doubt in intelligence development through this technology. In fact, the fuzzy part of the name indicates the understanding of fuzzy representation. A fuzzy representation paves new paths of being partially true information instead of being fully true or false.

One of the examples of fuzzy logic is search engine Google. Once you enter an incorrectly spelled topic for search, the system give results on the basis of proximity of search. The incomplete or ambiguous data is named as fuzzy data; therefore, this technology is named as fuzzy logic. Fuzzy logic is widely used in machine control. Prior to fuzzy logic, the logical theory was based on only two valued logics, one is true and other is false. Fuzzy logic is based on third approach that can go along with true and false. It is made up of certain rules and logical SQL query, which is named as fuzzy SQL query. Fuzzy logic requires sensors to respond in a fuzzy logical way for building AI. An arithmetic set theory problem is solved in this approach named as fuzzy arithmetic.

9.12.3 Fuzzy Control Systems

A fuzzy control system is conceptually a mathematical system that is able to analyze analog input values as logical variables. This overcomes the limitation of digital logic input systems, which could operate on discrete values of either 0 or 1 (true and false), while in the new approach; the system can take constant values between 0 and 1. These input variables are called fuzzy set in technological terms. A fuzzy logic system is regarded as a trusted control system building application. This technology is widely used in business not only for building systems but also for developing intelligent machines for consumers. Videocon was the first company to launch fuzzy logic in washing machines. This technology enabled washing machines to decide the type of cleaning by identifying the type and amount of dirt in clothes to be washed. This technology further led to the development of fully automatic washing machines, which washes and dries clothes simultaneously by selecting a single operation. Later on various other companies, such as Hitachi, Toshiba, Samsung, and LG, adopted the fuzzy logic technique to develop consumer durables.

9.12.4 Generic Algorithms

Generic algorithms use the application of mathematics and computer science. This technology is being used as software for various scientific, technical, and business applications. The generic algorithm software utilizes a set theory of arithmetical processes, which identifies the sets of process components that need to be formed. These sets are formed randomly and analyzed. The poor sets are continuously rejected to arrive at the best one. This is widely useful in situations where there are a number of possible solutions to a given problem. These options need to be evaluated to arrive at an optimum solution.

9.12.5 Virtual Reality

The virtual reality technology belongs to the creation of artificial visions through the use of computers. Therefore, it is also called computer simulated reality or Tele-Presence. The development of this technology has its roots in the development of more natural, realistic, and multisensory user interfaces in computers. The virtual reality technology uses multisensory computer input/output devices that can track the body movements of the user. It is able to create a three-dimensional virtual world through the identification of sounds and movements. It enables the computer to become more interactive with the user. The application of this technology ranges from medical science to physical and biological experiments. It is also widely used in entertainment, such as in virtual gaming. Computer-Aided Design (CAD) is among the most widely used application for business.

9.12.6 Intelligent Agents

The use of artificial intelligence has given birth to intelligent agent. An intelligent agent is a software based tool that is able to support various business and commercial processes. It behaves rationally in decision making especially in conditions where there are more than one alternative decision possible to one particular problem. It helps the user as an intelligent surrogate; therefore, it is named as intelligent agent.

A familiar example of an intelligent agent is Microsoft Office Assistant. This assistant is developed with all the procedural knowledge to work on Microsoft Office. This agent provides knowledge about all the applications, such as how to create a graph or table in a document. These agents are special purpose assistants who have answers of FAQs and various processes. The increasing use of Internet and complexity of operations on tools has popularized the use of intelligent agents.

Another example of an intelligent system is the camera and sensors in a robot. Through these tools, the robot perceives the environment.

An agent is called autonomous when it learns from its experience. There are broadly two categories of intelligent agents, which are discussed as following:

- **Physical Intelligent Agent:** Refers to physically built entities that are able to perceive through the sensors in its body and act through the parts of its body.
- **Temporal Intelligent Agent:** Refers to time based information storage systems that can provide data or instructions through computer programming.

9.13 Expert Systems

Experts systems are the most widely used applications of AI in business. These systems are intelligent knowledge-based information systems. They provide expertise for supporting various business functions. They can identify the user's requirement with the help of their intelligence. Let us understand more about expert systems in the upcoming sections.

The following are the components of expert systems:

- **Knowledge Base:** Refers to the essential components of expert systems. These systems are able to provide expert support with the use of knowledge base inbuilt in them. The knowledge base consists of facts and figures on various subjects and topics. It also consists of standard rules and relative subjects' knowledge.
- **User Interface:** Refers to the interactive user interface of expert systems. This interface understands user language and interacts in the same language with the user. This component creates expert system preferably referred by users.
- **Intelligent Agent:** Refers to one of the software components. Most expert systems also contain intelligent agent to support business professionals in performing their actions.

Expert systems are widely used in the following business functions:

- **Reasoning:** Involves logical operations and concept based reasoning.
- **Knowledge Support:** Involves knowledge of established rules, principles, and subjects.
- **Decision Support:** Involves rational agent functions to arrive at the best alternative decision.
- **Operational Support:** Involves support with the procedures of working and support by troubleshooting the problems in the system.
- **Control:** Involves expert control with information and intelligent measures.

As we know, expert knowledge through the system supports various business functions, such as human resource, production, and marketing. It saves the precious time that can be wasted while waiting for interaction with experts to share knowledge. An expert system is also able to provide knowledge of several experts at the same time. However, the main drawback of an expert system is that it is able to provide knowledge only in limited area. Moreover, being a system, it can be hacked and its knowledge can be misused. Apart from this, developing an expert system involves high cost and efforts.

Despite these limitations, expert systems are widely used system applications in business. Expert systems require knowledge engineering, development of neural network, installation of fuzzy logic, generic algorithms, and virtual interface development.

9.14 Cross Functional Information System

Cross functional information system allows you to use and share information among different departments in an organization. Therefore, they are called cross function information system as they cross departmental boundaries. The examples of cross functional information system are enterprise resource planning(ERP), customer relationship management(CRM), supply chain management(SCM) and knowledge management. All these system are inter-connected. The ERP focusses on the internal effieciency of an organization, CRM focusses on the relatioship with customers, SCM focusses on the relatioship with suppliers, and knowledge management focusses on the knowledge sharing. You will learn more about these systems later in the book.

9.15 Swarm Intelligence (SI)

The swarm intelligence is a special type of artificial intelligence. This type of intelligence is counted among the recent developments of AI. It is an approach towards behavior in a society by artificially intelligent systems. The technology of swarm intelligence is based on the group behavior shown by a decentralized and self-organized system. This technology was presented by Gerardo Beni and Jing Wang in 1989, while developing the cellular robotic systems.

SI systems usually consist of a number of intelligent agents interacting with one another as well as with their surrounding environment. As a distinct feature these systems do not have any central control unit structured in them for controlling the behavior of individual intelligent agents. It is the local interactions among the agents which guides their global behavior.

The application of swarm principles in robotics is called 'swarm robotics'. One of the successful applications of this technology in practical problem solving is ant colony optimization. In this application, researchers utilized the behaviors of ants in their society for solving problems in areas such as scheduling problems, routing, and assignments problems.

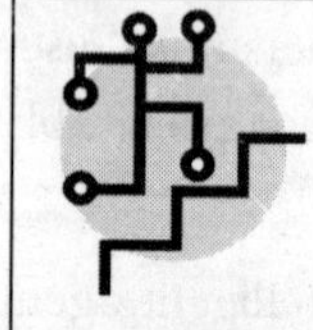

Activity-2

Find out some applications of swarm intelligence in business.

Case Study: The Sharp Technology and LCD television

LCD television sets are the most sold television sets in the market these days. This technology has been developed by pursuance of serial innovations without giving up. There was no compromise with what was determined to be achieved through the process of creating, sharing, guarding, and deriving knowledge. Sharp, a Japanese multinational corporation is regarded as the pioneer in LCDs since the 1970s. Sharp was the first to open a sixth-generation fabrication plant. This plant enabled the company to make LCD panels as large as 1,500 mm by 1,800 mm.

The company invented the first low-power electronic computer in 1973 with this technology. It was a synthesis of two technologies namely, liquid crystal display (known as LCD) and use of complementary metal oxide semiconductors (CMOSs). The technology experts at Sharp have given the name 'opto-electronics' to this synthesis of two different optical technologies. The success of this technology was the result of long phase of research and development conducted by the company experts. Sharp produced the first commercial LCD Television in1988.

In his famous book '*The New Dynamism of the Knowledge-Creating Company*', Hirotaka Takeuchi has mentioned that Katsuhiko Machida became the president of Sharp Electronics in 1998 and just in two months of time, he determined the objective of selling of all Sharp televisions in the domestic market was to be converted into the sale of flat-screen LCD television sets by 2005. By then, Sharp no longer produced the traditional technology tube (Catholic Ray Tube) televisions for the Japanese market. The company president has set an example of knowledge creation and learning. He formulized that innovation is being willing to think big and tackle a goal others deem too risky. This proved a great prediction for market and came up as an outstanding decision by the company by 2006. The sales reports after the Christmas 2006 were revealed and the CRT television became obsolete overnight. The sale of LCD televisions also conquered the sale of Plasma televisions and shifted the television market into the market of LCD screens. Many companies including Samsung and Sony turned their production with this shift however, some of the companies, unfortunately, had to close the production.

Questions:

Q1. Evaluate the performance of Sharp in terms of development of LCD television and competition in television market.

Q2. How do you find the decision of President of Sharp Corporation in terms of decision making?

*(*Case study presented is the proprietary information of the respective organization, and is used here specifically and only for educational purpose.)*

9.16 Summary

Knowledge is the refined form of information for an organization. Knowledge management is the process of knowledge acquisition, storing knowledge, and disseminating knowledge among the knowledge workers. Knowledge support system is a system that collects information, processes it to derive knowledge, stores this knowledge, and provides it to the users. The storage of knowledge is called knowledge base, as this facilitates easy access to the knowledge. A well-defined directory for the employees in an organization that creates a network among the experts and the knowledge seekers by using communication technology is called a knowledge network. Those people who have knowledge creation as their primary work are called knowledge workers. An organization uses knowledge as a tool for competitive advantage. Various competitive strategies can be developed with a knowledge management approach. These strategies include creation of knowledge-based company and learning organization. Knowledge management also builds a value chain for an organization as a strategic advantage. In a nutshell, effective knowledge management is an extremely crucial task for an organization. This importance of knowledge has turned it into an organizational asset which needs to be protected from unauthorized access and misuse.

Intelligence is the ability to understand, learn, and perform logical actions. Computer science has developed artificial intelligence that enables machines to behave rationally. This technology has faced ups and downs during the development phase. This has been a widely used technology in business functions and also in developing machines. Artificial intelligence is brought with several distinct technological applications which include knowledge base, neural network, fuzzy logic, generic algorithms, and virtual reality. The software with intelligence inbuilt is called intelligent agent. The most widely used business application of artificial intelligence is in the form of expert systems. Expert systems are able to provide support in decision making, business operations, and control with the knowledge base and artificial intelligence it consists of. The chapter has detailed all the important aspects of knowledge management and artificial intelligence.

9.17 Key Terms

- **Intangible:** Refers to something that cannot be seen, felt, heard, smelled or touched.
- **Explicit:** Refers to something that is expressed and clear.
- **Tacit:** Refers to something that is unexpressed and wordless.
- **Knowledge portal:** Refers to an online accessible store of knowledge which allows knowledge sharing and editing.
- **Artificial intelligence:** Refers to such type of intelligence that is not human but is created by human efforts.
- **FAQs:** Stand for Frequently Asked Questions. These are the sources of knowledge where answers of these questions are stored once answered by an expert.
- **Intellectual property:** Refers to such property that is the creation of mental efforts and does not possess form of physical property. The value of such things makes them to be referred to as property.
- **Cardinal tools:** Refer to those tools which do not possess any definite mathematical value instead are measured through comparison.
- **Set Theory:** Refers to the branch of mathematics that involves study of set of objects.
- **SQL query:** Refers to a computer programming language.
- **Analog Input:** Refers to defined set of inputs in computers.
- **Arithmetical Processes:** Refer to mathematical processes able to perform calculations with variables.

9.18 Exercise

Multiple Choice Questions

Q1. Knowledge is the processed form of ________.

a. Wisdom　　b. Data

c. Information　　d. Strategy

Ans. c

Q2. Knowledge culture relates to__________.

a. Knowledge management　　b. Knowledge filtering

c. Knowledge sharing　　d. Knowledge import

Ans. c

Q3. Knowledge that can be expressed verbally refers to which type of knowledge?

a. Management knowledge　　b. Self-managed knowledge

c. Explicit knowledge　　d. Tacit knowledge

Ans. c

Q4. Tacit knowledge is __________.

a. Verbal

b. Written

c. Expressed

d. Difficult to be expressed verbally

Ans. d

Q5. _________ is effective and adequate management of communication of knowledge in an organization.

a. Knowledge network

b. Knowledge acquisition

c. Knowledge management

d. Knowledge base

Ans. c

Q6. Which of the following methods involves identification of general formulae while solving any problem in organization?

a. Interview Method

b. Observation Method

c. Expert Opinion

d. Protocol Method

Ans. d

Q7. By the year______, organizations had started setting up separate systems for separate departments and provided coordination among the system users

a. 1984

b. 1986

c. 1987

d. 1990

Ans. c

Q8. ___________represents the organized storage of knowledge with or without the use of computer that facilitates ease of access to knowledge whenever required.

a. Knowledge base

b. Database

c. Knowledge source

d. Knowledge management

Ans. a

Q9. Knowledge Collaboration System is _____

a. Knowledge Creating System

b. Knowledge Acquisition System

c. Knowledge Network

d. Knowledge Support System

Ans. d

Q10. Which of the following refers to a strategic advantage with knowledge management?

a. Value chain with KSS

b. Learning Organization

c. Knowledge Creating Company

d. All of them

Ans. d

Short Answer Type Questions

Q1. Explain the dimensions of knowledge.

Q2. What is knowledge culture?

Q3. What are the different types of knowledge?

Q4. Explain the concept of knowledge network.

Q5. What do you mean by a learning organization?

Q6. Mention the main characteristics of a learning organization.

Q7. What is KSS? What are the components of a KSS?

Q8. What is a knowledge base?

Q9. What are the different types of KSS?

Q10. What is a knowledge creating company?

CHAPTER 10

Information System Security and Control

CHAPTER STRUCTURE

CHAPTER OBJECTIVES

- Elaborate on the ethical aspects of information technology
- Describe the importance of ethics in IT
- Explain the means of achieving ethics in IT
- Explore the ethical challenges of IT
- Elaborate on security management and control
- Discuss on management of risks
- Explain the requirements of a regulatory system

10.1 Introduction

The business functions today are largely based on the information system which has grown with the advances in information technology. It seems that information technology has spread its wings at every nook and corner of business. However, while the contribution of IT in business is commendable, damage happening to business enterprises due to misuse of IT is equally noteworthy. Undoubtedly, technology is a double edged sword. With one edge it provides numerous benefits while with the other it can cause harm as well. Some incidences in real life have proved that the more we develop in the brighter side; the dark side will also keep on increasing. The data and information stored in computer's memory can be accessed for use and misuse both. The trap of network can be accessed by such users who can harm the health of business and economy. Such incidents include violation of rights of an individual or a corporation. These issues have attracted the attention of system developers to maintain the usability of information systems.

Concerns related to system security and reliability maintenance have developed security passwords, controlled access and various regulations related to the use of information systems. Therefore, organizations are required to protect their data and information from unauthorized access. They are also required to prevent unethical practices performed by those who have been granted permission for access.

The chapter explores the ethical aspects of information technology by examining the importance of ethics in information technology and finding out the ways that help in achieving ethics in the use of information technology. The chapter discusses about the ethical challenges in information technology and explains its security management and control. Along with discussing about various security issues it explains the management of risk involved in application of information technology in business. It also discusses about the regulations and legal aspects related to information technology. Towards the end, it discusses about the enterprise resource planning, customer relationship management and supply chain management.

10.2 Ethical Aspects in Information Technology

The advancement of IT has affected business as well as society as a whole. IT brings serious threats of unauthorized and unethical usages besides its benefits. Information technology involves a large number of ethical issues which affect the larger society. These social issues, if not checked, can result in serious consequences. For instance, an employee who has access to the confidential organizational information can sell the information to another organization for monetary benefit. Similarly, any organization can try to get unauthorized access to other organization's data. Such practices cause harm to the security, integrity, and profit of an organization. These issues pose serious threat to the confidentiality and privacy of an individual, as well as an organization.

Before understanding the ethical aspects, let us first understand the meaning of ethics.

Ethics, as defined by Manuel G. Velasquez, refers to the "the process of examining the moral standards of a person or society to determine whether these standards are reasonable or unreasonable in order to apply them to concrete situations and issues". According to Epicurus, ethics refer to "the science that deals with things to be sought and things to be avoided with ways of life and with the chief aim of life". It is obvious from these definitions that, ethics relate with behavior of an individual. This behavior is judged on moral grounds. This judgment allows one to decide what 'should be' and what 'should not be' done in practice.

The categories of ethical aspects in IT are shown in Figure-1, as follows:

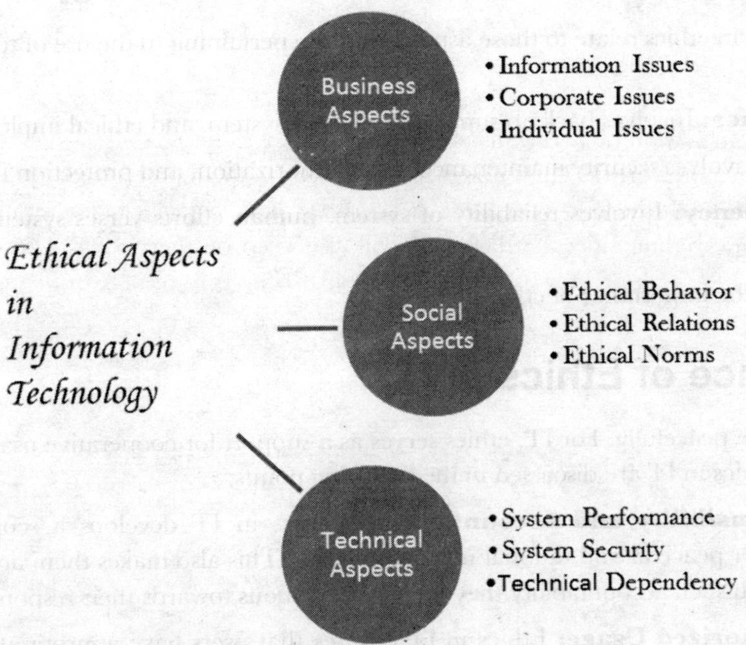

Figure-1: Major Aspects of Ethics in IT

As shown in Figure-1, three major aspects of ethics in IT include business aspects, social ethics, and technological aspects. Let us discuss in detail about each one of them.

10.2.1 Business Ethics in Information Technology

A business is responsible for understanding the criticality of ethical issues and resolving them. As per the theory of stakeholders in business, management of a business should be based on moral values. Business professional come across a number of ethical issues on daily basis. Some of these issues are as follows:

- **Information Issues:** Include data protection, information storage, and access rights.
- **Corporate Issues:** Include ethics in organizations, fair trade practices, fair competitive practices, and corporate social responsibility.
- **Individual Issues:** Include moral behavior, cooperation, prudence, rational practices, and humanization of organization culture.

10.2.2 Social Ethics in Information Technology

A society is a unit made of individuals. Therefore, a society is also responsible for maintaining ethical parameters in the use of IT. As per the theory of social contract all the individuals in the society have some ethical boundaries. The actions of individuals should not violate this contract else there can be harm to the individuals. A society includes following two types of aspects in ethical IT:

- **Ethical Behavior:** Includes social security, social justice, and morality. The elements of society shape the behavior of the individuals that forms the society.
- **Ethical Relations:** Include social integrity, social values, customs and beliefs.
- **Ethical Norms:** Includes social rights, duties, social regulations and legal foundations.

10.2.3 Technological Ethics in Information Technology

The technological aspects in ethics relate to those aspects that are pertaining to the use of technology. These aspects are categorized as follows:

- **System Performance:** Involves back up support, quality of system, and ethical implementation of systems.
- **System Security:** Involves security maintenance, user authorization, and protection from virus.
- **Technical Dependency:** Involves reliability of system, human efforts verses system performance, and human control over technology.

Let us now discuss about the importance of ethics in IT.

10.3 Importance of Ethics in IT

Ethics support in living life peacefully. For IT, ethics serves as a support for cooperative usage and restrict misuses. The major advantages with ethics in IT are discussed in the following points:

- **Cultivating Responsibility and Accountability:** Ethics in IT develops a scope of responsibility among business enterprises for peaceful and rational utilization of IT. This also makes them accountable for any unethical business practice. With such accountability they are made cautious towards their responsibility.
- **Preventing Unauthorized Usage:** Ethics in IT ensures that users have appropriate authority to access an IT facility. Unauthorized access harms confidentiality of information of an individual, as well as an organization.
- **Protecting Cumulative Rights:** Ethics in IT safeguards the rights of all the parties by establishing ethical responsibility. One unethical practice may provide prosperity to one organization; however, it may harm other organizations. Ethics protect the rights of all the individuals and businesses. Ignorance of IT ethics will lead to situations where all businesses indulge in unethical practices which in turn cause harm for all of them.
- **Building Reliability:** Ethics in IT improves the reliability on IT tools and devices by preventing unauthorized practices. Individuals and organizations store and share confidential information with the help of IT tools. Ethical aspects are needed to be followed so that users can take advantage of IT applications. In the absence of ethics IT usage would have suffered from lack of reliability.
- **Eliminating Risk:** Ethics in IT reduces the risk involved in the deployment of IT applications. Risk with IT relates with system failure, theft of data, and loss of critical information. The ethical guidelines help in increasing trust and reducing the risk.
- **Reducing Conflicts:** Ethics in IT reduces the possibility of conflict among the users of IT in business. Ethics clarify the limitations and liabilities of organizations which help in minimizing such conflicts. In the absence of ethical norms there is a high possibility of conflict among the different users of IT services and tools.

Let us now discuss the achievement of ethics in IT.

10.4 Achieving Ethics in IT

Capabilities and knowledge acquired with IT also bring some ethical responsibilities. These ethical responsibilities are the pre-requisites of deployment of technological resources to secure the beneficial usage while avoiding misuse at the same time. IT has made collection, storage, and transmission of data and information very easy. However, in the same time it has posed threat to the privacy and confidentiality of individuals and organizations. Therefore, it is essential to build ethical norms in the usage of IT. Figure-2 shows the mean of achieving ethics in IT, as follows:

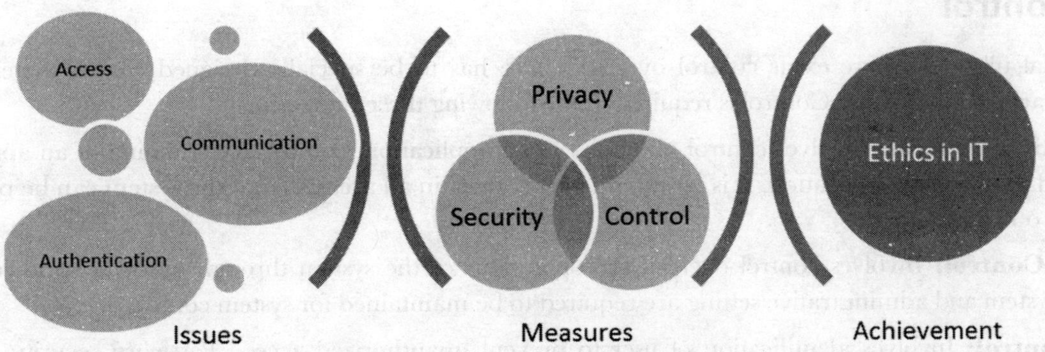

Figure-2: Achieving Ethics in IT

As shown in Figure-2, the issues related to access to IT, communication technology, and authentication of IT requires to be regulated. The measures for privacy, security, and control of IT help in establishing ethics. Let us discuss about privacy, security, and control in detail now.

10.4.1 Privacy

Maintaining privacy refers to maintaining confidentiality of information related to an individual or an organization. The regulations that support privacy consider that every individual has the right not to publicize everything related to them. The issue of privacy includes the following:

- **Access to Personal Information:** Refers to access to such information which an individual may or may not permit to be shared. For example, the personal contact number, address, and relationship status are some of the personal information of an individual. Such information should not be made public without the consent of the individual.
- **Maintenance of Confidentiality:** Involves protection of confidential records, information or data. For example, if an employee, who has access to confidential company information, intends to make it available for the competitor, it is unethical. Organizations sometimes ask the employees to enter into an agreement of fair use of organizational data.
- **Ethical Responsibility of Business:** Involves fair disclosure of terms of employment, policy and procedures to be followed, and equal treatment for all the employees. Hurting the sentiments of any employee intentionally is unethical practice by employer.
- **Adequate Disclosure:** Involves maintaining balance between right to information and privacy of an individual. The data that is not required to be disclosed should not be disclosed. Also, if it becomes necessary to disclose any such information prior consent must be taken from the individual whom this information belongs to.
- **Personal Communication:** Involves unauthorized access to a personal communication between two parties without their consent. Every individual has the right to express his or her feelings to the extent it does not hurt the sentiments of anybody else. Accessing the personal email inbox and reading personal mails of an individual is unethical.

Right to privacy is also one of the basic human rights and ethical practices avoid violation of this right. Let us now discuss control as a measure of achieving ethics in IT.

10.4.2 Control

IT is beneficial till when there exists control over it. There has to be specially designed control system established through software and hardware. Control is required in the following three dimensions:

- **Application Control:** Involves control on access to an application, control over running of an application, and controlled usage of an application. It is required to set control in all areas so that the system can be protected from virus and other such threats.
- **System Control:** Involves control over all the operations of the system through hardware and software. Data security system and administrative setting are required to be maintained for system control.
- **User Control:** Involves identification of user to prevent unauthorized access. Password security system allows only those users to access the data who confirm being authorized by password. Sometimes the access is prohibited for minors to maintain user control parameter as access to such information by minors is unethical.

Let us now discuss security as a measure of achieving ethics in IT.

10.4.3 Security

In IT, Security refers to protection from damage. It is very essential to develop adequate security measures for IT usage. The unsecure application of IT may result in ethical issues. IT is required to be secured on the following grounds:

- **Secure from Unauthorized Access:** Ensures protection of data and information to be accessed by anybody who is not authorized to access it. If unauthorized access is not prevented, unauthorized user can steal, destroy or harm the data resource of an organization.
- **Secure from Misuse:** Ensures that any private or confidential data is not used to cause harm for an individual or organization. If some hacker has hacked a website or personal account, he would not be allowed to manipulate the data or information therein. A common example of misuse of IT is when anybody has stolen your mobile phone, it is your responsibility to report this and stop the services available on that phone to prevent misuse.
- **Secure from Virus:** Ensures that data stored or knowledge with an organization is protected from being harmed by virus in the system. If a virus attacks a computer system it can harm all the function of it. It can also be transferred from one system to another. Therefore, it is required to format the system and secure it from virus entrance.
- **Secure for Privacy:** Prevents any harm to the privacy. The network accessed and computer systems should provide security to the privacy of the user. Some websites that utilize the personal information of user should disclose it in their privacy policy.

IT, if not secured properly, can be used for unethical practices and crime. Therefore, it is necessary to maintain adequate security standards with the use of IT.

10.5 Ethical Challenges of IT

IT has direct effect on individuals, society, and government. The first and foremost effect of IT is on individuals. For example, telecommunication system has revolutionized the way an individual used to communicate with other individual. This brought a change in the society; people started using phones to communicate with each other instead of meeting personally. This also resulted in the formation of various telecom regulatory authorities.

We have discussed how we can achieve ethics in IT, still in the pursuance of those measures there are some challenges faced. The use of IT can be made in pursuance of some unethical practices. These unethical practices are threatening not only for business but also for individuals and societies. For example, the telecommunication technology can be used for social development but at the same time it can be used for committing serious crimes in society. Internet which integrates the whole world as a common place has been utilized for fraudulent practices also. Such incidences include cyber-crime, hacking, unauthorized usage, piracy, and threat of virus and worms. Let us discuss about them in brief.

10.5.1 Cyber Crime

Crime is an act done by a person which is wrong in the eyes of law. *According to* ***Lord Atkin*** *"the criminal quality of an act cannot be discovered by reference to any standard but one: is the act prohibited with penal consequences"*. While breach of criminal law is the conventional crime, the breach of cyber ethics is cyber-crime. It is a recent and far more complicated form of crime. The standard definition on the topic says, "Any criminal activity that uses a computer either as an instrumentality, target or a means for perpetuating further crimes comes within the ambit of cyber crime".

Cyber crime has categorized computer crime into three main categories

- **Crimes Harming individual:** Includes transmission of any threat or harassment through IT and those that are supposed to mislead or harm individuals in the society.
- **Crimes Harming property:** Involves harming others property through IT. Sending a virus in the system and stealing data by trespassing security of other's system are some of such crimes.
- **Crimes Harming society:** Involves an intension of harming the society. Using IT to support terrorism is included in this category. Other such examples are cracking the security of any government or military agency and use of social sites for social disruption.

10.5.2 Hacking

Hacking is a crime that relates to the unauthorized access to the use of a computer or a network. A hacker breaks the security system of a computer or network and avails access to it. Hacking may result in serious cyber crimes while some people find it a fun activity. The cyber thieves utilize such tools that are able to scan the weakness in the software of the website. They use remote service to enable one computer in a network to execute program on another computer. This technique leads to 'sniffers (Refers to any software or hardware of a computer that can capture and execute passing over a digital network.)' which is able to find the password. There are also such cases noticed where a hacker only accesses the document and reads it. He neither steals the document nor damages it. It becomes even more difficult to deal with such kind of hacking. Mostly, the hackers are skilled people who are experts in computer hardware and software. These people may form a group and teach other people the hacking tricks. For example, hacking of a bank's website can result in serious financial scam.

A hacker's attack is mainly classified into two categories - passive or active. Passive attacks try to gather information about the system without making any changes to the state of the system; whereas, an active attack makes changes to the system or network they are attacking. A passive attack is a violation of confidentiality of information. On the contrary, an active attack affects the authenticity, integrity, and availability of data. Depending upon their origin, attacks can also be categorized as inside or outside. If an attack originates from within the security boundaries of an organization, then such an attack is called as an inside attack. This type of attack is usually caused by an insider of the organization who has access to more resources than he/she is authorized to. In an outside attack, the source of attack originates usually from outside the security boundaries of a company, such as the Internet.

Hacker attacks can also be categorized into the following four categories:

- **Operating Systems:** Specifies that most of the operating systems are installed with the default settings, resulting in exposure to vulnerabilities. In addition, it is difficult to apply patches to such vulnerabilities.
- **Applications:** Specifies that usually the code written for applications is not tested for vulnerabilities. This results in paving way for hackers to exploit programming loopholes in the applications. For example, in case of open source applications, a hacker can very easily have access to the code.
- **Shrink-wrap Code:** Specifies that usually the commonly-used applications contain some additional features that most of the users are not familiar with. A hacker can exploit such features to gain access to an application. One such feature is macros in Microsoft Word that facilitates a hacker to execute malicious programs within the application.
- **Misconfigurations:** Specifies that computers can be very easily misconfigured or when left with the lowest common security settings, increases the chances of a potential hacker attack.

10.5.3 Cyber Theft

Cyber theft is a committed stealing or damaging database in a computer by unauthorized entrance to a computer network. Such practices are serious theft to intelligence and strategic business. The issues in cyber theft relate with theft of money or money's worth by using IT tools as major weapon for theft. Cyber thefts result from unauthorized or fraudulent access in a network. In most cases cyber theft is committed through Internet. In a basic example, if one company steals the tender details of other company, while submitting its own tender, it will take advantage of such details. This is an unethical practice which can be used to harm others for one's own advantage. Another example can be stealing of confidential data of a country's military intelligence. One of the known examples of cyber theft is that of Citibank. In 1994, a theft of 11 million USD was committed by a hacker who used Internet to break the security system of the bank. Such incidents cause big threats to organizations from cyber theft.

10.5.4 Unauthorized Usage

The challenge of unauthorized usage is also called resource theft. When any IT resource, after being accessed or hacked unethically, is used by those hackers, it becomes unauthorized usage. It is observed that in organizations where Internet has been provided for official usage, employees are using it for playing games or such non-productive activity.

This usage also relates with the unauthorized use of an electronic instrument such as credit card. It does not recognize whether the owner is using the card or somebody else. It creates an unauthorized flow of money from the card holders account till the services on the card are not stopped. Unauthorized usage can be made of electronic properties, network accounts, and email accounts. Unauthorized usage is a serious threat to privacy and individuality.

The unauthorized usage of official resources (such as, computers and networks) for executing another job or personal business is called 'moonlighting'. It has become serious business challenge with the use of IT. Organizations may block some websites so that such practices can be controlled.

10.5.5 Software Piracy

The crime of copying software without being authorized for its use is named as software piracy. If someone has to use any particular software, he/she is required to buy its usage authorization. It is to keep in mind that what we pay for a software before we use it, permits its usage but it does not makes the user owner of the that software. It covers following actions:

- Unauthorized installation of software
- Unauthorized use of software
- Unauthorized distribution of software

Piracy has been a big concern of software companies since long time. The harms of software piracy are listed as following:

- Loss of revenue for software makers
- Compromised quality of software
- Loss of tax revenue for the government

The pirated software is not allowed to be upgraded and when connected to Internet, comes up with the threat of hackers and viruses.

There are many regulations formed to discourage software piracy but none of them are enough to provide foolproof security to this computer crime.

10.5.6 Piracy of Other Intellectual Property

Intellectual property is referred to such intangible property that has been created by individuals and corporates for their personal benefit or usage such as, copyright, trade mark, patent, and digital data. It is created through human intelligence and mental efforts. It is therefore, unethical to copy or steal the creativity and efforts of someone else. The technology which contributes to the creation and security of documents over computer is the same that contributes in copying it easily. The dissemination of this copied document is also very quick and easy.

10.5.7 Viruses and Worms

Viruses are special type of programs which are used to change or harm the computer functions. These are also called malicious programs. A computer virus is a set of software programs which is able to increase its size by itself and infect another programs or documents in a computer. A virus is able to copy itself and increase its number in a quick manner. Some viral codes serve the execution of this program. Virus generally does not damage hardware or original program; instead they damage data file and memory. Damage from virus is also noticed in the memory of a computer.

The subsets of virus are named as worms. Worms are different from viruses in the way they increase their size. They copy themselves across the network while virus increases by attaching itself to a file. After attaching itself to a file the virus runs by itself as and when the file is opened.

For example, in March 1999, a virus names as 'The Melissa' was noted on internet. Shortly after that it spread throughout the computer systems of United States and Europe. According to estimation this virus caused damage worth 80 million dollars to the computers around the world.

There are basically four categories of computer viruses that are discussed as follows:

- **Boot Sector Virus:** Resides in the boot sector of a computer such as a floppy disk. It attaches itself to the prime active part of the disk that a computer reads during boot up time of a computer.
- **Master Boot Records Virus:** Resides in the memory section of a computer. It corrupts the memory boot record system of the computer. It affects the memory support of a computer.
- **File Infector Virus:** Infects the program files and corrupts them from their executable codes. They normally reside in the memory of the computer. They infect other files also when any infected program is run from floppy disk.
- **Macro Virus:** Infects programs created by functions which give an option of Marcos such as Microsoft World and Microsoft Power point. Macro is the option that allows creation of mini-programs which are helpful in the execution of a series of operations. This type of virus affects the functions created using macro options.

10.5.8 Social Engineering and Phishing

Social engineering is a method of gaining access to a system or network by deceiving the users of the system and encouraging them to provide sensitive information required to bypass the security of the system. It is important to understand social engineering as it is one of the commonly used techniques of a hacker to attack a system by manipulating its human resource.

Phishing is a process of acquiring sensitive information such as important user credentials, bank details, and credit card details by impersonating a legitimate user using an electronic communication. E-mails received from famous websites are common means to entice the users. A phishing attack is performed by using e-mails or instant messaging that usually makes the users to enter information at a fake website claiming to be a legitimate one. In a phishing attack, e-mails are sent to the victim pretending to be sent by a bank or other financial organization. The e-mail might contain certain links prompting the user to enter important bank information such as passwords or Personal Identification Numbers (PINs) to confirm banking information or reset passwords. When the user clicks the link, the user is redirected to a fake website and the banking information submitted by the user is transferred to the hacker. The hacker then uses this information for financial gain or to carry out attacks. An example of phishing attack is an e-mail that claims the sender has a lot of money but requires your help to get out of the country. The victims of such attacks are usually common people who are not much aware of phishing attacks.

After understanding the challenges to security, let us now understand the management of security and control.

10.6 Security Management and Control

Technology is evolving day by day and so is the need for security. The products, now-a-days, available in the market are focused more on ease of use, which often results in overlooking the security aspect of the products. Most of the times, the vulnerabilities in a network are overlooked by system designers till the time the system is deployed. Computers are more focused on performing routine activities; thereby, making it difficult for system administrators to explicitly allocate resources for securing systems. For example, in case of large networks that are spread over a wide area, it becomes difficult for the system administrator to check all the log files generated by all the systems, identify vulnerabilities of each and every system, and apply security patches to individual systems. In addition, the easy availability of a lot of free automated tools and codes for hacking a system on the Internet has also increased the need to secure a system against potential threats.

As we have discussed the rapid growth in the application of IT has emerged various ethical challenges. These ethical challenges are met through management of security and control over the process. Security represents a state of well-being of information and infrastructure of an organization where the chances of data theft, data tampering, and disruption of information and services are as minimum as possible. There are three major issues in security management and control which are shown by Figure-3:

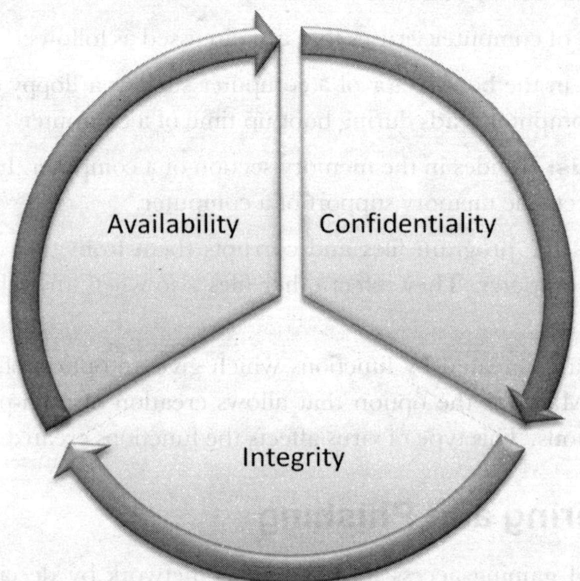

Figure-3: Issues in Security Management

Figure-3 shows that all the security management issues are divided in three categories as confidentiality, integrity, and availability. These issues are collectively referred to as CIA, or key security standards. These are discussed as follows:

- **Confidentiality:** Refers to the maintenance of security of confidential information, documents or other intellectual property. For the purpose of maintenance of confidentiality, management can create non-disclosure policy, privacy agreement, and security from viruses. The aim of confidentiality maintenance is to check unauthorized access by limiting the access. Confidentiality is lost when anybody who is not allowed access can access the confidential data in an organization.

- **Integrity:** Refers to the maintenance of reliability on IT. For this purpose, it has to be ensured that data or any other document has not been altered inappropriately. This segregation in data has to be prevented from both incidences of being done intentionally or accidently. It also includes reliability of data sources. The integrity is lost when the data is changed in an inappropriate manner.
- **Availability:** Refers to the in-time availability of information. Information is worth a lot if it is provided in time while information not available in time is not of any use. For this purpose, the technical aspects should be utilized for management of back up support. Sometimes the availability of system user is also required. Availability can be lost intentionally or accidently.

10.6.1 Internet-worked Security

All the above discussed issues relate with security from threat of unauthorized access to a network from outside the network. There can be threat within the network also. The major challenge in this measure of security is of balancing between the access to a network and security standards. Many organizations attempt to resolve their business requirements through intranet and extranet as there are high security issues with the use of Internet such as hacking and cyber theft. These security issues are required to be managed by security managers in an organization through various security measures. These measures include encryption, firewalls, virus protection, and email monitoring. Let us discuss about these security measures.

Encryption

This is a technique which converts the data into a form not easily understandable by everyone, to protect it from getting damaged. The converted form of data is named as 'cipher text'. It is basically reformatting of the original document or file with an intention to protect it from being harmed or copied. Sometimes, it is also used to hide some part of a document. In this privacy system text is scrambled and a passkey is assigned to convert it into readable form. The process of getting the encrypted text into its readable form is named as decryption.

Firewalls

The connection of an organization's network to another network (such as Internet), involves a threat for free movement of organizational data. This data needs to maintain the CIA level of security. For this purpose there is a separation created through firewalls. It protects the data on intranet from being accessed through Internet. Firewall is basically a structure of network components that exist between intranet and Internet.

Firewall is a part of a computer system or network that is designed to inspect incoming and outgoing network traffic, and alter the traffic flow by dropping or passing certain packets. It is designed to block unauthorized access while permitting authorized communications. Firewall is a device or a set of devices that is configured to permit or deny network transmissions on the basis of certain rules and criteria. A firewall inspects all the messages that enter or leave the company's Intranet and blocks those that do not meet the specified security criteria. It analyzes the incoming data to determine the IP address of the machine from which it is coming and the content that it contains. Next, the firewall checks if the content is compliant with rules that you have already configured. It also analyzes the information at the application level and determines whether or not the application should send or receive data through the port with which you are connected.

A firewall also prevents computer hackers to access your computer through the Internet by blocking back doors or open ports that connect your computer with Internet. This protects your system from being attacked by viruses from the Internet.

10.6.2 Virus Protection

As we have discussed that viruses and worms cause major challenge in security management with IT, therefore, virus protection is essential. To protect from viruses another program has been developed called as anti-virus. An anti-virus software program is able to identify and remove virus and worms from a computer. When an anti-virus program is run in a computer it scans and removes virus from it. Another protection tool is a spyware which can identify and stop any viruses and thereby restricts the entry of threats into the system. Anti- viruses are required to be updated on regular intervals. Updating an anti-virus updates the list of virus in its dictionary.

10.6.3 E-mail Monitoring

The facility of electronic mailing system, popularly known as email, is provided by almost all employers to their employees these days. The reason behind is to strengthen the communication and information sharing among employees. It has been observed that some people act as misusing this facility. Personal use of official emails and causing any type of threat or harm to company property are unethical practices. For example, some employee may forward company secrets to other people. Such threats of this facility are checked with email monitoring system. In this system the employer can access and check the emails (the received mails and the sent mails both) of all the employees.

Another ethical issue of privacy is violated with email monitoring system but it is also necessary for avoiding harmful results of email facility. Employers can also monitor the official telephones and radio facilities to avoid misuse of IT.

10.6.4 Other Security Issues

Apart from the issues discussed above some other measures are also used for security management and control. These are securing with security codes, maintaining back up support, system monitoring, and disaster recovery. These measures are helpful in maintaining the general security standards and ensuring least harm to an organization at a time when any such issues arise. Let us discuss these measures in brief.

Security Codes

This is the most commonly used form of system and document security. A password is created by the user so that unauthorized access can be stopped. This password is also called security code. Before displaying the document or navigating to the desired page, the user of the system is made to confirm the security code of a system. Entry is restricted till the correct code is not confirmed.

The security code system is used for computer systems, document sharing on network, personal accounts on network, and mobile phones.

Backup Files

Creating back up support of documents or files is necessary to minimize the loss from security breaks. It basically helps at the time of virus attack and any type of damage caused for the data already saved. Supporting with back up refers to copying a document or a file to another computer or location in the network so that if there is any reason causing inability to access that document, it can be accessed from there. Back up has become a routine activity for business organizations.

System Monitoring

Systems are monitored by system administrators in organization. The act of system monitoring is similar to supervision on the resources accessed through the system, the applications used in the system, and exercising proper control over it. The administrator is required to be able to check what is happening with the other systems, for example, what commands are run in the system, who is logged in which system, how many of system applications are being currently used. Any unethical usage of system can be checked and stopped in this way.

Disaster Recovery

Disaster with a computer system refers to any mishap with system operations. The attack of virus and worms problem in system functioning, and system failure are some examples of disasters that may come up while using an information system. Recovery is the tool which is used to support organizations in situations of such disaster with information system. The recovery tool helps in getting back the same database back.

Biometric Security

Security standards that utilize biological characters of a person to maintain security standards are included under this type of security system. This system follows some indicators of human body that are distinct from person to person such as, fingerprints of human beings. These indicators are identified to set and maintain the security of the system. This system is assumed as one of the best systems as there is nil chance of unauthorized access with biometric security unless the whole security system is brought to failure. A microphone or optical device is utilized under this system which is able to convert it into digital form. All the mentioned identifications compare the data taken from identification system with that already saved in the system. For example, companies take the thumb impression of their employees for their attendance. There is least possibility of proxy with this system and employees are not required to carry any punching card.

10.7 Management of Risks

Risk is involved with every benefit especially in business. Although it can be minimized, it requires proper management and control over resources. Risk in IT refers to the possibility of adverse impact brought with the indulgence of IT in business. It is the overall risk involved in the use of IT including the threats and challenges. In the same way management of risk in IT relates with management of aggregate of risk it involves. Well-managed risks bring profit while, failure to manage risk brings loss. Business professional engage themselves in the management of risks to acquire more and more profits for their business.

With the emergence of IT age, the necessity of management of risk related to the use of IT in business has become very important. Risk management involves four steps mainly as shown in Figure-4:

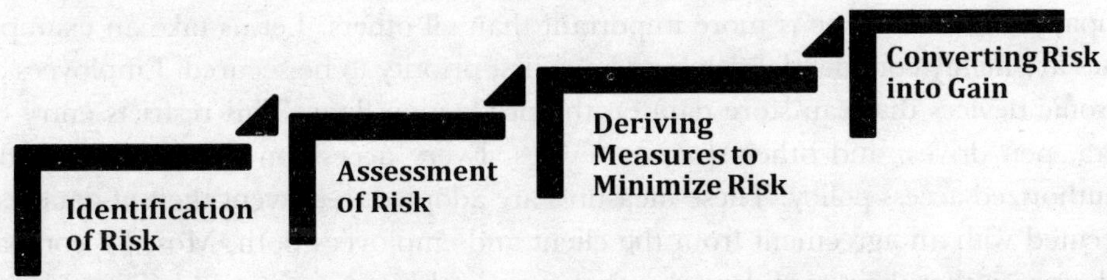

Figure-4: Risk Management Process

Let us understand risk management process, as shown in Figure-4, with an example of SDLC:

- **Identification of Risk:** Involves recognizing the risks (financial and technical) in the process of system development in an organization. These risks are identified at every step of SDLC.
- **Assessment of Risk:** Involves measurement of risk from all its possible sources. It consists of inter- organizational and intra-organizational sources of risk. The current and anticipated risks are visualized and measures are found to minimize them. In SDLC the system characteristics are analyzed along with the constraints. The impact of system development is anticipated so that the assessment of risk can be performed. After risk assessment is done a report of risk assessment is also prepared.
- **Deriving Measures to Minimize Risk:** Involves developing measures that can minimize the risk. It involves anticipated as well as unforeseen risks of the process of system development. System vulnerability and chances of failure are to be minimized. It generally follows the way of prioritizing the risks, evaluating their impact, and controlling the risks.

- **Converting Risk into Gain:** Involves converting the minimum possibility of adverse impact into the possibility of positive impact on business. An effective system design reduces the risk in SDLC. Strengthening of security system and control on system functions are the steps that are generally utilized in converting risk into gain.

The process of risk management can be applied in all the areas where IT is utilized for business so that IT implementation becomes successful for the business.

10.8 Requirement of Regulatory System

So far in the chapter, we have discussed that there are a number of threats to the security of IT devices and tools. Therefore, there is an urgent need of for legalization of IT usage. The crimes that are emerging in this sector are also growing fast. The regulatory authorities and government has also recognized this fact as a pressing need and formulized a legal framework of the use of IT. Following points support the requirement of IT regulatory system:

- Regulations set an equal and fair measure to control the actions of people.
- Regulations allow legal proceedings for a crime that gives the accused change to present his/her point.
- Regulations define each crime and specify the limit of excuses for them.
- People are bound by regulations and modify their actions accordingly.

All these points show that for the security and control of IT a regulatory framework is required. The legal proceedings are must to control the usage of IT and prevent it from being misused. Keeping the same in mind, most countries have passed regulatory acts that bound the people of the country. The Data Protection Act by British Government and Information Technology Act in India are some of the examples of such regulatory actions. Let us discuss the main aspects of the regulatory system in the use of IT.

10.8.1 Security Policy

Most organizations formulate their own policies to maintain the security standards with the use of IT. These policies are company specific generally and may take form of agreement between employer and employee. This is because different companies have different levels of security management. For one company one issue is more important than the other while for another company any other issue is more important than all others. Let us take an example of a call center where customer's details are highly confidential data and have first priority to be secured. Employees are not allowed to take any type of electronic devices that can store data on the production floor. This restricts entry of employees with mobile phones, camera, pen drives, and other storage devices. Every access on the production floor has to be in compliance with the authorized access policy. These measures are adopted to prevent theft of data, especially in BPOs. These policies are executed with an agreement from the client and employees both. Most IT companies follow email monitoring of its employees so that their confidential software and solutions are not transmitted to others. The major aspects of security policy of organizations include the following:

- Creating terms and conditions to comply with data security standards.
- Conducting orientation program to ensure new employees understand the criticality of data security.
- Monitoring systems of every employee to ensure there is no unauthorized usages.
- Appointing of security officers to set and execute compliance rules.
- Punishing for non-compliance such as issuing warning letter or terminating employment

It is the responsibility of every organization to maintain security and balance between privacy and control. The deployment of this responsibility is important to meet with ethical challenges of IT.

Activity-1

Find out the security policy of some major organizations in India.

____

____

____

10.8.2 Legal Actions

Technology is the conductor of change. It has changed individuals, society, and government. Since it has been used on massive basis, there emerged a need for some legal steps. The three types of main legal actions are in the field of copyright protection, data protection, and IT usage.

Cyber crimes involve criminal activities, such as fraud, theft, forgery, and defamation that are subject to the Indian Penal Code (IPC). In cyber crimes, a computer can be either used as a tool or as a target object or both. In India, the unlawful use of computers has given birth to new age of cyber crimes that are addressed by the Information Technology Act, 2000. A separate set of laws, known as cyber laws or Internet laws, has been designed to regulate the cyber crimes.

Following are the two categories of cyber laws:

- **Computer as a Target:** Specifies that a computer is used as a tool to attack other computers, such as virus and worm attacks.
- **Computer as a Weapon:** Specifies that a computer is used as a weapon to commit crimes, such as credit card frauds, cyber terrorism, and pornography.

Let us discuss the main regulatory actions taken in these fields.

Copyright Act

Copyright is a legal right provided to secure the creative work. The scope of creative work covers literature, drama, music, and other artistic works including cinematography and sound recordings. Copyright Act of India was enforced in 1957. This Act prevents reproduction and public transmission of such work by anyone while such works belong to some other individual. This right protects the creativity of people by giving it legal frame. The protection to creativity is also a safeguard towards the economic and social development of a country.

A similar Act named as Digital Millennium Copyright Act [DMCA] has been enforced by United States. This Act protects the digital creativity also. This Act covers the creation, transition, or application of IT devices, software, or services. The Act protects Internet Service Providers in case of violation of copyright Act by of the users they provide service to.

Data Protection Act

Various regulations have been enacted for the purpose of data protection. In our country, a prescribed format of legalizing data protection is provided under the IT Act 2000. Section 43 of the Act protects data from unauthorized access to a computer system. The violation of this may cause penalty up to one crore rupees. The unauthorized downloading, extraction and copying of data are also covered under the same penalty. Section 65 specifies that any action that knowingly or unknowingly hides, destroys, alters or causes harm to others' data is illegal. Any person found guilty in such action will have to bear penalty of imprisonment or fine up to 2 lakh rupees. Section 66 protects from hacking by causing imprisonment of three years or fine up to two lakh rupees or both on the person or institution involved in hacking. Section 70 protects the data stored under a protected system. Any access or attempt to access any secure system is illegal. Such actions may cause imprisonment up to ten years with fine. Section 72: The section protects the right of confidentiality and privacy of the data. Any action violating this right may cause imprisonment up to two years with or without fine up to one lakh rupees.

The British Government has executed Data Protection Act (DPA) since 1984. This Act has been modified recently in 1998. The Act aims at securing the personal data that belongs to the people of the country. It maintains privacy of individuals from unauthorized access to their personal information. The personal data, as specified, includes data that reflects the personal identity of a person such as, names, data of birth, addresses, telephone numbers, and e-mail ids. It protects all the data that is stored and accessed with any IT device and medium. It required the organizations that deal with personal data to be registered with the information commissioner for regulatory reason. It protects personal data from unlawful usage or access.

United States has adopted the approach of self-regulation with legal framework in data protection. Data has been categorized in different categories under the Act and have been given priority on the basis of their importance. More attention is provided to the higher importance deserving category of data. In 1974, The Privacy Act was passed in US. This Act established standards for reasonable, ethical and justifiable access to data by government agencies. An Electronic Communications Privacy Act was also enacted to prevent the intervention of electronic communications to the privacy of individuals. It also excludes the access to stored data without the consent of the owner. Regulations for internet service providers and access of data through internet have also been executed.

Hacking Regulations

Every country has its own laws for protecting information against hacking attacks. While performing ethical hacking for international organizations, you must check the laws of the specified nation to ensure that the testing performed is as per the cyber laws of the concerned country. With the help of Internet, you can very easily access the data stored on remote servers that might be located in another country. However, in such cases, the laws of that country are applied if you hack a system. Remember that even if your intentions are good but still as a hacker if you break the laws of the country, you will be prosecuted. Therefore, it is recommended that you must study the laws of the country prior to performing an ethical hacking for an international organization. In some countries, the laws may not be that strict as it is in case of United States. Therefore, it becomes quite easy for an ethical hacker to conduct a penetration testing in such countries where the laws are not very strict.

An ethical hacker must be familiar with the penalties of hacking a system before indulging in any hacking activity. Prior to hacking a system, the ethical hacker must get a signed legal document from the target organization. Ethical hackers should know when and where to use their hacking skills and understand the consequences of misusing these skills.

IT Act in India

The Information Technology (IT) Act, 2000 consists of 94 sections that are grouped into 13 chapters. There are four schedules included in this IT Act. This Act was later amended in 2008 and includes 124 sections and 14 chapters. The amendments made in 2008 have replaced Schedules I and II and deleted Schedules III and IV. The IT Act 2000 addresses issues, such as legal recognition of electronic records, legal recognition of digital signatures, secure electronic record, secure digital signature, and license to issue digital signature certificates. The IT Act 2000 amended in 2008 has brought several additional new sections in it regarding offences, such as cyber terrorism and data protection.

India stood as the 12th country in the world to adopt cyber laws. The IT Act of India was legislated on May 17, 2000. The Act aims at the regulation of the use of Information Technology. It aims mainly to legalize and regulate the system of electronic data interchange, electronic communication, and electronic commerce. This Act extends to the whole of India and also applies to any offence or contravention there under committed outside India by any person. The Act covers use of all the computer systems and networks located in India. Let us have a look on the main features of this Act:

- Chapter 1 of the Act deals with important definitions of the terms used in the regulation. It sets the scope of meaning of key terms of which the Act comprises of.
- Chapter 2 covers regulations regarding digital signature. It provides legal recognition to digital signature.
- Chapter 3 deals with electronic governance. It legalizes the use of electronic records in government organizations and establishments.

- Chapter 4 involves attribution, acknowledgment and dispatch of electronic records and their certifying authority.
- Chapter 5 comprises of Secure Electronic Records and Secure digital signatures. It establishes the rules and regulations related to the Electronic Gazettes.
- Chapter 6 covers Regulation of certifying Authorities.
- Chapter 7 deals with digital signature and details its certification with the duties of subscribers.
- Chapter 8 involves duties of subscribers.
- Chapter 9 comprises of penalties and adjudication the cyber regulations appellate Tribunal. It covers penalty for damaging a computer or computer system.
- Chapter 10 details about the establishment of the Cyber Regulations Appellate Tribunal to secure justice in such cases.
- Section 85 of the Act specifies the corporate social responsibility of a business. As per the Act the directors and managers of a corporation are responsible to uphold the corporate responsibility with pursuance of law and IT ethics. Any violation of IT ethics or this law that is conducted with the knowledge of these authorities holds them responsible for not stopping it.

The Act contributes significantly in empowering organizations to fight against cyber crimes. It also protects the rights of consumers in carrying on with electronic business.

10.9 Enterprise Resource Planning (ERP) System

One of the most important cross functional information systems includes ERP system. An ERP system integrates all the core business processes, such as purchase management, inventory management, production and distribution management, human resource, finance and sales. It produces a common database for all these business processes. The following are the major benefits of an ERP system:

- Supports the organization with an integrated view of business processes
- Provides quality information to support all the business processes
- Provides enterprise wide information to managers for effective decision making
- Supports organizational change and provides flexibility of business processes

Many renowned organizations, such as Microsoft, Cisco and Coca-Cola, have adopted the ERP system to increase operational effectiveness. However, installing an ERP system incurs heavy costs for an organization.

10.10 Customer Relationship Management (CRM) System

As we know, the success of an organization directly depends upon the level of customer satisfaction. Therefore, it is important for an organization to build rapport with the customers, identify their needs and expectations, and fulfill them. Maintaining successful relationships with the customers helps organizations to attract new prospects and gain market share. CRM is a tool that helps in determining mutually satisfying goals between the organization and its customers. A CRM system provides information related to the existing and potential customers of an organization. It also provides information related to customers' preferences and their feedback and facilitates customer interaction. Figure-5 shows the uses of CRM system in an organization:

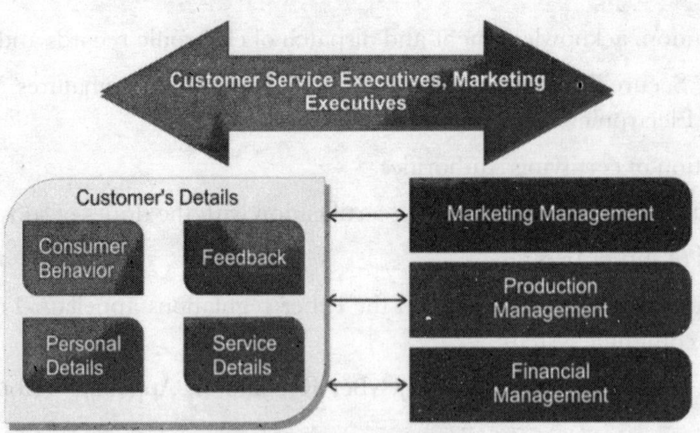

Figure-5: CRM System

10.11 Supply Chain Management (SCM) System

An SCM system is a cross-functional information system that is able to adjoin business processes from an organization to suppliers on one hand and to customers on the other hand. It helps in planning, organizing, directing, and controlling all the activities related to procurement of required materials in an organization. The system also helps in coordinating and integrating the links involved in this process. These links include suppliers, transporters, wholesalers, retailers, and customers. Figure-6 shows the SCM system:

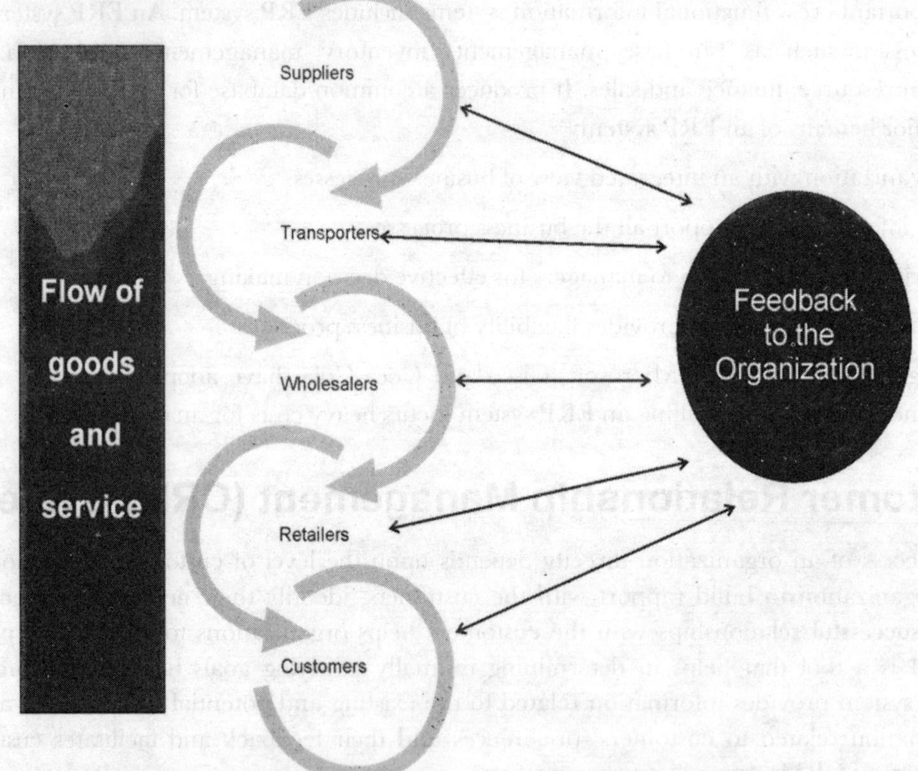

Figure-6: Basic Structure of Supply Chain Management

As shown in Figure-6, an SCM system coordinates the activities involved in the procurement of raw materials utilized in the production of finished goods. Supply chain management is a tactical task for every organization since it has a direct effect on the efficiency of the business. Therefore, an organization should have an effective SCM system. An SCM system helps an organization in:

- Providing effective and timely feedback and control
- Avoiding unnecessary delays in product delivery
- Preparing effective production planning
- Establishing effective delivery pattern
- Maintaining good relations with retailers, wholesalers, and suppliers

Case Study: Medical Industry and IT Ethics

Along with other professional sectors the medical industry has also been impacted by IT revolution. This has opened scope for various medicines, online consultation, and online purchase of medicines. Internet has provided access to these all. According to a research conducted around 52 million adults in USA, or 55% of those who have Internet access, have used the Internet to find information related to health or medical sector. The number of adults using the Internet for health information, shopping for health products, and communicating with providers, was expected to reach 88.5 million by 2005 and after that, at approximately twice the rate of the overall online population. The profession of doctors which was earlier regarded as less affected by consumerism and more driven towards human benefits, has also been segregated with high profit intensions. The major ethical issues with IT in medical industry relates to unlicensed, unqualified, or unprofessional medical service providers. There are many medical service centers run by medical service providers who are not eligible to provide it well. This is really a treat to the life of individuals who trust such services.

Ethical norms are required to regulate the doctor-patient relationship, online consultation and support, privacy and security of information available on Web. To regulate the ethical practices in medical industry and restrict such life-threatening practices government should make legal establishments. One of the largest medical service providers in the United States, the American Medical Association (AMA), has established the Code of Medical Ethics to be followed by its members. This code fulfills the requirements of definite ethical course of action in the medical service industry since the mid of 1840's. The code emphasizes that "the primary goal of the medical profession is to render service to humanity" while highlighting that "reward or financial gain is a subordinate consideration and under no circumstance may physicians place their own financial interests above the welfare of their patients." The Council of Medical Specialty Societies had published agreement statement in 1997 on the ethics of medicine, reminding the physicians that "the practice of medicine is rooted in the convention of trust among patients, physicians, and society. The ethics of medical industry must try to balance the responsibility of the physicians to each patient and the professional, collective obligation to all who need medical care."

Questions:

Q1. What are the ethical issues with IT in medical industry?

Q2. How can we regulate ethics in medical industry? Give two examples.

10.12 Summary

There are many benefits of IT in all the spheres of human life but we need to be cautious about its usage. This is mainly because of the ethical issues emerging with the use of IT. The ethical aspects with IT cover the professional, technical, and social aspects of human life. Ethics are importance in IT with reasons to ensure its safe and beneficial usage. Maintenance of privacy, devising security, and exercising control over the applications of IT are the aspects to achieving ethics in IT. There are various ethical challenges with which IT suffers from, which includes cybercrimes, hacking, piracy, and threat of viruses. There are three areas of management of security which are confidentiality, integrity, and accountability. Measures have also been developed to fight against such challenges of IT. These measures include password security, encryption, firewall, e-mail monitoring, and anti-virus protection mainly. Risk management approach is required to be adopted while implementing any IT tool so that any loss can be protected. For the protection and maintenance of ethics in IT, legal systems have also been established that aims at securing copyright and preventing data theft. IT Act in India has set regulatory measures for usage of IT to maintain the ethical aspects.

10.13 Key Terms

- **Sniffers:** Refers to any software or hardware of a computer that can capture and execute data passing over a digital network.
- **Cipher text:** Refers to encrypted text.
- **Executable codes:** Refers to codes that allow a computer to access any specific file by using them as programmable codes, such as .com, .sys.
- **Marco:** Refers to a feature of Microsoft World and Microsoft Power Point that allows recording a particular text and saves effort of typing it repeatedly.
- **Microsoft Word:** Refers to a software application or program that allows creating, editing, and saving documents electronically.
- **Microsoft PowerPoint:** Refers to an application or program that allows creating and displaying presentations on computers.
- **Proxy:** Refers to substitution of one person by another for pretending one's presence while one is not present.
- **SDLC:** Refers to System Development Life Cycle.

10.14 Exercise

Multiple Choice Questions

Q1. DMCA refers to ____________.

a. Digital Millennium Copyright Act
b. Digital Millennium Copyright Activities
c. Digital Millennium Copyright Action
d. Digital Millennium Computer Act

Ans. a

Q2. Which of the following is not a business aspect of IT ethics:

a. Information Issues
b. Corporate Issues
c. Individual Issues
d. System Security

Ans. d

Q3. The Information Technology Act, 2000 consists of _____ Sections.

a. 90 b. 92

c. 93 d. 94

Ans. d

Q4. __________include data protection, information storage, and access rights.

a. Information issue b. Corporate issue

c. Individual issue d. Social issue

Ans. a

Q5. Control measure of achieving ethics in IT does not deal with________?

a. Application control b. System control

c. Maintenance control d. User control

Ans. c

Q6. In IT, security refers to ______________

a. Protection from virus only b. Protection from damage

c. Protection from terrorists d. Defense system

Ans. b

Q7. Any criminal activity that uses a ______________ either as an instrumentality, target or a means for perpetuating further crimes comes within the ambit of cyber crime.

a. Computer b. Monitor

c. Telephone d. Mobile phone

Ans. a

Q8. Transmission of any threat or harassment through IT and those that are supposed to mislead or harm the individuals in the society is included in ______________

a. Cyber crimes that harm individuals b. Cyber crimes that harm society

c. Cyber crimes that harm business d. All of them

Ans. a

Q9. The challenge of unauthorized usage is also called

a. Software hacking b. Hardware hacking

c. Cyber Theft d. Resource Theft

Ans. d

Q10. The crime of copying software without being authorized for its use is named as ______________

a. Round Cyber Theft b. Resource Theft

c. Hacking d. Software Piracy

Ans. d

Short Answer Type Questions

Q1. What do you understand by ethical aspects in IT?

Q2. Discuss importance of ethics in IT.

Q3. How does privacy relate to IT ethics?

Q4. What is cyber crime?

Q5. What are virus and worms?

Q6. What do you mean by Security in IT ethics?

Q7. Write short notes on Disaster recovery.

Q8. What are the major aspects of security policy in an organization?

Q9. Discuss the main features of IT Act in India?

Q10. What is software piracy?

Glossary

Antivirus

It refers to software that is designed for preventing, identifying, and removing malware, including malicious codes and computer viruses.

Application software

It sits over the system software and focuses on executing a particular kind of application.

Assembler

It refers to the language processor that converts a program written in an assembly language (code) into the machine language (code).

Bar code reader

It is an input device that reads the combination of black color parallel lines of varying widths.

Cell

It refers to the intersection of a row and a column.

Compiler

It refers to the language processor that is used to convert or translate the HLL program code into the machine code (object code in one go and displays all the errors of the program along with the line numbers.

Computer hardware

It collectively defines the physical components of a computer.

Computer

A computer is an electronic device, which takes input from the user in the form of data, processes that data according to the instructions given by the user, and displays the output on the screen.

CPU

CPU stands for Central Processing Unit. It processes the instructions given to it by successful coordination between different parts of the computer.

Data Dictionary

It is a collection of all the system elements creating a form of dictionary.

Data flow diagram (DFD)

It is a technique used in the requirements analysis process. It shows the data flow between the functions of each program.

Data packet

It is a basic unit of communication on a network.

Database

It is a collection of related records stored together in a logical way.

Encryption

It is a technique which converts the data into a form not easily understandable by everyone, to protect it from getting damaged.

Executive Information System (EIS)

It provides critical information to the executive and top-level managers for making strategic decisions.

Extranet

It refers to a network owned by an organization. The employees can access the extranet even when they are outside the office for official task.

File

It is a collection of similar type of data appearing under a single name.

Flash memory

Pen drive and SD cards are the examples of flash memory. These devices get integrated with a universal serial bus (USB) connector.

Flat-file database

It refers to a database file that consists of a single table. This database file is also called sequential file.

Graphical User Interface (GUI)

GUI is an interface that uses the advantages of the graphical capabilities of a computer to allow the users to work with the programs easily.

Hacking

It is a crime that relates to the unauthorized access to the use of a computer or a network.

Information System(IS)

It is defined as an arrangement that processes data and provides meaningful information.

Input device

A device that lets you enter data or instructions in a computer is known as an input device.

Interpreter

It refers to a language processor that converts a program written in HLL into the machine language. It converts and executes the program line by line.

Intranet

It refers to a network specific to an organization. It serves the needs of the employees of the organization. Intranet cannot be accessed outside the office or for browsing the Internet.

IP address

It is a unique address to identify every device on a TCP/IP network.

Job scheduling

It is a process of assigning tasks to CPU according to their priority levels and available resources.

Keyboard

It is an input device that contains keys to feed information into the computer.

Knowledge management

It is the effective and adequate management of communication of knowledge in an organization.

Knowledge Support System (KSS)

It is a computer based knowledge management application that supports effective and efficient knowledge management.

Language processor

It is a type of system software that helps to translate the source code developed by using a High Level Language into the machine code.

Local Area Network (LAN)

It refers to a privately owned network of an organization, which is used to connect a computer with other hardware, such as a printer in an office or at home.

Magnetic storage device

Hard disk and tape drives are the examples of magnetic storage devices. These devices use a magnetic head to read and write data.

Management Information System (MIS)

It provides information on various business aspects to managers. It generates information for monitoring performance and maintaining coordination.

MICR

MICR stands for Magnetic Ink Character Reader. MICR is the character recognition system that uses a special ink referred as *magnetic ink* and characters to facilitate a secure way of information processing.

Monitor

It is an output device used to display the output of a program.

Mouse

It is a handheld device that allows you to control your computer without typing instructions from the keyboard.

MS-Access

It is a database application that allows to store data in the form of various objects, such as tables, reports, and forms.

MS-Excel

It is a spreadsheet application that is used to manipulate and organize data in the form of rows and columns.

MS-PowerPoint

It is a presentation software. It can hold a collection of slides, where each slide displays some information in the form of text, graphics, audio and video.

MS-Word

It's a word processing application software that allows to create professional-looking documents easily and quickly.

Network

It is a group of interconnected systems sharing services and interacting with each other through a shared communication link.

OMR

OMR stands for Optical Mark Recognition. OMR is the process of extracting the human marked data from the forms that are usually related to the surveys and various types of tests.

Operating System

It is a set of programs that controls the hardware of a computer and enables it to communicate and operate with the computer software.

Optical storage devices

CDs (compact disc) and DVDs (digital versatile disc) are the examples of optical storage devices. These discs work on the principle of electro-mechanics.

Output device

It is an electronic equipment connected to a computer and is used to communicate the results of the data processing.

Plotter

It is bigger size as compared to a printer. A plotter produces high-quality color graphics hard-copy output.

Presentation

It is a sequential collection of slides, where each slide displays some information in the form of text or graphics.

Primary Key

It refers to a unique key that does not allow to insert duplicate information in a specific field of a table.

Primary storage devices

They are also known as internal/ main/primary memory. These are storage locations that hold memory for short periods of time while the computer is on. RAM is an example of a primary storage device.

Printer

It is an output device that prints images, numbers, alphabets, and graphs on a sheet of paper.

Processor management

It refers to the task of managing processes (tasks or jobs) allocated to a processor.

Protocol

It defines a common set of rules and signals that computers on the network use to communicate with one another.

Relational database

This database consists of multiple tables. Data can be accessed from different tables by creating relation between them. To create a relation between different tables, there must be one common field in each table.

Ribbon

It is as an interface that contains an arrangement of command buttons and icons, and manages commands as a set of tabs.

Router

It is a networking hardware device that connects LANs and WANs on the Internet.

Scanner

It is an input device that can transfer typed or handwritten texts, graphs, diagrams, and photographs to the computer.

Search engine

It is an application used to search for information on the Internet according to a specified criterion.

Secondary storage devices

They are used to store a large amount of data permanently, which is not possible by using the primary memory. Some of the common secondary storage devices are hard disk, CDs and flash memory.

SmartArt graphics

It is a graphics tool generally used at a large level to design a set of presentation objects, such as flow charts, decision trees, and Venn diagrams.

Speaker

It is an output device that converts the electric signals received from the computer into sound waves.

Storage devices

Storage devices are used to store data. Broadly, they are classified as primary storage devices and secondary storage devices.

System software

Operating system and device drivers comes into this category. This type of software drives the computer hardware.

Topology

It is the physical layout of the network. It defines the set of rules that govern data communication.

Uniform Resource Locator (URL)

It is a simple string of characters used to represent and identify a Web page or Web site.

Virtual storage

It is a primary storage that does not actually exist; however, it gives an illusion of the primary storage to the programmers.

Virus

It is a computer program that infects the computer by giving erroneous results on various operations.

Waterfall model

It is the basic model of system development and follows a flow of steps beginning from feasibility check until system maintenance in a sequence.

Wide Area Network (WAN)

It is a type of network used to cover a wide geographical area or region, which can be interconnected with LANs.

Worksheet

In Excel, it is the place where you enter data or records and perform various operations.

Index

K

M

N

O

P

R

S

T

W